Human Freedom, Divine Knowledge, and Mere Molinism

Human Freedom, Divine Knowledge, and Mere Molinism

A Biblical, Historical, Theological, and Philosophical Analysis

TIMOTHY A. STRATTON

foreword by Kirk R. MacGregor

WIPF & STOCK · Eugene, Oregon

HUMAN FREEDOM, DIVINE KNOWLEDGE, AND MERE MOLINISM
A Biblical, Historical, Theological, and Philosophical Analysis

Wipf & Stock
An Imprint of Wipf and Stock Publishers
199 W. 8th Ave., Suite 3
Eugene, OR 97401

www.wipfandstock.com

PAPERBACK ISBN: 978-1-7252-7611-6
HARDCOVER ISBN: 978-1-7252-7612-3
EBOOK ISBN: 978-1-7252-7613-0

Manufactured in the U.S.A.   09/10/20

To my wife, Tia, and my son, Ethan:
Thank you for your love, grace, and patience.
Thank you for exuding all of these properties
while I worked on this long project.
I love you! This book is dedicated to the two of you.

Contents

Illustrations

Foreword

DR. TIM STRATTON HAS the rare and precious gift of taking highly complex issues in philosophical theology and making them easily understandable to laypeople at the same time as he shows their tremendous importance for scholars in the disciplines of philosophy and religion. This book will be profitably and enjoyably read by laypeople and scholars interested in various themes, including biblical exegesis, the history of Christian thought, metaphysics, epistemology, systematic theology, and practical Christian living. This book has several aims. It attempts to spell out how to best comprehend the sovereignty and providence of God biblically, philosophically, and theologically. It attempts to spell out how to best comprehend human freedom and responsibility biblically, philosophically, and theologically. It attempts to show how thinkers such as Augustine, Pelagius, Aquinas, Erasmus, Luther, Calvin, Molina, Arminius, and Edwards have shaped the contours of the contemporary debate concerning God's sovereignty and our free choice. It attempts to defend Molina's proffered reconciliation of sovereignty and free choice on non-soteriological matters at least (what Stratton cleverly dubs in a Lewisian fashion "mere Molinism") and on soteriological matters at most. Along the way, it attempts to provide many convincing original arguments for soft libertarian freedom (libertarian freedom on some matters) and divine possession of middle knowledge. It attempts to show how some of the most successful arguments for God's existence are bolstered by mere Molinism and to show how some of the most powerful arguments against God's existence are decimated by mere Molinism. Finally, it attempts to show the tremendous pragmatic explanatory power of mere Molinism in disclosing how infallible, inspired Scripture can freely be written by human beings, how God could use evolution to create life on earth, how God loves his people, and how our prayers make a vital difference in the overall fabric of the world.

In my judgment, Stratton succeeds admirably in achieving all these aims. Stratton crafts excellent definitions of divine sovereignty, divine providence, and libertarian freedom, careful all the while to obviate prevalent misconceptions of each. Extremely valuable to the historical theologian is Stratton's demonstration that, on non-soteriological matters, Augustine, Aquinas, Luther, and (amazingly) Calvin held to soft libertarian freedom. Moreover, Stratton illustrates that the Canons of Dort say nothing that rules out soft libertarianism outside the salvific arena. These factors alone make the book well worth reading. Stratton reveals how the exhaustive divine determinism of many prominent contemporary Calvinists is indebted neither to Calvin nor to Dort but to Edwards, whose reasons for exhaustive divine determinism are more philosophical than biblical or theological. Calvinists who defend exhaustive divine determinism (a view that even Turretin denied) need to be reminded that, though fully intending to give exclusively biblical reasons for their view, unwittingly read the Scriptures through the presuppositional lenses of Edwardsian metaphysics. On the other hand, Arminians who infer that Arminius himself believed the anti-Calvinist polemics of his post-Dort advocates need to be reminded that Arminius needs to be allowed to speak for himself and, when he does, paints a far different and more nuanced picture than the one many Arminian theologians have unwittingly presupposed.

Turning to mere Molinism, Stratton ingeniously offers several cleverly styled "Free-Thinking Arguments" for soft libertarianism, one of mere Molinism's two ingredients. The terminology is clever because Stratton is deliberately giving the lie to the notion that atheists and agnostics are the true freethinkers. On the contrary, he proposes that a consistent atheist or agnostic cannot be a freethinker at all, since their positions rule out the logical prerequisites to free thought! However, the mere Molinist can truly be a freethinker. Epistemologically, Stratton argues that human beliefs are rational, that humans can deliberate, and that humans can affirm knowledge claims only if they possess soft libertarian freedom. Stratton also proves to my satisfaction that compatibilism is not a genuine third option mediating between determinism and soft libertarianism, as Guillaume Bignon, Matthew Hart, and Paul Helm assert, but instead collapses back to determinism. Biblically, Stratton reveals that his "Omni Argument," his "Divine Desire v. Divine Determinism Argument," and God's testing of various individuals give more than adequate justification for soft libertarianism. I particularly appreciated Stratton's strong defense and careful articulation of the grammatico-historical exegesis of Scripture, his stress on the importance of logic in formulating theological systems, and his incisive discussion of the nature of objective truth.

In defense of mere Molinism's second ingredient, namely God's middle knowledge, Stratton puts forward many novel and powerful arguments. Theologically, these include the "Maximal Greatness and Middle Knowledge Argument," the "Omniscience, Omnipotence, and Middle Knowledge Argument," and the "Mere Molinism Argument" (humorously abbreviated the MMA). He also surveys strong arguments for middle knowledge from other contemporary philosophers and theologians, displaying his thorough acquaintance with the literature. One extremely important consequence of these arguments is that mere Molinism can bring peace between Calvinists and Arminians despite their disagreements. Thus one can be a mere Molinist while a five-point Calvinist, and one can be a mere Molinist while an unflinching Arminian. Stratton provides an excellent rationale as to why atheists and agnostics fervently oppose mere Molinism, which seems odd at first glance—why would they care whether or not a God whose existence they at best disbelieve or at worst deny possesses middle knowledge and whether or not humans possess soft libertarian freedom? The answer, according to Stratton, is that mere Molinism dissolves the best atheist and agnostic arguments against God's existence while rendering highly probable the best theistic arguments for God's existence. Stratton shows that mere Molinism solves the problems of moral evil and natural evil, the two most prevalent anti-theistic arguments. He also shows that mere Molinism furnishes the power to ground the *kalām* cosmological argument, the fine-tuning design argument, and the axiological argument. Accordingly, mere Molinism should prove to be both intellectually and emotionally satisfying to any Christian who is fully apprised of its support. I recommend this book to anyone who is even remotely interested in the topics of divine sovereignty and human freedom.

Dr. Kirk R. MacGregor
Associate Professor of Philosophy and Religion
Chair, Department of Philosophy and Religion
McPherson College

Acknowledgments

IT IS APPARENT FROM any dissertation or even any essay—which has footnotes—that the writer is standing on the shoulders of others who have researched similar areas. I am grateful for how they have first inspired my interest and then influenced the unique direction taken in this book.

I wish to thank my mom and dad (Russ and Suzy) for always wanting to discuss my research with me. Thank you for helping me with tuition. Thank you for your prayers. Thank you for raising Jessica and me exactly the way you did!

David Oldham: Thank you for granting me access to your nearly infinite personal library. Moreover, thank you for discussing this topic with me over countless cups of coffee. Your editing suggestions were perfect. I could not have completed this project if it were not for your support. You are a scholar with the heart of a pastor. I've learned so much from you. I cannot thank you enough.

Kirk MacGregor: Here's a counterfactual: if it were not for your work, my work would not exist! Thank you for always being an email away when I need advice or direction. I value your friendship.

William Lane Craig: Thank you for inspiring my research and your encouragement to continue. You were the one who first challenged my deterministic view and introduced me to Molina's ideas. Your work ultimately changed my life! I am grateful.

Jacobus Erasmus: Thank you for reviewing all of my syllogisms, catching a few mistakes, and offering suggestions to fix them. In my opinion, you are the most underrated philosopher in the world today! I am honored to count you as a colleague and a friend.

Mike Licona: Thank you for introducing me to North-West University and specifically to my supervisor, Professor Coetzee. Your friendship and advice have been invaluable!

Andre Rusavuk: Thank you for the great block quote suggestions and book recommendations pertaining to my research.

Clay Jones: Thank you for helping me see the problems with determinism and the importance of libertarian freedom when solving the "Problem of Evil."

Acknowledgments

R. Scott Smith: Thank you for allowing me to develop many of these ideas under your watchful eye when I was enrolled at Biola. I am so thankful that you were my primary reader of my thesis. That project inspired my doctoral research.

Kevin Lewis: Although we disagree on some of the finer points of theology, you sharpened me and pushed me to think correctly about God. Thank you!

Sean McDowell: Thank you for allowing me to develop some of these initial concepts while enrolled in your class at Biola and also for being the second reader for my MA thesis. I am grateful for your continued sharpening.

To the FreeThinking Ministries team (present and past members): Timothy Fox, Adam Coleman, Jacobus Erasmus, Scott Olson, Shannon Byrd, Jonathan Thompson, Braxton Hunter, Elliott Crozat, Brady Cone, and Richard Eng. Thank you for letting me run many of these ideas by you. Thank you for interacting with me, challenging me, arguing with me, and ultimately, making my case stronger. It is also essential to thank so many others who are part of the extended FreeThinking Ministries team and those who contribute to the website as guest authors. I am grateful for each of you.

To the FreeThinking Ministries board members: Jason Combs (EIC), Mike Main, Roger Allmand, Adrian Boykin, Frank Kovacs, Dustin Bailey (and former members: Paul Bauman and Kevin Andres). Thank you for making it possible to do this specific ministry while simultaneously pursuing a terminal degree in this field.

Pastor Mike Shields: Thank you for seeing the need for the church to answer tough questions and making my first steps of graduate work possible.

Dave Rozema: Thank you for the many philosophical talks at church! Although I have never been officially enrolled in your philosophy class, you have had a significant impact on my thinking.

Professor Callie Coetzee: Thank you for accepting my research proposal and taking me under your wing. I am eternally indebted to you!

And my dog, Rondo: You literally sat by my side through every word I typed in this dissertation. I needed your company. Thank you!

Finally, I want to thank my Lord and Savior Jesus Christ! You are my everything. I pray this project brings you glory.

Abbreviations

ANF   *Ante-Nicene Fathers.* Edited by Philip Schaff. Translated and edited by Alexander Roberts and James Donaldson. 10 Vols. Edinburgh: T & T Clark, 1867 to 1885. *CCEL*

BDB   Francis Brown, S. R. Driver, and Charles A. Briggs. *Enhanced Brown-Driver-Briggs Hebrew and English Lexicon of the Old Testament.* Oxford: Clarendon Press, 2000. http://judaisztika.hu/downloads/BDB.pdf.

CCEL   Christian Classics Ethereal Library. Grand Rapids, MI. https://www.ccel.org/.

CBSC   *Cambridge Bible for Schools and Colleges.*

CE   *The Catholic Encyclopedia.* Edited by Charles G. Herbermann, et al. 16 vols. New York: Robert Appleton Company, 1907. https://www.ecatholic2000.com/cathopedia/title.shtml. http://www.newadvent.org/cathen/.

CGT   *Cambridge Greek Testament for Schools and Colleges.*

DB   *A Dictionary of the Bible.* Edited by James Hastings. 4 vols. Edinburgh: T. & T. Clark, 1899.

DV   Aquinas, Thomas. *Questiones Disputatae de Veritate.* Translated by James V. McGlynn. Chicago: Henry Regnery, 1953. https://dhspriory.org/thomas/QDdeVer.htm.

EBC   Expositor's Bible Commentary. Edited by Frank E. Gaebelein. 12 Vols. Grand Rapids: Zondervan, 1978 to 1992.

ESV   *English Standard Version.* Wheaton: Crossway Bibles, 2008.

ICC   Briggs, Charles A., et al., eds. *International Critical Commentary.* New York: Charles Scribner's Sons.

IEP   *Internet Encyclopedia of Philosophy.* Edited by James Fieser and Bradley Dowden. https://www.iep.utm.edu/.

NCBC   New Century Bible Commentary.

NICNT   New International Commentary on the New Testament.

NIGTC   New International Greek Testament Commentary.

NIV   *New International Version.* Colorado Springs: International Bible Society, 1984.

NLT   *New Living Translation.* Wheaton: Tyndale House, 2006

NPNF1   *Nicene and Post-Nicene Fathers.* Series 1. Edited by Philip Schaff. 14 vols. Repr., Peabody, MA: Hendrickson, 1994.

NSHE   *The New Schaff-Herzog Encyclopedia of Religious Knowledge.* Edited by Samuel M. Jackson. 13 vols. Repr., Grand Rapids: Baker, 1952. CCEL.

PC   Spence, H. D. M. and Joseph S. Exell, eds. *The Pulpit Commentary.* 32 vols. New York: Funk & Wagnalls.

SC   Cook, F. C., ed. *Speaker's Commentary.* Vol 2. New York: Scribner's Sons, 1880. http://classicchristianlibrary.com/library/cook_fc/Cook-Holy_Bible_Commentary-NT-v2.pdf

SEP   *The Stanford Encyclopedia of Philosophy.* Edited by Edward N. Zalta. https://plato.stanford.edu/

ST   Aquinas, Thomas. *Summa Theologica.* Translated by Fathers of the English Dominican Province. New York: Benziger Bros, 1947. CCEL edition.

TNTC   Tyndale New Testament Commentary. 20 vols. Edited by Leon Morris.

WJA   Arminius, Jacobus. *The Works of James Arminius.* Translated by William R Bagnall. 3 vols. Buffalo, NY: Derby, Orton, and Mulligan, 1853. https://www.ccel.org/ccel/arminius/works https://www.ccel.org/ccel/arminius/works1. http://www.ccel.org/ccel/arminius/works2.html. http://www.ccel.org/ccel/arminius/works3.html.

1

Introduction, definitions, and methodology

THE QUESTION OF THE relationship between the terms "determinism" and "human free-dom" has occupied the thinking of human beings for centuries. Though it is often suggested that Homer, Socrates, Plato, Aristotle, and their writings are the seminal sources of the debate, recent research suggests that the modern use of "free will" has its roots in Stoicism.[1] But the debate must not be merely relegated to the ivory towers of philosophers in academia. It has been and remains a debate in theological and religious venues.[2] Even in philosophical discussions terms are utilized—especially to define or describe what "determinism" means—that are more commonly used in religious contexts. And though those using such terms may not be religious or arguing from a religious perspective, the terms themselves many times have theological and religious connotations: "fate," "karma," "destiny," "predestination," "decree," "election," "fortune," and "the force,"[3] for instance. Sometimes these terms are used in an ominous sense of humanity being *controlled* (causally determined) by a force—heredity (genetics), parentage (culture),

---

1. Frede, *Free Will*, 4: "The assumption that the Greeks all along must have been thinking of human beings as having a free will seems truly astounding nowadays. For, if we look at Greek literature from Homer onwards, down to long after Aristotle, we do not find any trace of a reference to, let alone a mention of, a free will. This is all the more remarkable, as Plato and in particular Aristotle had plenty of occasion to refer to a free will. But there is no sign of such a reference in their works." Regarding the roots of free will in Stoicism and Epictetus in particular, see Frede, *Free Will*, ix and 66–88, 125–52). Pigliucci, "Stoicism," defines the Greek philosophy which began about 300 BC as a philosophy that promoted the pursuit of virtue—"wisdom, courage, justice and temperance"—as the chief means to happiness. There was also a strong emphasis on logical thinking and cause and effect relationships.

2. The discussion—especially in chapters 3–11 and 14—will illustrate the debate in theology.

3. Hill, *Star Wars*, defines the term as used in *Episode IV: A New Hope* [a 1977 movie], Obi-Wan-Kenobi explains the Force to Luke Skywalker as 'an energy field created by all living things. It surrounds us, penetrates us, and binds the galaxy together.'"

nature, or even the gods—and the choice of term often identifies the source of the control, whether supernatural (good or evil), the forces of natural law, or some other cause.

Perhaps an illustration of this interplay of philosophy and theology can be seen in what might be labeled a determinism of two sorts: "scientific" determinism and "theological" determinism, both of which stand in contrast to a third variable: libertarian free will.

SCIENTIFIC DETERMINISM.

Scientific determinism arises from the belief that all that exists is nature. It stands to reason that, if nature is all that exists, then everything about humanity would be caused and determined by the laws or forces of nature. However, if everything about a human being is caused or determined by external factors, then this would imply that human beings do not possess the freedom to think or act in a manner opposed to what physics and chemistry dictate. Consequently, it would seem that human beings do not have genuine responsibility for their thoughts, beliefs, behaviors, or actions. Sam Harris, the well-known atheist and naturalist, arrives at the same conclusion about scientific determinism: "Free will is an illusion. Our wills are simply not of our own making. Thoughts and intentions emerge from background causes of which we are unaware and over which we exert no conscious control. We do not have the freedom we think we have. Free will is actually more than an illusion (or less), in that it cannot be made conceptually coherent. Either our wills are determined by prior causes and we are not responsible for them, or they are the product of chance and we are not responsible for them."[4]

Many scholars are not as honest and forthright as Harris about the implications of determinism. Nevertheless, this is the view of scientific determinism: all events are determined by natural causes.

THEOLOGICAL DETERMINISM.

The primary concern of this study is to critically evaluate, not only scientific determinism, but also the issue as to how Scripture and theologians relate their understanding to the issue of human freedom. In contrast to scientific determinism, then, is what might be called theological or divine determinism. The latter has its origins, not only in certain interpretations of select biblical passages, but also in the Bible's implications on the behavior of Christians. Although seminal sources extend back to St. Augustine and the Pelagians,[5] the issue broke out more recently in the Reformation and, espe-

---

4. Harris, *Free Will*, 5.

5. There are, however, numerous examples of references to free will prior to Augustine. For example, Justin Martyr (AD 100–165): "But lest some suppose, from what has been said by us, that we say that whatever happens, happens by a fatal necessity, because it is foretold as known beforehand,

cially, with the spirited debate between the humanist Desiderius Erasmus and the reformer Martin Luther. Erasmus wrote a short treatise called *Discourses on the Freedom of the Will* to which Luther wrote an extensive refutation called *On the Bondage of the Will*. In short,[6] Erasmus argued that God created humanity with genuine human freedom and, although infected with sin, humanity nevertheless maintains that freedom and, therefore, is responsible for both good and evil choices. Luther, however, argued otherwise: humanity does *not* possess free will (at least in soteriological matters) and, as a result, humanity is completely dependent on God to free them from the bondage of their fallenness and their bondage to Satan.[7]

John Calvin's comment, though similar to Luther's, is more well-known and quoted: "But those who, while they profess to be the disciples of Christ, still seek for free-will in man, notwithstanding of his being lost and drowned in spiritual destruction, labor under manifold delusion, making a heterogeneous mixture of inspired doctrine and philosophical opinions, and so erring as to both."[8] Later Calvin added, "Creatures are so governed by the secret counsel of God, that nothing happens but what he has knowingly and willingly decreed."[9]

Lest one conclude that this is a centuries-old debate and shed from current thinking, one need only to consult the writings of more modern Calvinists[10] who, often basing their arguments on certain biblical passages (such as Romans 9), presuppose that God causally determines all things and, thus, humans are not free. Moreover, since these contemporary Calvinists also affirm that they offer their objections as knowledge claims, they unintentionally join forces with naturalists. Indeed, some Calvinists deny human freedom with as much vigor as does Harris and his atheistic colleagues. Consider, for example, these words from R. C. Sproul: "We cannot soft-pedal

---

this too we explain. We have learned from the prophets, and we hold it to be true, that punishments, and chastisements, and good rewards, are rendered according to the merit of each man's actions. Since if it be not so, but all things happen by fate, neither is anything at all in our own power. For if it be fated that this man, e.g., be good, and this other evil, neither is the former meritorious nor the latter to be blamed. And again, unless the human race has the power of avoiding evil and choosing good by free choice, they are not accountable for their actions, of whatever kind they be" (Martyr, *First Apology*, 470 [chap. 43]). Another example is Irenaeus (AD 120–202) who wrote: "If then it were not in our power to do or not to do these things, what reason had the apostle, and much more the Lord Himself, to give us counsel to do some things, and to abstain from others? But because man is possessed of free will from the beginning, and God is possessed of free will, in whose likeness man was created, advice is always given to him to keep fast the good, which thing is done by means of obedience to God" (Irenaeus, *Against Heresies*, 1284; [4.37.4]). Nagasawa, *Human Free Will*, has compiled a list of such pre-Augustine examples that is ten pages long!

6. This is discussed in greater detail in chapters 6–11.

7. See chapters 6–11.

8. Calvin. *Institutes*, 1.15.8; [172]. The former designation (1.15.8) is Calvin's designation; the number following [172] is from the CCEL edition.

9. Calvin, *Institutes*, 1.16.3; [177].

10. For example, Schultz, "No Risk"; Bavinck, *Reformed Dogmatics*; Kane, *Contemporary Introduction*; Muller, "Grace, Election"; and Schreiner and Ware, *Grace of God*.

this dilemma by calling it a mystery; we must face up to the full import of the concept. If free will means autonomy, then God cannot be sovereign. If man is utterly and completely free to do as he pleases, there can be no sovereign God. However, if God is utterly sovereign to do as He pleases, no creature can be autonomous."[11]

This, then, is the view of theological determinism or what this author refers to as exhaustive divine determinism (EDD): all events are causally determined by God.

LIBERTARIAN FREE WILL.

In light of the previous descriptions of determinism (both scientific and theological) it is vital clearly to define what stands in contrast to it: libertarian free will (LFW) or simply *libertarian freedom*. Aquinas defines human freedom as the absence of any outside force that would prevent a person from weighing alternatives and making his own choices.[12] Importantly, Aquinas is not suggesting that there are no external influences (such as persuaders or persuasions) that put pressure on a person to think, weigh, and decide on a certain action. Such influences abound, both from natural and supernatural sources. However, as Aquinas notes, libertarian freedom implies that, despite the strength of the external influences, they do not necessarily causally determine the choices a person makes.

Libertarian freedom may be defined, essentially, as the conjunction of a rejection of compatibilism (which will be defined in chapter 12) along with the claim that humans (at least occasionally) possess free will. That is to say, the advocate of libertarian freedom affirms that people possess "freedom of moral and rational responsibility"[13] and "that the freedom necessary for responsible action is not compatible with determinism."[14] Thus, in simple terms, libertarian freedom *sometimes* refers to a categorical ability to act or think otherwise, and it *always* refers to source agency without any ultimate external deterministic causes. The former is sufficient for libertarian freedom, while the latter is necessary. With that said, one of the main aims of this study is to argue for a stronger model description or definitional model of libertarian freedom.

Consequently, the primary use of the term "libertarian freedom" in this study will usually refer to the idea corresponding to what most people seem to think of when they use the term "free will," namely, the categorical ability to choose among a range of alternative options, each of which is consistent or compatible with one's nature. This concept of libertarian freedom can be more clearly articulated with the following common illustration [author's adaptations]:

11. Sproul, *Can I Know?*, 7–8.

12. See chapter 5 and the extensive survey and documentation of Aquinas's view of human freedom.

13. Moreland and Craig, *Philosophical Foundations*, 267.

14. Moreland and Craig, *Philosophical Foundations*, 2nd ed., 303.

> Imagine a man whose brain has been secretly implanted with electrodes by a mad scientist. The scientist, being a . . . supporter [of politician X], decides that he will activate the electrodes to make the man vote for . . . [politician X] if the man goes into the polling booth to vote for . . . [politician Y]. On the other hand, if the man chooses to vote for . . . [politician X], then the scientist will not activate the electrodes. Suppose, then, the man goes into the polling booth and presses the button to vote for . . . [politician X]. In such a case it seems that the man freely votes for . . . [politician X] (he is responsible for his vote). Yet it was not within his power to do anything different![15]

This thought-experiment suggests that, in order for a person's will to be free, his choices, actions, and some of his beliefs must really be "up to" him and not due only to external factors. This is known as "agent causation" and implies *libertarian* freedom. An agent, although unable to physically act otherwise in this case, is free to think otherwise and make his or her own decisions (at least some of the time) according to reason and without being completely controlled by deterministic laws of nature or some other external cause. Moreover, if humans are free to make their own choices through reasoning and freely weighing alternatives, then they may be held responsible and accountable for their choices and free actions. This, then, is the essence of libertarian freedom.

More specifically, J. P. Moreland suggests that the following are four essential ingredients of libertarian freedom: For any person *P* and some event or action *e*, *P* freely brings about *e* if:

- *P* is a substance that has the active power to bring about *e*.

- *P* exerts his/her active power as a first unmoved mover (an "originator") to bring about *e* [in thought or action].

- *P* has the categorical ability to refrain from exerting his/her power to bring about *e* [nothing causally determines *P* to not do otherwise].

- *P* acts for the sake of reasons [thoughts], which serve as the final cause or teleological goal for which *P* acted.[16]

It follows from this that if *P* has this ability, then *P* also possesses responsibility.[17]

THE CENTRAL RESEARCH QUESTION.

The central research question which is the subject of this study is: "Does humanity possess libertarian freedom, and if so, are human freedom and genuine responsibility logically compatible with God's complete sovereignty and predestination"?

15. Craig, "Free Will." Quotation slightly altered to not identify any particular politician.

16. Moreland, *The Recalcitrant Imago Dei,* 44.

17. A more comprehensive definition of libertarian free will is offered in chapter 12.

The alleged dilemma.

While such deterministic language—as noted above—is used in some theological and philosophical circles, there is inherent in the human psyche a rebellion against any sense that individuals do not control their own destinies, that is, that all of a person's thoughts and actions are at the mercy of and are being controlled by someone or something else. People intuitively sense that they are—and must be—free in their thinking, decisions, and at least in some of their actions.[18] Perhaps it is this inner intuition that has moved many Christians to argue against determinism, arguments which will be explored in later chapters.

These apparent polar opposites—namely, determinism and freedom—have engaged the minds of many Christians, especially Christian philosophers and theologians, as they have sought to understand, define, and reconcile what seems irreconcilable. Of course, between these two ends of the spectrum, there are those who describe their position in terms other than determinism or freedom (though one's view usually tends toward one end or the other of the spectrum). There are also others who believe that there can be harmony between determinism and freedom. An example of the latter is Francis Turretin, who remarks with unusual frankness and candor: "God on the one hand by his providence not only decreed but most certainly secures the event of all things, whether free or contingent; on the other hand, however, man is always free in acting and many effects are contingent. Although I cannot understand how these can be mutually connected together, yet (on account of ignorance of the mode) the thing itself is (which is certain from another source, i.e., from the word) not either to be called in question or wholly denied."[19]

It is with this latter position—one seeking to affirm both freedom and determinism or divine providence, despite the tension that would incline one to either extreme—that prompted this writer to explore the issue as to how the two might be harmonized. It seems clear that the Bible teaches two important propositions, namely, that (1) God is sovereign, provident, and in control of *all* things all the time, and that (2) humans possess libertarian freedom and are genuinely responsible for at least *some* things at some times, such as their thoughts, and actions. Chapter 2 examines the biblical passages in support of these two propositions. However, to conclude, as does Turretin, that neither (1) nor (2) can be denied—and both accepted—even though they seem irreconcilable, leads to what William Lane Craig has called an interpretative "*cul de sac*" and, therefore, demands that the person "reassess whether [he] has, indeed, rightly interpreted Scripture."[20]

18. Aquinas's definition of actions as having five aspects is very helpful. They are as follows: "intention, deliberation, decision, exertion using means, and results" (summarized in Highfield, "God Controls," 161). A similar list is found in Jas 1:13–15: *temptation, desire, enticement, conception, sin,* and *death.*

19. Turretin, *Institutes,* 512.

20. Craig, "Response to Paul Kjoss Helseth," 55.

An important question, then, is: "Can one, to the satisfaction of both sides of the debate, show theologically and philosophically that predestination and election can be affirmed together with genuine human libertarian freedom"? The argument here is that this can be done responsibly while neither denying divine providence or human freedom nor appealing to mystery and *merely* acknowledging, as does Turretin, that both are taught in Scripture.

Basic research questions.

The above problem may be addressed by answering the following research questions:

1. How is one to understand divine sovereignty/providence from a philosophical, a theological and a biblical perspective?

2. How is one to understand human freedom and responsibility from a philosophical, a theological, and a biblical perspective?

3. How did some of the prominent historical Christian thinkers contribute to the debate about predestination, sovereignty/providence, and freedom; and how can their work help in addressing the central research question?

4. How do the writings of Luis de Molina offer insights and a possible solution to the central research question?

5. How do some of the prominent contemporary Christian thinkers contribute to the issue at hand, and how can their work help in addressing the central research question?

6. How does the discussion of human freedom and predestination contribute to the field of apologetics and practical Christian living?

The central hypothesis.

This study concludes that humans do possess libertarian freedom. Moreover, by building on the work of Luis de Molina—one of the great historical figures that contributed to the debate surrounding the central research question—divine providence and libertarian freedom can be reconciled without neglecting, diminishing, delimiting, or destroying either concept as taught in the Scriptures. Though others have made such an attempt—and with some of their reasoning, this writer would agree—the hypothesis staked out here is unique to his own research. Unique arguments are offered supporting the key "ingredients" of Molina's hypothesis.

RESEARCH METHODOLOGY.

The research methodology taken in this study involves a literature study, review, and critical analysis of the discussions, surrounding divine predestination, human libertarian freedom, and related topics, that appear in some of the leading academic journals and in relevant books. Importantly, this study was conducted in line with the ethical rules and guidelines as formulated by the North-West University—from which the author received his PhD—and in particular its Institutional Research Ethics Regulatory Committee.

The Protestant-Reformed tradition.

The discussion above might suggest that this approach completely departs from the Reformed tradition, or that arguments are being raised against essential Reformed positions. It is important, therefore, to note that this study unabashedly approaches the investigation from a Protestant-Reformed perspective. The author of this book has been a Protestant pastor in the Evangelical Free Church of America and, furthermore, considers himself Reformed.

What does it mean to be "Reformed"? The term is being used here in the sense that North-West University (South Africa) defines it:

> The Faculty of Theology of the North-West University practises the science of Theology on a Reformational foundation. In this way it recognises its historical links with the Reformation of the sixteenth and seventeenth centuries, [and] implies recognition that the Word of God, the Bible, originated through the inspiration of the Holy Spirit and that the Bible is therefore inspired and authoritative. In our practice of Theology as a science, we recognise and respect the Reformed view of God and the written Word of God as the particular revelation of God. This is the basis on which all paradigms (including our own) are subjected to constant critical and reformative study."[21]

The study which follows, then, is an attempt to practice theology on a Reformational foundation, which entails a constant, critical examination and scrutinizing of even this writer's own Reformed beliefs. As this study will show, some of the beliefs and teachings of many Reformed colleagues—in particular, the view that humanity lacks libertarian freedom or, in other words, the view that God causally determines all things—will be questioned. However, in the end, the crucial tenet of Reformed theology, namely, that God predestines and is sovereign over all things, will be affirmed and defended together with the view that humans possess libertarian freedom.

---

21. From North-West University website: http://theology.nwu.ac.za/theology-reformational -foundation.

Truth.

What is truth? People have been asking this question for centuries. In fact, Pilate asked Jesus this same question over two thousand years ago (John 18:38). Pilate may have been expressing his own skeptical philosophy, but there is such a category of "truth." In this study "truth" is defined as a statement or a proposition that corresponds to ontological reality. "Reality" simply refers to the way things are (apart from human opinion). In Col 1:16 it appears that the Apostle Paul believed that ultimate reality is grounded in the nature of God. Accordingly, the view here is that God is necessary, and all other actual things—*visible and invisible*—are contingent upon God, who is the ultimate reality. Although people may have different views of—or opinions about—reality, they cannot all be correct in their assessment of reality. Therefore, those who utter propositions corresponding to ultimate reality (or God) make truth claims.

It is important to distinguish between ontological reality and epistemology. Ontological or objective truth refers to the way things are regardless of whether human beings possess knowledge of reality. There is, therefore, no such thing as "my truth," or "your truth," "his truth," or "her truth." Objective truth is independent of a person's opinion; indeed, it is the judge, the standard or benchmark of all statements or beliefs.[22] Epistemology, in contrast, refers to how people come to know, or gain knowledge of reality. While truth is to be found in many disciplines, this author affirms that the Bible is the inspired, authoritative, and inerrant source of truth. This requires, therefore, that there be careful and the accurate interpretation of it.

Grammatico-historical method for biblical interpretation.

The discipline of how to interpret the Bible is called "hermeneutics." Often the discipline is associated in Christian circles as only related to a way of understanding and interpreting the Bible, but the word and the discipline have a wider context. It was an ancient response against the allegorical interpretation of philosophical treatises and other writings.[23] By "allegorical" is meant an interpretive explanation—often some hidden meaning—versus what is the plain meaning of the words as the author intended them to communicate. Philo would be an example of this in biblical interpretation.[24]

---

22. Howe, "How to Interpret (Part 2)," has a humorous way of arguing for absolute truth: "Whether someone is willing to admit it or not, everyone believes there is truth and that truth is absolute. Some people call themselves relativists. A relativist claims that there is no absolute truth, but even the relativist believes relativism is absolutely true . . . The fact is, there is absolute truth, and this truth does not change just because someone doesn't like it or agree with it, and it does not change depending on one's worldview. Truth is the same for everyone at all times."

23. Mantzavinos, "Hermeneutics."

24. Lévy says that Philo (20 BC–AD 40) himself defined the "allegorical" method in *Praem.* (*On Rewards and Punishments*) 61–65 as there being "secret ['*hidden*'] meanings, reachable only with God's help . . . For him, allegory assumes importance when literal interpretation encounters difficulty, for example, when it suggests conclusions in contradiction with God's absolute perfection. In *Leg.* 2.19, he

The hermeneutic followed in this study is based on several ingredients:[25]

1. The interpreter must seek to understand the meaning of the words in the sense intended by the author(s) for his contemporary readers.

   The pursuit of the interpreter is not to determine what a text means to him or her but particularly what it meant to the writer and then how it would be understood by the original readers. This means that one must understand how an author uses terms, which may be different than they are used in other books of the Bible, elsewhere, or today. This is sometimes denoted as "context" study: the immediate context (chapter), book, author, the great corpus of Scripture, other contemporary writings of the same time period and location, etc. This also means that the reader must distinguish what the text actually states ("exegesis") from application (how this might relate to a person's life today).[26]

2. The interpreter recognizes the importance of the original languages in the Bible: Hebrew, Aramaic, and Greek.

   Every translation reflects a person's understanding of the foreign language and his/her ability in that particular language. Some terms, tenses, pronouns are difficult to put into a translation without it becoming cumbersome for the reader. Rarely will the translation result in any difficulty for the reader to understand the original writer's meaning, but knowing the original language often enhances nuances not easily translatable. Howe's challenge of language study is well-balanced and helpful: "It's not necessary for everyone who wants to study the Bible to be a scholar in the original languages of the Bible . . . [But] serious Bible study requires some study in the original languages . . . Learning the basics of language, how to do word studies, and how to consider the way a word functions in a sentence, helps you to understand what the Bible is saying."[27]

3. The interpreter seeks to *determine* the meaning of the words in the *historical/cultural settings in which the material was written.*

   Today, it is easy for people whose worldview or culture is different from those in biblical times to read the Bible from their own perspective, but that often leads to misunderstandings. Howe illustrates this principle from Genesis 11 and the account of building the tower of Babel. Some interpreters have said that the tower was built to protect against a huge flood. But the question must be asked: "Why did these people begin to build a tower"? . . . By investigating ancient religious practices and beliefs, we discover that it was generally held to be true that

---

does not hesitate to say that the creation of Eve from one of Adam's ribs was a most improbable myth, if taken literally. It becomes likely only if one understands that 'ribs' are in fact the powers of Adam's mind" (Lévy, "Philo.").

25. Adapted from Howe, "How to Interpret (Part 2)."

26. Adapted from Howe, "How to Interpret (Part 2)."

27. Howe, "How to Interpret (Part 1)."

a person's god dwelled on a mountain . . . Since there were no mountains in the *plains of Shinar* . . . the people decided to construct a mountain in which their god(s) could dwell.[28]

4. The word "*grammatico*" does not necessarily mean literal, but takes into consideration the kinds of literature: the genres and compositional devices commonly employed in the time period the original author lived.[29]

This means that one must consider the many different genres of Scripture and interpret them accordingly. Such genres would include poetry, parables, "types," and apocalyptic writings. A fine discussion of these different genres is found in Osborne.[30] Michael R. Licona is clear: "For our purposes, we only need to recognize that the New Testament Gospels bear a strong affinity to Greco-Roman biography. Accordingly, we should not be surprised when the evangelists employ compositional devices similar to those used by ancient biographers. In fact, we should be surprised if they did not."[31]

Licona's words imply the importance of understanding not only the correct genre in which an author wrote, but also the compositional devices employed within the particular genre. If one errs on the proper understanding of genre or compositional device by the original author, one is apt to also err regarding the correct interpretation of the original author's ancient writing. Licona adds:

> God's Word is rich and beautiful. We can learn new things from it our entire lives. The deeper I study it, the more impressed with it I become. And there will still be much, much more for us to see. I, for one, love God's Word and I'm by no means trying to lessen its value or cast doubt on its reliability. However, I think we can misread it when we do so through modern lenses, as though the Gospels were written using modern literary conventions. Why would we demand that they be? Realizing that the Gospel authors felt free to report with some elasticity makes some uncomfortable. It made me uncomfortable at first. But a principle I have come to live by is this: I must accept the Gospels as God has given them to us rather than forcing them into a mold of how I think He should have. If I fail to do this, I may believe I have a high view of Scripture when, in reality, I merely have a high view of *my* view of Scripture. That would constitute misguided piety.[32]

In other words, if one reads ancient writings through modern lenses, mistakes are likely to follow. It is necessary to view ancient writings through ancient lenses to reach

28. Howe, "How to Interpret (Part 1)."

29. Kaiser and Silva, *Introduction,* 100, illustrate this in Kaiser's discussion of Caiaphas's comment that it is better that *one man* (Jesus) *die . . . than the whole nation perish* (John 11:49–52). Caiaphas did not make reference to the "substitutionary" death of Jesus, though John takes his words as a "prophecy" of that very act. Kaiser calls this "tak[ing] a man's own words and turn[ing] them back against him."

30. Osborne, *Hermeneutical Spiral,* 149–260.

31. Licona, *Why Are There Differences?,* 5.

32. Licona, *Are We Reading?*

correct interpretations. This is best accomplished by possessing a proper understanding of genre, compositional devices, and other literary conventions in which the original author of a particular book of the Bible and/or any other ancient writing employed.

One important footnote to the above discussion is that the interpreter should ask the questions: "Does this interpretation square with other passages of Scripture? Does it square with the nature of God (as illustrated by John 1; Col 1 and 2; Heb 1; Rev 1; and John 14:8–9)"?[33]

Rational principles and logic.

Luther referred to philosophy as the work of the devil[34] and the "devil's whore."[35] Yet, it was speculative philosophy from which he turned away.[36] Indeed, he was nicknamed "the philosopher"[37] because of his reasoned arguments, which are notably evident in his response to Erasmus: *The Bondage of the Will*. Logic is bedrock in that it underlies all use of language and communication. Therefore, all philosophical speculation, theological conversation, hermeneutical interpretations, scientific hypotheses, mathematics, and conclusions based on the historical method entail the reality of logical laws. Osborne says that:

> The theologian must truly be a renaissance person, for it is necessary to exegete the Scriptures, collate the theological threads via biblical theology, be aware of the development of dogma throughout church history, then contextualize all this for the modern situation; and at each stage philosophical reasoning plays a critical role. In a very real sense, the theologian is asked to be an expert exegete, historian, and philosopher . . . Philosophy helps the theologian to avoid subjective reasoning and to ground theological formulations in critical reasoning, coherence, and rationality . . . [It] is a supplement to theology in helping the latter reformulate biblical truths rationally and coherently in order to address the current situation. They are not equal partners, for theology contains the ultimate truth, but philosophy forces the theologian to be both logical and open to new expressions/clarifications of the timeless truths . . . Most theologians today argue that inductive and deductive methods must be integrated in constructing theological systems.[38]

33. The writer is indebted for this hermeneutical principle to his pastor, Adrian Boykin. His phrasing reflects the Reformed hermeneutic that "Scripture interprets Scripture."

34. Osborne, *Hermeneutical Spiral*, 296.

35. Amos, "How Useful Is Philosophy"? In a more negative vein, see Fitzgerald, "Luther and the Divorce."

36. Dragseth explains: "In the context of the medieval debate, Luther rejected philosophy as an adequate discipline in the most important discussions concerning human nature. He turned away from speculative philosophy" (Dragseth, "Martin Luther's Views").

37. Stepp, "Martin Luther."

38. Osborne, *Hermeneutical Spiral*, 296.

It would be impossible to engage in any of the above disciplines if there were no logical absolutes providing parameters to help a person reach conclusions that follow from given premises. Even interpreting Scripture correctly presupposes and depends on the laws of logic.

There are three fundamental Laws of Logic that are always required in rational interaction:

- *The Law of Identity*: Something is what it is: "A" is "A." Things that exist have specific properties that identify them.

- *The Law of Non-Contradiction*: "A" cannot be both "A" and "Non-A" at the same time, in the same way and in the same sense. "When two claims contradict one another, one . . . must be false."[39]

Wayne Grudem states it well: "Contradictions aren't acceptable in the study of systematic theology, since there aren't any contradictions in the Bible."[40] This presupposition is supported by Scripture itself. For example, Psa 119:160 states that *the sum of your words is truth* and this implies, in turn, that God's Word, which Christians believe is true in all that it teaches, will be logical when studied in the context as a whole. This is obvious because truth and logic are inextricably linked; one cannot be without the other since truth assumes logic and vice versa. As Grudem put it: "There are many times we need to acknowledge mystery, paradox, and things we can't fully understand. But that's different from saying there's a [logical] contradiction. God never asks us to believe a contradiction."[41]

- *The Law of Excluded Middle*: A well-defined proposition is either true or false. There is no middle position. For example, the proposition that "A proposition is either true or false" is either true or false.

These laws are just as necessary to keep a person grounded in rationality as the law of gravity is necessary to keep them grounded on the earth. The laws of logic are tools which help a person to objectively determine true or false propositions, inferences, and deductions. For example, if a scientific conclusion is logically incoherent, then the conclusion must be mistaken. Rosenblum and Kuttner's maxim cannot be stated too emphatically: "A [scientific] theory leading to a logical contradiction is necessarily an incorrect theory."[42] Logical laws apply to everyone regardless of when or where he lives, that is to say, the laws of logic transcend humanity and are objectively true. In fact, truth and logic are inextricably linked; one cannot have one without the other. Thus, if Christians claim that Christianity is true, then the affirmations of

---

39. Howe, "How to Interpret (Part 2)."

40. Grudem, *Systematic Theology*, 12.

41. Grudem, *Systematic Theology*, 12.

42. Rosemblum and Kuttner, *Quantum Enigma*, 95.

Christianity must be logical (even if people cannot fully understand all the affirmations). Therefore, heavy emphasis is placed on truth and logic throughout this study.[43]

Original languages.

In a study that is the scope of the current study, many of the primary sources are in languages other than English. These sources are identified in the bibliography, both for the original language and the translation, where possible. When biblical studies are used, the most current Hebrew (Aramaic) and Greek critical texts have been consulted. When sources are in other languages, the most recent translations have been consulted (e.g., Luther) or where there are different translations of the primary source (e.g., Calvin who wrote in both Latin and French), a comparison of the primary languages is helpful for determining the meaning. Some sources (e.g., Luis de Molina's writings) have not been translated into English and, therefore, secondary sources or translations have been consulted.

CHAPTER OUTLINES.

Chapter 2: A survey of biblical data on God's sovereignty and human freedom.

The objective of the second chapter is to set the scene for why this study's central research question involves reflection from both theological and philosophical perspectives. Chapter 2 argues that Scripture, or God's revelation of the truth, affirms both that God has a plan for history and that the actors on the stage of life do their own thinking and make their own decisions (at least on occasion) and, for this reason, experience the consequences of their actions. It would be irresponsible, of course, for a person to defend his view of divine providence by simply appealing to cherry-picked, biblical passages. Therefore, in this chapter, biblical passages are offered which support both sides of the debate. No attempt is made to argue in favor of a certain position. This will serve as the foundation for setting forth premises and drawing conclusions that take into consideration the whole of Scripture.

Chapters 3–11: A survey of human freedom during the Pre-Reformation, Reformation, and Post-Reformation periods.

No discussion of this subject can or should be understood, constructed, or defended without interacting with the great Christian thinkers of the past. They have also struggled with attempts to harmonize divine providence with human freedom and responsibility. By answering the questions and arguments posed by others (including

---

43. Chapters 12–13 and 15–16 are specifically focused on logical argumentation.

secular, orthodox, and heretic thinkers), Christians of the past have proposed unique solutions to the issue at hand. The fruit of their study and interaction with opposing points of view prove to be of great help to theologians and philosophers today. It is evident that contemporary debates about divine providence have been largely influenced by this rich past. Therefore, in chapters 3–11 a broad historical picture of the nature of the debate with an intentional emphasis on the issue of human freedom and determinism is offered. Other matters of theology and soteriology may be interesting, but the purpose of these chapters is to draw out, from the writings of past thinkers, their views on the subject at hand. These chapters, then, describe the historical background of the central research question of this book by surveying the theology of great past thinkers over a number of centuries.

Chapters 12–13: Arguments in favor of libertarian freedom.

These chapters take a philosophical turn and provide pivotal arguments to help a person discern which theologians of the past were correct or on the right path. In it, reasoned (and sometimes unique) arguments against exhaustive divine determinism or theological determinism are offered as well as arguments in favor of human libertarian freedom. An important part of these arguments is to have a careful definition of the term "libertarian freedom" or "libertarian free will." The chapters, therefore, include a meticulous analysis of libertarian freedom. Furthermore, in the chapters, a critical engagement with relevant, contemporary scholars is offered in order to arrive at some conclusions regarding determinism and free will. The objective of these chapters, then, is to highlight, and provide initial grounds for, the (somewhat unique) position that is argued for in subsequent chapters.

Chapter 14: God's sovereignty and human freedom: A Spanish theologian solves the mystery.

This chapter is an introduction to Luis de Molina, the Spanish Jesuit, who has been relatively unknown in Protestant circles, though in recent years has gained prominence in theological and philosophical circles. Molina broke fresh ground in the debate concerning divine providence in his attempt to reconcile human freedom and God's sovereignty. He appeals to God's omniscience or, more specifically, what he terms God's "middle knowledge" as a particularly convincing argument for harmonizing the two seeming "opposites." As impressive as Molina's ideas were, his ideas were criticized by the Dominicans of his day, who felt that he was out of step with Catholic doctrine, especially that of the great theologian Thomas Aquinas. This chapter provides a historical survey of Molina and his contribution to the debate.

Chapter 15: A defense of divine middle knowledge and Molinism.

Chapter 15 takes another philosophical turn. It critically examines the theology of Luis de Molina which was explored in the previous chapter and also provides arguments concluding that aspects of his theological view probably correspond to reality. Most Christian theologians, with the notable exception of open theists, believe that God knows everything related to the world of God's creation, including the complete future, and God has had this knowledge from at least the moment of creation. Of course, this belief suggests that nothing that God knows will fail to happen. However, this creates a difficult problem for determinists, whether scientific determinists or divine determinists: "Can human beings be in any sense 'free' if God foreknows all their actions"? It is here that Molina's "middle knowledge" proposal sheds light on, and provides a coherent solution to, the issue of divine providence and human freedom and responsibility. At the same time, the chapter will attempt to show that Molina's proposal is compatible with Reformed theology.

Chapter 16: The apologetic significance of Molinism.

This chapter seeks to integrate all the above chapters and demonstrate the practical applications of these matters. It also seeks to illustrate that, although the topic at hand is rather academic in nature, it is extremely relevant to the kingdom of God in the "real" world of everyday life. Understanding history (especially the history of Christianity), theology, and philosophy significantly enhances one's ability to support evangelistic efforts through apologetic argumentation, whether in academic settings, the neighborhood, and/or the workplace. Christians, whether they be academics, pastors, or lay people—if they study the contributions of others and those discussed here—will gain the ability to answer more of the tough questions that often arise over the course of ministry and life.

CONCLUSION.

In many ways this research project reveals the writer's own journey to understanding divine providence and human freedom, through an exploration of Scripture, history, theology, and philosophy. Each of these disciplines should be integrated in order to discern the true meaning of Scripture. Scripture is the foundation, but interpreting it correctly is often a process of reflecting on and evaluating the thinking of great leaders, theologians, and philosophers of both the past and the present.

2

Biblical foundations
Determinism and human freedom

WHILE THIS DEBATE ABOUT the nature of human freedom on the one hand and the various perspectives of determinism on the other will continue to be pursued by philosophers and theologians, attempts at resolving what appears to be an antinomy have a bit more urgency among Christians who are committed to the authority of the Bible. The issue might be framed this way: In the pages of Scripture there are numerous examples of (1) statements of God not only sovereignly moving history in a definite direction but also directly acting on human beings influencing their thinking and actions so that they carry out his will. (2) On the other hand—sometimes in the same context—there seem to be statements, thinking, decisions, and actions to the effect that the individual acted freely on his own volition or for which there appeared to be no outside control, no compelling influence, or anything causing or forcing the individual to act one way instead of the other.

No debate or possible solution of this perceived antinomy can be intellectually argued unless one is aware of the weight of the biblical data supporting both a view suggesting that God causally determines *all* things and the data supporting the view that human beings are responsible for *some* things. What follows, then, are selections of texts either commonly cited or relevant to each position. Some of the texts which follow merit comment, while there are others for which the meaning is abundantly clear.[1]

BIBLICAL DATA SUPPORTING DETERMINISM.

The *Stanford Encyclopedia of Philosophy* defines "determinism" this way: "The *world* is *governed by* (or is *under the sway of*) determinism if and only if, given a specified *way*

---

1. Unless otherwise stated, scriptural quotations are from the *ESV* translation.

things are at a time t, the way things go *thereafter* is *fixed* as a matter of *natural law*."[2] This is otherwise known as scientific or causal determinism in which all things are governed by the forces of nature (i.e., physics and chemistry). On this common view, human beings are not in control or responsible for anything they think or believe or how they act or behave. These things are not "up to the person." On a deterministic paradigm these things are "up to" (so to speak) the laws and forces of nature. In the biblical context determinism means the *way things go* is up to God and fixed by God. There are many examples in the Bible which seem to illustrate this. To make them more simply seen, they have been arranged into categories.

General.

> *But our God is in the heavens; he does whatever he pleases* (Psa 115:3; see also 135:6).
>
> *Declaring the end from the beginning, and from ancient times things which have not been done, saying, "My purpose will be established, and I will accomplish all my good pleasure"* (Isa 46:10).

This second passage certainly seems to imply that all events occurring—from the distant past to the end of time—had been declared by God to occur exactly as they occurred. Or as Calvin put it in his commentary on Isa 46:10, "Even the prophecies would have no certainty or solidity, if the same God who declares that this or that thing shall happen had not the events themselves in his power."[3] This leads some to conclude that there is no room for human free will.

> *All the inhabitants of the earth are accounted as nothing, but he does according to his will in the host of heaven and among the inhabitants of earth; And no one can ward off his hand or say to him, "What have you done"?* (Dan 4:35).[4]

Nebuchadnezzar's affirmation—which Daniel seems to record with approval—explicitly states that nothing and no one can prevent the will of God from occurring. Charles notes that the phrase *host of heaven* "embraces all the superhuman powers and is used sometimes of the angels and sometimes of the stars."[5] The addition of the words *the inhabitants of earth* make universal the *"no one."* If God's will/plan is always fulfilled, can there be any room for the free will of humanity?

---

2. Hofer, "Causal Determinism."

3. Calvin, *Isaiah,* 284.

4. See also Job 9:12: *Were he to snatch away, who could restrain him? Who could say to him, "What are you doing"?* and Job 42:2: *I know that you can do all things, and that no purpose of yours can be thwarted.*

5. Charles, *Daniel,* 48.

Sovereign over the affairs of men.

Before looking at specific texts from Scripture, it would be valuable to define what is meant by "sovereign" and "sovereignty." Philpott, while acknowledging that "some scholars have doubted whether a stable, essential notion of sovereignty exists,"[6] argues that "there is in fact a definition that captures what sovereignty came to mean in early modern Europe and of which most subsequent definitions are a variant: *supreme authority within a territory* . . . A holder of sovereignty derives authority from some mutually acknowledged source of legitimacy—natural law, a divine mandate, hereditary law, a constitution, even international law . . . But if sovereignty is a matter of authority, it is not a matter of mere authority, but of supreme authority."[7]

In the discussion which follows, the "supreme authority" is God, the Almighty One. Declarations of his sovereignty in the Scriptures are abundant:

> Now they told David, "Behold, the Philistines are fighting against Keilah and are robbing the threshing floors." [2] Therefore David inquired of the Lord, "Shall I go and attack these Philistines"? And the Lord said to David, "Go and attack the Philistines and save Keilah." [3] But David's men said to him, "Behold, we are afraid here in Judah; how much more then if we go to Keilah against the armies of the Philistines." [4] Then David inquired of the Lord again. And the Lord answered him, "Arise, go down to Keilah, for I will give the Philistines into your hand." [5] And David and his men went to Keilah and fought with the Philistines and brought away their livestock and struck them with a great blow. So David saved the inhabitants of Keilah. [6] When Abiathar the son of Ahimelech had fled to David to Keilah, he had come down with an ephod in his hand. [7] Now it was told Saul that David had come to Keilah. And Saul said, "God has given him into my hand, for he has shut himself in by entering a town that has gates and bars." [8] And Saul summoned all the people to war, to go down to Keilah, to besiege David and his men. [9] David knew that Saul was plotting harm against him. And he said to Abiathar the priest, "Bring the ephod here." [10] Then David said, "O Lord, the God of Israel, your servant has surely heard that Saul seeks to come to Keilah, to destroy the city on my account. [11] Will the men of Keilah surrender me into his hand? Will Saul come down, as your servant has heard? O Lord, the God of Israel, please tell your servant." And the Lord said, "He will come down." [12] Then David said, "Will the men of Keilah surrender me and my men into the hand of Saul"? And the Lord said, "They will surrender you." [13] Then David and his men, who were about six hundred, arose and departed from Keilah, and they went wherever they could go. When Saul was told that David had escaped from Keilah, he gave up the expedition. [14] And David remained in the strongholds in the wilderness, in the hill country of the wilderness of Ziph. And Saul sought him every day, but God did not give him into his hand (1 Sam 23:1–14).

6. Philpot, "Sovereignty."
7. Philpot, "Sovereignty."

God is the revealer of his sovereign plans which enable David to be victorious. But verses 6–14 introduce a fascinating twist in understanding God's plan. God tells David what in fact the people of Keilah *would* do *if Saul threatened to destroy the city* because David was inside its walls. Though God speaks to David in real time, what he reveals was one of the *possible* circumstances that God *knew* would occur. MacGregor draws out the significance of this example by saying "The knowledge mediated here did not constitute predictions of the future (foreknowledge), for Saul did not actually come to Keilah and the citizens of Keilah never actually handed over David to Saul."[8] The critic might reply, "This merely was a possibility, not unlike any person who would offer his counsel." Not so! People at best can give a conjecture—an uncertain possibility—but in the text God—the God of truth—declares what would certainly happen given those circumstances.

> O LORD, the God of our fathers, are you not God in the heavens? And are you not ruler over all the kingdoms of the nations? Power and might are in your hand so that no one can stand against you (2 Chr 20:6).
>
> Even from eternity I am he, and there is none who can deliver out of my hand; I act and who can reverse it? (Isa 43:13).
>
> If it is of God, you will not be able to overthrow them; or else you may even be found fighting against God (Acts 5:39).
>
> Peter answered him, "Though they all fall away because of you, I will never fall away." [34] Jesus said to him, "Truly, I tell you, this very night, before the rooster crows, you will deny me three times." [35] Peter said to him, "Even if I must die with you, I will not deny you"! And all the disciples said the same (Matt 26:33–35).

Gibson notes the polar opposites: Peter is determined not to deny Jesus (free choice), but the Savior's prophecy will be fulfilled: "Jesus sees it all, and gives him warning in the very plainest words. But Peter persists. He vainly imagines that his master cannot know how strong he is, how burning his zeal, how warm his love, how steadfast his devotion. Of all this he is himself distinctly conscious. There is no mistake about it."[9]

One could give numerous examples where a man of God prophesies about a future event and then Scripture states sometime later that what was predicted occurred *"according to the word of . . . "* (e.g., 1 Kgs 15:29; 16:12, 34; etc.). Prophecies of a true prophet, that is, one who speaks for God, will be fulfilled/occur and thus seem to support determinism.

> You will say to me then, "Why does he still find fault? For who resists his will"? On the contrary, who are you, O man, who answers back to God? The thing molded will not say to the molder, "Why did you make me like this," will it? Or does not the potter have a right over the clay, to make from the same lump one

8. MacGregor, "Monergistic Molinism," 81–82.

9. Gibson, *Matthew*, 397.

vessel for honorable use and another for common use? (Rom 9:19–21; see also
Isa 45:9–10).

Romans 9 is probably the most common passage of the Bible offered in support of a divine deterministic view. Sanday and Headlam devote a lengthy excursus
to showing this throughout history. In short, they note that "St. Paul in this section
(verses 19–29) expands and strengthens the previous argument. He had proved in
verses 14–18 the absolute character of the divine sovereignly from the Old Testament;
he now proves the same from the fundamental relations of God to man implied in
that fact which all his antagonists must admit: God had created man . . . He would
not exist but for the will of God, and whether his lot be honourable or dishonourable,
whether he be destined for glory or eternal destruction, he has no ground for speaking
of injustice."[10]

Not every scholar would state the case so strongly, but one cannot escape the
case that Paul's analogy of comparing humanity to clay in the hands of a divine potter
suggests that God is the determiner of man's destiny.

Sovereign over nature.

> *You are the Lord, you alone. You have made heaven, the heaven of heavens, with
> all their host, the earth and all that is on it, the seas and all that is in them; and
> you preserve all of them; and the host of heaven worships you* (Neh 9:6).
>
> *For from him and through him and to him are all things. To him be glory forever*
> (Rom 11:36).
>
> *For by him all things were created, in heaven and on earth, visible and invisible,
> whether thrones or dominions or rulers or authorities—all things were created
> through him and for him.* [17] *And he is before all things, and in him all things hold
> together* (Col 1:16–17).
>
> *He upholds the universe by the word of his power* (Heb 1:3).

Soteriological sovereignty.

> *But to all who did receive him, who believed in his name, he gave the right to
> become children of God,* [13] *who were born, not of blood nor of the will of the flesh
> nor of the will of man, but of God* (John 1:12–13).
>
> *No one can come to me unless the Father who sent me draws him. And I will
> raise him up on the last day* (John 6:44).

10. Sanday and Headlam, *Romans*, 266.

Certainly, at face value, these verses seem to suggest that it is God who decides who is saved (whom he *draws*), leaving the question about what that means for those who are *not* drawn. However, it suggests that there are some who are not "drawn," and thus will have their eternal destiny away from God. Godet does not address the undrawn, but makes it clear that "the same God who sends Jesus for souls, draws each soul to Jesus. Both these divine works correspond with and complete one another. The happy moment when they meet in the heart, and when the will is surrendered, is that of the gift on God's part, of faith on man's. Jesus adds that, as in salvation the initiative belongs to the Father, so the completion is the task of the Son. The Father draws and commits; the Son receives, keeps, and quickens, until the glorious climax, the resurrection at the last day."[11]

This is another important text which demands more exegetical discussion, but for now it seems to be an example of determinism in the salvation of sinners; they cannot save themselves.[12]

> And when the Gentiles heard this, they began rejoicing and glorifying the word
> of the Lord, and as many as were appointed to eternal life believed (Acts 13:48).

Of these words, Calvin wrote: "We need not doubt that Luke calls those τεταγμένοι [*appointed*] who were chosen by the free adoption of God. For it is a ridiculous cavil to refer this unto the affection of those who believed, as if those received the gospel whose minds were well-disposed. For this ordaining must be understood of the eternal counsel of God alone."[13]

Gloag in his commentary on Acts, however, says that "the interpretations which have been given to it [this text] are numerous, and so different that it has been adduced in proof of opposite doctrines."[14] He has a lengthy discussion on the different views and the strengths and weaknesses of each. Here it is good enough to acknowledge the strength of Calvin's "deterministic" point of view. This appears to document an instance of people believing—and thus being saved—only because they were exactly the people who were determined by God to have eternal life.

> When Rebekah had conceived children by one man, our forefather Isaac,
> [11] though they were not yet born and had done nothing either good or bad—in
> order that God's purpose of election might continue, not because of works but be-
> cause of him who calls— [12] she was told, "The older will serve the younger." [13] As
> it is written, "Jacob I loved, but Esau I hated" (Rom 9:10–13).[15]

11. Godet, *John*, 238.

12. See Aquinas's view in chapter 5.

13. Calvin, *Acts*, 844.

14. Gloag, *Acts*, 39.

15. The following verses are also relevant here: 14 *What shall we say then? Is there injustice on God's part? By no means! 15 For he says to Moses, "I will have mercy on whom I have mercy, and I will have compassion on whom I have compassion." 16 So then it depends not on human will or exertion, but on*

Not a few scholars think similarly to Sanday and Headlam: "As will become more apparent later, St. Paul's argument is to show that throughout God's action there is running a 'purpose according to election.' He does not therefore wish to say that it is merely God's love or hate that has guided Him . . . [Quoting Gore,[16] he concludes:] There was from the first an element of inscrutable selectiveness in God's dealings within the race of Abraham."[17]

The reader cannot miss this "selectiveness" since the text seems to state that God loves some humans and hates others and further, he "elects" those he loves, while rejecting those whom he hates.[18]

> *Predestined according to his purpose who works all things after the counsel of his will* (Eph 1:11).

Paul with the combination of the words—*predestined, purpose, counsel of his will*—seems to do what Abbot concludes: "Here the combination *counsel of his will* seems intended to express emphatically the absolute self-determination of God, or to use other words—and especially the words *all things*—seems to imply an exhaustive view of predestination."[19]

> *But God, being rich in mercy, because of the great love with which he loved us,[5] even when we were dead in our trespasses, made us alive together with Christ— by grace you have been saved— [6] and raised us up with him and seated us with him in the heavenly places in Christ Jesus, [7] so that in the coming ages he might show the immeasurable riches of his grace in kindness toward us in Christ Jesus.[8] For by grace you have been saved through faith. And this is not your own doing; it is the gift of God, [9] not a result of works, so that no one may boast. [10] For we are his workmanship, created in Christ Jesus for good works, which God prepared beforehand, that we should walk in them* (Eph 2:4–10).[20]

God, who has mercy. 17 For the Scripture says to Pharaoh, "For this very purpose I have raised you up, that I might show my power in you, and that my name might be proclaimed in all the earth." 18 So then he has mercy on whomever he wills, and he hardens whomever he wills. 19 You will say to me then, "Why does he still find fault? For who can resist his will"? 20 But who are you, O man, to answer back to God? Will what is molded say to its molder, "Why have you made me like this"? 21 Has the potter no right over the clay, to make out of the same lump one vessel for honorable use and another for dishonorable use? 22 What if God, desiring to show his wrath and to make known his power, has endured with much patience vessels of wrath prepared for destruction, 23 in order to make known the riches of his glory for vessels of mercy, which he has prepared beforehand for glory? (Rom 9:14–23).

16. Gore, "The Argument," 40.

17. Sanday and Headlam, *Romans*, 246–47.

18. See the "Omnibenevolence of God" in chapter 13.

19. Abbott, *Ephesians*, 20–21.

20. Boice and Ryken put rather explicitly what they consider Paul saying: "Like a spiritual corpse, he is unable to make a single move toward God, think a right thought about God, or even respond to God—unless God first brings this spiritually dead corpse to life" (Boice and Ryken, *The Doctrines of Grace,* 74).

Therefore, God sends them a strong delusion, so that they may believe what is false, [12] in order that all may be condemned who did not believe the truth but had pleasure in unrighteousness (2 Thes 2:11–12).

To those who are elect exiles of the Dispersion in Pontus, Galatia, Cappadocia, Asia, and Bithynia, [2] according to the foreknowledge of God the Father, in the sanctification of the Spirit, for obedience to Jesus Christ and for sprinkling with his blood (1 Pet 1:1–2).[21]

Summary.

Regardless of which position a person holds, he or she cannot deny how compelling are the above examples for the case of God's total sovereignty. The question is raised: "Does exhaustive divine sovereignty negate human libertarian freedom"? That question cannot be answered without looking at the Scripture texts which seem to affirm it.

BIBLICAL DATA SUPPORTING HUMAN FREEDOM.

There is also much to commend the biblical data supporting the case for human freedom. These passages cannot be ignored. The *Stanford Encyclopedia of Philosophy* defines "freedom" this way: "The power to choose otherwise."[22] This ability to choose otherwise is commonly referred to as libertarian free will (LFW). However, some have argued that the ability to choose otherwise is merely a sufficient condition for LFW, not a necessary condition. The necessary condition for LFW is that of being a first mover.[23] Whatever influences (strong or otherwise) are present on a person at a given time, if one is free and responsible, then he or she has the ability to think, decide, and act (or not act) on his or her own. With this in mind, LFW can be defined as the conjunction of (1) a rejection of compatibilism (the belief that all things are caused and determined by God or nature and the fact that humans are still free and responsible for some things) (2) along with the claim that humans (at least occasionally) possess free will.[24] For the purpose of this study, however, reference to LFW will typically and simply mean what most people probably think of when they use the term free will. Simply put, libertarian freedom is at least the ability to choose between or among a range of alternative options each of which is compatible with one's nature at a given moment.

---

21. Other examples of *chosen, elect,* etc., are Rom 11:5; Eph 1:4–6; Col 3:12; 1 Thes 1:4; Jas 2:5; and 1 Pet 2:9.

22. Rowe, "Divine Freedom."

23. Chapter 1 gave a preliminary definition of LFW, but there will be further discussion about these philosophical issues later.

24. Kevin Timpe is the source of this definition for academic discourse (via personal email: 30 August 2017).

The following is a selection of examples of Scriptures which speak of a person's freedom. Again, these are arranged into categories:

General.

After these things God tested Abraham (Gen 22:1).

Though the same word in Hebrew can be translated *test* or *tempted*, here it must be understood in the sense of *test*, because God never solicits a person to sin (Jas 1:13). Though testing comes from God, it is a very man-centered experience. Willis describes this experience this way: "The suggestion in Deut 8:2; 2 Chr 32:31; and Psa 26:2 is that the divine proving or testing of man is to bring out the real feelings and motivations of the heart. According to Gen 22, God tested Abraham's faith to see if he really put God's will above what seemed to be logical, his love for Isaac, and the dreams of the future which God's promises had aroused in his breast."[25] The tested individual, then, is being given the opportunity—the freedom—to demonstrate by the choices he makes what sort of person he really is. Testing also presupposes that the one giving the test is not at the same time compelling the individual to act or decide in any given way.

> *If you turn at my reproof, behold, I will pour out my spirit to you; I will make my words known to you.* [24] *Because I have called and you refused to listen have stretched out my hand and no one has heeded,* [25] *because you have ignored all my counsel and would have none of my reproof,* [26] *I also will laugh at your calamity* (Prov 1:23–26).

Describing this individual, Bridges writes: "And think of his knowledge, instead of being a delight, being *hated; his fear not chosen*; none of his gracious *counsel* regarded; all his *reproof despised*. Is it not just, that the sinner, thus obstinately bent upon the choice of *his own way*, should not only gather, but *eat the fruit of it*"?[26] Awesome is the power of free choice—even against God himself. A person who refuses the mercy and counsel of God does so to his/her own detriment. As Bridges suggests, this verse seems to contradict the view that God causes and determines all thoughts, actions, beliefs, and behaviors of all humans all the time.

> *The kingdom of heaven may be compared to a king who gave a wedding feast for his son,* [3] *and sent his servants to call those who were invited to the wedding feast, but they would not come* (Matt 22:3).

This is a problematic text, because the pericope ends with the words: *Many are called but few are chosen.* Yet the text clearly focuses on the fact that the call—though given by God—is resisted, yes, rejected by those he has invited. People were genuinely

---

25. Willis, *Genesis*, 291. See also Heb 11:17–19.
26. Bridges, *Proverbs*, 10.

invited to join the kingdom of heaven—implying that they could accept God's invitation—yet these individuals would not come on their own volition or free will. In this specific example, Jesus is referring to the Jewish leaders's rejection of him and his mission and thus the results: both the destruction of their city and being cast out into *outer darkness.*

In the spirit of coming to grip with the text, the comments of the great Baptist scholar John Broadus are instructive: "This selection of the actually saved may be looked at from two sides. From the divine side, we see that the Scriptures teach an eternal election of men to eternal life, simply out of God's good pleasure. From the human side, we see that those persons attain the blessings of salvation through Christ who accept the gospel invitation and obey the gospel commandments. It is doubtful whether our minds can combine both sides in a single view, but we must not for that reason deny either of them to be true."[27]

> O Jerusalem, Jerusalem, the city that kills the prophets and stones those who are sent to it! How often would I have gathered your children together as a hen gathers her brood under her wings, and you were not willing! (Matt 23:37).

Commentators have noted that the double address to the city expresses the deep compassion of the Savior. He desired the response to be different. But the people of Jerusalem had a will that opposed the will of God and by their rebellion forfeited God's plan for their best. Plummer summarizes well: "His mission to them as their Saviour is closed. If that relation to them is ever to be renewed, the initiative must come from them. What He has said and done for them ought to have sufficed for their conversion, and no more teaching will be granted to them. The little that still remains to be given will be for those who have accepted Him, for the faithful few among His disciples. But opportunity for conversion will always remain open, and it is for them to see if they will avail themselves of it."[28]

> If anyone's will is to do God's will, he will know whether the teaching is from God or whether I am speaking on my own authority (John 7:17).
>
> If you abide in me, and my words abide in you, ask whatever you wish, and it will be done for you (John 15:7).

Prayer implies a freedom in real time to entreat God for his responsive action to meet a need a human being has. The great Greek scholar and expositor J. B. Westcott says: "The petitions of the true disciples are echoes (so to speak) of Christ's words. As He has spoken so they speak. Their prayer is only some fragment of His teaching transformed into a supplication, and so it will necessarily be heard. It is important to notice how the promise of the absolute fulfillment of prayer is connected with the personal fellowship of the believer with Christ, both in the Synoptics and in St. John

---

27. Broadus, *Matthew*, 450. This is similar to the conclusion of Turretin in chapter 1.

28. Plummer, *Matthew*, 235.

. . . It shall come to pass for you. The result is not due to any external or arbitrary exertion of power, but to the action of a law of life."[29]

> *No temptation has overtaken you that is not common to man. God is faithful, and*
> *he will not let you be tempted beyond your ability, but with the temptation he will*
> *also provide the way of escape, that you may be able to endure it* (1 Cor 10:13).

Paul's teaching is that God has provided (at least some) humans with an ability not to sin; they are able to not fall into temptation. Robertson and Plummer in their excellent commentary argue that:

> The σὺν [*together*] and the articles imply that temptations and possibilities of escape always go in pairs: there is no πειρασμὸς [*temptation*] without its proper ἔκβασιν [*escape*], for these pairs are arranged by God, who permits no unfairness. He knows the powers with which He has endowed us, and how much pressure they can withstand. He will not leave us to become the victims of circumstances which He has Himself ordered for us . . . The power to endure is given σὺν τῷ πειρασμῷ [*together with the temptation*], the endurance is not given; that depends on ourselves.[30]

Accordingly, whenever people sin, it is not that they had to; there was a genuine *ability to do otherwise* because *a way of escape* was available for them to choose. It is important to notice that there is a range of alternative options, each of which are compatible with a Christian's regenerated nature. Therefore, when people can and do freely choose to sin and were *able* not to sin, it follows that they are genuinely respons-*able* for their sin, not God.

> *So, whether you eat or drink, or whatever you do, do all to the glory of God*
> (1 Cor 10:31).

Paul has been discussing principles for determining whether a believer can/should eat things offered to idols (9:1). As he concludes his discussion, he gives this general principle: the believer can choose among the options, but he is commanded to make sure he makes a choice that glorifies God.

> *For you have been called to live in freedom, my brothers and sisters. But don't use*
> *your freedom to satisfy your sinful nature. Instead, use your freedom to serve one*
> *another in love* (Gal 5:13).[31]

Freedom is clearly stated here by Paul, but he goes on to add that there are choices as to how that freedom appropriately is to be expressed: not with behaviors which

29. Westcott, *John, Greek Text*, 201. For more on the relationship of prayer and human freedom/determinism, see chapter 16.

30. Robertson and Plummer, *1 Corinthians*, 209.

31. Quoted from the *NLT*.

come from a person's *sinful nature* (which Paul implies one "could" do), but with a commitment to love one another (which one "ought" to do instead).

> *For God gave us a spirit not of fear but of power and love and self-control*
> *(2 Tim. 1:7).*
>
> *Whoever is slow to anger is better than the mighty, and he who rules his spirit*
> *than he who takes a city (Prov. 16:32).*
>
> *For this very reason, make every effort to supplement your faith with virtue,*
> *and virtue with knowledge, and knowledge with self-control, and self-control*
> *with steadfastness, and steadfastness with godliness, and godliness with brotherly*
> *affection, and brotherly affection with love (2 Pet 1:5, 7).*

The Bible contains many passages calling Christians to exercise self-control and self-discipline. Indeed, self-control is the opposite of control by something or others. If one is ever in control of the self (the thing one refers to as "I"), then does it not follow that there must be some sense of personal freedom?

> *And the dead were judged by what was written in the books, according to what*
> *they had done (Rev 20:12).*

Hengstenberg makes an interesting contrast between the books that are the basis of the last judgment: "The single book of life opened is opposed to the many books of works, that are also opened. The difference as to the many and the one is either to be explained on the consideration, that but few are saved, or because the book of life contains simply the names, while the books of the dead contain the long array of their evil deeds."[32] Judgment for the unbelievers, then, is based on deeds done, and thus on both personal responsibility and freedom of action because a person cannot be judged for what he cannot avoid doing, especially if it was causally determined by someone or something other than the defendant.

Soteriological.

> *If you obey the Lord your God and keep his commands and decrees that are writ-*
> *ten in this Book of the Law and turn to the Lord your God with all your heart*
> *and with all your soul.* [11] *Now what I am commanding you today is not too dif-*
> *ficult for you or beyond your reach.* [12] *It is not up in heaven, so that you have to*
> *ask, "Who will ascend into heaven to get it and proclaim it to us so we may obey*
> *it"?* [13] *Nor is it beyond the sea, so that you have to ask, "Who will cross the sea to*
> *get it and proclaim it to us so we may obey"?* [14] *No, the word is very near you;*
> *it is in your mouth and in your heart so you may obey it.* [15] *See, I set before you*
> *today life and prosperity, death and destruction.* [16] *For I command you today to*
> *love the Lord your God, to walk in obedience to him, and to keep his commands,*

---

32. Hengstenberg, *Revelation*, 378.

decrees and laws; then you will live and increase, and the Lord your God will bless you in the land you are entering to possess. [17] *But if your heart turns away and you are not obedient, and if you are drawn away to bow down to other gods and worship them,* [18] *I declare to you this day that you will certainly be destroyed. You will not live long in the land you are crossing the Jordan to enter and possess.* [19] *This day I call the heavens and the earth as witnesses against you that I have set before you life and death, blessings and curses. Now choose life, so that you and your children may live* [20] *and that you may love the Lord your God, listen to his voice, and hold fast to him. For the Lord is your life, and he will give you many years in the land he swore to give to your fathers, Abraham, Isaac and Jacob* (Deut 30:10–20).[33]

This passage is particularly eye-opening because Moses seems to command the unregenerate Israelites to make a genuine choice to follow God or not. He says they have options from which to choose. They are to choose between life and death, between blessings and curses. Moses pleads with them to choose life, making it clear that the Israelites actually possess the *ability* to make this choice. That is to say, this choice is "up to them" and not causally determined by things external to them. Further, he makes it clear that this is not only something they possess the ability to do, but moreover, it is not even *too difficult* for them to make this choice. He says, "You may do it." The *ESV* reads, *so that you* can *do it.* This seems to be not only biblical support of libertarian freedom to choose otherwise; but libertarian freedom regarding an offer to choose God, or at the least, not to reject him.

And Jesus said to his disciples, "Truly, I say to you, only with difficulty will a rich person enter the kingdom of heaven. [24] *Again I tell you, it is easier for a camel to go through the eye of a needle than for a rich person to enter the kingdom of God."* [25] *When the disciples heard this, they were greatly astonished, saying, "Who then can be saved"?* [26] *But Jesus looked at them and said, "With man this is impossible, but with God all things are possible"* (Matt 19:23–26).

At least, these words speak of choice. Roger Olson's comments on them are forceful: "What sense does this verse make in light of irresistible grace? Is Jesus saying it is harder *for God* to save a rich man than a poor one? How could that be? If everyone, without exception, only gets into the kingdom of God by God's work alone without any required cooperation on his or her part, then Jesus's saying makes no sense at all."[34] Olson reflects his Arminian position. If God gives grace to all and sovereignly chooses to create a world in which everyone is extended free choice, then there is no basis for merit.

God our Savior, who desires all people to be saved and to come to the knowledge of the truth (1 Tim 2:3–4).

33. Quoted from the *NIV.*
34. Olson, *Against Calvinism,* 165.

This text is one of the most controversial texts on the subject of human free will and determinism. As Humphreys says, "Chrysostom's comment is 'if he willed to save all, do thou will it also; and if thou willest, pray for it' . . . Thus, the Greek fathers accepted St. Paul's words in their *prima facie* sense. The Latin fathers seek to guard their application; and St. Augustine actually says 'by *all* understand "all the predestined" because men of all sort are among them.'"[35]

It could be argued that this verse implies human freedom in a libertarian sense because, if God desires all to be saved, then it seems the only reason some are not saved is because of their own free will. This passage demands more work exegetically, but, for here, it can be cited as evidence of human freedom.

> *Have I any pleasure in the death of the wicked, declares the Lord God, and not rather that he should turn from his way and live?* (Ezek 18:23).[36]
>
> *The Lord is not slow to fulfill his promise as some count slowness, but is patient toward you, not wishing that any should perish, but that all should reach repentance* (2 Pet 3:9).
>
> *We destroy arguments and every lofty opinion raised against the knowledge of God, and take every thought captive to obey Christ* (2 Cor 10:5).

Denney, commenting on these words of Paul, says:

> Men do certainly fortify themselves against the Gospel in their thoughts. The proud wisdom of the Greek was familiar to the Apostle . . . The expression has sometimes been censured as justifying the . . . taking away freedom of thought in religion. To think of Paul censuring the free exercise of intelligence in religion is too absurd; but he would have dealt very summarily with theories, ancient or modern, which serve no purpose but to fortify men . . . He would have spoken of sin and judgment, of reconciliation and life in Christ, till these great realities had asserted their greatness in the mind, and in doing so had shattered the proud intellectual structures which had been reared in ignorance or contempt of them . . . The Apostle had to beat down all the barriers by which men closed their minds against this supreme revelation.[37]

In Paul's evangelism there is every evidence of human interaction and reasoning and effort to win over the minds of his listeners. Though done in the power of God, there is a contest going on in the hearts and minds of men; people freely can reject the message and thus are responsible for their own thoughts (at least some of them). Paul's words are the words of debate. No, they are stronger: the thoughts freely held by some must by persuasion be *taken captive*. Thus, a vigorous argument is to be made

---

35. Humphreys, *Timothy and Titus*, 94–95.

36. See also Jer 48:31: *Therefore, I wail for Moab; I cry out for all Moab; for the men of Kir-hareseth I mourn.*

37. Denney, *2 Corinthians*, 142.

against the thinking in the minds that hold some back from living according to the law of Christ in the power of the Spirit.

Paul states that *we* are—and implies that we ought—to take our thoughts captive to obey Christ. An application of Paul's teaching could be that people are responsible "free thinkers" of the libertarian variety. Accordingly, Paul seems to suggest that all of a person's thoughts are not causally determined and forced upon them from external sources; humans possess the ability to think otherwise, that is to say, they are responsible for their own thoughts (at least some of them).

Paul, then, is clear that anyone can be taken captive by incorrect thinking (See also Col 2:8), but ought to do otherwise. It follows that humanity is engaged in a battle, a battle *not against flesh and blood* (Eph 6:12). Whether a person realizes it or not, he is in a battle waged in the mind and for the mind! It was Paul's strategy in the power of the Spirit to take thoughts adverse to *the knowledge of God* captive. People can freely choose to—and do—oppose the truth, and it is the challenge of believers to challenge their thinking and choices.

TEXTS WITH BOTH A FLAVOR OF DETERMINISM AND HUMAN FREEDOM.

In addition to the above examples, there are other occasions where statements of God's sovereignty and a person's freedom of thought and action occur simultaneously in the context: chapter, paragraph, and even the same sentence. It is these which are especially thought-provoking *and* press the serious student of the biblical text to seek an explanation and/or a solution to what seems logically impossible. Consider the following:

Pharaoh.

> *Still Pharaoh's heart was hardened, and he would not listen to them, as the Lord had said. Then the Lord said to Moses, "Pharaoh's heart is hardened; he refuses to let the people go"* (Exod 7:13–14).
>
> *But when Pharaoh saw that there was a respite, he hardened his heart and would not listen to them, as the Lord had said . . . But Pharaoh hardened his heart this time also, and did not let the people go* (Exod 8:15, 32).
>
> *But the Lord hardened the heart of Pharaoh, and he did not listen to them, as the Lord had spoken to Moses . . . But when Pharaoh saw that the rain and the hail and the thunder had ceased, he sinned yet again and hardened his heart, he and his servants* (Exod 9:12, 34).

> *Then the Lord said to Moses, "Go in to Pharaoh, for I have hardened his heart and the heart of his servants, that I may show these signs of mine among them"* (Exod 10:1).[38]

So, which one is it? Did Pharaoh harden his own heart or did God harden Pharaoh's heart? The Bible claims both to be true, but after considering the logical law of non-contradiction, can both of these biblical statements be true? J. S. Banks, though in an article written over a century ago, expresses the dilemma well:

> The moral difficulty of this subject is the ascription in Old Testament of the hardening of men's hearts to God . . . First of all, the result is twice foretold. The Lord says, *I will harden his heart* (Exod 4:7). In the case of the first five plagues and the seventh . . . the phrase is *Pharaoh hardened his heart* or *his heart was hardened* . . . In the sixth, eighth, and ninth . . . the phrase is *the Lord hardened his heart* . . . Thus, the result is not ascribed to God only; both the divine and the human agencies are recognized. Whatever God had to do with the result, Pharaoh's freedom of action was not interfered with . . . At each stage Pharaoh might have yielded instead of refusing . . . It shows us, that divine appeals and commands never leave men as they find them. If not yielded to, they increase insensibility, benumb and gradually deaden moral feeling. This effect is contrary to the divine purpose, and is entirely man's fault; but it is natural and inevitable. The more powerful the appeals, the more rapid the hardening process, until God's Spirit withdraws, and leaves man to his own ways (Rom 1:28). Looked at from the human side, Pharaoh, like every smaller transgressor, is seen acting with perfect freedom, consciously pitting his own will against God's, despising louder and louder warnings of ruin, self-punished and self-destroyed. Looked at from the divine side, God is seen commanding, forewarning, repeating rejected opportunities, doing everything to ensure submission and safety . . . It is evident that we have here again the old problem of reconciling the divine foreknowledge and government with human freedom and responsibility. Each element is attested by its own evidence. Both are necessary to a complete explanation. The two regions meet at some point invisible to human eye and undefinable in human speech and thought.[39]

The pertinent question is raised: Who is doing the "hardening"? According to the biblical text, both Pharaoh and God are said to be engaged in this activity. It appears, then, that God is influencing Pharaoh to carry out his plan, and yet at the same time Pharaoh is acting on his own, perhaps protecting his sovereign rule or determining to keep from losing the valuable asset of Israel's labor.

---

38. See also Exod 7:22; 8:19; 9:7, 35; 10:20, 27; 11:10; and 14:8.

39. Banks, "Hardening," 302–3.

The sons of Eli (1 Sam 2:12–17, 22–25, especially verse 25).

> Now the sons of Eli were worthless men. They did not know the Lord. [13] The custom of the priests with the people was that when any man offered sacrifice, the priest's servant would come, while the meat was boiling, with a three-pronged fork in his hand, [14] and he would thrust it in to the pan or kettle or cauldron or pot. All that the fork brought up the priest would take for himself. This is what they did at Shiloh to all the Israelites who came there. [15] Moreover, before the fat was burned, the priest's servant would come and say to the man who was sacrificing, "Give meat for the priest to roast, for he will not accept boiled meat from you but only raw." [16] And if the man said to him, "Let them burn the fat first, and then take as much as you wish," he would say, "No, you must give it now, and if not, I will take it by force." [17] Thus the sin of the young men was very great in the sight of the Lord, for the men treated the offering of the Lord with contempt . . . [22] Now Eli was very old, and he kept hearing all that his sons were doing to all Israel, and how they lay with the women who were serving at the entrance to the tent of meeting. [23] And he said to them, "Why do you do such things? For I hear of your evil dealings from all these people. [24] No, my sons; it is no good report that I hear the people of the Lord spreading abroad. [25] If someone sins against a man, God will mediate for him, but if someone sins against the Lord, who can intercede for him"? But they would not listen to the voice of their father, for it was the will of the Lord to put them to death.

The historian here describes the aggressive, sinful actions of Eli's sons: (1) they forcefully took portions of people's sacrifices in disregard to the Mosaic regulations and to the officiating Levite's rebuke (for which no recorded reprimand was made by their father *but* was by the officiating Levite); and (2) they became sexual predators of the women who assisted in the duties associated with Tabernacle rituals (for which their father gave a very stern warning). If the words at the end of verse 25—*for it was the will of the Lord to put them to death*—had not been included in the historian's account, the reader would have assumed the young men were making their own choices and doing whatever they wished despite being confronted and knowing that what they were doing was evil. Commentators usually ignore God's sovereignty enshrined in these difficult words. Unusual is Smith who notes that: "Man can bring upon himself neither good nor evil except by the working of God's will, and the punishment of sin is as thoroughly a part of God's will as the rewarding of righteousness. An intense conviction of the personality of God was the very foundation of the religious life of the Israelites, and lies at the root of the words of Eli here and of those of Job."[40] Surely the sense of determinism is in the writer's words in verse 25, but, it is important in this discussion to note that the words which follow seem to state that God's response is not *prior* to the evil they did but afterwards (2:30–34): *Because the sons did not honor*

---

40. Smith, *2 Samuel*, 41.

me . . . I will.[41] And because of Eli and his sons's sins, God revokes his promise, which sounds not like predestination but punishment *subsequent* to their sins. Thus, the sovereign will of God (determinism?) is clearly stated, but the reader sees what appears to be the free act of the sons and what appears to be God's subsequent judgment for their behavior and thus, their responsibility and accountability.

Absalom's treason (2 Sam 16:15—17:14).

> *Now Absalom and all the people, the men of Israel, came to Jerusalem, and Ahithophel with him.* [16] *And when Husham the Archite, David's friend, came to Absalom, Hushai said to Absalom, "Long live the king! Long live the king!"* [17] *And Absalom said to Hushai, "Is this your loyalty to your friend? Why did you not go with your friend"?* [18] *And Hushai said to Absalom, "No, for whom the Lord and this people and all the men of Israel have chosen, his I will be, and with him I will remain.* [19] *And again, whom should I serve? Should it not be his son? As I have served your father, so I will serve you."* [20] *Then Absalom said to Ahithophel, "Give your counsel. What shall we do"?* [21] *Ahithophel said to Absalom, "Go in to your father's concubines, whom he has left to keep the house, and all Israel will hear that you have made yourself a stench to your father, and the hands of all who are with you will be strengthened" . . .* [17] *Moreover, Ahithophel said to Absalom, "Let me choose twelve thousand men, and I will arise and pursue David tonight.* [2] *I will come upon him while he is weary and discouraged and throw him into a panic, and all the people who are with him will flee. I will strike down only the king" . . .* [5] *Then Absalom said, "Call Hushai the Archite also, and let us hear what he has to say."* [6] *And when Hushai came to Absalom, Absalom said to him, "Thus has Ahithophel spoken; shall we do as he says? If not, you speak."* [7] *Then Hushai said to Absalom, "This time the counsel that Ahithophel has given is not good."* [8] *Hushai said, "You know that your father and his men are mighty men, and that they are enraged, like a bear robbed of her cubs in the field. Besides, your father is expert in war; he will not spend the night with the people . . .* [11] *But my counsel is that all Israel be gathered to you, from Dan to Beersheba, as the sand by the sea for multitude, and that you go to battle in person.* [12] *So we shall come upon him in some place where he is to be found, and we shall light upon him as the dew falls on the ground, and of him and all the men with him not one will be left" . . .* [14] *And*

41. The full account of 2:30–34 follows: *Therefore the Lord, the God of Israel, declares: "I promised that your house and the house of your father should go in and out before me forever,"* but now the Lord declares: *"Far be it from me, for those who honor me I will honor, and those who despise me shall be lightly esteemed.* [31] *Behold, the days are coming when I will cut off your strength and the strength of your father's house, so that there will not be an old man in your house.* [32] *Then in distress you will look with envious eye on all the prosperity that shall be bestowed on Israel, and there shall not be an old man in your house forever.* [33] *The only one of you whom I shall not cut off from my altar shall be spared to weep his eyes out to grieve his heart, and all the descendants of your house shall die by the sword of men.* [34] *And this that shall come upon your two sons, Hophni and Phinehas, shall be the sign to you: both of them shall die on the same day."*

Absalom and all the men of Israel said, "The counsel of Hushai the Archite is bet-ter than the counsel of Ahithophel." For the Lord had ordained to defeat the good counsel of Ahithophel, so that the Lord might bring harm upon Absalom.

When David hears that Ahithophel is part of the treason, he is heart-broken and prays that God will bring Ahithophel's counsel to naught, that though Ahithophel had a reputation for wisdom. Ahithophel counsels Absalom to take two actions: lay with David's concubines (understood as a step of a new king) and then attack David imme-diately. Absalom accepts the first, but seeks Hushai's counsel before doing the second. He—as a loyal adviser to David—gives advice contradictory to Ahithophel and by so doing keeps David and his men from likely disaster. There is every indication—were it not for 17:14—that this is deliberation freely given and a decision freely made. The words of Smith are very emphatic: "The Lord had appointed; literally, *and Jehovah had commanded to bring to nought . . .* So plain did it seem to the writer that Absalom's suc-cess depended upon rapid action, that nothing less than the direct interference of the divine providence could account for the infatuation of Absalom and his counsellors."[42]

In the same context, then, there seems to be evidence of determinism (*com-manded*) and free deliberation.

David's sin in taking a census (2 Sam 24:1–10; cf. 1 Chr 21:1–8).

Again the anger of the Lord was kindled against Israel, and he incited David against them, saying, "Go, number Israel and Judah." ² So the king said to Joab, the commander of the army, who was with him, "Go through all the tribes of Israel, from Dan to Beersheba, and number the people, that I may know the number of the people." ³ But Joab said to the king, "May the Lord your God add to the people a hundred times as many as they are, while the eyes of my lord the king still see it, but why does my lord the king delight in this thing"? ⁴ But the king's word prevailed against Joab and the commanders of the army . . . ¹⁰ But David's heart struck him after he had numbered the people. And David said to the Lord, "I have sinned greatly in what I have done. But now, O Lord, please take away the iniquity of your servant, for I have done very foolishly."

Then Satan stood against Israel and incited David to number Israel. ² So David said to Joab and the commanders of the army, "Go, number Israel, from Beer-sheba to Dan, and bring me a report, that I may know their number." ³ But Joab said, "May the Lord add to his people a hundred times as many as they are! Are they not, my lord the king, all of them my lord's servants? Why then should my lord require this? Why should it be a cause of guilt for Israel"? ⁴ But the king's word prevailed against Joab . . . ⁶ But he did not include Levi and Benjamin in the numbering, for the king's command was abhorrent to Joab. ⁷ But God was displeased with this thing, and he struck Israel. ⁸ And David said to God, "I

42. Smith, *2 Samuel*, 418.

> *have sinned greatly in that I have done this thing. But now, please take away the*
> *iniquity of your servant, for I have acted very foolishly."*

This quotation has a little different twist in that it appears from the two accounts that the Lord "incited" David and yet Satan "incited" David to do what was an act of pride and disobedience to the Lord. Joab knew it was wrong and warned David that it would *be a cause of guilt for Israel.* But David insisted, refusing to listen to his general. There is every indication that David deliberately rejected what he later admitted was wise counsel. Yet at the same time the historian notes that David did not act on his own initiative: He was incited[43] by God and Satan. The action David took was the will of God because the anger of the *Lord* was kindled against Israel. Again, both human freedom (on David's part) and divine determinism (God's incitement of David and his judgment on Israel for her sin) are both part of the historical account.

God pronounces judgment on Ahab and his family (1 Kgs 21:20–29).

> *Ahab said to Elijah, "Have you found me, O my enemy"? He answered . . . "I*
> *[the Lord] will bring disaster upon you. I will utterly burn you up, and will cut*
> *off from Ahab every male, bond or free, in Israel.* [22] *And I will make your house*
> *like the house of Jeroboam the son of Nebat, and like the house of Baasha the*
> *son of Ahijah, for the anger to which you have provoked me, and because you*
> *have made Israel to sin."* [23] *And of Jezebel the Lord also said, "The dogs shall eat*
> *Jezebel within the walls of Jezreel.* [24] *Anyone belonging to Ahab who dies in the*
> *city the dogs shall eat, and anyone of his who dies in the open country the birds*
> *of the heavens shall eat . . . "* [27] *And when Ahab heard those words, he tore his*
> *clothes and put sackcloth on his flesh and fasted and lay in sackcloth and went*
> *about dejectedly.* [28] *And the word of the Lord came to Elijah the Tishbite, saying,*
> [29] *"Have you seen how Ahab has humbled himself before me? Because he has*
> *humbled himself before me, I will not bring the disaster in his days; but in his*
> *son's days I will bring the disaster upon his house."*

This is an amazing text. On the one hand God pronounces judgment on Ahab and his family, that not one of his descendants will be left. Yet when Ahab shows a brokenness which God notes in real time, God changes his pronounced judgment and shows Ahab mercy. It is hard to understand this without asking if this does not illustrate not

---

43. The Hebrew word here used here סוּת is translated *"allure* in 2 Chr 18:31 *and* God *allured them away from him . . . So also* Job 36:16: *He allureth thee* out *of the mouth of distress, freedom hath seduced thee;* for meaning *seduce, entice,* see also v 18. [Another use of the word is translated] *instigate,* in bad sense, c. acc. pers., + בְּ *against,* 1 Sam 26:19; 2 Sam 24:1; Jer 43:3; Job 2:3; c. acc. pers. alone 1 Kgs 21:25; 2 Kgs 18:32 = Isa 36:18; see also 2 Chr 32:15; Deut 13:7; Jer 38:22; + inf. 1 Chr 21:1; 2 Chr 18:2; 32:11" (Brown et al., 694).

only human freedom to respond to God's plan but also God's freedom to change in real time in response to man's repentance.[44]

It is interesting that commentators accept both God's sovereignty and human freedom. Hammond is but one example: "The Searcher of hearts saw in it [Ahab's repentance] a genuine self-abasement . . . There is no injustice here—no threat of punishment against the innocent instead of the guilty—as might at first sight appear. For in the first place, God knew well what the son would be, and in the second place, if the son had departed from his father's sins, he would have been spared . . . The sentence would have been revoked. Judgment was deferred to give the house of Ahab another chance. When Ahab lapsed into sin, he suffered in his own person; when his sons persisted in sin, excision befell the family."[45]

Prophets who prophesy, but their prophecies (true and false) are controlled by God (Ezek 14:6–11).

Therefore, say to the house of Israel, Thus says the Lord God: Repent and turn away from your idols, and turn away your faces from all your abominations. [7] For any one of the house of Israel, or of the strangers who sojourn in Israel, who separates himself from me, taking his idols into his heart and putting the stumbling block of his iniquity before his face, and yet comes to a prophet to consult me through him, I the Lord will answer him myself. [8] And I will set my face against that man; I will make him a sign and a byword and cut him off from the midst of my people, and you shall know that I am the Lord. [9] And if the prophet is deceived and speaks a word, I, the Lord, have deceived that prophet, and I will stretch out my hand against him and will destroy him from the midst of my people Israel. [10] And they shall bear their punishment—the punishment of the prophet and the punishment of the inquirer shall be alike—[11] that the house of Israel may no more go astray from me, nor defile themselves anymore with all their transgressions, but that they may be my people and I may be their God, declares the Lord God.

The prophet very likely thought he had a word from God. He acts as he understands and speaks, unconscious that he has been deceived by God. Thus, the text indicates both God's sovereign control and the prophet's free expression. (See also 1 Kgs 22:23; 2 Chr 18:21.)

The great scholar E. H. Plumptre mixes both of these perspectives and does so by saying God's sovereign action is in response to man's sin: "The teaching of modern

44. Some have charged God with doing precisely what he said he would, apparently cancelling his mercy, but a careful reading of the text and the fulfilment documented in the next chapter (1 Kgs 22) clarifies what God did. He did not rescind his judgment of Ahab; he postponed the disaster to fall on his family until after Ahab's death. It would not fall in his lifetime.

45. Hammond, *1 Kings*, 512.

thought is to soften language like this into "I have permitted him to be deceived." The distinction was seldom, if ever, present to the mind of the Old Testament, or indeed of the New Testament, writers. It is Jehovah who sends the *lying spirit* in 1 Kgs 22:20–23. It is he who in the latter days shall send men *strong delusions* that they shall believe a lie (2 Thes 2:11). In both cases it is implied that the delusion is a righteous punishment, is indeed the natural, because the divinely appointed, punishment of the sin."[46]

Jesus and Judas (Luke 22:21–22).

> But behold, the hand of him who betrays me is with me on the table. [22] For the Son of Man goes as it has been determined, but woe to that man by whom he is betrayed!

In those two short sentences there are two statements of Jesus that described an action determined for Jesus's betrayor: Before the act—Judas's betrayal—Jesus predicts (prophesies) it (verse 21) and then Jesus says *it has been determined*. At the same time Jesus makes it clear that Judas is responsible for his action: *woe to that man*. Plummer says, "It is part of the divine decree that the death of the Christ should be accompanied by betrayal . . . [and] although God knows from all eternity that Judas is the betrayer of the Christ, yet this does not destroy the freedom or responsibility of Judas."[47] This is a very clear example which shows that determinism—rightly understood—need not mean that the sinner can blame God for being judged.

Peter's sermon (Acts 2:22–24; 3:13–18).

> Men of Israel, hear these words: Jesus of Nazareth, a man attested to you by God with mighty works and wonders and signs that God did through him in your midst, as you yourselves know— [23] this Jesus, delivered up according to the definite plan and foreknowledge of God, you crucified and killed by the hands of lawless men. [24] God raised him up, loosing the pangs of death, because it was not possible for him to be held by it . . .
> [13] The God of Abraham, the God of Isaac, and the God of Jacob, the God of our fathers, glorified his servant Jesus, whom you delivered over and denied in the presence of Pilate, when he had decided to release him. [14] But you denied the Holy and Righteous One, and asked for a murderer to be granted to you, [15] and you killed the Author of life, whom God raised from the dead. To this we are witnesses . . . [17] "And now, brothers, I know that you acted in ignorance, as did also your rulers. [18] But what God foretold by the mouth of all the prophets, that his Christ would suffer, he thus fulfilled.

46. Plumptre, *Ezekiel*, 248.

47. Plummer, *Luke*, 500.

The people crucified and killed Jesus, asking for a murder to be released, though they did it in ignorance. These decisions and actions originated with the people. But it was *according to the definite plan and foreknowledge of God*. It was God's plan that they carried out. F. F. Bruce notes these in his comment on verses 3:14–18: "This is what *you* did, but *God* restored him to life again . . . Again, it is clear how the apostolic preaching in Acts loves to emphasize the contrast between men's treatment of Jesus and God's."[48]

The prayer meeting (Acts 4:23–28).

> *When they were released, they went to their friends and reported what the chief priests and the elders had said to them.* [24] *And when they heard it, they lifted their voices together to God and said, "Sovereign Lord, who made the heaven and the earth and the sea and everything in them,* [25] *who through the mouth of our father David, your servant, said by the Holy Spirit, 'Why did the Gentiles rage, and the peoples plot in vain?* [26] *The kings of the earth set themselves, and the rulers were gathered together, against the Lord and against his Anointed'—*[27]*for truly in this city there were gathered together against your holy servant Jesus, whom you anointed, both Herod and Pontius Pilate, along with the Gentiles and the peoples of Israel,* [28] *to do whatever your hand and your plan had predestined to take place."*

The previous chapter records how the Jewish leaders opposed the believers's witness, like the Psalmist put it: *Gentiles raging and plotting*. The people (two individuals specifically mentioned by name) were initiating, but God was *doing whatever* [his] *hand and* [his] *plan had predestined to take place*.

Gloag, in his classical commentary, put it well:

> They thought to do their own will, but in reality, they were fulfilling the purpose of God. He makes the actions of His enemies subservient to His purposes. "The death of the Lord," as Meyer observes, "was not the accidental work of hostile willfulness, but, on the contrary, the necessary result of the divine determination, which must use the free action of man as its instruments." This determination of God, however, must be explained in such a manner as to make it consistent with the free agency of men. Herod, and Pontius Pilate, and the Gentiles, and the people of Israel, though acting as the instruments of God's will, were not freed from moral responsibility, nor was their guilt thereby in the least degree extenuated.[49]

---

48. Bruce, *Acts*, 82.
49. Gloag, *Acts*, 160.

SUMMARY.

The purpose of this chapter has been to affirm that there are two positions illustrated and, therefore, found in the Bible: human libertarian freedom/responsibility and God's total sovereignty. Documentation of these has been provided by surveying the chief, relevant biblical data that support the providence of God over *all* things, and on the other hand by examining the Scriptures implying human freedom and genuine responsibility over *some* things. Both appear to be taught in holy writ, yet they might seem to be logically incompatible. The question, then, is raised: Are these clear examples of contradictions in the Bible (and thus, reason to doubt the inerrancy or reliability of Scripture), or is there a way to logically reconcile all these statements? Must readers shrug their shoulders and retreat to mystery, or can Christians provide a logically coherent answer to this vital question? One matter is certain: A solution cannot occur by denying free will (by some flavor of divine determinism), nor by denying God's sovereignty. Whatever solution is proposed, it cannot be affirmed by diminishing the role of the one or the other.

The above discussion also has provided the backdrop of heated debate behind the doors of the church for the past five hundred years or so. Some Christians think it is more important to affirm the total sovereignty of God, while others believe one ought to allow for human freedom and responsibility lest they make God the author of evil and evil himself. The motives behind these two groups of Christians are both righteous; however, these doctrinal debates have been a sword dividing the Body of Christ—sometimes with vitriol!

In the following chapters there will be (1) a discussion of the competing views held by Christians; (2) a philosophical analysis of their strengths and weaknesses; and (3) a proposal as to what is the best logical explanation and the best biblical interpretation.

3

A survey of human freedom during the pre-Reformation period

Augustine (AD 354–430)

THE MAJORITY OF ALL theological and philosophical positions typically stands on the foundations of significant writers from the past. Though some make far greater contributions than others, any author who ignores the work of other theological thinkers weakens his own arguments and forfeits the enhancements of those who have previously researched the same subject. In the spirit of that attitude, this chapter (and the chapters 4–11) will explore what notables have written on the subject of human freedom. For simplicity, the chapters are divided as the "Pre-Reformation Period" and the "Reformation Period and Post-Reformation Periods." This chapter will begin the focus on the "Pre-Reformation Period."

Three notable figures will readily come to mind to those familiar with the time period. St. Augustine by far is the most prominent, not only in his day but throughout the years of history since then. Today he still is widely read and that in numerous languages. But, because his work was significantly impacted, or better, his views were altered by a second writer, the influence and teaching of this second person must be considered. To be specific, this second writer had such an impact on what Augustine wrote earlier in life that Augustine's last contributions—if read alone anonymously— would not sound like the earlier Augustine at all. Further, much of the theological and philosophical discussion from that day to the present interacts with Augustine and this second writer: a monk named Pelagius. It is surprising, then, that Pelagius's recorded thought is miniscule in comparison to the corpus of Augustine's writings, and in fact, most of what is known about Pelagius comes not from his own writings, but from those who opposed him, most significantly Augustine himself.

A third theologian/philosopher—Thomas Aquinas—also must be considered, because, when the Reformation movement was germinating and then began, he had already established himself as the most prominent Roman Catholic scholar and a prolific author. Indeed, he was the person who, along with his writings, might be seen as the "other side" in Reformation studies. Prominent later leaders—Luther, Calvin and Molina—responded to his *magnum opus: Summa Theologica*. But his work is profoundly insightful both for modern theologians, and especially for students of the philosophy of religion.

Because Pelagius was responding to Augustine's early writings, a discussion of Augustine and his early and later writings will be the first focus.

AUGUSTINE, BISHOP OF HIPPO (AD 354–430)

Augustine in his autobiography *Confessions* describes how, after living a life of sexual impurity and pursuit of understanding various philosophies, he became a Christian at the age of thirty-two. He attributes his conversion as the fruit of (1) careful searching for the truth[1] and (2) the powerful influence and faithful prayers of his godly mother Monica. He was a prolific author, and sixteen centuries later his influence is still felt. Two books in particular are still widely read and known: *Confessions* (written between AD 397 to 401) and *City of God* (written in AD 426). But among the most influential writings in philosophical and theological circles—especially which are relevant for an understanding of his view of free will and God's sovereignty—are Augustine's "A Treatise on Nature and Grace" (written AD 415), "On Grace and Free Choice (written AD 426), and *On the Free Choice of the Will* (which he wrote and revised off and on over a period of eight years from AD 387 to 395). Interestingly, this latter work is summarized by Augustine in what he called *Retractationes* (English: *Reconsiderations*), in which he not only catalogues his writings, giving their chronological order, but also gives a concise presentation of the essence of their contents.[2]

But any discussion of *On the Free Choice of the Will* must be seen and understood by Augustine's later work "A Treatise on Nature and Grace," a treatise that specifically

---

1. This personal search influenced Augustine's thinking of the requirement for all persons. They must deliberately search for the truth, after which the will makes progress "upward" toward wisdom and God's way. (See, for example, 3.22.64, [218], and see the discussion later in this essay. All quotations and the documentation from Augustine's chief works (others are clearly documented otherwise) are from the fine translation and editing of Peter King, *On the Free Choice*. The quotations will have both the sections of Augustine's work (e.g., 3.22.64) and, where relevant, page numbers [n] in King's translation.

2. In the introduction to this work he says "The reader who reads my works in the order in which they were written may learn something of how I progressed as I wrote them" (Augustine, *Retractationes*, Prologue, 3; [104]). This comment is very relevant to the author's summary of Augustine's "A Treatise on Nature and Grace, Against Pelagius" (not to be confused with *On Grace and Free Choice*) and the author's assessment (at the end of this essay) of the apparent shift in Augustine's view of free will.

addresses the heresy of a monk named Pelagius[3] and clarifies the necessary influence and role of God and his grace in the choices every person makes.

On the Free Choice of the Will is written as a dialogue between Augustine and a fellow priest named Evodius, who asks his counsel on a question that has befuddled philosophers and theologians for centuries. The following brief excerpt introduces the subject at hand and the flavor of the interactions that will follow between the two in all three chapters ("books" as they are called) of Augustine's work:

> Evodius (E): *Please tell me whether God is not the author of evil.*[4]
>
> Augustine (A) = *Evil could not occur without an author. But if you ask who the author is, no answer can be given, for there is not just a single author—rather, evil people are the authors of their evildoing* (1.1.1.4).
>
> E = *Perhaps no one sins unless he has learned how. But if that is true, I ask: From whom did we learn how to sin? How is it that we do evil?* (1.1.2.4).
>
> A = *You are raising a question that hounded me while I was young; when I was worn out it caused my downfall, landing me in the company of heretics* (1.2.4.10).
>
> A = *We believe that everything that exists comes from the one God, although God is not the author of sins. But this is the sore point: If sins come from the souls that God created, and those souls come from God, how is it that sins are not almost immediately traced back to God?*
>
> E = *You have now stated plainly what keeps troubling my thoughts, pushing and dragging me into this very investigation* (1.2.5.12).

Twenty-five years after writing *On the Free Choice of the Will*, Augustine admits that

> The discussion [in *On the Free Choice of the Will*] was undertaken on account of those who deny that the origin of evil lies in the free choice of the will, and who contend that, if this is so, God as the Creator of all natures ought to be blamed . . .[5] Now since this was the question at hand, there was no examination of grace in these books [that is, the three volumes or books of which *On the Free Choice of the Will* consists], by which God so predestines the people He elects that He Himself even prepares the wills of those among them who are already making use of free choice. Whenever an opportunity to mention this grace came up, it was mentioned only in passing and not defended by detailed reasoning as though it were the subject being dealt with. For it is one matter to look into the origin of evil, another to look into how we may return to our former good or reach a greater good.[6]

---

3. See a fuller discussion of Pelagius's teaching, commonly known as *Pelagianism* later in chapter 4.

4. See chapter 16 for an answer to this question commonly known as the "Problem of Evil."

5. Specifically, Augustine is making reference to the Manichaeans, who "introduced some unchangeable nature of evil that is co-eternal with God" (Augustine, *Retractationes*, 1.9.2; [127–28]).

6. Augustine, *Retractationes* 1.9.2; [127–28].

In those words Augustine described his continuing pursuit of how to harmonize the two seemingly polar opposites of human freedom on the one hand and God's sovereignty, foreknowledge, and man's needed grace for salvation on the other.[7] It is vital to note the distinction that must be made between the ability to freely choose among a range of alternative options in general, and the ability to freely choose regarding moral, ethical, and soteriological matters. Be that as it may, it is this writer's conclusion that Augustine never was able to show how the two could be logically compatible. Rather, he settles for accepting *both* (1) man's free will (which is brilliantly argued in *On the Free Choice of the Will*) and (2) the need for God's grace *sovereignly given* to respond rightly (which is explicitly stated and exegetically supported in "A Treatise on Nature and Grace").[8] It is the purpose of the following discussion to provide a concise, documented summary of Augustine's argument[9] and then to explain how he failed in his reasoning.

ON THE FREE CHOICE OF THE WILL.

In brief, this is the argument of *On the Free Choice of the Will*:

1. Premise #1: God is totally good, and anything which comes from his hand is good.

2. Premise #2: Free will is a gift from his hand, given to all mankind and, therefore, free will is a good gift.

3. Premise #3: This free will was "good" when given to Adam and Eve but—though flawed in people ever since—still enables every person to choose to do good *or* to make destructive decisions, which in turn makes their own wills ever more damaged and prone to evil.

This argument will now be more thoroughly explained and briefly illustrated in Augustine's lengthy treatise.

---

7. Brown summaries the dilemma well: "God's activity and human free choice appear to be exclusive alternatives. For if we say that God's foreknowledge is absolutely certain, or that God is the cause of every activity, or that God's grace is necessary for us to choose the good, then it is hard to explain how our choices can be free. On the other hand, if we claim that our choices are really free, it seems we must deny that God has any part in them, either knowing them with certainty or causing them. This means that God is not omniscient or omnipotent. The issue of free choice also plays a critical role in that other vexed philosophical puzzle—the problem of evil. For if we do not have free choice, we are not to be blamed or praised for our actions; rather, it is all God's doing. God becomes responsible for moral evil, either by causing it Himself or by punishing us who are not responsible for it" (Brown, "Augustine on Freedom," 30). Brown expresses the dilemmas well, but the author is not as pessimistic as he appears to be by his framing of the opposites.

8. See also another treatment in Augustine, "On Grace and Free Will."

9. The summary will follow Augustine's argument sequentially so the reader can easily follow the treatise *On the Free Choice of the Will* in Augustine's own words.

Premise #1: God is good, sovereign, and just (1.2.5.12–13).

Augustine argues that God is wholly good and, therefore, is the giver of only "good" gifts. With this few would argue. But, since the question at issue is the origin of evil, Evodius acknowledges that he does not understand how a good God could give a gift (free will) and have it denominated "good" but which would result in the bad and evil decisions people would make and the damages such decisions would wreak not only in their own lives but also in others. Perhaps freedom was not actually a "good gift" or, if it was, that God should not have given it in the first place. He is puzzled because of what this thinking would suggest if taken to its logical end. In his own words he asks Augustine: "I ask whether free choice itself, through which we are found guilty of having the ability to commit sin, ought to have been given to us by him who made us. It seems that, if we lack it, we would not be bound to sin. My fear is that in this way God will also be reckoned as author of our evildoings (1.16.35.117)."[10] With this comment of Evodius, Book 1 of *On the Free Choice of the Will* ends.

Premise #2: God has given people free will, and free will is a good gift.

Augustine is dogmatic about this, and it is a crucial premise of his reasoning. To him, though free will is a "good" gift—it provides an ability to choose between a range of alternative possibilities—for "acting rightly" or for "sinning" (2.1.3.5–7). Though this second premise seems intuitively reasonable, Augustine also believes that the "fact that a person cannot live rightly without it [without free will, it] is therefore a sufficient reason why it should have been given [by God] to him." Further, if people do not have free will, they cannot justly be punished by God. If they are not free, then ultimately, they are causally determined or controlled by someone or something else. In defending this Augustine writes: "When God punishes the sinner, what does He seem to be saying but: 'Why did you not make use of free will for the purpose for which I gave it to you'?—that is, for acting rightly" (2.1.3.6).[11]

This is clear enough, but Evodius's question (as quoted above) still is an issue: If free will results that some will choose against wisdom and sin and thus receive God's judgment, why did not God just *not* give it and choose some other "gift" that would not have led to sinners's damnation? (See also Evodius's question in 2.1.4.8).

---

10. Evodius is dealing with Augustine's statement that, because God is good, he only gives good gifts, and, therefore, human freedom is a good gift. Evodius does not see how this conclusion does not make God blameworthy because the good gift has resulted in evil behavior. Yet his question is itself troublesome because human freedom does not necessitate sin. Human freedom, therefore, does not make us blameworthy because of the *ability* to commit sin, but blameworthy because we sin. Human freedom, however, does give the ability to commit sin or not to commit sin.

11. This later will come back to haunt Augustine because the Pelagians will conclude this as support of their belief that people on their own can choose to seek God.

Augustine seems to suggest that Evodius's question is "*blasphemous*" because a good God cannot be "*faulted*" for the gifts he gives. He says to Evodius (2.2.4.10):

> But if you hold that God gave us free will . . . I want you to tell me briefly whether we should say that God ought not to have given what we acknowledge he gave:
>
> 1. Now if it is *uncertain* whether God gave it, we rightly ask whether it was well given. Then if we find that (*a*) it was well given, we also find that it was given by Him from whom all goods are given to the soul; or if we find that (*b*) it was not well given, then we realize it was not given by Him Whom it is blasphemous to blame.
>
> 2. On the other hand, if it is *certain* that God gave it, then, no matter how it was given, we must recognize that it should neither (*a*) not have been given, nor (*b*) have been given otherwise than it was given. For it was given by Him Whose deed cannot be faulted in any way.

At this point Augustine seems to dodge the question raised by Evodius, and it is hard not to conclude that one of Augustine's solutions to the problem of evil (as not coming from God) is by denying that anything evil can come from his hand. To suggest that God ultimately is the source of evil—by giving people free will—is to fault the one who *cannot be faulted in any way* and to *blaspheme* him. A good God only gives good gifts.

Augustine, therefore, must explain how a good gift could be utilized, yet with evil being the result. To that end, he gives considerable space to arguing that what a person sees in this world can be classified in three ways from inferior to the highest: (1) What merely exists [such as a rock]; (2) what is alive [e.g., plants, animals, and humans]; and (3) what understands [human beings] (2.5.11.43). A person's five senses perceive the first two, and above it is one's "internal sense," which judges the data received by the senses (2.5.12.48). And above this internal sense is the ability to reason (2.6.13.51),[12] which is given to human beings (2.11.31.125).

Augustine then asks if there might be anything more superior than reason, which he answers himself, identifying it as God (2.6.14.54–55; see also 2.15.39.154) and truth and wisdom (2.13.35.137).[13] Human reason is changeable (different people reason and reach differing conclusions), but there exists that which is not changeable (2.6.14.55–57). Numbers are an example of this unchangeable quality: $2 + 2 = 4$ (2.10.29.119). While unchangeable wisdom exists and should be pursued

12. "Ability to reason," that is, to judge concepts and ideas as good, bad, better, the best, worse, etc. (See chapter 12).

13. "Wisdom is the truth in which the highest good is recognized and grasped" (2.9.26.100) . . . "You will not deny that there is unchangeable truth, containing everything that is unchangeably true. You cannot call it yours or mine or anyone else's. Instead, it is present and offers itself in common to all who discern unchangeable truths" (2.12.33.130–31).

(2.10.28.111), people do not choose it as their "highest good" (2.9.27.106), and thus do not live wisely. This can be seen as analogous to God's other good gifts. For example, the eyes (or hands or feet) of human beings were given for good, but they can be misused for evil (2.18.48.182–84). What would a person be without hands or feet? Thus, as it is good to have limbs, and such gifts come from God—the giver of the good—they like free will can be misused.

Evodius understands the analogy, but he is still unconvinced and asks: "First, then, I would like you to prove to me that free will is something good; then I will grant that God gave it to us, since I acknowledge that all good things are from God" (2.18.49.186).[14]

Augustine seems to be frustrated by his consistent questioning. He replies, "Since you grant that the eye in the body is a good thing, even though its loss does not prevent one from living rightly, does not free will, without which no one lives rightly, seem to you to be something good"? (2.18.49.188). But Evodius objects: "I agree. But one point bothers me. Our question is about free will; we see that it uses other things for good or not. How is it also to be counted *among* the goods [i.e., rationality, morality, love] we use"? (2.19.51.189–90). He accuses Augustine of not comparing equal categories: human members (hands, feet, etc.) are not in the same family of ideas as free will is.

To him Augustine replies:

> When the will adheres to the common and unchangeable good, it achieves the great and fundamental goods of a human being, despite being an intermediate good. But the will sins when it is turned away from the unchangeable and common good, towards its private good, or towards something external, or towards something lower. The will is turned to its private good when it wants to be in its own power ... Evil is turning the will away from the unchangeable good and towards changeable goods. Yet, since this *turning away* and *towards* is not compelled but voluntary, the deserved and just penalty of unhappiness follows upon it (2.19.53.199–200).

Thus, for Augustine, it is the human will which is the arbiter, the functional operant, of the human freedom God has given to all people. But he must have realized that he really had not addressed Evodius's concern because he goes on to say:

> But perhaps you are going to raise the question: Since the will is moved when it turns itself away from the unchangeable good towards the changeable good, where does this movement come from? It is surely evil, even if free will should be numbered among good things on the grounds that we cannot live rightly without it. If this movement, namely turning the will away from the Lord God, is undoubtedly a sin, then surely can we not say that God is the author of sin? Therefore, this movement will not be from God. Then where does it come

14. In later discussions evidence will be given which will show that human freedom is a good gift. See chapters 13 and 16.

from? If I were to reply to your question that *I do not know*, perhaps you will then be the sadder, but I will at least have replied truthfully (2.19.53.199–201, author's *emphasis*).[15]

And then he adds:

Do not hesitate to attribute to God as its Maker everything in which you see number and measure and order. Once you remove these things entirely, absolutely nothing will be left . . . Thus, if every good were taken away, what will be left is not something, but instead absolutely nothing. Yet every good is from God. Therefore, there is no nature that is not from God. Thus, see what the movement of 'turning away' pertains to. We admit that this movement is sin, since it is a defective movement, and every defect is from nothing. Be assured that this movement does *not* pertain to God! . . . Yet this defective movement, since it is voluntary, is placed within our power. If you fear it [that is, fear of the movement toward sin], you must not will it; if you do not will it, it will not exist (2.20.54.203–5).

What Augustine does here is to go back to what he has stated at the beginning. Nothing but good comes from God. He then seems to solve the problem of evil by saying that—since all good comes from God—evil could not have come from him. In other words—if he stopped here—he would be assuming the conclusion, not explaining the origin of evil.

But Augustine has not finished his argument. He too understood the weakness of his argument thus far, so in Book 3 he gets to the core of the issue.

Premise #3: The person determines whether he chooses wisdom or to live unwisely.

Although Augustine especially addresses this in Book 3, he touched on it earlier in Book 2: "Nobody loses truth and wisdom against his will . . . It is not possible for anyone to be physically separated from it. Instead, what we call 'separation' from truth and wisdom is a perverse will that takes delight in inferior things, and nobody *unwilling wills anything*" (2.14.37.144, author's *emphasis*). It is important in his thinking to affirm that a person who acts *unwisely knows* wisdom (2.15.40.160), and that this *known* wisdom entreats the person to do what is good (2.16.41.163),[16] but the one who sins chooses not to follow it.

15. Augustine stumbles at this point. Later he will show that the ability to freely choose comes from God, but the free choice for good or evil is made by the person. Notice Premise #3 in the next section.

16. Augustine prays: "Wisdom! The sweetest light of a mind made pure! Woe to those who abandon you as guide and wander aimlessly around your tracks, who love indications of you instead of you, who forget what you intimate. For you do not cease to intimate to us what and how great you are" (2.16.43.168).

Evodius's further questions:

If free will is a good gift, why do some choose wisely and others turn away?

Book 3 sharpens Augustine's argument, partly because Evodius gets more direct in his questions. Evodius does not understand how—if free will is a good gift from God, and he has made man good—why in some people that freedom is used to make choices for God and in others to turn away from him. In his own words:

> It has been made completely clear to me that free will should be counted among good things . . . We are therefore also compelled to admit that free will was given by the divinity, and ought to have been given. If you think the time is right, I want to know this from you: Where does the movement come from by which the will is turned away from the common and unchangeable good and is turned to its private goods, or to goods belonging to another, or to lower goods—all of which are completely changeable? . . . If free will was given in such a way that it has this movement as something natural, then it is turned to these [lesser goods] by necessity, and no blame can be attached where nature and necessity predominate (3.1.1.1).

What is puzzling to him is that he is compelled to admit that "turning away" from God is evil and that the one who does so is justly blameworthy (3.1.1.2).[17] And he wishes to acknowledge that God is good and has given people a good gift in free will, but he is still puzzled how a good gift results in evil. If God is not the source of evil—he shudders even to think this—then who or what is its source? What is it in human freedom that causes some to turn away from the good, from wisdom? (Does this not beg the question in favor of causal determinism?)

If God "foreknows," how is it that a person does not sin by "necessity"?

But this is not the whole of Evodius's struggle. He looks at the wider theological picture of the Scripture's teaching on God's foreknowledge and how that relates to human freedom. "It perplexes me beyond words how it could happen that [1] God has foreknowledge of everything that will happen, and yet [2] we do not sin by any necessity . . . Since God had foreknown that he was going to sin, it was necessary that what He foreknew would be the case would happen. So how is the will free where such

---

17. Evodius's question is so very important. To express his intellectual struggle another way, he is asking if God—in giving mankind free will, something "good"—constituted his gift in such a way *that it built into man the natural tendency* on the part of some to choose God's way and on the part of others to turn away from wisdom and God. He readily sees the evil exposed when a person uses that freedom to turn away from what God had has called good, but he is baffled that it occurs because of God's good gift. If God made human beings this way, how can they be blamed for what they naturally do? To use his words: "I do not *know* whether there is any blame in leaving the unchangeable good behind to turn to changeable goods" (3.1.1.2).

unavoidable necessity is apparent"? (3.2.4.12–15). This is no small problem, not only for free will but also for the problem of evil. If God "foreknows" that some will *"necessarily"* choose the good, while others will reject the way of wisdom, how does that not make him the ultimate cause for both? Because this is a core issue, Augustine spends a significant time responding. His reasoning can be summarized in three statements: (1) He says that the questions about foreknowledge Evodius asks are asked typically by two sorts of people: (a) People who believe that no providence rules in human affairs, and (b) people who believe that God's providence is weak[18] or unjust or evil (3.2.5.16–17). (The reader might wonder if Augustine's response was not a bit unfair *if* it was a way to "punish" Evodius for his question.)

(2) His second response to Evodius is far more substantive. He says Evodius's question is based on a false premise that is apparent in the following syllogism:

- Premise #1: God foreknows everything that will be.

- Premise #2: Everything God foreknows happens not by will but by necessity. (See also 3.3.6.24).

"You [Evodius] fear that by this train of reasoning we infer either the negation of [Premise #1], which is irreligious, or, if we cannot deny [1], we infer instead the negation of [2]" (3.3.6.21–23).

The problem with Evodius's reasoning is that Premise #2 is false. The correct premise—Augustine insists—is that "we sin not by necessity but by the will." This sounds like a word game, but Augustine is making a philosophically very important point that surrounds the word "necessity." *Necessity* implies that the person is compelled, that it is impossible for him/her to avoid what is foreknown. But Augustine's "correction" of Evodius's premise states that, while it is true that if something or some action is foreknown, a person will do precisely what is foreknown, he/she—in the context of making the choice in real time—could actually make a different choice or no choice at all. In other words, the choosing remains free. But—looking back after the decision—the decision made would have been foreknown of God. What a person *will* do is different from saying what a person "necessarily" must do. *Necessity* implies a fatalistic determinism.[19]

---

18. Like Gregory Boyd and open theists today. See chapter 16.

19. William Lane Craig explains this with an excellent illustration: "The reader should now be able to see that the argument for theological fatalism commits a fairly common logical fallacy. In effect the fatalist argues:
Necessarily, if God foreknows x, then x will happen.
God foreknows x.
　　　　　Therefore, x will necessarily happen.
But such reasoning is universally recognized to be logically fallacious. It is like reasoning:
Necessarily, if Jones is a bachelor, Jones is unmarried.
Jones is a bachelor.
Therefore, Jones is necessarily unmarried.
But Jones is not *necessarily* unmarried. He just *is* unmarried. He is perfectly free to be married; no

(3) In his third response, Augustine argues that we "will" by our will: "Although God foreknows our future wills, it does *not* follow from this that we do not will something by our will . . . a blameworthy will, if anything of the sort is going to be in you, will not thereby *not* be your will, merely because God foreknows that it is going to be" (3.3.7.27–29).

Evodius is tracking along with Augustine in that he wants to avoid implying that a person sins because of being compelled—or causally determined—by God and at the same time he wishes to affirm that "our will remains free," but he reiterates his question more clearly: "I confess, I do not yet see how these two things are not in conflict with each other: (*a*) God's foreknowledge of our sins, and (*b*) our free will in sinning. For we must allow both that God is just and that He has foreknowledge. Yet I would like to know the following":

A. How does God justly punish sins that necessarily happen?

b. How is it that future events God foreknows do not happen necessarily?

c. How is whatever necessarily happens in His Creation not to be imputed to its Creator? (3.4.9.37).

Augustine tries to reply using a human illustration: human foreknowledge does not make a person do what one might foreknow. But Evodius immediately objects because only God can have perfectly certain and infallible foreknowledge (3.4.10.38–3.4.11.41); any human foreknowledge is subject to error. Augustine admits the weakness of his argument because if foreknowledge made man's actions compulsory, then

---

necessity compels him to be unmarried . . . The valid form of the argument is:

Necessarily, if God foreknows x, then x will happen.
God foreknows x.
Therefore, x will happen.

It is fallacious to infer that x will *necessarily* happen. It just will happen. It is entirely possible that x *will* fail to happen. Of course, if it were to fail to happen, God would not have foreknown x. From God's foreknowledge of x we can be absolutely sure that x will occur. But it does not have to occur; it is possible for it to fail to happen.

What is impossible is a situation in which God foreknows x and x fails to happen, for this would be a logical contradiction. It is impossible for both God to foreknow that Jones will mow the lawn and Jones to refrain from mowing the lawn . . .

God's foreknowledge is *chronologically* prior to Jones's mowing the lawn, but Jones's mowing the lawn is *logically* prior to God's foreknowledge . . . Once we understand the logical priority of the events to God's knowledge of them, we can see more easily why the fact of God's foreknowledge does not prejudice anything. The reason God foreknows that Jones will mow his lawn is the simple fact that Jones will mow his lawn. Jones is free to refrain, and were he to do so, God would have foreknown that he would refrain. Jones is free to do whatever he wants, and God's foreknowledge logically follows Jones's action like a shadow, even if chronologically the shadow precedes the coming of the event itself. In short, the argument for theological fatalism is simply fallacious. From God's foreknowledge of a free action, one may infer only that that action will occur, not that it must occur. The agent performing the action has the power to refrain, and were the agent to do so, God's foreknowledge would have been different" (Craig, *Only Wise God*, 72–74).

neither punishment nor reward could be appropriately given to them because they are not earned.

Augustine especially reacts to Evodius's third question—*How is whatever necessarily happens in His Creation not to be imputed to its Creator?*—by reminding and cautioning him that humans are not able to understand God's ways: "Nor can you think of anything better in Creation that has escaped the Maker of Creation . . . They [people like Evodius!] declare: 'He should have made us such that we always want to enjoy His unchangeable truth and never want to sin'" (3.5.13.49–51). The fact is, Augustine suggests, that human beings "reason and evaluate matters differently" (3.5.17.61).

Augustine, then, gets highly theological to demonstrate that both the one whose nature is not corrupted is good and the one whose nature is corrupted was—before his corruption—good, and that God should be praised when a person does rightly and praised when the sinner is justly punished (3.13.36.128).

What causes the "will" to make its choices?

Evodius remains unconvinced and does not feel that Augustine has addressed his concerns. Though he agrees "that it is completely true that it cannot happen in any way that our sins are assigned rightly to our Creator" (3.16.46.160), he says that he

> Would still like to know why *this* nature, which God foreknew would not sin, does not sin, and why *that* nature, which He foresaw would sin, does sin. I no longer think it due to God's foreknowledge that the former does not sin and that the latter is compelled to sin. Yet nevertheless, if there were no cause, rational creatures would not be divided into (*a*) those who never sin; (*b*) those who persevere in their sinning; and (*c*) those who sometimes sin and sometimes are turned to acting rightly, the group 'intermediate' between (*a*) and (*b*). What is the cause dividing rational creatures into these three groups? [Is Evodius by these groups assuming causal determinism?]
>
> Now I do not want you to reply: "the will." I am looking for the cause of the will itself. It is not without cause that the first group never wills to sin, the second group always wills to sin, and the third sometimes wills to sin and sometimes does not, despite the fact that they are all of the same kind. This alone seems clear to me: The threefold will of rational creatures is not without cause. But what the cause is I do not know" (3.17.47.161–63).

Augustine replies by noting the fallacy of an infinite regress: "The will is the cause of sin, but you are searching for the cause of the will itself. If I were able to find this cause, are you not also going to ask about the cause of this cause that has been found? What will limit our investigation"? (3.17.47.161–63).

So, what is the ultimate cause? Augustine's response: "Either the will is the first cause of sinning, or no sin is the first cause of sinning. No sin is rightly assigned to anyone but the sinner. Therefore, it is rightly assigned only to someone who wills it. I do not know why you want to look any further." Only a few sentences later, however, Augustine states: "Whatever the cause of the will is, if it cannot be resisted there is no sin in yielding to it; but if it can be resisted, let someone not yield to it, and there will be no sin" (3.18.50.170; see also 3.18.51.174).

Augustine has no doubt that human nature in his day is in the same bondage of which Paul speaks: *I do not do the good I will, but the evil I hate, that I do* (Rom 7:19). This he attributes, not to the way God made man, but to God's judgment—the "penalty"—for his disobedience. Indeed: "If this is not a penalty but human nature instead, they are not sins. If there is no getting around the way human beings were naturally made, so that they could not be better, then they do what they should when they do these things" (3.18.51.174).

Both of these last quotations are remarkable admissions, because they reveal that Augustine has really grasped the problem of evil. The "free will to act rightly . . . [relates to] human beings [as they] were originally made" (3.18.51.179). On the other hand, "Someone loses what he was unwilling to use well, although he could have used it well without trouble had he been willing" (3.18.51.178).

Free will was good for Adam and Eve, but it has been seriously damaged, though people can still make good choices.

In short, human free will was "good" as it came from the Creator, and mankind as originally created was able to use his free will to do what was good and wise (3.18.52.179). But with the fall—the "punishment" enacted because of Adam and Eve's disobedience—people do what they will out of ignorance or bondage (3.19.54.185–3.20.55.187). Yet "anyone willing to turn back to God . . . [is] able to overcome even what they have been born with" (3.20.56.188; see also 3.22.64.217). To say it more precisely, one might say that free will remains a good gift but fallen human beings, who before were able to exercise it "rightly," afterward do not readily choose the good as they previously were able, though they still can.

This naturally led Augustine to discuss four theories of the origin of the soul.[20] When he has finished, he says: "It is quite clear that souls suffer punishments for their sins by the most upright and supremely just and unshaken and unchangeable majesty and substance of the Creator. These sins, as we have been discussing for a long time, should be attributed to their own will. Nor should any further cause of sins be looked

---

20. He summarizes: "There are [therefore] four theories about souls: [1] Souls come from a stock. [2] Souls come about anew in each individual born. [3] Souls already exist somewhere and they are sent by God into the bodies of those who are born. [4] Souls already exist somewhere and they descend of their own accord into the bodies of those who are born" (3.21.59.200).

for (3.22.63.216) . . . The soul is not held guilty because it is naturally ignorant and naturally incapable, but rather because it did not make an effort to know, and because it did not work enough to acquire the ability to act rightly" (3.22.64.218).

Augustine realizes the weakness of his argument.

One might get the impression from Augustine's discussion of the will that it is the person alone who determines his destiny, depending on the choices he or she makes. Even those who choose rightly do it on their own; they *make an effort to know* and they *work enough to acquire the ability to act rightly.* According to Augustine, they make the right choices (although they could have done otherwise), and, therefore, are given divine help. "[The] soul is ignorant of what it ought to do, precisely because it has not yet received it [i.e., the truth]. But it will receive this, too, if it uses well what it *has* received: the power to search diligently and religiously, if it is willing" (3.22.65.223).

Augustine puts great emphasis on the effort of the individual in pursuing wisdom. It is this personal and diligent searching that makes the difference. To the Calvinist's ear, this sounds like what is often called an "Arminian" view of salvation. And Augustine himself—twenty-five years later—realized this weakness and lack of precision on this point in his book when the Pelagian heretics maintained—from reading his *On the Free Choice of the Will*—that "the will is so free that they leave no place for God's grace" (*Retractationes* 1.9.3; see also 1.9.4). He documents how strongly he argued for such freedom by listing quotes from *On the Free Choice of the Will* in almost the entirety of *Retractationes* (1.9), but he says he did so because he was not arguing against the Pelagians but the Manichaeans (*Retractationes* 1.9.3–1.9.7).

Augustine should not be that hard on himself because—though he does not specifically discuss "grace" in *On the Free Choice of the Will*—he implies it near the end of Book 3: "Yet the Creator of the soul is praised on all sides for implanting the capacity for the highest good from these beginnings; assisting our progress; perfecting and satisfying those who make progress; ordaining the most just damnation for the sinner—that is, for someone refusing to lift himself up to perfection from his beginnings or now relapsing from some progress—according to his deserts" (3.22.65.221).

But this response leads to more questions: God on the one hand "assists" and "perfects" those who choose to make "progress" upward, but on the other hand "ordains the most just damnation for the sinner . . . who refuses to lift himself up." It is easy to conclude at least that special grace is given to the one, while the other is damned who wasn't given grace. (More on this later when Augustine's "A Treatise on Nature and Grace" is explored.) This sounds something akin to the "irresistible grace" of Calvinism.

As Augustine brings his discussion to an end, he addresses what some people who think they are "clever" (to use his word) ask, and his reply is profoundly helpful in understanding his position on free will: "If the First Man was created wise, why was he led astray? But if he was created foolish, how is God not the author of vices, since foolishness is the ultimate vice"? (3.24.71.240).

Augustine shows the error of such thinking by splitting the horns of the false dilemma offered by "clever" people by providing a third possibility. There is an "intermediate [state] between foolish and wisdom" (3.24.71.241). God creates people having this intermediate state, a state in which they can and do receive his precepts. When a person chooses/wills to do right, he begins to become wise. Contrariwise, if he chooses/wills to ignore or reject such precepts, he is on the road to becoming foolish (3.24.73.252–54). With each choice one either is gaining wisdom (learning)[21] or he is becoming more foolish or perverse in his way.[22] "It is one thing to be rational, another to be wise. By reason one becomes capable of apprehending a precept, to which one ought to be faithful, so that one does what is prescribed . . . Observance of the precept takes in wisdom . . . There are two ways for someone to sin before becoming wise: (a) he does not accommodate himself to receiving a precept; (b) he does not observe it once received" (3.24.72.245–47).

Thus, Adam—though sinless—became a sinner while in the "intermediate state" when he freely chose to turn against God's precept and ate of the forbidden fruit (3.24.72.249). What happened in the Garden of Eden is a paradigm of what happens to everyone since then. There is no absence of influences both for good and for evil, but the will is not chained nor does it lack the freedom to make one decision or another or none at all. Because this discussion is so very important to understand, Augustine's own words are worthy of being quoted:

> Adam was provided with impressions on each side, one from God's precept and the other from the serpent's suggestion (3.25.75.258) . . . Neither what the precept given to Adam by the Lord was, nor what the suggestion given to him by the serpent was, lay in his control (3.25.75.257) . . . What anyone accepts or rejects is in his power [and] . . . there is no power over which impression he is affected by . . . As a rational substance, it [he] accepts what it [he] wants from each source, and, on the basis of what it [he] accepts, there follows its [his] deserved happiness or unhappiness (3.25.75.256–75) . . . Whoever wills surely wills *something*. But he cannot will unless this "something" is either suggested externally through the bodily senses or enters into the mind in hidden ways (3.25.75.259).

Summary of Augustine's argument in *On the Free Choice of the Will.*

In these words, one finds the essence of Augustine's argument: free will is a good gift. With it every person has been given the ability to reason, implying the libertarian

21. See discussion in chapter 16.

22. Augustine says Paul was speaking of this in Rom 1:22–32 (3.24.72.249).

ability to accept reasonable thoughts and beliefs and reject unreasonable thoughts and beliefs. But there are inside and outside influences (or as Augustine calls them "impressions") which act on or influence a person while reasoning. Specifically, there are "influences" from God *and* on the other hand from sources antagonistic to God's way. But people are not always compelled or causally determined to choose one way or another or to make no choice at all. They (at least occasionally) truly have a free will: the ability to choose among a range of alternatives/options, each consistent and compatible with their nature.

As late as AD 412, when Augustine wrote *On the Spirit and the Letter,* he still affirms his understanding of free will as a God-given "good" gift, but—because he is interacting with what he senses is a misunderstanding by Pelagius and his followers—he gives more details. There are two gifts from God: (1) the freedom to make/will choices and (2) influences ("incentives") to will to believe. These incentives—he explains—are both external (via "evangelical exhortations") and internal in a person's decision-making faculties. He words his understanding very carefully:

> The very will by which we believe is reckoned as a gift of God, because it arises out of the free will which we received at our creation . . . This will is to be ascribed to the divine gift, not merely because it arises from our free will, which was created naturally with us; but also because God acts upon us by the incentives of our perceptions, to will and to believe, either externally by evangelical exhortations, where even the commands of the law also do something . . . or internally, where no man has in his own control what shall enter into his thoughts, although it appertains to his own will to consent or to dissent . . . To yield our consent, indeed, to God's summons, or to withhold it, is . . . the function of our own will.[23]

AUGUSTINE "RECONSIDERS" HIS THINKING: GRACE IS GIVEN TO SOME.

Near the end of his life Augustine says in his *Retractationes*: "Of our own accord we were able to fall, namely by free choice, but not also to rise up" (1.9.6). It is vital to note that Augustine continues to affirm a limited freedom (the ability to freely fall), but this claim for inability on one's own "to rise up" *seems* to be singing a different "tune" than what has been argued in *On the Free Choice of the Will.* He wrote two more definitive works—" A Treatise on Nature and Grace" (AD 415) and "On Grace and Free Choice"

---

23. Augustine, "Spirit and Letter," 346. This sentence is the epitome of choosing among a range of options. Augustine in the *City of God* is explicit: "From him [God] come all powers, but not all wills (5.8) . . . Just as he is the creator of all natures, so is he the giver of all power of achievement, but not of all acts of will. Evil wills do not proceed from him because they are contrary to the nature which proceeds from him" (5.17) (Augustine, *City of God*, NPNF1: 222, 497). The author owes this bibliographic note to Brown, "Augustine on Freedom," 58.

AD 426)—where this changed position is made clear. Augustine himself says that he wrote this latter treatise because "there are some persons who suppose that the freedom of the will is denied whenever God's grace is maintained, and who on their side defend their liberty of will so peremptorily as to deny the grace of God. This grace, as they assert, is bestowed according to our own merits."[24]

The decade before Augustine's death seems to be a period of transition for him. He still struggles with how to harmonize human freedom and God's grace regarding moral, ethical, and soteriological issues. This is seen in his *Letter to Valentinus 214* in which he expresses concern for some in Valentinus's monastery who "preach grace in such a manner as to deny that the will of man is free . . . I wish you to understand in accordance with this faith, so that you may neither deny God's grace, nor uphold free will in such wise as to separate the latter from the grace of God, as if without this we could by any means either think or do anything according to God, which is quite beyond our power."[25] Later he says "that man's will is free, and . . . there is also God's grace, without whose help man's free will can neither be turned towards God, nor make any progress in God."[26]

One cannot miss his dilemma. He wants to affirm that any turning toward and to God cannot be traced to a person's own efforts, yet turning away is due to a person's own free will. But some of his statements in "A Treatise on Nature and Grace"—directed against the Pelagians and their teaching—seem to be like the expression: "What the big print giveth, the small print taketh away." What he has stated as freedom of the will—uncoerced and in its own power—in his *On the Free Choice of the Will* seems to be contradicted in this later writing. In a chapter entitled "*The Wills of Men Are So Much in the Power of God, That He Can Turn Them Whithersoever It Pleases Him,*" he writes: "If this divine record [the Scriptures he quotes] be looked into carefully, it shows us that not only men's good wills, which God Himself converts from bad ones, and, when converted by Him, directs to good actions and to eternal life, but also those which follow the world are so entirely at the disposal of God, that He turns them wherever He wills, and whenever He wills, to bestow kindness on some, and to heap punishment on others, as He Himself judges right by a counsel most secret to Himself, indeed, but beyond all doubt most righteous."[27]

The titles of several following chapters document this same point of view:

- Chapter 42: *God Does Whatsoever He Wills in the Hearts of Even Wicked Men.*

- Chapter 43: *God Operates on Men's Hearts to Incline Their Wills Whithersoever He Pleases.*

---

24. Augustine, *Retractationes* 2:68; [*NPNF1*:141].

25. Augustine, "Letter to Valentinus," 1214.

26. Augustine, "Letter to Valentinus," 1216.

27. Augustine, *On the Free Choice*, 41.

- Chapter 45: *The Reason Why One Person Is Assisted by Grace, and Another Is Not Helped, Must Be Referred to the Secret Judgments of God.*

In each of these chapters Augustine provides biblical citations which he feels support and provide the basis of the chapter heading. If one did not know otherwise, the reader of "A Treatise on Nature and Grace" might think he was reading the work of a different author than the one who penned *On the Free Choice of the Will.* Even a casual reader can see this contrast.

What is rather matter-of-factly stated in "A Treatise on Nature and Grace" is more clearly explained in his *City of God:* "We are driven to believe that the holy angels never existed without a good will or the love of God. But the angels who, though created good, are yet evil now, became so by their own will . . . These angels, therefore, either received less of the grace of the divine love than those who persevered in the same; or if both were created equally good, then, while the one fell by their evil will, the others were more abundantly assisted, and attained to that pitch of blessedness at which they became certain they should never fall from it."[28]

In the last treatise (AD 429) Augustine wrote—"On Predestination and Perseverance"—it is clear that he has moved to a deterministic, double predestination position regarding soteriological matters: "He chose them in Christ before the foundation of the world as those to whom He intended to give His grace freely—that is, with no merits of theirs, either of faith or of works, preceding; and does not come to the help of those who . . . He wills not to come to their help, since in His predestination he, *secretly* indeed, but yet righteously, has otherwise determined concerning them."[29]

In the end, Augustine has to admit as he states in his *Retractationes* (2.1): "I have tried hard to maintain the free choice of the human will, but the grace of God prevailed." In other words, since logically the two views—human freedom and God's determinism[30]—cannot be harmonized, one must rest the argument as being only understandable by God: *the Secret Judgments of God.* It is for this reason that it was stated earlier in this essay that Augustine failed in his attempt to harmonize the two."[31]

A footnote must necessarily be added. Since "A Treatise on Nature and Grace" was written to address the Pelagian heresy, Augustine may well have focused on the necessity of God's grace in soteriological matters and thus perhaps overstated his

28. Augustine, *City of God,* 493. Here both freedom and grace seem to be implied.

29. Augustine, "On Predestination," 25, author's *emphasis.* See also 35–36. The writer is indebted to Gene Fendt, "Between a Pelagian Rock," for these bibliographic citations.

30. The word "determinism" is used here instead of "sovereignty," because in the view of this writer the two terms must be distinguished. An explanation will be given later in chapters 12 and 16.

31. Wolfson says that "In the *Confessions,* immediately after the prayer [which upset Pelagius; see below], Augustine wrote his own commentary on it. In that commentary he made it clear that grace did not follow free will, as something merited and auxiliary, but preceded it and created it. A similar view was expressed by him in another work ("On Diverse Questions from Simple," 1.7) which had appeared about three years prior to the appearance the *Confessions*" (Wolfson, "Philosophical Implications," 555).

case. This may explain why the reader of *On the Free Choice of the Will* may see it as a treatise on human freedom, while a reader of "A Treatise on Nature and Grace," while championing God's grace, may see it as a treatise on soteriological determinism. Maybe, if Augustine had not been dealing with the serious heresy of Pelagianism, he would have argued that God's grace is given to all, but it was not an "irresistible" grace. If a person by the exercise of his will, chooses to act wisely and respond to God's grace, he or she nevertheless can claim no credit, or merit for the forgiveness received as the result. He or she simply responded to God's grace.[32] But the person—who resists or neglects God's grace—has himself forfeited the only opportunity for pardon. Either way, God's grace is given to all and is the ultimate influence in the salvation of the believer. Although Augustine became more "Calvinistic" in his later years, he never appears to have rejected a limited libertarian freedom in issues unrelated to soteriological issues.

32. Interestingly, Augustine in the *City of God* says, "For the evil of the soul, its own will takes the initiative; but for its good, the will of its Creator makes the first move" (2:13.15).

4

A survey of human freedom during the pre-Reformation period

Pelagius (AD 354? to 418)

PELAGIUS WAS A BRITISH monk about whose early life little is known. Even primary sources of his writings[1] are hard to come by (three are included in Jerome's writings), but for the most part what Pelagius taught is gleaned from others (the most prominent being Augustine) who quote him in their evaluation and condemnation of his theology. He was a well-studied theologian, who was as comfortable in Latin as he was in Greek. When he was about fifty-five, he traveled to Rome and was startled by what he saw in the church.[2] Indeed, these so-called "believers" were so decadent in their behavior that he was motivated to find out how there could be such a disconnect between church attendees and godly behavior. When he heard of Augustine's prayer from his *Confessions*—"*My whole hope is in Thy exceeding great mercy and that alone. Give what Thou commandest and command what Thou wilt. Thou commandest continence from us, and when I knew, as it is said, that no one could be continent unless God gave it to him, even this was a point of wisdom, to know whose gift it was*"[3]—he believed he had found the cause for this inconsistency.[4] What caught his eyes and what he objected to especially were the words: *Give what Thou commandest* [and] *no one could be continent unless God gave it to him.* Pelagius understood the words to imply that what God commanded people to do, they

---

1. Only two complete works of Pelagius exist: his *Commentary on the Letters of St. Paul* and a "Letter to Demetrias." Only his *Commentary on Romans* and his "Letter to Demetrias" are available in English.

2. Fox, "Biblical Theology," 171.

3. Augustine, *Confessions*, 10.29.40; [169]. Augustine himself claims that Pelagius heard the prayer from a Bishop in Rome ("On Perseverance," 20.53; [1475]). See Wolfson's insightful comments in footnote #123 in chapter 3.

4. Kelly, *Early Christian Doctrines*, 357.

could not do on their own; the "commandment" could only be done by the "gift"—the enablement—of God. He wondered: "Does that not crush human freedom? How, then, could God hold people accountable for what they could not humanly do? Could this explain the moral depravity he was witnessing in Rome"?[5]

Harry Wolfson's essay puts this controversy in the historical context of the prior thinking of the church[6] which had been deeply influenced by Philo (c. 20 BC to AD 40). Among those so influenced were Clement of Alexandria, Justin Martyr, Tertullian, and especially Origen. Wolfson says that Philo spoke of human freedom as being the power to choose between two impulses, one evil and the other good. Divine grace was given to the person who sought to do good despite the stronger pull of evil. "Grace" as defined this way was a "merited" grace.[7] According to Wolfson this was the philosophy of the church up until Augustine, who reversed the construct: grace did not follow man's appeal for divine help, but preceded it and thus was the energizing principle for man to cry out for help, for grace. Therefore, any attempt to understand Pelagius's response to Augustine must be seen in this divide precipitated by Augustine's teaching.

THE THEOLOGICAL ERROR OF PELAGIUS.

Pelagius's thinking, despite his commendatory crusade for godliness, led him (and his key followers Coelestius and Julian) to theological positions that finally resulted in his being declared a heretic by the church. For this reason, Rees in the title of his book calls him "the reluctant heretic,"[8] reluctant because it was not his motive to go against church doctrine but to call people to holiness. But his teachings certainly were

---

5. An interesting perspective has been suggested by J. N. L. Myres that Pelagius—precisely because of his revulsion of the moral decadence he saw—responded to how "grace" (*gratia*) was used in the public sphere. It denoted the "corruption in the courts, for official hanky-panky of all kinds in public life; for the irrational, unpredictable, or capricious as contrasted to the rational, the dependable and the intelligible in all human relationships" ("Pelagius and the End," 22–23). Did the Augustinian emphasis on the grace of God result in a laissez faire attitude to doing what was right and holy? Certainly, Pelagius had not mistaken the use of the term in Augustine's teaching later, but could he have responded so harshly at first because of misunderstanding Augustine's use of the word?

Three years after Myres's essay, Liebeschuetz ("Did the Pelagian Movement"?, 231) wrote an article in which he clearly shows that favors ("graces"—Χάριτας) were rampant abuses, but he fails to relate this use of the term to Augustine's use of God's grace and his attack on Pelagius's works-centered theology. Indeed, Pelagius's concern was more on a person's freedom of will.

6. Wolfson, "In our judgment, Pelagius, on the problem of freedom, represents the original Christian belief. It was Augustine who introduced something new from without. On the showing of his own statements, his doctrine of grace is only a Christianization of the pagan Stoic doctrine of fate" (Wolfson, "Philosophical Implications," 562).

7. See Wolfson, ("Philosophical Implications," 554–55). Pelagius—according to Augustine—put it this way: "What is good is more easily fulfilled if grace assists" (Augustine, "Against Two Letters of Pelagius," 2.8.17; [1114]).

8. Rees, *Pelagius.*

seen then—and are today as well—as contradictory to orthodoxy. What were those teachings? Hodge[9] summarizes his essential teachings well:

1. People cannot be responsible for any behavior that they cannot help doing by their own efforts. Thus, for Pelagius free will meant the ability to do what was right and good. This must be seen and understood as his reaction to Augustine's determinism.[10]

2. Sin is the deliberate choice to do what the person recognizes and understands to be evil.

3. There is no such thing as "original sin," that is, that the sin of Adam has "infected" everyone since then and thus explains our proclivity to doing evil. We sin because of the pattern and influences of those around us. Adam was merely the first of many bad examples. His sin injured only himself, not his descendants. A corollary premise for Pelagius's belief was that if our "nature is sinful, the God as the author of nature must be the author of sin."[11]

4. Not only did Adam's sin have no effect on his descendants, but Pelagius said it was possible for some people to live without sin.[12] "Pelagius taught that some men had no need for themselves to repeat the petition in the Lord's prayer, 'Forgive our trespasses.'"[13]

---

9. Hodge, *Systematic Theology*, 152–54. The statements which follow are not verbatim quotes (some are and are documented), but are a summary of Hodge's discussion. He documents his summary with some references often in Latin. Another valuable source is Kelly (*Early Christian Doctrines*) who documents his conclusions with Pelagius's own words. Wolfson's article, "Philosophical Implications," is also helpful.

10. Wolfson documents this deterministic orientation of Augustine (at least in his later writings) that Pelagius could not accept: "In another place, he raises again the question, 'Can men do anything by the free determination of their own will'? and again his answer is: 'Far be it, for it was by the evil use of his free will that man destroyed both it and himself.' Man thus, both sins and does good not by freedom of choice but by necessity. This necessity is described by Augustine by two terms, one applied to the necessity by which one sins and the other to the necessity by which one refrains from sinning and acts righteously . . . Augustine goes on to maintain that, just as man is powerless to resist his concupiscence, so he is also powerless to resist the grace bestowed upon him by God; and consequently, just as by the necessity of his concupiscence man must sin, so by the necessity of grace man must refrain from sinning and act righteously. This irresistibility of grace is expressed by him in passages wherein he speaks of the human will as being 'indeclinably (*indeclinabiliter*) and invincibly (*insuperabiliter*) influenced by divine grace' and of God as he 'whom no man's will resists when he wills to give salvation.'" (Wolfson, "Philosophical Implications," 556–58).

11. Hodge, *Systematic Theology*, 153.

12. Later as Pelagius was confronted with his teaching he replied: "I did indeed say that a man can be without sin and keep the commandments of God, if he wishes; for this ability has been given to him by God. However, I did not say that any man can be found who has never sinned from his infancy to his old age but that, having been converted from his sins, he can be without sin by his own efforts and God's grace, yet not even by this means is he incapable of change in future" (Olson, *Against Calvinism*, 270).

13. Hodge, *Systematic Theology*, 154.

5. It was but a short step for Pelagius to declare that some men—regardless of their being pagan, Jews, or Christians—could be saved without the gospel. They could "fully obey the law and attain eternal life,"[14] though those who have the opportunity to hear the gospel would find it easier to reach that end.

6. Grace was defined differently by Pelagius. Grace was not as Augustine defined—divine enablement to respond to the Gospel—but is the "natural faculties of reason and free will, the revelation of truth . . . and all the providential blessings and advantages which men enjoy."[15]

Wolfson's explanation is very helpful here, because Pelagius does not mean that God's grace does not play a part: "But as in Philo and the rabbis and the Church Fathers before him, Pelagius draws a distinction between man's freedom of doing evil and his freedom of doing good. In both cases the choice of his will is absolutely free. But in the effectuation of his choice there is a difference. Once man has chosen to do evil, he is left to himself to carry out the decision of his will. God will neither help him nor hinder him. But once man has chosen to do good, and meets with difficulty in carrying out the good decision of his will, God will come to his help. This is Pelagius's conception of grace—a grace which is merited and only auxiliary."[16]

PELAGIANISM.

The words "Pelagius" and "Pelagianism" are found often in theological literature, but the essence of his beliefs and how they are a rather strong rebuttal to Augustine's doctrine of "original sin" are not so well known. One of the best sources is to be found in A. H. Strong's *Systematic Theology* and his excellent summary of Wiggers:[17]

1. Adam was created mortal, so that he would have died even if he had not sinned.

2. Adam's sin injured, not the human race, but only himself.

3. New-born infants are in the same condition as Adam before the Fall.[18]

14. Hodge, *Systematic Theology*, 154.

15. The six summaries are from Hodge, *Systematic Theology*, 152–54, and #6 is quoting Hodge, *Systematic Theology*, 154. Kelly also comments on #6 this way: "By grace, however, he really meant (a) free will itself, or the possibility of not sinning with which God endowed us at our creation; (b) the revelation, through reason, of God's law, instructing us what we should do and holding out eternal sanctions; and (c), since this has become obscured through evil custom, the law of Moses and the teaching and example of Christ. Thus, grace on his view is in the main *ab extra*; it is 'a grace of knowledge' or, as Augustine put it, a grace consisting in 'law and teaching.'" (Kelly, *Early Christian Doctrines*, 359).

16. Wolfson, "Philosophical Implications," 556–58.

17. Wiggers, *Historical Presentation*, 59. Actually, the points below—while they accurately may be descriptive of Pelagius's thinking—were actually the essential beliefs of a lawyer named Caelestius, who was greatly influenced by Pelagius. See also Pohle, "Pelagius and Pelagianism," 101–2.

18. Kelly, in *Early Christian Doctrines*, 358, notes that Pelagius thought every child received a soul created immediately by God.

4. The whole human race neither dies on account of Adam's sin, nor rises on account of Christ's resurrection.

5. Infants, though not baptized, attain eternal life.

6. The law is as good a means of salvation as the gospel.

7. Even before Christ some men lived who did not commit sin.[19]

Refutation of Pelagianism.

Many, especially those in a reformed tradition, recognize why such teachings were condemned by the church as heretical. The official position of the western church was articulated in AD 418 (also the year Pelagius died) at the Council of Carthage, though other councils weighed in over one hundred years afterward. At Carthage two hundred bishops published eight canons stating where Pelagius and his followers erred in their teachings. Specifically, they were the following:

1. Death did not come to Adam from a physical necessity, but through sin.

2. New-born children must be baptized on account of original sin.

3. Justifying grace not only avails for the forgiveness of past sins, but also for the avoidance of future sins.

4. The grace of Christ not only discloses the knowledge of God's commandments, but also imparts strength to will and execute them.

5. Without God's grace it is not merely more difficult, but absolutely impossible to perform good works.

6. Not out of humility, but in truth must we confess ourselves to be sinners.

7. The saints refer the petition of the Our Father, "Forgive us our trespasses," not only to others, but also to themselves.

8. The saints pronounce the same supplication not from mere humility, but from truthfulness.[20]

---

19. Examples include "Abel, Enoch, Joseph, Job, and, among the heathen Socrates, Aristides, Numa" . . . [Then Pelagius adds that] the virtues of the heathen entitle them to reward . . . [They] were not indeed without evil thoughts and inclinations, but these are not sin. Sin consists in acts. We are born, not full, but vacant of character. In every man there is a natural conscience; he has an ideal of life; he forms right resolves; he recognizes the claims of law; he accuses himself when he sins" (Strong, *Systematic Theology*, 597)

20. Pohle, "Pelagius and Pelagianism," 101–2.

Pelagianism and Augustine.

The purpose of including Pelagius in the list of leading theologians is the part he played in the corrective action taken by Augustine, especially in the latter's "A Treatise on Nature and Grace" (which has been discussed in detail above). Further documentation also can be found in the collected "Anti-Pelagian" writings.[21]

Roger Olson has provided an excellent account of how Pelagius and his followers looked at free will:

> Augustine defined free will simply as doing what one wants to do. For him, "In brief, then, I am free with respect to any action (or that action is in my power) to the extent that my wanting[22] and choosing to perform that action are sufficient for my performing it." Just so long as a person does what she wants to, her action is "free." This is quite different, of course, from defining free will as the "ability to do otherwise," which is probably the view Pelagius and his followers held. For Augustine, people are free to sin but not free not to sin. That is because, they want to sin. The Fall has so corrupted their motives and desires that sinning is all they want to do apart from God's intervening grace. Thus, they are sinning "freely."[23] Pelagius and his followers would almost certainly reject this idea of free will and argue that a person is only truly free if he could either sin or not sin.[24]

SEMI-PELAGIANISM.

Semi-Pelagianism[25] is so called because it was an attempt to bridge the divide between Pelagius and Augustine. The key leaders of this movement—which were not homogeneous in their teachings—were John Cassianus, Vincent Lerinensis, and Fautus of Rhegium.

Cassianus.

Cassianus taught that the effects of Adam's sin on his posterity were the following:

1. All descendants became mortal.[26]

21. See most of Augustine's writings about Pelagianism in vol. 5 of *NPNF1*.

22. As will be seen later, "wanting" was the key factor in Edwards's position, not of free will, but of his view of divine determinism. See chapter 11.

23. Is a sinner free to choose among a range of alternative sins? If so, they have libertarian freedom, in at least some choices.

24. Olson, *The Story of Christian Theology*, 273. This sounds like what is referred to today as compatibilistic free will, as opposed to libertarian freedom. This will be discussed further in chapter 12.

25. Unless otherwise noted, the summary or quotes are from Hodge, *Systematic Theology*, 166–67.

26. Pelagius's friend, Caelestius, who was more forthright than he, said "Adam was born mortal

2. Man's knowledge and understanding of God deteriorated, especially after the flood.

3. The soul of man was weakened and needed God's grace.

4. A person could not save himself. (Pelagius said that persons could save themselves by obedience to God's law, even without the gospel.)

5. People are not spiritually dead, only sick, and thus needed the help of the Great Physician. Pelagius himself declared that God does not "bestow special favour upon some;" He is no "acceptor of persons."[27]

6. Sometimes a person begins the work of conversion; sometimes God. (Augustine said it was all of God.)[28]

7. Predestination is based on God's fore-*seeing* man's response.[29]

Lerinensis.

Lerinensis taught that:

1. The Augustinian doctrine of original sin made God the author of evil; for, he says, it assumes that God has created a nature, which acting according to its own laws and under the impulse of an enslaved will, can do nothing but sin.

2. Heresy is the teaching that grace saves those who do not ask, seek, or knock, in evident allusion to the doctrine of Augustine that it is not of him that willeth, nor of him that runneth, but of God who showeth mercy.[30]

Fautus.

Fautus completely distanced himself from Pelagius's doctrine of original sin:

1. He agreed with Augustine that as the result of Adam's sin people have become morally corrupt.

2. No one is born without sin because of Adam. (Pelagius taught that Adam's sin damaged only himself.)

---

and would have died even if he had not sinned" (Kelly, *Early Christian Doctrines,* 361).

27. Kelly, *Early Christian Doctrines,* 360.

28. That being said, one should note the discussion in the essay on Augustine and how he in his earlier writing suggested that it is the will of man which responds to the influence of God's grace.

29. Kelly, *Early Christian Doctrines,* 371.

30. Hodge, *Systematic Theology,* 166–67.

3. The souls of people are prone to evil and without divine assistance incapable of doing anything spiritually good. (Pelagius taught that all people—even pagans—could do good enough to even be accepted by God.)[31]

Fautus's position—as reflected in the above three principles—indicates that he was not "Pelagian." His position seems to be in the orthodox camp.

Semi-Pelagianism condemned.

In the end, semi-Pelagianism was condemned at the Council of Orange (AD 529) and "the following propositions were established:

1. As a result of Adam's transgression both death and sin have passed to all his descendants.

2. Man's free will has consequently been so distorted and weakened that he cannot now believe in, much less love, God unless prompted and assisted thereto by grace.

3. The saints of the Old Testament owed their merits solely to grace and not to the possession of any natural good.

4. The grace of baptism enables all Christians, with the help and co-operation of Christ, to accomplish the duties necessary for salvation, provided they make the appropriate efforts.[32]

5. Predestination to evil is to be anathematized with detestation.

6. In every good action the first impulse comes from God, and it is this impulse which instigates us to seek baptism and, still aided by Him, to fulfil our duties.[33]

PELAGIANISM AND ARMINIANISM.

The above discussion makes it clear that both Pelagianism and Semi-Pelagianism are contrary to scriptural teaching. But often the terms are also used to malign those who would call themselves Arminians.[34] A footnote is therefore appropriate. James Pedlar is very helpful in distinguishing the two belief systems. For simplicity, they differ in several ways:

---

31. Hodge, *Systematic Theology*, 166–67.

32. Many Calvinists would disagree with this statement, especially the last words: "provided they make the appropriate efforts."

33. Kelly, *Early Christian Doctrines*, 371–72.

34. See a later discussion of Arminius in chapter 9.

1. Contrary to Pelagius and many of his followers, Arminians affirm the doctrines of original sin and total depravity.

2. Arminians affirm that people cannot turn to God by their own efforts. God's grace draws a person to seek for and receive his pardon.

3. Arminians affirm that God's grace also is necessary to live in a way which pleases him.[35]

In short, Pedlar concludes, "What is distinctive about the Arminian position (as opposed to monergistic Reformed accounts) is that God's grace is *resistible*, meaning that we can refuse his gracious offer of salvation. However, that hardly means that one's *acceptance* of God's gracious offer is some kind of Pelagian or Semi-Pelagian meritorious 'work.'"[36]

35. Pedlar, "Why Arminian Theology."
36. Pedlar, "Why Arminian Theology."

5

A survey of human freedom during the pre-Reformation period

Aquinas (AD 1225/1227 to 7 March 1274)

"THOMAS AQUINAS" IS THE anglicized form of the Italian *Tommaso d'aquino*, that is, the "Thomas of/from Aquino," a district/county in central Italy, just outside Rome. He was a nobleman: his father Landulf was the Count of Aquino, a knight of King Roger II; and his mother Theodora[1] was the Countess of Teano, a town just north of Naples. He was one of nine children.[2] Little is known of his five sisters, but his three brothers were military men. At five years of age, he was sent to the Benedictine Monastery of Monte Cassino, where his uncle Sinibald was the abbot. Then, when war broke out about AD 1236, he was sent to the University of Naples where his education included the *Trivium* (grammar, rhetoric, and logic) and the *Quadrivium* (arithmetic, geometry, music and astronomy). It was also at Naples that he became a Dominican.[3] This latter decision led to an intriguing family drama. Not only did Aquinas's family not approve his becoming

---

1. "Peter Calo relates that a holy hermit foretold his career, saying to his mother Theodora before his birth: 'He will enter the Order of Friars Preachers, and so great will be his learning and sanctity that in his day no one will be found to equal him.'" This prophecy was remarkably fulfilled! "About the year 1236 [when] he was sent to the University of Naples, Calo says that the change was made at the instance of the Abbot of Monte Cassino, who wrote to Thomas's father that a boy of such talents should not be left in obscurity. At Naples his . . . chronicler says that he soon surpassed Martini [one of his instructors] at grammar . . . Thomas could repeat the lessons with more depth and lucidity than his masters displayed . . . Later when he was at Cologne, he studied under a professor named Albertus Magnus, who after hearing 'his brilliant defense of a difficult thesis . . . exclaimed: "We call this young man a dumb ox, but his bellowing in doctrine will one day resound throughout the world."'" (Kennedy, "St. Thomas Aquinas," 663–64).

2. As the heading above noted, scholars are not certain of the date of Aquinas's birth. See Philip Schaff, *History of the Christian Church: Middle Ages,* 512.

3. The Dominicans were also called the "Order of Preachers" because of their emphasis on preaching and teaching (Brown, "Thomas Aquinas").

a Dominican, they were distressed to the degree that Aquinas's mother had her military sons kidnap him[4] and hold him in captivity for approximately two years, during which time they did everything they could do to dissuade their brother from the direction he had chosen. Among their methods was to hire a prostitute who, when she visited his room was driven away by Aquinas with a tool from the fireplace.[5] This response is an important element to any discussion of Aquinas's life not only because of the influence this had on his life[6] but because it is evidence that beyond being an academic, he was a godly young man.

The Dominicans sent Aquinas to Rome, but he was there only briefly and then left for studies at the Dominican University of Saint Jacques in Paris, from which he received his MA in AD 1245. Further studies began there and continued at the Dominican house of studies in Cologne, in both places under his professor Albert the Great, who was one of the greatest influences on his life. His studies under him were in Old and New Testaments, in the philosophy of Aristotle, and especially in the *Sentences* of Peter Lombard. This latter book—a primer for understanding the faith—was very important because it furnished the outline of what became Aquinas's *magnum opus: Summa Theologica*,[7] (hereafter simply identified as *ST*). Interestingly and significantly, when he was sent to Paris to teach in the Dominican University (AD 1251), his prescribed responsibility was to teach the *Sentences*, out of which came the publication of his commentaries on Lombard's work. It was also while in Paris that he began his pursuit and research for the ThD degree from the University in Paris, finally being awarded that degree in AD 1257.[8]

For the next seventeen years he taught in various places, though mostly at his alma mater in Paris but also in Rome. It was during this time that he did much writing on biblical subjects (commentaries on *Job*, *Isaiah*, *Jeremiah*, and *Lamentations*), a sort of harmony of the Gospels (*Catera Aurea*), works on apologetics (e.g., *Summa Contra Gentiles*—a work on the truth of the Catholic faith), and his *ST*.[9]

Though he died relatively young (at forty-seven or forty-nine years old), he had a very fruitful life as a priest, preacher, teacher and author. A study of his teaching

---

4. Hampden, *Life of Thomas Aquinas*, 23.

5. Hampden, *Life of Thomas Aquinas*, 25.

6. Kennedy writes: "When the temptress had been driven from his chamber, he knelt and most earnestly implored God to grant him integrity of mind and body. He fell into a gentle sleep, and, as he slept, two angels appeared to assure him that his prayer had been heard. They then girded him about with a white girdle, saying: 'We gird thee with the girdle of perpetual virginity.' And from that day forward he never experienced the slightest motions of concupiscence" (Kennedy, "Thomas Aquinas," 664). This is no small commendation in the age of unfaithfulness among clergy!

7. Schaff, *History of the Christian Church: Middle Ages*, 507. Actually, Aquinas started a revision/updating of the *Sentences*, but he soon gave that up, and it became his *ST*. By anyone's estimation, *ST* should not be called a "primer" but a theological treatise of great sophistication and scholarship! (See also Kennedy, "St. Thomas Aquinas").

8. Brown, "Thomas Aquinas."

9. Hampden, *Life of Thomas Aquinas*, 44–46.

ministry reveals many moves (at the direction of his superiors) from university to university, at none of which had he a long tenure. Of him Brown wrote: "In his lifetime, Thomas's expert opinion on theological and philosophical topics was sought by many, including at different times a king, a pope, and a countess. It is fair to say that, as a theologian, Thomas is one of the most important in the history of Western civilization, given the extent of his influence on the development of Roman Catholic theology since the fourteenth century."[10] Among his writings are some sixty papers and books.[11]

His legacy—in life and as a scholar—was recognized almost fifty years after his death (18 July AD 1323) when he was elevated to "Saint" by Pope John XXII.[12] Almost five hundred years later (AD 1879) Pope Leo XIII pronounced that Aquinas and his writings should be recognized as the definitive Catholic theology.[13]

AQUINAS: HIS UNDERSTANDING OF HUMAN FREEDOM AND THE SOVEREIGNTY OF GOD.

There is no lack of references to human freedom in the writings of Aquinas, a sampling of which is given below. The selections are not intended to represent his thinking in any preconceived way. They have been chosen so that researchers can know the way he expressed himself in his own words and also have representative sources to which to go for additional study. Though the following examples come from different periods in Aquinas's life, they should not be studied as if they reflect an "early" Aquinas and a "later" Aquinas, that is, to say that they are not to be seen as a "development" or more maturity in his thinking on human freedom.[14]

1. *We have free-will with respect to what we will not of necessity, nor [of] natural instinct (ST 1.19; [256]).*[15]

2. *On the part of the agent, a thing must be, when someone is forced by some agent, so that he is not able to do the contrary. This is called "necessity of coercion." Now*

10. Brown, "Thomas Aquinas."

11. For a listing, a brief annotation of his more important works, and an excellent bibliography, see Brown, "Thomas Aquinas."

12. An excellent summary of Aquinas's life and his philosophical writings is found in Brock, *Philosophy of St. Thomas*, 1–24.

13. Lindsay, "Thomas Aquinas," 250.

14. "Though there are significant developments in [Aquinas's] thinking, there is also enormous continuity. His major conclusions can all be found in his first important work, the *Commentary on the Sentences*. He shifted in his emphases, but he did not change his mind radically. One cannot seriously speak of an 'Early Aquinas' and a 'Later Aquinas.' He was a man of many thoughts, but he always had a single vision, albeit one presented with varied nuances and with different degrees of attention to detail" (Davies, *The Thought of Thomas*, viii, quoted by Hartung, "Thomas Aquinas," 12–13).

15. Aquinas, *Summa Theologica*. Henceforth, this book will be identified as *ST*. The page numbers [256] are from the Christian Classics Ethereal Library edition, and the other nomenclature (*ST,. . .*) is the schema that Aquinas himself used. The *italics* (in #1–9) are verbatim quotes of Aquinas.

> *this necessity of coercion is altogether repugnant to the will. For we call that violent which is against the inclination of a thing . . . Therefore, as a thing is called natural because it is according to the inclination of nature, so a thing is called voluntary because it is according to the inclination of the will. Therefore, just as it is impossible for a thing to be at the same time violent and natural, so it is impossible for a thing to be absolutely coerced or violent, and voluntary (ST 1.82; [920]) . . . The will does not desire of necessity whatsoever it desires (ST 1.82; [922]).*

3. *Man has free-will: otherwise counsels, exhortations, commands, prohibitions, rewards, and punishments would be in vain (ST 1.83; [931]).*

4. *Although free-will* [Liberum arbitrium—i.e., free judgment] *in its strict sense denotes an act, in the common manner of speaking we call free-will, that which is the principle of the act by which man judges freely (ST 1.83; [933]).* This is from an important section of ST entitled "On Free Will," more of which will be unpacked later.

5. *The proper act of free-will is choice: for we say that we have a free-will because we can take one thing while refusing another; and this is to choose. (ST 1.83; [935]). Free choice designates something which is open to opposites and by no means determined to one of them (Aquinas, Questiones Disputatae, 24.4).*[16]

6. *Man does not choose of necessity. And this is because that which is possible not to be, is not of necessity. Now the reason why it is possible not to choose, or to choose, may be gathered from a twofold power in man. For man can will and not will, act and not act; again, he can will this or that, and do this or that (ST, FS 13.6; [1455]).*[17]

7. *Some have held that the human will is necessarily moved to choose things . . . But this opinion is heretical. For it takes away the reason for merit and demerit in human acts, as it does not seem meritorious or demeritorious for persons to do necessarily what they could not avoid doing. It is also to be counted among the oddest philosophical opinions, since it is not only contrary to faith but also subverts all the principles of moral philosophy. For if nothing is within our power, and we are necessarily moved to will things, deliberation, exhortation, precept, punishment, and praise and blame, of which moral philosophy consists, are destroyed (Aquinas, De Malo 6; [257]).*[18]

8. *Without any doubt it must be affirmed that man is endowed with free choice. The faith obliges us to this, since without free choice there cannot be merit and demerit, or just punishment and reward. Clear indications, from which it appears that man*

16. *Questiones Disputatae de Veritate* (Aquinas, "Questions/Disputations Concerning Truth"). Hereafter, this will be identified as *DV*.

17. See also *ST*, FS.6.3; [1383], quoted later in this essay.

18. *De Malo* means "Concerning Evil." From this point on this will be noted as *DM*.

freely chooses one thing and refuses another, also lead us to this. Evident reasoning also forces us to this conclusion (DV 24.1).

9. *For free-will is applied to those things that one wills not of necessity but of one's own accord: wherefore in us there is free-will in regard to our wishing to run or walk . . . Now man to the exclusion of other animals is said to have free-will, because he is inclined to will by the judgment of his reason, and not by natural impulse as brute animals are . . . Again, according to the Philosopher (Ethic. ii. 9; vi.) will is of the end, but choice is of the means to the end . . . Now Choice is always an act of free-will . . . Further, through having free-will man is said to be master of his own actions . . . This may also be gathered from the very signification of the word. For the free is that which is its own cause according to the Philosopher at the beginning of the Metaphysics (ii. 9.) (Aquinas, Summa Contra Gentiles, 1.88; [185–86]).*

The numbers prior to each of the above do not identify a ranking of importance, but are provided to document the summary statements below. Some items may be overlapping, but the objective is to show that the definition given for free will flows directly from Aquinas's words.

1. Free will means that persons do not make decisions of "necessity" [1,9], that is, that they do not *do necessarily what they could not avoid doing* [7].[19]

2. Free will means that a person does not do what he/she does by *natural instinct* [1] or *impulse* [9].

3. Free will predicates *free rational judging* [4]. This is a very important concept and principle in Aquinas's thinking.

4. Free will as a concept is necessary if there is to be moral responsibility and re-wards or punishments [3, 7, 8].

5. Free will means that a person has a range of options from which to choose [5], *for man can will and not will, act and not act; again, he can will this or that, and do this or that* [6].

6. Free will means that a person is not powerless and is not *necessarily moved to will things* [2,7].

7. Aquinas's concept of human freedom identifies a logical order: free will→choice (means to an end)→willing (end) [9].]

   A. Choice is an act of the will: *Now Choice is always an act of free-will.*

   B. Free will shows that a person is *master of his own actions.*

8. Free will means that the causation of action is free, coming from within the person, not from an outside cause [9].

19. The numbers in [1] are references to the items directly above in the previous section.

Considering these statements, it would appear that Aquinas could have given his agreement to these conclusions:

1. A person is "uncaused" when making a given choice. This does not preclude outside influences.

2. Aquinas's thinking supports the Principle of Alternate Possibilities (PAP): A person is morally [and rationally] responsible for her act only if she could have done otherwise than she does.[20]

3. The person has the ability to choose among a range of possible alternatives, each consistent and compatible with and according to his nature.[21]

Aquinas: Libertarian free will.

Before exploring further if Aquinas's view of human freedom is what today is called "libertarian free will," it is important to be clear about what are the bookends of his definition. The one end is that free will means that no "outside" cause determines/compels (causally determines) a person's choices (See #8 in the summary above). But the other bookend is equally important: free will does not mean always freedom to do what one chooses to do or be or not to do or be. In *DV* Aquinas explains: "In man's activity two elements are to be found: (1) the choice of a course of action; and this is always in a man's power; and (2) the carrying out or execution of the course of action; and this is not always within a man's power; but under guidance of divine providence the project is sometimes brought to completion, sometimes not. Thus, a man is not said to be free in his actions but free in his choice, which is a judgment about what is to be done. This is what the name *free choice* refers to."[22]

This is significant because many people mistakenly believe that "a man is said to be endowed with free choice inasmuch as he is the master of his own *actions*."[23] A simple illustration shows why this is a misunderstanding. A person looks in the refrigerator and discovers that there is no milk. He thinks about his family's needs and decides to go to the store and pick up a gallon. He goes outside—the temperature is twenty-five below zero—and the car will not start. He chose freely, but he could not act on his choice.[24]

20. Definition [less the addition in brackets] is from Markovits, "Ethics."

21. Compare the summary of Lonergan "A free act has four presuppositions: (A): a field of action in which more than one course of action is objectively possible; (B) an intellect that is able to work out more than one course of action; (C) a will that is not automatically determined by the first course of action that occurs to the intellect; and since this condition is only a condition, securing indeterminacy without telling what in fact does determine, (D) a will that moves itself" (Lonergan, *Grace and Freedom*, 96).

22. Aquinas, *DV* 24.1.

23. Aquinas, *DV* 24.1, author's *emphasis*.

24. Another way of approaching this is: if one freely chooses to keep driving straight and not to turn

This is a profoundly important distinction, especially as it relates to the biblical concept of "grace." Can one *alone*—without God's enablement—become, as Jesus put it, born again or become holy in living? Far too often the answer to this question has created sharp (sometimes hostile) division between Arminians and Calvinists. But Aquinas shows a possible way out of this dilemma. God is an influence on *all* people to "seek him and his righteousness." He is one of many influences; some unlike him are evil. But his divine influence (grace) is sufficient for *all* to choose to receive his pardon.[25] But should a person—responding to his "prevenient grace" (or a less controversial term "sufficient grace")—freely choose to act on his gracious offer, if he chooses to desire his pardon, it is God's grace alone that enables him to become reborn or to take a step toward God's holiness.[26] Thus, for example, in Rom 8 believers are urged to *not present the members of our bodies to sin* (a free decision) yet are told *by the Spirit they are to put to death the deeds of the body.* Choices are freely made in response to outside influences (including God's influences on humanity) but the actions are divinely enabled to carry out those choices.[27] To say it another way, every

---

the steering wheel to the right or left, then he is freely choosing to drive straight. Unbeknownst to the driver, however, the steering wheel "locked up" (due to faulty manufacturing), and it was impossible to turn it to the right or to the left—even though he did not will or choose to turn to the right or left. So, the driver is freely choosing to do the only thing he could do (even though he did not know it). It seems the driver can be held responsible for driving straight based on his intent to not turn right or left.

Suppose, however, that the driver chose to turn right and was physically unable to make the turn. Can the driver be held responsible for not making the turn? Certainly not! He intended to make the turn and tried to make the turn. He used his libertarian freedom to choose to do something he just could not do. So, in a case like this, the driver possesses libertarian freedom to "choose" but not to "do."

25. The critics to whom Aquinas is responding have said (incorrectly), "Free choice is said to be a capability of the will and reason by which good is chosen with the help of grace or evil is chosen without it. But there are many who do not have grace. Hence, they cannot freely choose good; and so they do not have free choice regarding good things" (Aquinas, *DV* 24.1).

26. Again, the critics to whom Aquinas is responding have said (incorrectly), "Anselm says that if we had the power of sinning and not sinning, we should not need grace. But the power of sinning and not sinning is free choice. Then, since we need grace, we do not have free choice" (Aquinas, *DV* 24.1). A person can see this blunder more fully in what the critics go on to say: "Each thing is named from the best, as is gathered from the Philosopher. But as applied to human actions 'the best' means meritorious acts. Therefore, since man does not have free choice as to these, because *'without me you can do nothing,'* as is said in John (15:5) with reference to meritorious acts, it seems that man should not be said to be endowed with free choice" (Aquinas, *DV* 24.1).

27. This goes back to Aquinas's distinction between *sensible* and *rational* appetites (which will be discussed in the pages ahead). Animals which have only the *sensible* appetite act automatically to outside stimuli. Their actions are inherent in them, whether those actions have beneficial results or are harmful. Humans, however, do not have within them such freedom to act; they have freedom to choose. They cannot act on their choice to follow the influence of God to obey and seek him. He enables them. But when they spurn and reject God's way, they do themselves harm and the more they disobey, the more they are in bondage. Holiness is a divine enablement as we make our choices, choices for which we have sufficient grace. Aquinas says it this way: "The slavery of sin does not imply force, but either inclination, inasmuch as a preceding sin in some way leads to following ones, or a deficiency in natural virtue, which is unable to free itself from the stain of sin once it has subjected itself to it" (Aquinas, *DV* 24:1).

time God gives a command, he also provides the ability to carry out this command. For example, when Jesus commanded Peter to get out of the boat and walk on water, God provided Peter the ability to walk on water.

But does this mean that Aquinas's thinking fits into the modern philosophical concept of "libertarian free will"? Scott MacDonald frames the question well: "When we in the late twentieth century ask whether someone is an incompatibilist about free choice, we mean to be asking whether that person denies that someone's choosing freely on some occasion is compatible with her choice's being wholly determined or necessitated on that occasion by antecedent causal conditions . . . Aquinas [does not fit that description. He] is clearly an incompatibilist of some sort, [but] it's not at all clear that *his* incompatibilism commits him to *ours*."[28] Then he goes on to add: "I have an ulterior motive in taking up these matters. I think Aquinas's account of incompatibilist free choice is especially interesting and attractive because, if I am right about its structure and essential nature, it stakes out a moderate libertarianism that avoids some of the common and particularly damaging criticisms directed against a traditional form of libertarianism. If Aquinas's account is defensible, it preserves genuine indeterminacy in human agency while at the same time securing a necessary connection between an agent's free choices and her reasons for acting."[29]

Aquinas's view of human freedom, then, is far more complex than the quotations above may indicate. But this writer finds—like MacDonald—it is both fascinating and challenging to understand.

Aquinas: Libertarian free will (A clarification).

This brief essay, then, seeks to unpack the essence of Aquinas's thinking and to do that by specifically addressing four areas that need clarification:

1. Clarification #1: Does God possess libertarian freedom?

2. Clarification #2: The Latin behind terms which look like human freedom: *liberum arbitrium* and *electio*.

3. Clarification #3: Aquinas's term which comes into English as "appetite."

4. Clarification #4: The interplay of "will" and "reason"—indeed the whole person—in acts of the will.

28. MacDonald, "Aquinas's Libertarian Account," 311–12. *Italics* are MacDonald's.

29. MacDonald, "Aquinas's Libertarian Account," 311–12.

CLARIFICATION #1: DOES GOD HAVE LIBERTARIAN FREEDOM?

This may appear to be a strange question because the subject under consideration is human freedom, but the answer to this question—posed by Aquinas himself—gives flavor to the larger topic of what "freedom" actually entails. In *ST* he writes:

> We have free-will with respect to what we will not of necessity, nor by natural instinct . . . Hence . . . animals, that are moved to act by natural instinct, are not said to be moved by free-will. Since then God necessarily wills His own goodness, but other things not necessarily . . . He has free will with respect to what He does not necessarily will . . .
>
> Since the evil of sin consists in turning away from the divine goodness, by which God wills all things . . . it is manifestly impossible for Him to will the evil of sin; yet He can make choice of one of two opposites, inasmuch as He can will a thing to be, or not to be. In the same way we ourselves, without sin, can will to sit down, and not will to sit down.[30]

Thus, according to Aquinas, freedom in God is "limited" to what he is—"good"—and thus evil is impossible with him. But he nevertheless has free will in areas consistent with his nature. That is to say, God is free to choose among a range of equally good options. Based on the illustration that Aquinas gives about human freedom in areas not related to moral issues—such as sitting or not sitting—God is free in areas compatible with his goodness: to create the universe or not to create the universe, or perhaps whether it is to rain in Spain today or not to rain in Spain (or some other place).[31]

Another important difference is that human beings are contingent. God is a necessary and eternal being, and thus, Aquinas contends: "The divine nature is uncreated and is its own act of being and its own goodness. Consequently, there cannot be in it any deficiency either in existence or in goodness." Further, "Knowing also is found to be a different sort in man than in God and in the angels. Man has a process of knowing which is obscured and gets its view of the truth by means of a discourse. From this source comes his hesitation and difficulty in making decisions and in judging."[32] God is all-knowing; he does not learn, nor forget. Thus, human beings are contingent beings whom God has created for good, but who have also been given the freedom to reject it or not.

CLARIFICATION #2: THE LATIN BEHIND THE TERMS: LIBERUM ARBITRIUM AND ELECTIO.

In every discipline there is a vocabulary to be learned. And this is especially true when research is made of a theological or philosophical work written in a foreign language.

30. Aquinas, *ST* 1.19.10; [256].

31. This important concept will be more thoroughly explored and unpacked in chapter 15.

32. Aquinas, *DV* 24.3.

Aquinas writes in Latin[33] and, without the benefit of understanding what is the meaning of the Latin terms he uses, one might reach conclusions which he would never have intended.

Probably the most notable example is the term used by Aquinas for free will: *liberum arbitrium*. The words themselves look like and appear to fit the definition of unqualified libertarian free choice, but that is not Aquinas's meaning. He uses the term in conjunction with another Latin term *electio* ("choice"), and this gives a different flavor of what human freedom really consists. *Electio* is an act of the will (in conjunction with a person's reason) but proposes to the will what it infers as a best suggestion (among a range of contenders) for a given action in a set of circumstances. *Electio*, however, is not a final selection but is the product of the interaction between the mind's reasoning and will, which "will" ultimately issues a decision and subsequent action. This rational, weighing process (between the mind and will) Aquinas calls *liberum arbitrium* and the proposed best suggestion is *electio*. To use Aquinas's words: "'Free-will' (*liberum arbitrium*) . . . is nothing else but the power of choice (*electio*) . . . But to 'choose' (*electio*) is to desire something for the sake of obtaining something else: wherefore, properly speaking, it regards the means to the end . . . Wherefore it is evident that as the intellect is to reason, so is the will to the power of choice (*electio*), which is free-will (*liberum arbitrium*)."[34]

He is even more explicit in *DV*: "Free choice (*liberum arbitrium*) is therefore the will. The term does not designate the will absolutely, however, but with reference to one of its acts, to choose (*electio*) . . . Free choice (*liberum arbitrium*) does not refer to the will absolutely but in subordination to reason."[35]

Aquinas's scholar Eleonore Stump—to whom this writer is indebted for a careful analysis of these Latin terms—admits that "Although "*liberum arbitrium*" means "free judgment," Aquinas sometimes sounds as if *liberum arbitrium* is just the power of the will to do otherwise than it does . . . Nonetheless, it is a mistake to suppose that "*liberum arbitrium*" is Aquinas's term for the freedom of the will in general . . . Even understood narrowly as confined to the power of the will producing *electio*, *liberum arbitrium* isn't a property of the will alone. It can be understood as a property of the will only insofar as the will itself is understood to be the rational appetite and to have a close tie to the intellect."[36]

This association of the will with what Aquinas calls the "*rational* appetite" or human reasoning is probably the most important principle for understanding Aquinas's concept of free will. How the "will" is related to thinking and reasoning will be traced much more extensively in the fourth clarification below (and in later chapters),

33. The Latin for the above terms can be found in texts which show the Latin and an English translation in parallel columns.

34. Aquinas, *ST* 1.83; [619–20].

35. Aquinas, *DV* 24.6.

36. Stump, "Aquinas's Account," 586–87.

but for now the point is that one must be careful to understand the Latin behind English translations (or any other translation) for key terms. But one must hasten to add, however, that what appears to be confusing in terminology will be clarified by what follows in clarification four below. In short, human freedom as understood by Aquinas is a process involving the whole person: passions, rational thinking, and will.

CLARIFICATION #3: AQUINAS'S TERM WHICH COMES INTO ENGLISH AS "APPETITE."

Aquinas's use of *"appetite"* as a theological/philosophical term is a foreign and often a puzzling concept to the beginning reader of Aquinas, though a person who is conversant with Aristotle's writings[37] will recognize how dependent Aquinas is on him for the terms and even the three categories which are delineated.[38] Despite it being obscure at first, it really is a very simple concept. As human beings, we have appetites, that is, desires for any number of things: food, relationships, sex, etc. So "appetites" are hungers, desires, bents, inclinations,[39] movements toward what is "good," that is, for what God has made his creation (plants, animals, human beings) to aspire to and be like.[40] One way for beginners to understand as they read is mentally to translate the term "appetite" with the word "inclination" each time they encounter the word. Specifically, Aquinas identifies three categories of appetites, beginning with the lowest order in plants and inanimate things and ascending to the highest order in human beings. His fullest explanation is quoted below:

> Man has free-will: otherwise counsels, exhortations, commands, prohibitions, rewards, and punishments would be in vain. In order to make this evident, we must observe that some things act without judgment; as a stone moves downwards; and in like manner all things which lack knowledge. And some act from judgment, but not a free judgment; as brute animals. For the sheep, seeing the wolf, judges it a thing to be shunned, from a natural and not a free judgment, because it judges, not from reason, but from natural instinct. And the same thing is to be said of any judgment of brute animals. But man acts from judgment, because by his apprehensive power he judges that something should be avoided or sought. But because this judgment, in the case of some particular act, is not from a natural instinct, but from some act of comparison in the reason, therefore he acts from free judgment and retains the power of

---

37. Aristotle, *De Anima*. The specific section that is especially helpful begins with 2.1; [52]. In 2.4; [63], Aristotle speaks of the "faculties" as "cognitive, sensitive and nutritive."

38. Augustine, *On the Free Choice* (2.5.11.43–2.11.31) also uses these three categories.

39. It is interesting that Aquinas himself uses "appetite" and "inclination" synonymously (*ST* 1.80; [910]).

40. Aquinas, *ST* 1.59; [658]: "Since all things flow from the divine will, all things in their own way are inclined by appetite towards good, but in different ways."

being inclined to various things. For reason in contingent matters may follow opposite courses, as we see in dialectic syllogisms and rhetorical arguments.[41]

Thus, there are three appetites:[42]

1. *Natural* appetite: These are inclinations "without knowledge" or "without judgment," that is, no reasoning is involved. These are "things . . . which act, not from any previous judgment, but, as it were, [are] moved and made to act by others."[43] Aquinas has in mind two basic groups of "things:" plants and inanimate bodies. For example, it is the natural inclination of a stone to go downward, a fire to go up and set other things on fire,[44] a plant to turn toward the sun, and an arrow directed toward a target. The *natural* appetite, then, denotes a bent in the subject to do what has been "programed" into it. Though this is a simplistic explanation, Aquinas gives the illustration of a stone which obeys gravity, and it will fall unless some other force acts on it.

   The other two appetites belong to a far different category; they relate only to the "animal" world, the world of living creatures: creeping things, fowl, reptiles, animals, and human beings. Yet among these there is a clear line of division between non-human animals and human beings. Though the *sensitive* appetite can be involved in human choices and behavior, no animals have *rational* appetites. Animals do function "with some knowledge/judgment," that is, they do "learn" some things (such as—to use a modern example—learning to peck a button to receive food), but as will be seen they have "knowledge" only in a limited way. Unlike human beings, animals have no ability to reflect upon a range of possible alternatives and reason to logically abductive conclusions, for example. In this way human beings are like God, bearing the image of their Creator.[45]

2. *Sensitive* appetite: These are inclinations "with some knowledge" or "judgment." Another term which might describe this appetite is inclination and action by reflex. To throw more light on this, Aquinas adds that this *sensitive* appetite has two aspects functioning at all times: (1) *Concupiscible* and (2) *Irascible*. Both are Latin terms that have merely been transliterated into English, the first meaning "desire" and the second "anger."[46] Thus the concupiscible appetite is an inclination

---

41. Aquinas, *ST* 1.83; [931]. See also *ST* 1.59; [658–60].

42. Unless otherwise noted, all the definitions come from the quotation above or *ST* 1.59; [658].

43. Aquinas, *ST* 1.59; [652].

44. Aquinas, *ST* 1.80; [910].

45. Aquinas, *ST* 1.80; [910]. See also Aquinas, *DV* 24.2: "Brutes have a certain semblance of reason inasmuch as they share in a certain natural prudence, and in this respect a lower nature 'in some way attains to the property of a higher'. This semblance consists in the well-regulated judgment which they have about certain things. But they have this judgment from a natural estimate, not from any deliberation, since they are ignorant of the basis of their judgment."

46. Aquinas, *ST* 1.81; [915]. See also 1.82; [928–29] where Aquinas says "the concupiscible power is so called from '*concupiscere*' [to desire], and the irascible part from '*irasci*' [to be angry]."

for a good that is "pleasant to the sense (like 'sweetness'), suitable to nature, and fleeing from that which is harmful."[47] Aquinas illustrates this in the animal world with the sheep fleeing on seeing a wolf. The irascible appetite is an inclination for the good "as something which resists an attack on what is suitable and which wards off and repels what is harmful," as when an animal would fight to protect its young.[48]

It is also important to bear in mind that these two components of the *sensitive* appetite interact (and agree or conflict) with each other:

> Now these two are not to be reduced to one principle: for sometimes the soul busies itself with unpleasant things, against the inclination of the concupiscible appetite, in order that, following the impulse of the irascible appetite, it may fight against obstacles. Wherefore also the passions of the irascible appetite counteract the passions of the concupiscible appetite: since the concupiscence, on being aroused, diminishes anger; and anger being roused, diminishes concupiscence in many cases. This is clear also from the fact that the irascible is, as it were, the champion and defender of the concupiscible when it rises up against what hinders the acquisition of the suitable things which the concupiscible desires, or against what inflicts harm, from which the concupiscible flies. And for this reason, all the passions of the irascible appetite rise from the passions of the concupiscible appetite and terminate in them; for instance, anger rises from sadness, and having wrought vengeance, terminates in joy.[49]

3. *Rational* or *Intellectual* appetite: These are inclinations "with knowledge." This is the ability of the human being to reflect and reason to a decision or conclusion. Aquinas sometimes calls this the "will."[50]

Understanding the *natural* appetite is rather straight-forward, but how the *sensitive* appetite and *rational* appetite differ is quite important, and Aquinas makes his thinking clear: "In . . . animals, movement *follows at once* the concupiscible and irascible appetites: for instance, the sheep, fearing the wolf, flees at once, because it has no superior counteracting appetite. On the contrary, man is *not moved at once*, according

---

47. Aquinas, *ST* 1.82; [928].

48. Aquinas uses the example of fire (though he recognizes this is not animate): "In order to make this clear, we must observe that in natural corruptible things there is needed an inclination not only to the acquisition of what is suitable and to the avoiding of what is harmful, but also to resistance against corruptive and contrary agencies which are a hindrance to the acquisition of what is suitable, and are productive of harm. For example, fire has a natural inclination, not only to rise from a lower position, which is unsuitable to it, towards a higher position which is suitable, but also to resist whatever destroys or hinders its action" (Aquinas, *ST* 1.81; [915]).

49. Aquinas, *ST* 1.81; [915].

50. See Aquinas, *ST* 1.59; [664]: "Now it is quite evident from what has been said . . . that the object of the intellective appetite [is] otherwise known as the will."

to the irascible and concupiscible appetites: but he *awaits the command of the will, which is the superior appetite.*"[51]

Animals with their *sensitive* appetite respond reflexibly, while a human being's *sensitive* appetite may direct a person to respond in the same as an animal, for example, to flee, but that inclination is tempered by the will (*rational* appetite) not to run. Later Aquinas explains himself more definitively: "Now this necessity of coercion is altogether repugnant to the will. For we call that violent which is against the inclination of a thing. But the very movement of the will is an inclination to something. Therefore, as a thing is called natural because it is according to the inclination of nature, so a thing is called voluntary because it is according to the inclination of the will."[52]

He was even more clear earlier: "Such a judgment [from *sensitive* appetite] is not a free one, but implanted by nature . . . Only an agent endowed with an intellect can act with a judgment which is free."[53] Aquinas illustrates this with the emotion of anger. The *sensitive* appetite unleashes the emotion of anger, but it is the *rational* appetite which moderates it. "To get angry with moderation, for instance, implies something which goes beyond the capacity of the irascible power; for the irascible power cannot moderate the passion of anger by itself unless it is perfected by . . . the moderation of reason."[54]

There is an interesting recent, true story that illustrates the difference between *sensitive* appetite and *rational* appetite. A fifty-four-year-old woman in Indonesia named Wa Tiba went out to her vegetable garden and never returned. When the villagers checked on her by going to her garden, they did not find her, but they did find a python nearby that had eaten something so large that its stomach was greatly enlarged. They feared the worse had happened, and capturing the snake, they cut open the bloated area. Then they found what they had feared: the woman, though dead, fully clothed inside.[55]

The story and the accompanied video went viral. A South African friend, when he heard the story, said he had heard such accounts in his own country. And then he added that people there know that if such an attack were to occur, they should not fight the snake but act "dead" and also keep their hands outstretched so that if the

---

51. Aquinas, *ST* 1.81; [917], author's *emphasis*.

52. Aquinas, *ST* 1.82; [920].

53. Aquinas, *ST* 1.59; [662]. See also Aquinas, *DV* 1.1: "Brutes do not judge about their own judgment but follow the judgment implanted in them by God. Thus, they are not the cause of their own decision nor do they have freedom of choice. But man, judging about his course of action by the power of reason, can also judge about his own decision inasmuch as he knows the meaning of an end and of a means to an end, and the relationship of the one with reference to the other. Thus, he is his own cause not only in moving but also in judging. He is, therefore, endowed with free choice—that is to say, with a free judgment about acting or not acting."

54. Aquinas, *DV* 24.3.

55. Gibbens, "Woman Swallowed."

snake tried to swallow them up to the outstretched arms, it could not get beyond that point. Often, then, he said, the snake will try another approach like attempting to swallow via an arm. If it then failed, it would just give up and slitter away. (Whether these tactics actually work or do not is another story, but the point does illustrate the interplay of the *sensitive* appetite and the *rational* appetite.)[56]

The instinctive—and thinking—response (the *sensitive* appetite) that a non-human animal (and human being too!) would make would be to vigorously fight the snake, but such action would ultimately lead to being crushed by the coiled snake's strong muscles. But the *rational* appetite might operate this way. "I want to survive and must fight." But the "will" of the person would resist such a choice and interact with the mind which reminds the person of the wisdom of survival and, therefore, to reason: "To fight is to lose. Relax; act dead; make it impossible to be swallowed." The *rational* appetite so reasons to this *better* option (from within a range of other possibilities), and Aquinas would contend that the will agrees and finally directs the defensive action.

What animals would do from instinct—fight and perish—human beings, exercising their thinking capacity, can freely do against what they might naturally do to their demise.[57] This is precisely Aquinas's conclusion:

> Hence "they are moved by things seen," as Augustine teaches; and as Damascene says, they are driven by passions, because they naturally judge as they do about a particular thing seen or a particular passion. They are accordingly under the necessity of being moved to flight or pursuit by the sight of a particular thing or by a passion which is aroused. A sheep, for example, is under the necessity of fearing and fleeing at the sight of a wolf, and a dog under the influence of the passion of anger has to bark and pursue, intent upon hurting. But man is not necessarily moved by the things which he meets or by the passions which arise, *because he can admit or repress them.* Consequently, man has free choice, but brutes do not.[58]

Clarification #4: The interplay of "will" and "reason."

At the very beginning of Eleonore Stump's excellent essay "Aquinas's Account of Freedom: Intellect and Will," she lays out the essence of Aquinas's perspective of human freedom. It is a good abstract for the following discussion:

---

56. The author is neither endorsing, nor rejecting these tactics. The tactics may be merely anecdotal.

57. The writer's colleague has seen this occur when visiting a pig farmer. A pig got its head caught under a wooden fence and instead of just relaxing fought to its death. If it had relaxed—which is not instinctive—it could have survived.

58. Aquinas, *DV* 24.2, author's *emphasis*.

Contemporary discussions of free will tend to belong to an older, non-Thomistic tradition of thought . . . [in which] human freedom is a property of just one component of human mental faculties, namely, the will; and freedom consists in an agent's *ability to will autonomously* in general and *independently of the intellect in particular.* The influence of this tradition persists in contemporary discussion, both for libertarians and for their opponents . . . For Aquinas, *freedom with regard to willing is a property primarily of . . . [the whole] human being,* not of some particular component . . . Furthermore, the will is not independent of the intellect. On the contrary, the dynamic interactions of intellect and will yield freedom as an emergent property or a systems-level feature.[59]

For Aquinas, then, human freedom exists in the sense that nothing outside of the person compels him or her to make choices or to act in a certain way. Instead, the human being acts on the interaction of internal factors which involve the emotions, thinking, deliberating, evaluating, weighing, judging, and then ultimately deciding or willing. There are indeed outside influences, and to insist on human freedom does not mean an immunity to them. But these do not necessarily compel a person to act without the interaction of the internal factors previously mentioned. Freedom, therefore, is not a function of will alone as if it were an independent structure or entity.

Aquinas identifies this freedom as a function of the image of God uniquely found in human beings:

We are said to have free choice in so far as our acts are voluntary . . . According to the Philosopher, in everything which moves itself there is the ability to be moved and not be moved . . . Man is seen to be made to the image of God from the fact that he has free choice, as Damascene and Bernard both say . . . Whatever is endowed with free choice acts and is not merely acted upon . . . If the judgment of the cognitive faculty is not in a person's power but is determined for him extrinsically, neither will his appetite be in his power; and consequently, neither will his motion or operation be in his power absolutely . . . But to judge about one's own judgment belongs only to reason, which reflects upon its own act and knows the relationships of the things about which it judges and of those by which it judges. Hence the whole root of freedom is located in reason. Consequently, a being is related to free choice in the same way as it is related to reason.[60]

Further, the will should not be seen as merely a decision-making faculty, for decisions are never made independent of a person's reason. The ability to reason—and reach rational conclusions—should not be conflated with a cause (which can also be referred to as "a reason" for an effect). Rather, the ability to reason is the judging/

---

59. Stump, "Aquinas's Account," 856, author's *emphasis.*

60. Aquinas, *DV* 24.2.

weighing faculty of the person.[61] But reason, so argues Aquinas, does not work independently but jointly with the will and "reports" its findings and recommendations to it. But reason should not be equated with the will. Will, though part of the process when it resists what reason "suggests" and refers an issue back for more thinking and evaluating, eventually is the end of the process, the decision to act. Thus, one might look at the two as co-dependent, or as Aquinas puts it, "The will is called a mover which is moved,"[62] and "The intellect moves the will . . . [and] the will moves the intellect and all the powers of the soul."[63] In few other places does Aquinas make more clear the integrated interaction of these two aspects the soul. They are "two faculties which are ultimately interrelated and which are always working together in the closest conjunction with each other."[64]

Voluntary Action

Another way of considering human freedom is to ask what constitutes "voluntary" action. Aquinas sees it as having two essential elements:

1. An act is "voluntary" if the principle behind the movement is within the person.

2. An act is "voluntary" if the agent has some knowledge of its end.[65]

For example, "when a stone is moved upwards, the principle of this movement is outside the stone: whereas when it is moved downwards, the principle of this movement is in the stone."[66] Though the movement downward is intrinsic, since the stone is an inanimate object, it fails on the second element, *having no knowledge of its end.* But do non-human animals fit the condition of "voluntary"? Aquinas says "Yes," but it is an "imperfect" voluntary: "Consequently, perfect knowledge of the end leads to the perfect voluntary; inasmuch as, having apprehended the end, a man can, from deliberating about the end and the means thereto, be moved, or not, to gain that end. But imperfect knowledge of the end leads to the imperfect voluntary; inasmuch as the agent apprehends the end, but does not deliberate, and is moved to the end at once."[67]

"Voluntary" may suggest only taking action, but it also applies to non-action: "The word 'voluntary' is applied to that of which we are masters. Now we are masters

---

61. "Reason, whose function it is to refer and compare . . ." (Aquinas, *DV* 24.5).

62. Aquinas, *ST* 1.59; [659].

63. Aquinas, *ST* 1.82; [926]. See also Aquinas, *DV* 24.6: "The will in some sense moves reason by commanding its act; and reason moves the will by proposing to it its object, which is the end. Thus, it is that either power can in some way be informed by the other."

64. McInerny, *Philosophical Psychology,* 241.

65. Aquinas, *ST* FS 6; [1381].

66. Aquinas, *ST* FS 6; [1379–81].

67. Aquinas, *ST* FS 6; [1381].

in respect of to act and not to act, to will and not to will. Therefore, just as to act and to will are voluntary, so also are not to act and not to will."[68]

Some may suggest that fear in human beings promotes involuntary action and thus is an exception to human freedom. To be sure, fear comes from the outside, but it consists of the *sensitive* appetite, which in animals brings an involuntary action, but because human beings have a *reasoning* appetite, the immediate emotion (sensation) of fear is processed—as illustrated in the python story—and the action to take weighs different actions or lack of action. Thus, though the threat is from the outside, the reason suggests an action that is to act or not to act in a certain way or another. Aquinas says it this way: "Therefore, we must consider the nature of free-will, by considering the nature of choice. Now two things concur in choice: one on the part of the cognitive power, the other on the part of the appetitive power. On the part of the cognitive power, counsel is required, by which we judge one thing to be preferred to another: and on the part of the appetitive power, it is required that the appetite should accept the judgment of counsel."[69]

Aquinas also relates how the *sensitive* and *rational* appetites interact in moral decisions, a very important dimension of human freedom. As noted earlier, Aquinas contends that unless there is free choice, there cannot be moral responsibility.[70] This also means that no creature has built into him or her the ability to be absolutely good: "There is not and cannot be any creature whose free choice is naturally confirmed in good so that the inability to sin belongs to it by its purely natural endowments . . . A rational nature, accordingly, which is directed to good, taken absolutely, through many different actions, cannot have actions naturally incapable of going astray from good unless it have in it naturally and invariably the formality of the universal and perfect good. That can be had, however, only in the divine nature. For God alone is pure act."[71]

Though both appetites are created by God for the good, "a man who wishes to fornicate, for instance . . . although he knows in general that fornication is evil, nevertheless judges this present act of fornication to be good for him and chooses it under the aspect of good. As Dionysius says, 'no one acts intending evil."[72] Therefore,

68. Aquinas, *ST* FS 6.3; [1383].

69. Aquinas, *ST* 1.83; [935]. See also the *sensitive* appetite and the emotion of anger, discussed above (Aquinas, *DV* 24.3).

70. Aquinas, *ST* 1.3; [931]; *DM* 6; [57]; *DV* 24.1.

71. Aquinas, *DV* 24.7. Aquinas explores this extensively in Article 7, but it is beyond the scope of this essay.

72. Aquinas, *DV* 24.2. See also Aquinas, *DV* 24.8: "The will naturally tends to good as its object. That it sometimes tends to evil happens only because the evil is presented to it under the aspect of a good . . . There cannot be any sin in the motion of the will so that it tends to evil unless there previously exists some deficiency in the apprehensive power, as a result of which something evil is presented as good. This deficiency in reason can come about in two ways: either from reason itself, or from something extrinsic to it . . . Reason proves deficient because of something extrinsic to it when the lower powers are drawn to something intensely and the act of reason is consequently interrupted so

something has happened to the *rational* appetite. Though from the hand of God, it is inclined for the good, because of the fall (original sin), it is led to misunderstanding what is the "good" as it relates to specific decisions or acts.

A person can also use the very grace God has given badly: "Man has not entirely destroyed his [power of] free choice by using it badly . . . Nevertheless, a person can use his free choice badly even when it has the freedom of grace."[73] Thus, moral sin reflects damage[74] to a person's reasoning ability, the processing center, and not to some outside force, nor even to internal suggestions of the *sensitive* appetite: "The lower appetitive powers, that is, the irascible and the concupiscible, need habits by which the moral virtues are completed. That their acts should be moderate does not exceed human nature, but it does exceed the scope of the powers mentioned. It is accordingly necessary that what belongs to a higher power, reason, be impressed upon them.[75] We are moved by free choice inasmuch as by our free choice we choose to be moved; and the same is true of other acts."[76]

AQUINAS: GOD'S GRACE AND THE FALL OF MAN.

The mention of grace in the equation of human behavior and choices (in the previous paragraphs above) returns one to the key question of this thesis: "If every human being has been damaged by the fall, in what sense does he have freedom"? Or to ask it in another way, "If the *rational* appetite has been damaged by original sin, can human beings avoid sinning without divine grace"? Aquinas answers by noting the positions that he considers heretical:

> Opposite heresies have arisen regarding this question. Some, judging of the nature of the human mind after the manner of corporeal natures, have been of the opinion that man does from necessity everything to which they saw there was an inclination of the human mind. For the human mind has two contrary inclinations. One, from the instinct of reason, is to good. Noting this, Jovinian said that man cannot sin. The other inclination is in the human mind from

that it does not propose to the will its judgment about the good clearly and firmly." (See also *DV* 24.9).

73. Aquinas, *DV* 24.4.

74. Aquinas, *DV* 24.12. See also Aquinas, *DV* 24.8: "The will naturally tends to good as its object. That it sometimes tends to evil happens only because the evil is presented to it under the aspect of a good. But evil is involuntary, as Dionysius says. Consequently, there cannot be any sin in the motion of the will so that it tends to evil unless there previously exists some deficiency in the apprehensive power, as a result of which something evil is presented as good. This deficiency in reason can come about in two ways: either from reason itself, or from something extrinsic to it . . . Reason proves deficient because of something extrinsic to it when the lower powers are drawn to something intensely and the act of reason is consequently interrupted so that it does not propose to the will its judgment about the good clearly and firmly. For example, someone with a proper regard for the necessity of observing chastity may desire something contrary to chastity through a lust for what is pleasurable."

75. Aquinas, *DV* 24.4.

76. Aquinas, *DV* 24.5.

the lower powers, especially as corrupted by original sin. By this the mind is inclined to choose the things which are pleasurable to the carnal senses. Noting this inclination, the Manicheans said that man necessarily sins and cannot in any way avoid sin. Thus both, though by opposite paths, fell into the same inadmissible position, denying free choice; for man does not have free choice if he is driven with necessity to either good or evil.

On the other hand, there arose Pelagius, who, wishing to defend free choice, opposed divine grace and said that man is able to avoid sin without the grace of God. This error very evidently contradicts the teaching of the gospels, and has therefore been condemned by the Church.[77]

Aquinas: God's grace and the fall of man ("False" views).

Briefly, then, there are two positions with which Aquinas disagrees:

1. Though human beings are thinking beings, they do not differ from animals; they do what they do by nature or necessity. There are two different expressions of this erroneous position:

   A. Expression #1: The "instinct of reason" is predisposed to doing only good, that is, it does not and cannot sin.

   B. Expression #2: Human beings—damaged as they are from the fall (original sin)—are inclined to evil desires and thus you have the Manichean position *that man necessarily sins and cannot in any way avoid sin.*

Both of these expressions are forms of determinism and thus are a denial of free will.

2. Pelagianism: Human beings are free and thus can make morally good choices without the help of grace.[78]

Aquinas: God's grace and the fall of man ("Catholic" views).

In contrast to these heretical views, Aquinas says, "Now the Catholic faith takes a middle course, *so saving free choice as not to exclude the necessity of grace.*"[79] In other words, what Aquinas will set forth is a position between determinism on the one hand (the first position above) and on the other hand the Pelagianism that says human beings are truly free and do not need God's grace. So how does he explain this "middle course"?[80] He answers:

77. Aquinas, *DV* 24.12.
78. Aquinas, *DV* 24.12.
79. Aquinas, *DV* 24.12, Author's *emphasis*.
80. The importance for Aquinas's view of human freedom—as explained most thoroughly here in *DV* 24.12—merits more extensive quotations from his writings so that the explanation of his position

The "Catholic" view (No outside causation).

Aquinas reasserts that all decisions and behaviors flow from within, that is, from the interaction of reasoning and willing and thus are not causally determined by outside forces.[81]

The "Catholic" view ("Surprises").

"Surprises" [which are defined below], however, can lead to decisions and actions that otherwise would not occur, but this does not preclude the fact that—should the person have been more attentive—he or she could have done otherwise: "A sin or its avoidance can exceed the power of free choice . . . inasmuch as a particular sin occurs suddenly and more or less by surprise, thus escaping the election of free choice, *even though by directing its attention or efforts to it* free choice could commit the sin or avoid it."[82]

THE "CATHOLIC" VIEW ("SURPRISES:" FITS OF PASSION).

By "surprises" Aquinas means that temptations came rather *suddenly* and unexpectedly and as a result caught the otherwise thinking person off guard. He gives two examples of such occurrences,[83] one of which is *One can be surprised by a "fit of passion."*

> In the state of corrupt nature, it is accordingly not within the power of free choice to avoid all sins of this sort, because they escape its act, although it can prevent any particular one of those movements if it makes the effort against it. But it is not possible for man continuously to make the contrary effort to avoid movements of this kind on account of the various occupations of the human mind and the rest required for it. This comes about from the fact that the lower powers are not wholly subject to reason as they were in the state of innocence. It was then easy for man to avoid each and every one of these sins by his free choice, because no movement could arise in the lower powers except at the dictate of reason. In his present state, however, man is not, commonly speaking, restored by grace to this harmonious condition; but we look forward to it in the state of glory. In this state of misery, then, even after reparation by grace

is carefully documented.

81. Aquinas, *DV* 24.12.

82. Aquinas, *DV* 24.12, author's *emphasis*.

83. Aquinas also adds a third in *DV* 24.10: "The third [influence] is a false judgment of reason in regard to a particular object of choice. It comes either from one of the two influences mentioned above, the surge of passion or the penchant of habit, or else from a universal ignorance, as when one is of the erroneous opinion that fornication is not a sin." Thus, a carefully informed thinking process is imperative for godly living. "By means of the true judgment which he has of the principle, a man can do away with any errors that he may have fallen into regarding his conclusions. In the same way by being rightly disposed regarding the end, he can do away with every surge of passion."

man cannot avoid all venial sins. This is, however, in no respect prejudicial to the freedom of choice.[84]

Aquinas carefully stakes out what he means: (1) A person succumbs to sin because of the suddenness of the temptation and because of *various occupations of the human mind and the rest required for it* [distract it]. But he could have avoided sinning if he had *made more effort (which was within his ability) against it*. (2) The fall has damaged everyone's reasoning ability, that is, their ability to resist and deny *Sensitive* inclinations [*passions*], and thus fallen human beings have impaired *Rational* appetites. Further, grace in the present day has not restored this ability, though it will be restored in the world to come. (3) Thus, *after reparation by grace man cannot avoid all venial sins*. (4) But this impairment—which has and does impact a person so that he cannot successfully avoid all sins—does not diminish human freedom (it *is*, *however*, *in no respect prejudicial to the freedom of choice*). The skeptic wonders what meaning is intended for the grace Aquinas makes reference to here and why he felt he had to affirm immediately afterward that God's grace does not contradict man's freedom of choice. (He affirms this again after the second way a person can be surprised.)

The "Catholic" view ("Surprises:" Habit).

Aquinas defines "habit" in the same sense as Augustine: "A habit is that by which a person acts easily" (*DV* 24.4). "When we say that a man has free choice, we do not mean that he is actually judging freely, but that he has within himself that by which he can judge freely. Consequently, if the act of judging freely should contain anything which goes beyond the capacity of a power, then it will designate a habit or a power perfected by some habit. To get angry with moderation, for instance, implies something which goes beyond the capacity of the irascible power; for the irascible power cannot moderate the passion of anger by itself unless it is perfected by a habit by means of which there is impressed upon it the moderation of reason."[85]

"Habit," then, is just like it sounds. It is a pattern of responding based on practice. Giving in to a passion will pave the way to repetition of the response in the future, while resisting will make it easier to resist such stimuli in the future.

> A man . . . may not always have the habit of a vice, because from one act of lust, for instance, the habit of lust is not formed . . . [But] when something to be done which is conformable to the previous choice presents itself to a man so disposed, he straightway goes out to it in a choice unless he holds himself in check by much deliberation . . . [that is, he] resists[86] . . . Even though [he] has avoided

84. Aquinas, *DV* 24.12.

85. Aquinas, *DV* 24.4.

86. In *DV* 24.1, Aquinas explains himself: "The slavery of sin does not imply force, but either inclination, inasmuch as a preceding sin in some way leads to following ones, or a deficiency in natural virtue, which is unable to free itself from the stain of sin once it has subjected itself to it."

this one or that by employing as much deliberation as is required, [he] is still unable to keep consent to a mortal sin from sometimes stealing up on [him] . . . before so much deliberation . . . since it is impossible, because of the many cares with which the human mind is occupied, for a man always or for a long time to remain in such great watchfulness as is required for this.[87] Furthermore, *he is removed from this disposition only by grace*, by which alone the human mind is made to adhere by charity to the unchangeable good as its end.[88]

AQUINAS: GOD'S GRACE

This last statement about the need for grace appears to introduce a difficulty in Aquinas's argument for human freedom, that is, the freedom exercised by the interaction of reasoning and willing, not by any force from the "outside," as the grace from God would be. It appears that Aquinas also recognizes this inherent difficulty for he summarizes—or should one say—declares his conclusion despite the apparent antithesis:

> It is therefore clear from what we have said that we do not take away free choice, since we say that free choice can avoid or commit any sin taken singly; nor again do we take away the necessity of grace, since we say that man (even one having grace, as long as that grace has not been made perfect in the state of glory), because of the corruption of human nature called "fuel of sin," cannot avoid all venial sins though he can avoid each one. Since we say, moreover, that a man in the state of mortal sin and deprived of grace cannot avoid all mortal sins *unless grace should come to his aid* (though he can avoid each one singly) because of the habitual adherence of his will to an inordinate end (referred to by Augustine under the figure of the crookedness of a lower leg which brings on the necessity of limping).[89]

In other words, Aquinas affirms both the freedom to choose to sin or to avoid sinning, but at the same time insists on the necessity of grace.

The question of the place of "grace" in Aquinas is an important issue because it directly relates to his concept of human freedom. In *DV* 24—from which the quotations above are taken—he makes reference to grace several times. From his first usages of the word—*In his present state, however, man is not, commonly speaking, restored by grace to this harmonious condition; but we look forward to it in the state of glory. In this state of misery, then, even after reparation by grace man cannot avoid all venial sins*—one might conclude that he meant (to use contemporary terms) something like

---

87. Later in this same article (*DV* 24.1), Aquinas writes: "Man cannot be habitually disposed to sin for a long time without having unexpectedly presented to him a need for action. When that occurs, because of the inclination of the bad habit he slips into consent to a mortal sin, since it is not possible for a man long to be sufficiently attentive to the need of taking pains to avoid mortal sin."

88. Aquinas, *DV* 24.4, author's *emphasis*.

89. Aquinas, *DV* 24.1, author's *emphasis*.

"prevenient" [Arminian] or "irresistible" [Calvinist] grace, grace that leads to being "born again," that is, to receiving God's pardon and gift of eternal life, and the adjectivo description of grace *"commonly called"* and the words *after reparation by grace* seem to identify it this way. If this is correct, then Aquinas is saying that conversion does not correct the heart damage, damage which only will receive its cure at the resurrection (*in the state of glory*).

If, however, Aquinas is to be understood as using the term as a reference to a "special" dose of grace that is given in this world, he has been misunderstood. He says that, when such grace is received, a person is able to resist sin, especially sin related to his habit: *a man in the state of mortal sin and deprived of grace cannot avoid all mortal sins unless grace should come to his aid.* "Grace," then, for Aquinas clearly refers to what God gives—God as a source outside of the person—that influences the *rational* appetite (which is internal). Of course, in itself, God's grace as an influence in the time of temptation need not be understood as a compelling force. All sorts of influences—for good and evil—play into the equation and compete for the attention and action of the reason and the will. There is, therefore, nothing which would forbid God and his grace from being an influence on the reason and the will, but if it is effectual in enabling the avoiding of sin—as Aquinas says it is—one can rightly ask "Who receives it"? and "Why"? This also engages Aquinas. He continues:

Aquinas: God's grace: "Who receives it"?

He addresses his own questions: "Some of them [that is, "doctors" or theologians like Augustine] say that without habitual ingratiatory grace man can avoid mortal sin, though not without the divine help by which divine providence guides man to do good and avoid evil. This is true when the person has been willing to make an effort against sin; and as a result of it any single mortal sin can be avoided."[90] But these words have been puzzling to many because they surely seem to suggest that grace is given *"when the person has been willing to make an effort against sin."* If so, then, Aquinas views grace as *merited*. Perhaps those who resist this interpretation of his words note that he prefaced his comment with the word *some* and, thus, is not giving his consent. But the second sentence quoted above seems to indicate his assent to what these *doctors* have said. Perhaps what he goes on to say makes his position clearer: "It is not possible for an adult without grace to be only in original sin, because as soon as he has attained the use of free choice, if he has prepared himself for grace, he will have grace."[91]

Earlier, Aquinas seems very clearly to speak of "merited" grace: "Although man cannot by his free choice acquire the grace which makes works meritorious, he nevertheless can prepare himself to have grace, which will not be denied him by God if

90. Aquinas, *DV* 24.24.
91. Aquinas, *DV* 24.24.

he does what is within his power. Thus, it is not altogether outside the power of free choice to perform meritorious works, although the power of free choice does not of itself suffice for this, inasmuch as the manner of operating which is required for merit exceeds the capabilities of nature."[92] In other words, it is one thing to say that a person cannot do meritorious works in his own strength; they demand God's grace. It is far different to say that that enabling grace is given *if* a person *can prepare himself to have grace* by doing *what is within his power.*

Aquinas: In what sense is a person "free"?

If one were to stop here in his analysis of Aquinas's views, he would make a serious blunder in his conclusions, because Aquinas develops this subject further in later articles.[93] He asks the question: "Is free choice capable of good without grace"? To this he replies that a person *cannot*: "Commenting on the words of the Epistle to the Romans (7:15): *The evil which I hate, that I do,* the Gloss says: 'Man wills good naturally, to be sure; but this will always is without effect unless God's grace has strengthened his act of willing.' Without grace, then, man cannot accomplish any good."[94] But he goes on to say that this is a qualified "good." A person can do "good" things, such as giving alms to the poor. This is good in the sense "of the act," but is not the "good" in the "manner of acting," that is, it is not prompted by doing it from a heart responding to a person's love for God or doing it in his name. The latter is a grace-enabled "spiritual good" and is "the kind of good which is above human nature."[95]

But the issue that is more to the point is the question raised in very next article: "Can man without grace prepare himself to have grace"?[96] Aquinas sets his response in contrast with those who argue that a person "without grace can therefore prepare himself for grace." Those who argue this way, Aquinas says—and emphatically states—that God would not appeal to a person "to repent" or "to open the door" of his life to him if the person could not respond to it. He gives as an example what Anselm has written: "the reason why a person does not have grace is not that God does not give it, but that man does not accept it. But this would not be true if man were not able without grace to prepare himself to have grace. Man can, therefore, by his free choice prepare for grace."[97] This seems to be merited grace. With this Aquinas cannot agree, because "It is written (John 6:44): *No man can come to me, except the Father, who has sent me, draw him* . . . [And] in praying we ask of God to convert us to Himself, as is shown in the Psalm (84:5): *Convert us, O God our savior* . . . But it would not be necessary for man

---

92. Aquinas, *DV* 24.1.

93. Aquinas, *DV* 24.14–15.

94. Aquinas, *DV* 24.14.

95. Aquinas, *DV* 24.14.

96. Aquinas, *DV* 24.15.

97. Aquinas, *DV* 24.15, *Difficulties*, 3.

to ask this if he could by his free choice prepare himself for grace. It, therefore, seems that without grace man cannot do so."[98]

But what sort of grace? It does not mean, Aquinas argues, "habitual" giftings, because then one might wonder "why [it] is given to some and not to others"?[99] He rather sees God's grace given to all, grace which—rightly responded to—moves a person to call out to God for his saving grace. It is this appeal to God that is preparatory for the grace (a "secondary" installment) that leads to God's pardoning grace, "the forgiveness of sins." "Thus, when a man begins to prepare himself for grace by turning his will to God for the first time, he must be brought to this by some external occasions, such as an external admonition or a bodily sickness or something of the sort, or else by some interior instinct, as God works in the hearts of men, or even in both ways together."[100]

Opportunity to hear the gospel (external admonition), personal crisis or afflictions (2 Cor 4:17), or some other way that *God works in the hearts of men* are prompters for a person to cry out to God for his pardon. Aquinas acknowledges that this is a mystery, that how it occurs "cannot be known by man." It is hard not to conclude that this sounds much like what Arminius taught about God's grace: that he gives to everyone his "prevenient" grace, grace that can be rejected. If it is not rejected, the person will eventually call out to God in repentance and for mercy, and God in his grace grants his forgiveness. "It is accordingly evident that free choice cannot prepare itself for grace unless it is divinely directed to this end. And because of the two reasons given, God is supplicated in two different ways in the Scriptures to work this preparation for grace in us: (1) By asking that he convert us, turning us from the state in which we were to himself, as when it is written (Psa 84:5): *Convert us, O God, our salvation.* This is because of the first reason. (2) By asking that he direct us, as when it is written (Psa 24:5): *Direct me in your truth.*"[101]

Aquinas: Human freedom is not antagonistic to God's grace:

In Aquinas, then, human freedom must not be seen as antagonistic to the influence of God or his grace. God is an active influence on *all* human beings—*He is not willing that any perish* (2 Pet 3:9)—and thus his grace is given to all. That grace and influence can be resisted, ignored, and/or rejected. Each person has free choices. But to that grace—which is given to all—a person can make a positive response (calling out to God), resulting in God's giving that person enabling grace, grace that results in being pardoned for his sins (salvation). Or if the person is already a believer, his positive response to God's call to holiness results in being made holy by God's enabling grace.

98. Aquinas, *DV* 24.15, *To the contrary,* 1–2.

99. Aquinas, *DV* 24.15, *Reply,* 1–2.

100. Aquinas, *DV* 24.15, *Reply,* 1.

101. Aquinas, *DV* 24.15, *Reply,* 2.

Thus, a person who goes to his perdition can only blame himself for his destiny; he rejected God's grace, that could have led him to repentance and God's pardon. On the other hand, the believer can honestly admit, "I am who I am totally by the grace of God. I have not and could not ever merit the grace which was given to me and continues to be given to me. I could never save myself. When I understood God's gracious gift, I cried out to God for his mercy. And I still do." One sees this in Paul's exhortation in Romans. By God's grace a person is able to make a choice not to *give his members to sin,* which also involves his *present*[ing] *himself to God and his members as instruments of righteousness* (Rom 6:12–14). A person chooses, and God enables. Paul continues in Rom 8:12–13: *So then, brothers, we are debtors, not to the flesh, to live according to the flesh. 13 For if you live according to the flesh you will die, but if by the Spirit you put to death the deeds of the body, you will live.* Every person has a choice to resist sin, but he cannot become holy on his own; the Spirit is the one who graciously enables him "*to not live according to the flesh.*"

If this sounds more theological—just practical Christian living—rather than "philosophical," then the reader is reminded once again that Aquinas's writings were intended, not as a philosophical treatise, but for an audience of believers who wanted to understand their faith.

CONCLUSION.

While there are other Pre-Reformation scholars whose writings could have been reviewed in this chapter, the three which have been reviewed in the previous three chapters are the most notable because of their contributions to the specific subject of human freedom. No attempt has been made to relate them to the thesis of this book, though this is the subject of later chapters. Instead, here—as fairly as possible—the objective has been to trace their contributions, to understand what they have written, and then to critique them as to the consistency of their handling the pertinent issues. An important preliminary observation is that each of these thinkers—although there is a disagreement among them regarding the role of grace as it pertains to soteriological issues—appear to affirm a limited libertarian freedom, that is, that persons occasionally have the ability to choose among a range of various options, each of which is consistent and compatible with their natures.

6

A survey of human freedom during the Reformation and post-Reformation periods

Desiderius Erasmus (AD 1466–1536)

WHEN A PERSON THINKS of the Reformation, the names of its chief theologians—Martin Luther and John Calvin—figure predominantly. But the Reformation—yes, the whole Protestant movement and biblical studies—was heavily impacted by another person who may not be immediately associated with the Reformation at all: Desiderius Erasmus. He gave the world the first Greek, critical text of the New Testament that became the standard from his day on, being constantly revised as older manuscripts were discovered. But his influence goes far beyond this! His interaction—theological conflict—with Luther led to his publication of a "little book" published under the title *The Freedom of the Will*. To it Luther replied with what he himself called his most important writing: *The Bondage of the Will*. These two are most valuable in the discussion at hand: human freedom. Thus, the interaction of these two scholars cannot be ignored.

Calvin and his *magnum opus*—*The Institutes of the Christian Religion*—influenced the thinking of a branch of Christianity for years afterward, continuing even today. But another conflict brought a divide that also lives on. Arminius, a great scholar and pastor, reacted against the strict (hyper?) Calvinism that came after Calvin's death, viewing it and arguing against it as a deterministic theology. His position—expressed also after his death in a document called *The Remonstrance of 1610*—was forcefully confronted by the proceedings of the Synod of Dort that defined what has come to be known as the five points of Calvinism: TULIP.[1]

Thus, these five—Erasmus, Luther, Calvin, Arminius and the Synod of Dort—will be the centers of the focus which follows, with specific attention being to review

---

1. TULIP stands for Total depravity, Unconditional election, Limited atonement, Irresistible grace, and Perseverance of the Saints.

their contributions to the question of human freedom and deterministic theology. To these a brief essay will be appended to make note of the teachings of the prominent American Calvinist Jonathan Edwards whose influence continues in Calvinist circles to this day.

Desiderius Erasmus (AD 1466–1536)

Not much is known about Erasmus's early life, though near the end of life he admitted that he had been born out-of-wedlock[2] and that at the time his father was a priest. This may well have been a harbinger of Erasmus's later dissatisfaction with the church. His early education was at the prestigious school at Deventer, during which tragedy struck him at the critical age of thirteen, when both his parents died.[3] Afterward, he spent seven years at the monastery at Steyn. At twenty-five he became both a priest and a monk,[4] which laid a foundation for his religious views that shines through his writings. Though he studied at the University of Paris and Cambridge in England, Erasmus-scholar Ephraim Emerton describes his life well: "Erasmus led a life of an independent scholar, independent of country, of academic ties, of religious allegiance, of anything that would interfere with the free development of his intellect and the freedom of his literary expression."[5]

Though a monk, Erasmus was not interested in theology; he felt there was little intellectual stimulation in such a context. His interest was really in humanistic studies, and when he had the opportunity to study in England (AD 1499), he became acquainted with and was deeply influenced by the humanists John Colet and Thomas More.[6] What especially influenced his life was hearing Colet give expositions of the Pauline Epistles from the Greek, and, because it was so refreshing—it was not allegorical interpretation (which had characterized his education at the monastery and in Paris) but exegesis of what the text specially stated—he devoted himself to studies of Greek and Greek writers, translating many of them into Latin.[7] Though his *In Praise of Folly* (written in AD 1509) was not regarded by him as a serious piece of literature, it was well-received both by scholars and those outside the academic circle. It went through many editions. It not only was a satire of human nature, but it also criticized some of the foolishness, superstition, formalism, and corruption in the church, which interestingly were some of the very issues that Luther also found reprehensible in his *95 Theses*.[8] But by far his greatest contribution to the church—yes, the world—was

2. Schaff, *History: German Reformation*, 317.

3. Wilkinson, *Erasmus*, 36.

4. Wilkinson, *Erasmus*, 37.

5. Emerton, "Erasmus," 164.

6. Schaff, *History: German Reformation*, 320.

7. Schaff, *History: German Reformation*, 327.

8. Wilkinson, *Erasmus*, 68–70; Schaff, *History: German Reformation*, 317–29. Schaff, *History:*

his researching and printing of the first critical text of the New Testament in Greek: *Novum Instrumentum* (AD 1516). It consisted of the Greek text and Erasmus's own Latin translation in parallel columns and important annotations about the Greek text.[9] That text (later renamed *Novum Testamentum*) became the New Testament basis of Luther's German translation and Tyndale's English translation and the many English translations which followed. What Erasmus wrote in his preface to this text promoted such translations of the Bible in the vernacular of the people,[10] who could not understand the old Latin of the Vulgate: "Erasmus had in mind . . . that the New Testament should receive a central place in education . . . Therefore, he says that he has prepared his revised Latin version . . . [because] he wished the New Testament to be read and studied by large groups of people, for whom . . . a [new] Latin translation would thus be indispensable."[11]

ERASMUS AND HUMAN FREEDOM.

Erasmus's scholarship and skill in writing won him a place of honor in the world of the Reformation. Of him Schaff says his "fame . . . exceeded the fame of any other scholar in Europe."[12] He had friends who were in high places: kings, princes, philosophers, professors, and popes. Because of this he had friends on both sides of the conflict emerging between Luther and the Catholic Church. Some saw him as a Luther convert in disguise and urged him to "come out" and support Luther, while his Roman Catholic friends urged him to attack Luther and his theological views. Erasmus repeatedly refused to be a part of the fray. Indeed, he hated that the conflict was becoming more and more bitter and, worse, was dividing Christendom.[13] Finally, the pressure grew

---

German Reformation, 326, writes: "It was a common saying, to which Erasmus himself refers, that he laid the egg which Luther hatched." More detailed was Erasmus's discussion (1502) in his *Enchiridion militis Christiani* (*Manual of the Christian Knight*).

9. In Erasmus's introduction he writes: "I have revised the New Testament, as it is called, entirely in accordance with the original Greek . . . We have added our *Annotationes* in order that firstly they should enlighten the reader as to what has been changed and why, and secondly that they should explain everything which seems complicated, unclear or difficult" (De Jonge, "*Novum Testamentum*," 398).

10. Emerton, "Erasmus," 165: "All the writings of Erasmus were in Latin, but they were at once translated into the common languages of the European peoples, a process which received the hearty approval of Erasmus himself." Erasmus himself wrote: "I would wish that all women read the gospel and the Epistles of Paul. If only they were translated into all human tongues, so that not only the Scots and the Irish but also the Turks and the Saracens could read and study them. . . If only the peasant sang something from them at the plough, the weaver recited something to the measure of the shuttle, the traveler dispelled the tedium of the journey with such stories" (Do, "A Plea," 139–40).

11. De Jonge, "*Novum Testamentum*," 406.

12. Schaff, *History: German Reformation,* 321.

13. Emerton, "Erasmus," 165, says that "Erasmus was charged—and very justly—with having 'laid the egg that Luther hatched' [and Erasmus] half admitted the charge, but said he had expected quite another kind of bird." Erasmus, as he said of himself, was "a debater, not the judge; the enquirer, not

so intense that he published his *The Freedom of the Will* (AD 1524).[14] Because Luther responded to his position a year later with "page-by-page" arguments, it would be helpful here to briefly summarize Erasmus's arguments before looking at Luther's *The Bondage of the Will*.

THE INTRODUCTION TO THE FREEDOM OF THE WILL.

Erasmus begins his short book, not stating his position, but responding to Luther and/or his followers:

1. He attacks Luther's arrogance in thinking that his views alone were right and all the teachings of the Fathers for thirteen hundred years were in error: "Luther attributes very little importance to scholarship."[15]

2. He disassociates himself from Luther: "I have never sworn allegiance to the words of Luther."[16]

3. He argues that even Luther's friends do not agree among themselves with what Luther had written.[17]

4. He is appalled ("it is pernicious") that such a theological issue as human freedom should be aired to "common" ears ("the dull-witted"), rather than among scholars ("the learned-world" of "universities, councils, bishops, popes") and churchmen.[18]

5. He labels the whole subject as a trivial pursuit that "was more labor than fruit."[19]

These are important points, but one must move beyond these preliminary criticisms to the chief support Erasmus gives for why he believes in human freedom:

---

the dogmatist . . . It is better not to enforce contentions which may the sooner harm Christian accord that advance true religion" (Rupp and Watson, *Luther and Erasmus,* 38). Though Erasmus shared much of what Luther had written, his disagreement did not appear to issue in conviction based on those shared beliefs, while Luther—who admittedly was argumentative and combative—saw the conflict as a battle for truth, truth that determined the eternal destiny of the hearers.

14. All the Erasmus-quotes are from Rupp and Watson, *Luther and Erasmus.*

15. Rupp and Watson, *Luther and Erasmus,* 37, 42, 45.

16. Rupp and Watson, *Luther and Erasmus,* 36.

17. Rupp and Watson, *Luther and Erasmus,* 42.

18. Rupp and Watson, *Luther and Erasmus,* 42–43.

19. Rupp and Watson, *Luther and Erasmus,* 35. Erasmus says: "Therefore, in my judgment on this matter of free choice, having learned what is needful to know about this, if we are in the path of true religion, let us go on swiftly to better things . . . [We should not] through irreverent inquisitiveness rush into those things which are hidden, not to say superfluous" (Rupp and Watson, *Luther and Erasmus,* 39).

ERASMUS'S ARGUMENTS IN THE FREEDOM OF THE WILL.

Basically Erasmus's "little book" set forth seven arguments for human freedom:

1. *He defines "free choice" [as] a power of the human will by which a man can apply himself to the things which lead to eternal salvation, or turn away from them.*[20]

    Specifically, Erasmus is addressing free choice in the context of "salvation," but in other places in his discussion he seems to refer to all the choices that a person makes, those with eternal consequences and others which relate to "sloth, malice, and their incurable propensity toward all manner of evil."[21] Clearer is the example Erasmus gives later in his essay, quoting from *Ecclesiasticus* 15:14–17: "*God made man from the beginning, and left him in the hand of his own counsel. He added his commandments and precepts. If thou wilt observe the commandments, and keep acceptable fidelity forever, they shall preserve thee. He hath set water and fire before thee; stretch forth thine hand for which thou wilt. Before man is life and death, good and evil; that which he shall choose shall be given him.*"

    While the second and fourth sentences in this quotation from *Ecclesiasticus* relate to moral and life-destiny choices, the first and third relate to choices freely made that involve non-moral decisions.

2. *Erasmus admits that "there are many places in the Holy Scriptures which seem to set forth free choice. On the other hand, others seem to take it wholly away. Yet it is clear that Scripture cannot be in conflict with itself.*[22]

    Erasmus acknowledges that one can find scriptural support both for human freedom and determinism, and also admits that many "ancient" writers have argued for one side or another, but that he "as yet" had "no fixed conviction, except that I think there to be a certain power of choice."[23]

3. *He sees the determinism of Luther (and Wyclif and the later writings of Augustine) as not only obliterating human freedom, but as stating "that whatever is done by us is done not by free choice but by sheer necessity."*[24] (Emphasis is author's, which shows that choices include other matters than the faith that leads to forgiveness and pardon).

4. *A corollary of the previous argument is that such determinism not only makes God responsible but human beings both not responsible and, worse, unmotivated.*

    Augustine says somewhere, that "God works in us good and evil, and rewards his own good works in us, and punishes his evil works in us;" what a window

---

20. Rupp and Watson, *Luther and Erasmus*, 47.
21. Rupp and Watson, *Luther and Erasmus*, 41.
22. Rupp and Watson, *Luther and Erasmus*, 47.
23. Rupp and Watson, *Luther and Erasmus*, 37.
24. Rupp and Watson, *Luther and Erasmus*, 41.

to impiety would the public avowal of such an opinion open to countless mortals! . . . What weakling will be able to bear the endless and wearisome warfare against his flesh? What evildoer will take pains to correct his life? Who will be able to bring himself to love God with all his heart when He created hell seething with eternal torments in order to punish his own misdeeds in his victims as though he took delight in human torments? For that is how most people will interpret them.[25]

Erasmus accuses Luther—and Augustine—of double predestination: Some, who by the good works he "works" in them, he rewards with his pardon and others—in whom he also "works"—he punishes for their evil. "Why try to be different than what he has made us"? they might say. "God is unjust! How can we love him"?

5. *A further corollary is what such determinism does to prayer. Why pray if everything has already been determined?*[26]

6. *While Luther appeals to Scripture, the issue—Erasmus says—is not with suitable texts, but with the interpretation of them.*[27]

What need is there of an interpreter when the Scripture itself is crystal clear? But if it is so clear, why have so many outstanding men in so many centuries been blind, and in a matter of such importance, as these would appear? If there is no obscurity in Scripture, what was the need of the work of prophecy in the days of the apostles?[28]

7. *This last quotation from Erasmus's book introduces one of his major complaints. Apparently, Luther and/or his disciples had spoken of the gift of the Spirit as being the basis both for the accuracy of their position and their break with Catholic teaching.* Erasmus writes:

I do not intend this to refer specifically to Luther, [but] others . . . who, if there is any controversy concerning the meaning of the Scriptures, when we bring forward the authority of the Early Fathers, chant at once, "Ah! but they were only men." And if you ask them by what argument the true interpretation of Scripture may be known, since both sides are men, they reply, "By the sign of the Spirit."

But let us grant, as indeed we must, that it is possible that the Spirit might reveal to a single humble and unlearned man what he has not revealed to the wise and prudent . . . But if Paul in his time, in which the gift of the Spirit was

25. Rupp and Watson, *Luther and Erasmus*, 41.

26. Rupp and Watson, *Luther and Erasmus*, 43. See later in this book—in chapter 16—for a discussion of prayer and human freedom.

27. Rupp and Watson, *Luther and Erasmus*, 45.

28. Rupp and Watson, *Luther and Erasmus*, 44.

in full force, orders spirits to be tested whether they be of God, what ought to be done in this carnal age? How, then, shall we prove the Spirit? . . .

Moreover, if we grant that he who has the Spirit is sure of the meaning of the Scriptures, how can I be certain of what he finds to be true for himself? What am I to do when many bring diverse interpretations, about which each swears he has the Holy Spirit? . . .

Even supposing that the Spirit of Christ could have allowed his people to err in trivial matters on which the salvation of men does not greatly depend, how can it be believed that for more than thirteen hundred years he would have concealed the error in his Church and not have found anybody among so many saintly men worthy to be inspired with the knowledge of what these people claim to be the chief doctrine of the whole gospel?[29]

ERASMUS'S VIEW OF GRACE.

Erasmus concludes his treatise with a discussion of how grace relates to free will. In Adam and Eve, "the will was so upright and free that, apart from new grace, he could continue in innocence but, apart from the help of new grace, he could not attain the happiness of eternal life which the Lord Jesus promised to his followers."[30] After the fall, the will was corrupted, "but, by the grace of God, when sin has been forgiven, the will is made free to the extent that, according to the views of the Pelagians, even apart from the help of new grace it could attain eternal life . . . So, it is possible for man, with the help of divine grace (which always accompanies human effort), to continue in the right, yet not without a tendency to sin, owing to the vestiges of original sin in him."[31]

If this sounds unclear, it is because Erasmus himself is unclear on what position he takes on grace.[32] One thing he insists on, however, is that human beings do have free will. Indeed, the words of *Ecclesiasticus* quoted above "would be irrelevant if there were no strength of free choice at all in us. For although free choice is damaged by sin, it is nevertheless not extinguished by it. And although it has become so lame in the process that before we receive grace, we are more readily inclined toward evil than good, yet it is not altogether cut out."[33]

In the final paragraphs, Erasmus asks: "What, then, is free choice worth in us after sin and before grace"?[34] He is unclear and summarizes what he sees as three positions:

29. Rupp and Watson, *Luther and Erasmus*, 44.

30. Rupp and Watson, *Luther and Erasmus*, 48.

31. Rupp and Watson, *Luther and Erasmus*, 49.

32. Emerton identifies Erasmus's position as "easy going Semi-Pelagianism" (Emerton, "Erasmus," 165–66).

33. Rupp and Watson, *Luther and Erasmus*, 51.

34. Rupp and Watson, *Luther and Erasmus*, 51.

1. Grace "implanted by nature."

> This is common to all, and remains even in those who persist in sin: they are free to speak, be silent, sit down, get up, help the poor, read Holy Scripture, listen to sermons; but these things, in the opinion of some, in no way conduce to eternal life. Nor are there lacking those who, bearing in mind the manifold goodness of God, say that man can so far make use of benefits of this kind that he may be prepared for grace and so call forth the mercy of God.[35]

2. "Peculiar grace."

> The second is peculiar grace, with which God in his mercy arouses the sinner wholly without merit to repent, yet without infusing that supreme grace which abolishes sin and makes him pleasing to God. Thus the sinner assisted by a second grace . . . (operative grace) begins to be displeased with himself, although he has not yet put off all the desire of sin, yet by his alms and prayers and his devotion to sacred studies, and by listening to sermons, as well as by appeals to good men for their prayers and other deeds morally good, as they call them, he behaves as a candidate for the highest grace . . . This grace . . . is, by the goodness of God, not denied to anyone, for the divine benevolence supplies sufficient opportunities to each in this life by which he may recover, if he will, the use of the free choice that remains to him and put his powers at the disposal of that divine will which invites but does not constrain him forcibly to higher things. And this they consider to be within the power of our own choice . . . If he seeks it [this grace] with all his powers, no sinner ought ever to be secure, yet on the other hand, none ought to despair; and, moreover, no man perishes save by his own fault. There is, therefore, a natural grace; there is a stimulating grace (albeit imperfect); there is the grace that makes the will effective, which we called cooperating, which allows us to perform that which we have undertaken to do; there is a grace that carries things to a conclusion. These three they think to be one, although they are called by different names according to what they effect within us. The first arouses, the second promotes, the third completes.[36]

3. "The highest grace, *peculiar* grace."

Though Erasmus calls this grace an extreme view of *peculiar* grace, he makes clear how it differs from the previous view of grace:

> [This view is held by] those who, at the other extreme from Pelagius, attribute most of all to grace and practically nothing to free choice, yet do not entirely remove it, for they deny that man can will the good without peculiar grace, they deny that he can make a beginning, they deny that he can progress, they

---

35. Rupp and Watson, *Luther and Erasmus*, 52.
36. Rupp and Watson, *Luther and Erasmus*, 52–53.

deny he can reach his goal without the principal and perpetual aid of divine grace . . . But harder is the opinion of those who contend that free choice is of no avail save to sin, and that grace alone accomplishes good works in us, not by or with free choice but in free choice, so that our will does nothing more than wax in the hand of the craftsman when it receives the particular shape that pleases him . . . Hardest of all seems the view of all those who say that free choice is a mere empty name . . . but it is God who works evil as well as good in us, and all things that happen come about by sheer necessity.[37]

Though Erasmus understands these various views—and variation within them—he admits that it with this last view (the third view) that he finds himself in least agreement, especially the most rigid variations. This sets the table—as it were—for Luther to argue for human bondage and thus to support this last position.

---

37. Rupp and Watson, *Luther and Erasmus*, 53–54.

7

A survey of human freedom during the Reformation and post-Reformation periods

Martin Luther (AD 1483–1546)

LUTHER PROUDLY ADMITS THAT his parents were "peasants." Hans, his father was a miner and Margarethe, his mother was a carrier of wood from the forest. In fact, during his growing up years in Mansfield, Saxony, the family was so poor that it was necessary for Martin to sing in the streets to pay for his schooling.[1] He remembers his parents as being severe disciplinarians, but they brought him up as a strict Catholic, respecting priests and praying to God and the saints. His home education also included stories about the devil and witches[2] which filled him with terror.

After primary school, he attended the prestigious University of Erfurt, where he studied the classics and learned enough Latin to write fluently, though not with the finesse and wit of Erasmus. He also grew in his love of music which tempered his natural tendency to melancholy and fear of Satanic attack.[3] From this university he received his BA (AD 1502) and his MA (AD 1505), and then began studying law at the same school.

Though his father had in his own mind that Luther would become a lawyer, he—to his father's great disappointment—became a monk. Two events appear to lie behind his decision: the death of a close friend (killed in a duel or by lightening) and the occasion he was caught in a severe thunderstorm and a nearby lightning strike which filled him with such fear that he cried out to St. Anna for protection, promising to become a monk if she spared his life.[4]

---

1. Schaff, *History: The German Reformation*, 91.
2. Schaff, *History: The German Reformation*, 91.
3. Schaff, *History: The German Reformation*, 93.
4. Hay, *Luther*, 18.

Luther's decision to become a monk may have been a sudden, crisis decision, but his dedication as a monk was noted even by those who later opposed his teachings. His Augustinian order was known for its preaching, commitment to poverty, devotion to the Virgin Mary, the study of theology, and the reading of the Latin Bible. In addition, Luther had another obsession: his spiritual disciplines, which included bodily punishments[5] (by which he hoped to rid himself of his sin), fasting, and confessions weekly to a priest. Kittelson says during these times Luther remarked that "I lost touch with Christ the Savior and Comforter, and made of him the jailer and hangman of my poor soul."[6] When he officiated at his first mass (AD 1507), at which his father was in attendance, his sinfulness and the very idea of lifting the chalice which would become the blood of Jesus, caused him to become faint and stumble, spilling some of the precious wine. Schaff writes:

> The more he seemed to advance externally, the more he felt the burden of sin within. He had to contend with temptations of anger, envy, hatred and pride. He saw sin everywhere, even in the smallest trifles. The Scriptures impressed upon him the terrors of divine justice. He could not trust in God as a reconciled Father, as a God of love and mercy but trembled before him, as a God of wrath, as a consuming fire. He could not get over the words: "I, the Lord thy God, am a jealous God." His confessor once told him: "Thou art a fool, God is not angry with thee, but thou art angry with God." He remembered this afterward as "a great and glorious word," but at that time it made no impression on him. He could not point to any particular transgression; it was sin as an all-pervading power and vitiating principle, sin as a corruption of nature, sin as a state of alienation from God and hostility to God, that weighed on his mind like an incubus and brought him at times to the brink of despair.[7]

A person who significantly influenced Luther's life both while in the convent and long afterward was Johann von Staupitz. Though he was Vicar-General of the Augustinian convents of Germany, he was a mystic who urged Luther to look away from his focus on his sins and the personal merits he sought by spiritual disciplines to the merits of Christ's death on his behalf, from the condemning focus on law-keeping to a God who devotedly loved him. It was through his influence that Luther turned from the study of scholasticism to the study of Augustine and the Scriptures. Staupitz also urged him to become a priest and to pursue the DD degree at Wittenberg. Perhaps most significantly, it also was Staupitz's influence that led to Luther's freedom from guilt by justification by faith apart from human works or merit. This was not merely

---

5. Luther in his lectures on Genesis said, "Formerly, when I was a monk, I used to hope that I would be able to pacify my conscience with the fastings, the praying, and the vigils with which I used to afflict my body in a way to excite pity. But the more I sweat, the less quiet and peace I felt; for the true light had been removed from my eyes" (Luther, "Lectures," 326).

6. Kittelson, *Luther*, 79.

7. Schaff, *History: The German Reformation*, 98.

a new theology or interpretation, but a very personal, profound transformation. It brought peace, release from the torment of his ascetic punishments, and freedom from the bondage of law-keeping. It was this that drove him so dogmatically to insist on this "new Gospel" through all the personal attacks and very real threats to his life.[8]

Another huge influence was Luther's trip to Rome at Staupitz's request (AD 1510), not for his own personal benefit but to see if Luther could facilitate a better association with the Augustinians there. Luther, however, did take advantage of visiting the holy places there as part of his spiritual pilgrimage to find peace within and pardon for his sinfulness. Attention to shrines, relics, penances, and indulgences were valued by him at the time. Whatever benefit he sought to derive from ascending the twenty-eight steps of Scala Santa even on his knees was extinguished because of the astonishing decadence he found among the monks and priests. In contrast to the poverty that was a covenant he made as an Augustinian, he found their indulgence was in affluence. Further, they openly mocked the very rituals they conducted as modes of worship.[9]

After receiving his degree from the University of Wittenberg (AD 1515), he became a professor at the same institution, teaching biblical studies and preaching daily. Early in his ministry there, his teaching was not in the modern tradition of exegesis of the text, but in a more allegorical and Christo-centric/application that Erasmus despised.[10] Later, Luther moved away from this approach.

Luther's thinking—especially about the means of God's pardon—had been developing from the time of his acquaintance with Staupitz. But, if a turning point in his life that shaped his future were identified, it might be when Johannn Tetzel in AD 1516 began selling indulgences in Germany. Especially vexing were his words: "As soon as the coin in the coffer rings, the soul from purgatory springs."[11] The thought of buying forgiveness prompted Luther to write (AD 1517) his "Disputation of Martin Luther on the Power and Efficacy of Indulgences" to Albrecht von Brandenburg, his bishop and the Archbishop of Mainz. That document was allegedly nailed to the door of All Saints' Church in Wittenberg and came to be known as the *Ninety-five Theses*.[12] Whether it was nailed to the door or not, it was widely published, and this infuriated Pope Leo X, who not only found the theses against indulgences threatened his building of St. Peter's Basilica, but especially took Thesis #86—*"Why does the pope, whose wealth today is greater than the wealth of the richest Crassus, build the basilica of St. Peter with the money of poor believers rather than with his own money"?*—as an attack on himself. The fire now had been ignited that would find Luther increasingly an

---

8. Köstlin, "Luther," 91; Schaff, *History: The German Reformation*, 99–100.

9. Schaff, *History: The German Reformation*, 107–9; Hay, *Luther*, 24–25.

10. Schaff, *History: The German Reformation*, 105.

11. Schaff, *History: The German Reformation*, 127–29.

12. Schaff, *History: The German Reformation*, 130–32.

irritant to Rome and endangered by the religious authorities and civil leaders. He was excommunicated four years later (AD 1521) by Pope Leo.[13]

Much more could be added about Luther's colorful and significant history—the translation of the Bible into German (New Testament in AD 1522 and Old Testament in AD 1534), his marriage to the former nun Katharina von Bora (AD 1524), his use of singing in the church, his catechisms, etc.—but the focal point of the subject of interest here is his view on human freedom, as enshrined in what he[14] and others (e.g., Packer and Johnson) acknowledge as his most important book—*On the Bondage of the Will*[15]—to which this essay now turns.

LUTHER AND *ON THE BONDAGE OF THE WILL*.

One footnote, however, is worthy of being added because it traces the importance of Luther's book and his passionate and sometimes sharp statements to Erasmus and his short diatribe. *Bondage* was not merely a philosophical interaction and a petty dispute for Luther, as it was for Erasmus; it was a life or death issue to him and his hearers. His final words illustrate that. Reeves said Luther was asked on his deathbed: "Are you ready to die trusting in your Lord Jesus Christ and to confess the doctrine which you have taught in his name"? He answered "Yes," and then took his final breath.[16]

Free will and salvation

In Luther's introduction to *Bondage*—among other things—he upbraids Erasmus's dismissal of the importance of any discussion of "free-will" but especially his cavalier attitude toward biblical truth: "In a word, what you say comes to this: that you do not think it matters a scrap what anyone believes anywhere, so long as the world is at peace . . . When you tell Christian people to let this folly guide them in their labours, and charge them that in their pursuit of eternal salvation they should not concern themselves to know what is in their power and what is not—why, this is plainly the sin that is really unpardonable. For as long as they do not know the *limits of their ability*, they will not know what they should do; and as long as they do not know what they should do, they cannot repent when they err; and impenitence is the unpardonable sin."[17] This centers Luther's discussion of "free will" squarely in soteriology and thus, its importance for a person's eternal destiny. While he wishes people to think deeply about the nature of free will, Luther forthrightly announces his position, based on the premise that what God "foreknows" is not "contingent," (that is, shaped or determined by man's decision or

---

13. Schaff, *History: The German Reformation*, 185–87; Hay, *Luther*, 77–79.

14. Luther, *Bondage*, 40.

15. All quotations are from *On the Bondage of the Will* are from Luther, *Bondage*.

16. Reeves, *Unquenchable Flame*, 60.

17. Luther, *Bondage*, 69; 77–78, author's *italics*.

circumstances) but "necessarily" will happen: "It is, then, fundamentally necessary and wholesome for Christians to know that God foreknows nothing contingently, but that He foresees,[18] purposes, and does all things according to His own immutable, eternal and infallible will. This bombshell knocks 'free-will' flat, and utterly shatters it."[19]

But this idea of "necessity" troubles Luther: "I could wish, indeed, that a better term was available for our discussion than the accepted one, *necessity*, which cannot accurately be used of either man's will or God's. Its meaning is too harsh, and foreign to the subject; for it suggests some sort of compulsion, and something that is against one's will, which is no part of the view under debate. The will, whether it be God's or man's, does what it does, good or bad, under no compulsion, but just as it wants or pleases, as if totally free. Yet the will of God, which rules over our mutable will, is changeless and sure."[20]

This appears to be some form of compatibilism.[21] But Luther is not finished with his discussion of "necessity." While he understands that "necessity" has to be carefully defined as distinguishing what "will" happen from what "necessarily" will occur, he dismisses it as merely a "play on words": "I shall not find it hard to show how unreal the distinction is. By *necessity of consequence*, they mean, roughly speaking, this: If God wills something, then it must needs be; but that which thus comes to be is something which of itself need not be . . . This is to say that God's action is necessary, if He wills it, but the thing done is not in itself necessary. But what do they establish by this play on words? This, I suppose—the thing done is not necessary; that is, it has no necessity in its own that the thing done is not essential nature."[22]

Free will in "matters below."

Thus far Luther has argued that a person has an inability to respond to God; only God and his grace can enable that to occur and thus the term "free-will" cannot apply. This clearly confirms that Luther is monergistic versus Erasmus's synergism, which affirms that grace is given when a person does what he can, when he makes "use of benefits

18. Luther does not distinguish between foreknowledge and foreseeing, which philosophically are different concepts. See a later discussion in this chapter.

19. Luther, *Bondage*, 80. "For once it is granted and settled that 'free-will' has lost its freedom, and is bound in the service of sin, and can will no good, I can gather nothing from these words but that 'free-will' is an empty term whose reality is lost. A lost freedom, to my way of speaking, is no freedom at all, and to give the name of freedom to something that has no freedom is to apply to it a term that is empty of meaning" (Luther, *Bondage*, 148).

20. Luther, *Bondage*, 81. See Craig's discussion of "necessity" in footnote #19, p.50, and Craig, *Only Wise God*, 72–74.

21. See more on "compatibilism" in chapter 11.

22. Luther, *Bondage*, 82. Later Luther shows he dismisses this distinction and views foreknowledge as "necessity": "And if you do not allow that the thing which God foreknows is necessarily brought to pass, you take away faith and the fear of God, you undermine all the divine promises and threatenings, and so you deny Deity itself"! (Luther, *Bondage*, 213).

of this kind [given to all persons] that he may be prepared for grace."[23] Not so, Luther maintains. Spiritually there is a "bondage of the will,"[24] and he, therefore, would prefer in such a context that the term not be used. But a person *has* free-will in other matters: in mundane decisions, which Luther calls matters "below him:"

> If we do not want to drop this term altogether—which would really be the safest and most Christian thing to do—we may still in good faith teach people to use it to credit man with "free-will" in respect, not of what is above him, but of what is below him. That is to say, man should realise that in regard to his money and possessions he has a right to use them, to do or to leave undone, according to his own "free-will"—though that very "free-will" is overruled by the free-will of God alone, according to His own pleasure. However, with regard to God, and in all that bears on salvation or damnation, he has no "free-will," but is a captive, prisoner and bond slave, either to the will of God, or to the will of Satan.[25]

Luther later explains further what he means by "freedom below him" by challenging the very basis Erasmus gives for his position: *Ecclesiasticus* 15:14–7, especially verse 14: *"God from the beginning made man, and left him in the hand of his own counsel."*

> Here it speaks of man's creation . . . Then it [the text of verse 14] goes on: *and left him in the hand of his own counsel.* What have we here? Is this where "free-will" is erected? But there is no mention here of commandments . . . If anything is to be understood by *the hand of his own counsel*, what should rather be understood is the fact, recorded in Gen 1:25 that man was made lord of all things so that he might freely rule them, as Moses says: *Let us make man to have dominion over the fishes of the sea* (Gen 1:26). Nothing else can be evinced from the words. For there man certainly could act according to his own will, all these things having been put under his control . . . So, we learn from *Ecclesiasticus* that man falls under two kingdoms. In the one, he is led by his own will and counsel, not by any precepts and commandments of God; that is, in the realm of things below him. Here he reigns and is lord, being left in the hand of his own counsel.[26]

Luther clearly believes that there is human freedom in many decisions and actions a person is engaged in this world ("in the realm of things below him"). This might be termed what philosophers call "soft libertarian freedom" or "limited libertarian

---

23. Rupp and Watson, *Luther and Erasmus*, 52.

24. Luther, despite Erasmus's claim that he has set himself against the church leadership in the past, attributes his position as consistent what great churchmen have taught: "Lombard clearly agrees with Augustine that 'free-will of its own power has no power but to fall, nor avails but to sin.' Accordingly, in his second book *Against Julian* (8.23) Augustine calls it a *slave* will rather than a *free* Will" (Luther, *Bondage*, 142).

25. Luther, *Bondage*, 107.

26. Luther, *Bondage*, 150.

freedom," that is, limited to things other than soteriological matters. But "in the other kingdom, however, man is not left in the hand of his own counsel but is directed and led by the will and counsel of God. As in his own kingdom he is led by his own will, and not by the precepts of another, so in the kingdom of God he is led by the precepts of another, and not by his own will."[27] Thus, when the writer of *Ecclesiasticus* and Erasmus interpret the conditional phrase for obedience—"if you will"—as meaning "you can," they make a mistake. With such statements people are challenged to keep the law ("their duty") and find how impotent they are ("their inability").[28] In short, Luther declares that everyone has freedom in some things, but when it comes to the ability to turn to God from sin to obtain pardon, a person is a slave: there is a "spiritual" bondage of the will; a person cannot turn from his/her wicked way and obviously cannot merit God's forgiveness.

LUTHER AND MELANCHTHON.

Melanchthon—the acknowledged theologian of Lutheranism—explains Luther's position more thoroughly:

> Nor, indeed, do we deny liberty to the human will. The human will has liberty in the choice of works and things which reason comprehends by itself. It can to a certain extent render civil righteousness or the righteousness of works; it can speak of God, offer to God a certain service by an outward work, obey magistrates, parents; in the choice of an outward work it can restrain the hands from murder, from adultery, from theft. Since there is left in human nature reason and judgement concerning objects subjected to the senses, choice between these things, and the liberty and power to render civil righteousness, are also left . . . Therefore, although we concede free will the liberty and power to perform the outward works of the Law, yet we do not ascribe to free will these spiritual matters, namely, truly to fear God, truly to believe God, truly to be confident and hold that God regards us, hears us, forgives us, etc.[29]

The Reformed, systematic theologian clearly affirms limited libertarian freedom, but what must be factored into understanding Luther is that in his thinking Adam and Eve were free from the beginning, but—unlike humankind since the fall—were responsive to the Holy Spirit and "naturally wanted what God wanted."[30] Since the fall, man's thinking, choices, and behavior have become corrupt and now are under the domination of the evil one and, thus, humankind is in bondage to sin. This does not mean, however, that Luther believed that a person could not do the "works" of the

---

27. Luther, *Bondage*, 151.
28. Luther, *Bondage*, 155–57.
29. Melanchton, *Apology*, 23.18.
30. Rupp and Watson, *Luther and Erasmus*, 16.

law and do them with the "highest of zeal." But "doing" the law, he argued, is not the same as "fulfilling" the law:

> None were zealous for the works of the law but the best and most excellent men, and that only with their best and most excellent faculties, that is, their reason and their will . . . It makes no difference whether they exercised themselves in the law with the highest zeal, or with lukewarm zeal, or with none at all. They all could perform only works of the law; and works of the law do not justify . . . The real position in the sight of God is that those who are most zealous in the works of the law are furthest from fulfilling the law; for they are without the Spirit, Who alone fulfils the law. Men may try to keep it in their own strength, but they can accomplish nothing."[31]

Such "good works" would be included in what Luther calls deeds "from below." How these good works relate to a person's salvation is explained by an interesting insight by Rupp and Watson. Though human beings are in bondage, they can be "prepared" for the grace that will set them free.

> God's purpose is to save man from his evil bondage, and to this end he works by means of his Word and his Spirit . . . By his Word he confronts men outwardly, and by his Spirit inwardly . . . First, it is the function of the law, in what he calls its spiritual use, to bring home to men their sinful plight and their inability to save themselves from perdition. In this way, men are made ready for the gospel and its message of grace. Although, therefore, Luther repudiates the Scholastic idea that man can prepare himself for grace by "doing what in him lies," he does not deny that there is a preparation for grace; he affirms it, only as God's doing, not man's. Secondly, it is the function of the gospel, in what Luther calls its proper office, to bring home to man the grace and love of God and evoke in him the response of faith. Where and insofar as this happens, man is restored to his true and natural relationship to God, and thereby enters into the fullest freedom of which he is capable.[32]

Luther, therefore, was rejecting the view of human freedom that was the understanding of the Scholasticism of his day (and as some think Aquinas believed),[33] that a person could freely choose to live in such a way that would merit receiving the grace which alone could save. Instead, people merit only condemnation. Free will, according to Luther, has no application to and should not be used in connection with a person's salvation. In such a context it is blasphemous. But Luther does affirm that human beings are free to choose or not to choose in the mundane issues of life.

---

31. Luther, *Bondage*, 283–85.

32. Rupp and Watson, *Luther and Erasmus*, 19.

33. See documentation in chapter 5 which makes Aquinas's understanding unclear.

8

A survey of human freedom during the Reformation and post-Reformation periods

John Calvin (AD 1509–1564)

"Jehan Cauvin" in many ways is a surprising Reformation figure considering his background. His father—Gérard Cauvin—was secretary to the bishop of Noyon-la-Sainte (France), Calvin's hometown. He was the firstborn and had four brothers, two of whom died while very young, and the other two—Charles and Antoine—received a religious education preparatory for ministry. He had two sisters, one of whom (Marie) followed the path of her reformer brother to Protestantism, while the other appears to have remained in the Catholic church.[1] He had a painful childhood. His mother Jeanne Lefranc—whom he never mentions in any of his writings—died while he was very young.[2] His father was excommunicated because of some financial scandal (He was the financial official of his city.) and then died apparently after battling several years with testicular cancer when Calvin was twenty-two.[3] That same year his brother Charles—who was a prominent church official—was excommunicated for heresy and died six years later.[4] This turbulent childhood and the corruption in the Catholic church (e.g., selling religious offices/positions even to unqualified persons who were willing to pay for them) may well have made it far easier for the family to leave the church and associate with the Protestant movement that was spreading rapidly.[5]

Much of this turbulence occurred at a distance since Calvin had begun his university studies at the College de la Mache at fourteen where he mastered Latin. His short stay there was followed by studies in philosophy at the College de Montague.

1. Schaff, *History: Swiss Reformation*, 269.
2. Schaff, *History: Swiss Reformation*, 268.
3. Schaff, *History: Swiss Reformation*, 268.
4. Schaff, *History: Swiss Reformation*, 269.
5. Schaff, *History: Swiss Reformation*, 270.

Both of these were short in duration. At the direction of his father (because he felt that a career in law would be more prosperous than the priesthood), Calvin began studies (AD 1526) in law at University of Orleans from which he graduated (AD 1532), shortly after his father's death.[6]

Though by this time he had distinguished himself as a scholar, even publishing a commentary in AD 1532 on Seneca's *On Mercy*,[7] his troubles began when the new rector—Nicolas Cop—of the Collège de France (Collège Royal) gave his inaugural address hosted by the Church of the Mathurins (AD 1533). The address was written by Calvin, who was a friend of Cop. The address, Schaff says, "was a plea for a reformation on the basis of the New Testament, and a bold attack on the scholastic theologians of the day, who were represented as a set of sophists, ignorant of the Gospel. 'They teach nothing,' says Calvin, 'of faith, nothing of the love of God, nothing of the remission of sins, nothing of grace, nothing of justification; or if they do so, they pervert and undermine it all by their laws and sophistries. I beg you, who are here present, not to tolerate any longer these heresies and abuses.'"[8]

This infuriated those who were listening—not the least the political leaders and the clergy—and Calvin and Cop had to flee to Cop's home town of Basel. Indeed, Calvin's life from this point on was punctuated with persecution and adversaries and, therefore, he was often on the run.[9] Because of this Schaff called him a "wondering evangelist."[10] Despite such adversity, during this time he began writing the *Institutes of the Christian Religion*, the first edition of which was published in AD 1536. Like Aquinas's initial work on what became *ST*, Calvin wrote this short treatise of only six chapters as a primer for the Christian faith.[11] For a time, he was an associate of William Farel in Geneva and later became a pastor to various churches in Strasbourg. There he revised his *Institutes* (which now had become a theology) and began writing New Testament commentaries. He later (AD 1541) returned to Geneva with the city's blessing

6. Schaff, *History: Swiss Reformation*, 273.

7. Schaff, *History: Swiss Reformation*, 276. Schaff describes this book written when Calvin was only twenty-three as one which "moves in the circle of classical philology and moral philosophy, and reveals a characteristic love for the best type of Stoicism, great familiarity with Greek and Roman literature, masterly Latinity, rare exegetical skill, clear and sound judgment, and a keen insight into the evils of despotism and the defects of the courts of justice, but makes no allusion to Christianity. It is remarkable that his first book was a commentary on a moral philosopher who came nearer to the apostle Paul than any heathen writer . . . He freely quotes Aristotle, Plutarch, Virgil, Livy, Ovid, Horace, Pliny, Quintilian, Curtius, Macrobius, Terence, Diogenes Laertius, and especially his favorite Cicero, whom he was for some time in the habit of reading through once a year" (Schaff, *History: Swiss Reformation*, 276).

8. Schaff, *History: Swiss Reformation*, 285.

9. Jackson, "Calvin," 838.

10. Schaff, *History: Swiss Reformation*, 289.

11. Schaff, *History: Swiss Reformation*, 300. Jackson notes that Calvin said that "When it was then published it was not the copious and labored work which it is now, but only a small treatise, containing a summary of the principal truths of the Christian religion; and it was published with no other design than that men might know what was the faith held by those whom I saw basely and wickedly defamed by those flagitious and perfidious flatterers" (Jackson, "Calvin," 839).

and continued his writing there. Even during the years there, Calvin was caught up in the controversies which continued to rage, not only about some of his writings but because of other so-called "reformers," whose dogmatisms and sometimes foolish actions spilled over onto his work by false associations. He continued preaching and lecturing all this time and laboriously worked to complete a final edition (AD 1559) of the *Institutes* which had become eighty chapters, mostly by the adding of further material on the same subjects he had written briefly about previously.

Calvin was a prolific author. Among his writings are commentaries on every book of the New Testament with the exception of 2 and 3 John and Revelation. He wrote commentaries on the Old Testament books: the five books of Moses (the Pentateuch), Joshua, Psalms, and Isaiah. Later he authorized the transcription of his lectures on Jeremiah, Lamentations, Ezekiel (partial), Daniel, and the Minor Prophets. In addition he assisted Olivetan in a French translation of the Bible (AD 1535), penned many letters and treatises on various subjects, and composed a French doctrinal statement—the Gallic Confession (AD 1559)—which had international significance and, according to historian de Greef,[12] became the foundation for the Belgic Confession (AD 1561).

CALVIN AND HUMAN FREEDOM.

Calvin follows both Aristotle and Aquinas in his understanding of the will. "Let us, therefore, hold, for the purpose of the present work, that the soul consists of two parts, the intellect and the will (2.2.2.12),—the office of the intellect being to distinguish between objects, according as they seem deserving of being *approved or disapproved*—and the office of the will, to choose and follow what the intellect declares to be good, to reject and shun what it declares to be bad."[13]

Coming from the hand of God in creation, Adam and Eve had libertarian freedom to choose either the good or evil. "Adam, therefore, might have stood if he chose, since it was only by his own will that he fell; but it was because his will was pliable in either directions and he had not received constancy to persevere, that he so easily fell. *Still he had a free choice of good and evil.*"[14] With the fall, however, all mankind was darkened so that they are "blind" in their understanding, needing the "special illumination" of God.[15] This does not mean that all the understanding was darkness in every area. But it is with reference to the "First Table," that is, in a person's ability to see the truth and respond acceptably to God, that there is blindness. But "as to the precepts of the Second Table, there is considerably more knowledge of them, inasmuch as they are more closely connected with the preservation of civil society."[16] Therefore, Calvin

12. De Greef, "Calvin's Writings," 50–1.
13. Calvin, *Institutes*, 1.15.7; [171], author's *emphasis*.
14. Calvin, *Institutes*, 1.15.8; [171], author's *emphasis*.
15. Calvin, *Institutes*, 2.2.19–21; [238–40].
16. Calvin, *Institutes*, 2.2.24; [243].

believed that there was "light" in some areas, areas unrelated to the salvation and God's pardon. If the reason has "light" in even the smallest of areas, a person can have freedom in those specific areas to make choices.

This is a very important concept to bear in mind when it comes to understanding Calvin's view of human freedom. He explains this distinction between the "First Table" and the "Second Table," using the same terminology Luther used: "Things above" [Calvin: "Superior objects"] and "Things below" [Calvin: "Inferior objects"]: "To charge the intellect with perpetual blindness, so as to leave it no intelligence of any description whatever, is repugnant not only to the Word of God, but to common experience . . . Still it is true that this love of truth fails before it reaches the goal, forthwith falling away into vanity. As the human mind is unable, from dullness, to pursue the right path of investigation . . . Still, however, man's efforts are not always so utterly fruitless as not to lead to some result, especially when his attention is directed to inferior objects."[17]

Calvin introduces this same distinction with other terms "heavenly things" and "earthly things:"

> It may therefore be proper, in order to make it more manifest how far our ability extends in regard to these two classes of objects, to draw a distinction between them. The distinction is, that we have one kind of intelligence of earthly things, and another of heavenly things. By earthly things, I mean those which relate not to God and his kingdom, to true righteousness and future blessedness, but have some connection with the present life, and are in a manner confined within its boundaries. By heavenly things, I mean the pure knowledge of God, the method of true righteousness, and the mysteries of the heavenly kingdom. To the former belong matters of policy and economy, all mechanical arts and liberal studies. To the latter . . . belong the knowledge of God and of his will, and the means of framing the life in accordance with them.[18]

Calvin does not extensively spell out his concept of the freedom in "earthly things" in the *Institutes*, but he does in other writings: "There are two main parts in that light which remains in corrupt nature. Some seed of religion is sown in all; and also the distinction between good and evil is engraved on their consciences."[19] Muller cites another example: "In addition, at the very point that he cites Aristotle on necessity, Calvin recognizes that in Aristotle's view, the possibility of one or another of two things occurring stands opposed to necessity and that Aristotle understands some necessities to take the form of necessities of the consequence, having followed on a moment in which there

---

17. Calvin, *Institutes*, 2.2.12–3; [233–34].

18. Calvin, *Institutes*, 2.2.13; [234].

19. Calvin, *John*, John 1:5.

were alternative possibilities: 'when someone has thrown a stone, he can no longer take it back, *but it was in his power to hold on to it or to throw it'.*[20]

This last example from is especially helpful because it shows a window into what Calvin meant by "earthly matters." They include things as mundane as the decision a person freely makes when he picks up a stone. He can hold it, throw it, or do any number of other things: drop it, put it in his pocket, etc. When these distinctions are not considered or blurred, discussion of the "bondage of the will" could fallaciously lead to conclusions of exhaustive determinism, *for all human thoughts and actions.* Indeed, Muller concludes that "not a few of the proponents and critics of the Reformed doctrine of free choice and divine willing have confused the specifically soteriological determination of the Reformed doctrine of predestination with a 'divine determinism of all human actions,' presumably including such actions as buttering one's toast in the morning or taking what Jeremy Bentham once called an 'anteprandial circumgyration' of his garden."[21]

Calvin: The term "free will" is confusing.

This is also why Calvin dislikes the term "free will" because it is so easily misunderstood. Yet he briefly[22] alludes to a helpful way of distinguishing these concepts: "The schools, however, have adopted a distinction which enumerates three kinds of freedom: the first, a freedom from necessity; the second, a freedom from sin; and the third, a freedom from misery:[23] the first naturally so inherent in man, that he cannot possibly be deprived of it; while through sin the other two have been lost. I willingly admit this distinction, except in so far as it confounds *necessity* with *compulsion.*"[24]

Bernard, whom Calvin is referencing (as "schools"), identifies the first—freedom from necessity—as what distinguishes mankind from the animals because people have been made in the image of God. It is the freedom that means there are no outside forces which compel or coerce a person's choices. Bernard writes: "Take away free choice and there is nothing to be saved. Take away grace and there is no means of saving. Without the two combined, this work cannot be done . . . None but God can give it, nothing but free choice can receive it. What, therefore, is given by God alone and to free choice alone, can no more happen without the recipient's consent than without

---

20. Muller, *Divine Will*, 190, author's *emphasis.*

21. Muller, *Divine Will*, 222–23.

22. It is interesting that Muller is more specific: "He also made a concerted effort to avoid examination of non-soteriological issues concerning the intricacies of knowing and willing, whether divine or human" (Muller, *Divine Will*, 184). "Non-soteriological" refers to what Calvin called "earthly things."

23. The discussion which follows will focus only on the first: freedom from necessity. The third relates to eternity. The second, as will be noted blends in with the first, as it especially focuses on soteriological issues.

24. Calvin, *Institutes*, 2.2.5; [227–28].

the bestower's grace."[25] With those words Bernard makes an important distinction. There are some areas in which the will is free, but with reference to salvation a person is dependent on the grace of God. Bernard does not explain what those "free" areas might be—as Calvin did above with his distinction of "earthly" and "heavenly" matters—but he makes it clear that such freedom does not apply in the area of salvation. With this Calvin would agree, for he insists that when it comes to the knowledge of God, "man's keenness of mind is mere blindness."[26]

Calvin appears to alter his view on human freedom.

Yet Calvin does not always sing the same tune. He seems to back-track on what he has declared as areas of human freedom. In a later chapter in this same book he writes: "In those actions, which in themselves are neither good nor bad, and concern the corporeal rather than the spiritual life, the liberty which man possesses, although we have above touched upon it (*supra*, Chap. 2 sect. 13–17), has not yet been explained. Some have conceded a free choice to man in such actions . . . [However] I contend that whenever God is pleased to make way for his providence, he even in external matters so turns and bends the wills of men, that whatever the freedom of their choice may be, it is still subject to the disposal of God. That your mind depends more on the agency of God than the freedom of your own choice, daily experience teaches."[27]

Because of this apparent contradiction—which Calvin apparently(?) recognizes—he devotes a complete chapter in explaining himself. His thinking and arguments might be summarized as follows:

1. Argument #1: *One must make a distinction between saying that people sin from "necessity" and yet saying they sin "voluntarily."*

He agrees with Bernard's position: "Bernard says not improperly, that all of us have a will; but to will well is proficiency, to will ill is defect. Thus, simply to will is the part of man, to will ill the part of corrupt nature, to will well the part of grace" and thus, "I say that the will, deprived of liberty, is led or dragged by necessity to evil."[28] He—with Aquinas—says that, while God is totally good and can only do good, he freely does good.[29] The Devil, on the other hand, is evil, but he freely does evil. To say

---

25. Quotations of Bernard (*Treatise* 1.2) are from Brümmer, "Calvin, Bernard," 441.

26. Calvin, *Institutes*, 2.2.19; [239].

27. Calvin, *Institutes*, 2.4.6–7; [267–68].

28. Calvin, *Institutes*, 2.3.5; [252].

29. Aquinas, however, is not arguing like Calvin. The former speaks of divine freedom dealing with choices related to sitting or standing, sending rain or withholding rain, etc. God does not have freedom to do otherwise when it is opposed to his nature, and thus, theologians would argue God cannot choose to do evil. This does not necessarily mean that God does not possess a form of libertarian freedom known as "Source Incompatibilism." Kevin Timpe writes: "Source Incompatibilism is the claim that what is most important for an agent's free will is the agent being the [ultimate] source of her actions" (Timpe, *Free Will*, 12).

it another way, Calvin quotes Augustine: "Man through liberty became a sinner, but corruption, ensuing as the penalty, has converted liberty into necessity" and then he adds, "Whenever mention is made of the subject, he hesitates not to speak in this way of the necessary bondage of sin."[30]

It is hard for this writer not to conclude that by what he says he is evading the issue. One can readily agree that Adam freely chose—without compulsion—to disobey God. But how is it that a person does something "voluntarily" if the "*will is deprived of liberty*"?[31] Does not "necessity" refer to what a person *must* do because of his nature? True, prior to the fall (of the Devil and man), both had the freedom to choose among a range of options each compatible with their natures, but now, according to the Calvinistic view, they have only one option: evil. Only the grace of God can change this bondage in man by expanding his range of options, spiritually giving him the ability to respond to the good. Is not Calvin, then, assuming his conclusion, that is, that despite saying that people sin by necessity, they nevertheless have freedom? If the will responds to the person's reasoning (Calvin affirms this) and his understanding is corrupted (with this Calvin also agrees), does it not follow that the will only wills (in agreement with the intellect) what is evil?[32] Is this not implied by Calvin in *Bondage and Liberation*? "We say that man's *mind* is smitten with blindness, so that of itself it can in no way reach *the knowledge of the truth*; we say that his will is corrupted by wickedness, so that he can neither love God nor obey his righteousness."[33] There can be no freedom for man—elect or non-elect—apart from the grace of God.

Remarkably, Calvin quotes Augustine to the same effect, though he would prefer that the word "free-will" be "abolished" from theological vocabulary:

> Augustine hesitates not to call the will *a slave*. In another passage *he is offended with those who deny free will*; but his chief reason for this is explained when he says, "Only lest anyone should presume so to deny freedom of will, from a desire to excuse sin." It is certain, he elsewhere admits, that *without the Spirit*

30. Calvin, *Institutes*, 2.3.5; [253].

31. Lane distinguishes the way "free choice" is used in Calvin. One he calls "psychological freedom": "Human choice is free in the sense that is not coerced by external forces but moves voluntarily, of its own accord" (Lane, "Bondage and Liberation," 19). This is the way Aquinas uses the term. [It is interesting that another Calvinist scholar—G. C. Berkouwer (1962)—rejects this sense of "free-will." See Lane, "Did Calvin Believe"?, 80]. The other way Lane describes free choice he calls "ethical freedom" or "that a free will has the power to choose between good and evil by its own strength" (Lane, "Bondage and Liberation," 19).

32. It is hard to understand Lane's conclusion: "If Calvin appears to state that the will cannot but follow the intellect, this is because he is incautious in his use of language, not because he wished to affirm something that was patently false and which he was about to contradict" (Lane, "Bondage and Liberation," 17). That God's grace infuses the elect with "right reason" does not set aside that the will follows the reason, a reason enabled to see "light and truth" and, in the case of the non-elect—because of irremediable, dark reasoning—rejects the grace of God. The quotation above from Calvin's later publication *Bondage and Liberation* supports this conclusion.

33. Calvin, *Bondage and Liberation,* 320, author's *emphasis*.

> *the will of man is not free*, inasmuch as it is subject to lusts which chain and master it. And again, that nature began to want liberty the moment the will was vanquished by the revolt into which it fell. Again, that *man, by making a bad use of free will, lost both himself and his will*. Again, that free will having been made a captive, can do nothing in the way of righteousness. Again, that *no will is free which has not been made so by divine grace*. Again, that the righteousness of God is not fulfilled when the law orders, and man acts, as it were, by his own strength, but when the Spirit assists, and the will (not the free will of man, but the will freed by God) obeys. He briefly states the ground of all these observations, when he says, that man at his creation received a great degree of free will, but lost it by sinning.[34]

Perhaps it is fair to say that this particular discussion of "necessity" versus "voluntary" has led to a dead-end and is not fruitful. Augustine and Calvin are correct in concluding that, if the "will is not free," it leads to a form of fatalism: a person cannot not sin.

2. *Argument #2: Conversion of the will is the effect of divine grace inwardly bestowed.*

It is hard to reconcile any sense of freedom of the will with Calvin's concept of regeneration: "It may be proper to consider what the remedy is which divine grace provides for the correction and cure of natural corruption. Since the Lord, in bringing assistance, supplies us with what is lacking, the nature of that assistance will immediately make manifest its converse—viz. our penury [destitution] . . . But lest anyone should cavil that the good work thus begun by the Lord consists in aiding the will, which is in itself weak, the Spirit elsewhere [Ezek 36:26–27] declares what the will, when left to itself, is able to do . . . How can it be said that the weakness of the human will is aided so as to enable it to aspire effectually to the choice of good, when the fact is, that it must be wholly transformed and renovated"?[35]

The will must not be considered "weak," for that would suggest some natural ability or strength. In fact, it is hard like a "stone" (Calvin's illustration). Further, there is no sense in which the unregenerate cooperates with God and thus is prepared for his grace. He quotes Augustine's dictum: "Grace precedes every good work; the *will accompanying, not leading*; a handmaid, and not a guide."[36] This is precisely the argument used against Pelagius who spoke of grace being given because of a person's initiative or merit. Calvin says Augustine says it clearly: "Men . . . labour to find in our will something that is our own, and not God's; how they can find it, I wot not."[37] Calvin then explicitly expresses his own view: "The first part of a good work is the will, the second is vigorous effort in the doing of it. God is the author of both."[38] Thus, prior to the regenerative grace of God, a person does not have "free will"; there is an inescapable "bondage of the will" from

34. Calvin, *Institutes*, 2.3.8; [230], author's *emphasis*.

35. Calvin, *Institutes*, 2.3.6; [253].

36. Calvin, *Institutes*, 2.3.7; [254].

37. Calvin, *Institutes*, 2.3.7; [255].

38. Calvin, *Institutes*, 2.3.9; [257–58].

which only God can liberate the person. But Calvin implies a freedom of the will posterior to the regenerative grace of God, which seems to reflect Paul's words in 1 Cor 10:13.

3. *Argument #3: God both regenerates some and condemns/damns others.*

Calvin indicates his agreement with Augustine that "the truth which we are specially desirous to maintain [is] . . . that the grace offered by the Lord is *not merely one which every individual has full liberty of choosing to receive or reject*, but a grace which produces in the heart both choice and will."[39] With this an Arminian would agree![40] Yet Calvin goes on to say: "We know that divine grace is not given to all men, and that to those to whom it is given, it is not given either according to the merit of works, or according to the merit of the will, but by free grace: in regard to those to whom it is not given, we know that the not giving of it is a just judgment from God."[41]

What the "big print giveth, the small print taketh away!" How can such a statement not be understood by the damned as concluding they have no chance? They were not given the grace needed for regeneration. They, therefore, reject God because God has rejected them. Or to put it another way: Could they *voluntarily* respond to God and the offer of his pardon which they hear proclaimed to them but still be rejected by God? Calvin appears to just dismiss this argument with the words: "What matters it whether you sin with a free or an enslaved judgment, so long as you sin voluntarily, especially when man is proved to be a sinner because he is under the bondage of sin"?[42] Of course, fallen man sins, but the unregenerate have no hope of receiving the grace which alone can make them able to respond to God and sin less. "Therefore, while we all labour naturally under the same disease, those only recover health to whom the Lord is pleased to put forth his healing hand. The others whom, in just judgment, he passes over, pine and rot away till they are consumed."[43] Such teaching makes the criticism apparently valid that there is no need to exhort those who are not elect because they cannot respond, an argument that Calvin dismisses by saying that such exhortations will be the basis of the final judgment of non-elect.[44] Because (1) they hear the "exhortations" to turn to God and obey him and (2) they do not do either (because they cannot), these same exhortations unheeded will be the reason for their judgment.

---

39. Calvin, *Institutes*, 2.3.13; [262], author's *emphasis*.

40. Pelagius taught that a person could of his/her own initiative respond to God or reject his offer of pardon. Arminius denied this. A person cannot respond to God without his grace. But unlike Calvin, Arminius believed that such "grace" was given to all, but it was a grace which did not erase a person's freedom to accept or reject that grace. Calvin's concept of grace was an "efficacious" grace which was given only to the elect. (See also the later discussion of the *Canons of Dort* in chapter 10).

41. Calvin, *Institutes*, 2.3.14; [263].

42. Calvin, *Institutes*, 2.5.2; [272].

43. Calvin, *Institutes*, 2.5.3; [273].

44. Calvin, *Institutes*, 2.5.4–5; [273–74]. Much of this same discussion is visited again in Calvin's treatise of election in *Institutes*, 3.21–24; [766–822].

Calvin's detractor: Pighius

Calvin's very strong, deterministic soteriology did not fail to attract strong detractors soon after his publication of the *Institutes*. Albert Pighius, a Dutch Roman Catholic, especially did not like Calvin's treatment of human freedom and predestination, and, therefore, published in AD 1542 *De libero hominis arbitrio et diving gratia, Libri decem* (not available in English). Calvin responded a year later to the first part of Pighius's book (six of the ten chapters) with *The Bondage and Liberation of the Will*, specifically addressing Pighius's critique of what he had written about free will. In his final edition of *Institutes* Pighius is mentioned only once, but his arguments are apparent in Calvin's discussion. Basically, Pighius argued against two key positions he felt Calvin held:

1. *Everything happens by absolute necessity.*

Pighius accuses Calvin of affirming human freedom in name only because a person cannot avoid sinning. In this regard Pighius has sufficient grounds for his complaint, because Calvin explicitly states this in *Bondage and Liberation*:

> We are not Stoics who dream up a fate based on a continuous connection of events. All we say is that God is in charge of the world which he established . . . We say that those things which appear to be in the greatest degree due to chance happen of necessity . . . [We say that] nothing can happen other than what he decreed at the beginning. All things are subject to his power, and so there is no created thing which does not, either of its own accord or *under coercion*, obey his will . . . All the wicked are submissive to his authority, so that *they cannot move beyond what he has commanded*, since it pleases him to do so, and now *he drives them on* and guides them to execute his judgments.[45]

Calvin wants to defend God as someone who does not indifferently ("blindly and randomly") control all events (which is good and commendable), but he nevertheless affirms deterministic control which screams of unfairness and makes Pighius question how this does not rule out any sense of human accountability. It is hard to not agree with him when Calvin defines "necessity" as (1) "a fixed, steady state in which a thing cannot be otherwise than what it is" and (2) as excluding "the existence of alternative possibilities."[46] Lane—the editor of the English translation of *Bondage and Liberation*—recognizes this when he says, "It is not immediately obvious how the earlier statements [of Calvin] that God drives, forces, bends and constrains the wicked are to be reconciled with the later denials of coercion."[47]

Lane is right about the "irreconcilable" statements, but one does not have to go to an "earlier" or "later" Calvin to see this sort of contradictory statements. In the above citation "coercion" is defined as coming from God's eternal decree (thus what is outside

---

45. Calvin, *Bondage and Liberation*, 257–58, author's *emphasis*.

46. Calvin, *Bondage and Liberation*, 335.

47. Calvin, *Bondage and Liberation*, 26.

a person), yet just a few pages later in the same book—*Bondage and Liberation*—Calvin softens his position, redefining "coercion" and a person's freedom in the same way Aquinas did, that is, that a person freely makes choices when nothing outside his person compels him/her to make a certain choice or take a certain action. A person's own emotions, reason, and will account for what the person does. These are Calvin's words: [a free will is one which] "directs itself . . . is not taken by force or dragged unwillingly. [In contrast, a 'coerced' will is one which] "does not incline this way or that of its own accord or by an internal movement of decision, but is forcibly driven by an external impulse."[48] Aquinas acknowledges that there are outside "influences," but decisions are made by the individual's own reason and will. Calvin's position moves far beyond this: "nothing can happen other than what he decreed." Even with this, Calvin is uncomfortable because the term "freedom" is confusing. Lane notes that "if freedom is opposed to coercion, I both acknowledge and consistently maintain that choice is free, and I hold anyone who thinks otherwise to be a heretic. If, I say, it were called free in the sense of not being coerced nor forcibly moved by an external impulse, but moving of its own accord, I have no objection . . . In any case, it does not even seem to agree very well with the usage of Scripture. For freedom and bondage are mutually contradictory, so that he who affirms the one denies the other. Accordingly, if the human will is in bondage, it cannot be said at the same time to be free, except improperly."[49]

Yes, it is hard to use these terms in a deterministic context because they are so easily misunderstood.[50] In short, it is hard to accept on the one hand that it is only by outside enablement—that is, by a God-given grace, needed because of man's inability on his own to respond to God—that the elect find salvation and not also see the same decree—and outside decision—determines the damnation of the non-elect.[51]

2. *If God "decreed all from the beginning" did not this predestination include not only Adam's fall but all since then, some to damnation and some to salvation?*

48. Calvin, *Bondage and Liberation*, 279–80.

49. Calvin, *Bondage and Liberation*, 23.

50. Calvin, *Institutes*, 2.2.7; [229]: "I think we ought religiously to eschew terms which imply some absurdity . . . How few are there who, when they hear free will attributed to man, do not immediately imagine that he is the master of his mind and will in such a sense, that he can of himself incline himself either to good or evil? It may be said that such dangers are removed by carefully expounding the meaning to the people. But such is the proneness of the human mind to go astray, that it will more quickly draw error from one little word, than truth from a lengthened discourse. Of this, the very term in question furnishes too strong a proof. For the explanation given by ancient Christian writers having been lost sight of, almost all who have come after them, by attending only to the etymology of the term, have been led to indulge a fatal confidence."

51. These strong words of soteriological determinism by Calvin and Pighius's rebuttal that such determinism makes human accountability impossible are precisely the reasons that Molina proposed God having "middle knowledge," that is, that God knows how every person would freely act—and actualized a world where that freedom would occur. Thus, in the world that God created, he is sovereign ("nothing can happen other than what he decreed at the beginning") and yet humanity acts freely and consistent with God's foreknowledge. (See chapter 14 in this book for more on Molina's position.)

This issue is addressed in the *Institutes*.[52] A person can hear echoes of Pighius in the very question Calvin asks: "How is it that the fall of Adam involves so many nations with their infant children in eternal death without remedy unless that it so seemed meet ['pleasing'] to God"?[53] Yet, though he calls this decree "dreadful," he says that it is a natural consequent to God's foreknowledge. Some, he says, try to avoid this dreadful truth by speaking of what God "permits" but does not will it. Such thinking Calvin argues denudes the term "predestination" of all meaning: "I will not hesitate, therefore, simply to confess . . . that everything is necessary which he has willed; just as those things *will certainly happen* which he has foreseen" But Calvin admits that he has difficulty answering this objection, concluding that "their perdition depends on the predestination of God, the cause and matter of it is in themselves."[54] The non-elect are predestined to their doom, but nevertheless are responsible. Obviously, this will not satisfy those who have questions because such a conclusion does not seem to follow. And Calvin recognizes this: "Someone, perhaps, will say, that I have not yet stated enough to refute this blasphemous excuse. I confess that it is impossible to prevent impiety from murmuring and objecting . . . The reprobate would excuse their sins by alleging that they are unable to escape the necessity of sinning . . . We deny that they can thus be validly excused, since the ordination of God . . . is consistent with equity: an equity, indeed, unknown to us, but most certain."[55]

But as William Lane Craig has said elsewhere, to declare a doctrine on the basis of something "unknown" means adequate reasoning needs to be marshalled to explore the issue more carefully.[56]

Pighius has other arguments against Calvin, which even other opponents of Calvin recognized as semi-Pelagian, and thus are not relevant here.

Though much of this essay has identified the dynamics and arguments of those who have raised their disagreements with Calvin's teaching, it is important to take note of what was earlier stated, namely, his distinction of "inferior objects" from "superior objects" and "earthly things" (matters) and the "heavenly." In the former, there is *limited* libertarian freedom, that is, at least in some things, while in the latter there is only a granted, enabled "freedom" which comes from the efficacious grace of God.[57] Calvin's difficulty was how to align this sense of freedom to the determinism of predestination, election and God's absolute sovereignty.[58] This, of course, sets the stage for the position which will be developed in the later chapters of this book.

---

52. Calvin, *Institutes*, 3.23.7–14; [795–802].

53. Calvin, *Institutes*, 3.23.7; [796].

54. Calvin, *Institutes*, 3.23.8; [796], author's *emphasis*.

55. Calvin, *Institutes*, 3.23.9; [797].

56. Craig, "Response to Helseth," 55.

57. This "enabled freedom" is often called "compatibilistic freewill." See more in chapter 12.

58. Muller, Divine Will, 192–93, put it early: "This conclusion [that 'Calvin's approach to human freedom is untechnical and, consequently, somewhat vague, perhaps even imprecise'] does not indicate

9

A survey of human freedom during the Reformation and post-Reformation periods

Arminius (AD 1560–1609)

THE MAN WHOSE ANGLICIZED name is often expressed as James or Jacobus Arminius was born Jacobus Harmenszoon (literally, "Harmen's son") in Oudewater, Holland, in AD 1560. The town is noteworthy because it adopted the wave of Calvinism and anti-Catholicism that spread throughout the Netherlands, and for their views the citizens of the town paid a huge price: The king of Spain attacked the city and massacred all its people. Because a clergyman was mentoring the young Arminius after his father died, Arminius was not in Oudewater at the time or he would have experienced the same fate as his mother and sister.[1]

A year after the death of his family (AD 1575), Arminius—now a fifteen-year-old orphan—began his studies at the University of Leyden. After leaving Leyden he studied in Geneva under Theodore Beza, the most prominent "Calvinist" leader after Calvin's death.[2] MacCulloch calls Beza "the high priest of Calvinism."[3] After his studies in Leyden, Arminius became a minister in Amsterdam (AD 1588) and fourteen years later became a lecturer at the very university he attended as a student in Leyden. The years in Amsterdam were fruitful, but trouble began when Arminius (in AD 1592) was asked—to trip him up?[4]—to write an essay supporting his former

---

that Calvin was inconsistent . . . only that he focused on the issue of sin and grace while declining to elaborate on the broader philosophical issues. His thought does not fit a strict determinist pattern, but it is unclear how he understood alternativity in the general operations of intellect and will."

1. Brandt, *The Life of Arminius*, 32–39; Studebacker, "The Theology of Arminius," 4.
2. Studebacker, "The Theology of Arminius," 5.
3. MacCulloch, "Arminius and Arminians," 28.
4. Studebacker, "The Theology of Arminius," 6.

teacher's (Beza) position on predestination.[5] What he taught and wrote on that occasion—and on other occasions—however, fueled an often mean-spirited[6] controversy for the rest of his life both while in Amsterdam and later at the University of Leyden (AD 1603–1609). A fellow professor at this latter institution—Franciscus Gomarus— led the opposition, delivering a contrary view of predestination from what Arminius had just presented as a new faculty member. Gomarus was not interested in debate; his intent was to destroy.[7]

FIVE ARTICLES OF REMONSTRANCE.

Confusion about what Arminius believed only grew when, a year after his death, his "followers" published *Five Articles of Remonstrance* which gave shape to a more

---

5. Bangs, "Arminius and the Reformation," 155–57, says there was an *erroneous* report that Arminius had agreed with Beza's "Supralapsarianism" predestination theory but, when researching a response to anti-Calvinist [though a believer] Coornheart, he saw he could no longer hold to Beza's position and devoted himself to a careful study of the Scriptures and the godly leaders of the past. In fact, Arminius himself debunked his connection with Coornheart: "The rumor about my advising the students to read the works of the Jesuits and of Coornheert, I can call by no other name than a lie; for never to anyone, either by request or spontaneously, have I uttered a word on that subject. So far from this after the reading of the Scripture . . . I recommend that the Commentaries of Calvin be read, whom I extol in higher terms . . . for I affirm that in the interpretation of Scriptures Calvin is incomparable . . . so much so that I concede to him a certain spirit of prophecy in which he stands distinguished above others, above most, yea, above all" (Bangs, "Arminius and the Reformation," 163–64). Another valuable contribution on Arminius and Calvin is den Boer, "Cum delectu," 73–86. See also Arminius, *Works*, 1.1.

"Supralapsarianism" is a big word (*supra* = "before" and *lapsum* = "fall") denoting the Calvinistic doctrine that God elected some to salvation literally "before the fall." Boettner, "Predestination," 417, explains this term and its opposite in a very helpful way: "[For] infralapsarians . . . the order of events is: God proposed (1) to create; (2) to permit the fall; (3) to elect some out of this fallen mass to be saved, and to leave the others as they were; (4) to provide a redeemer for the elect; and (5) to send the Holy Spirit to apply this redemption to the elect. According to this plan, election follows the fall. According to the supralapsarian view the order of events is: God proposed (1) to elect some creatable men (that is, men who were to be created) to life and to condemn others to destruction; (2) to create; (3) to permit the fall; (4) to send Christ to redeem the elect; and (5) to send the Holy Spirit to apply this redemption to the elect. According to this plan election precedes the fall."

6. Richard Muller, "Arminius and the Reformed Tradition," 18, writes: "As the records of the seventeenth century indicate, the debate over Arminius's theology was intense, acrimonious, and proceeded on an *ad hominem* as well as on a confessional and dogmatic path. The level of anger and recrimination in the original debate can easily be seen in a comparison of the alternative histories of the controversy, notably the Reformed history presented as a preface to the Canons of Dort and the Remonstrant narrative written later by Limborch in response to the Reformed history."

7. It is interesting that Richard Muller, in the conclusion of his fine article on "Arminius and the Reformed Tradition," 47, gave this analysis of the difference between Arminius and Calvinism of his day: "Given the diversity of the Reformed tradition, notably the differences between Calvin and Bullinger on predestination and the sacraments, or the difference between Calvin and Vermigli on divine permission, there remains some validity in Bangs's comment that a comparison of Calvin with Arminius would yield 'possibly no less agreement or more dissent than would be found among later Calvinists.' One can certainly tabulate more similarities than differences, and not only between Arminius and Calvin: there are more similarities than differences between Arminius's and Gomarus's theologies."

defined essence of "Arminianism." Below is an excerpt (not a summary) from those articles, given in a rather lengthy quote deliberately provided because there has been so much controversy and misrepresentation.[8] The articles will appear in *italics* and the comments which follow are the author's summary, which will help the reader understand what gave rise to the Synod of Dort's "Five Points of Calvinism: TULIP."[9]

1. **Article #1:** *That God . . . before the foundation of the world, hath determined, out of the fallen, sinful race of men, to save . . . those who, through the grace of the Holy Ghost, shall believe on this his Son Jesus, and shall persevere . . . and, on the other hand, to leave the incorrigible and unbelieving in sin and under wrath.*

   Though not stated in so many words, these words are the Arminians's way of saying there is no double predestination.

2. **Article #2:** *Jesus . . . died for all . . . so that he has obtained for . . . all . . . redemption and the forgiveness of sins; yet that no one actually enjoys this forgiveness . . . except the believer.*

   This is an explicit statement against "limited" atonement: Jesus "died for all."

3. **Article #3:** *Man has not saving grace of himself, nor of the energy of his free will, [and] . . . can of and by himself neither think, will, nor do anything that is truly good . . . It is needful that he be born again of God in Christ, through his Holy Spirit.*

   Man is fallen, depraved, and powerless to even recognize and choose the good.

4. **Article #4:** *This grace of God is the beginning, continuance, and accomplishment of all good, even to this extent, that the regenerate man himself, without prevenient or assisting, awakening, following and co-operative grace, can neither think, will, nor do good, nor withstand any temptations to evil . . . But as respects the mode of the operation of this grace, it is not irresistible.*

   God gives grace to all, without which none can respond to God. Thus, a special grace ("irresistible") is not necessary for human response. All—having received this grace—can reject or not reject this grace.

5. **Article #5:** *It is ever through the assisting grace of the Holy Ghost . . . in all temptations, extends to them his hand, and if only they . . . desire his help, and are not inactive, keeps them from falling . . . But whether they are capable, through negligence, of forsaking again the first beginnings of their life in Christ, of again . . . turning away from the holy doctrine . . . of losing a good conscience, of becoming devoid of grace, that must be more particularly determined out of the Holy Scripture, before we ourselves can teach it with the full persuasion of our minds.* [/NL 1–5]

---

8. A fuller quotation of these "Articles" may be found later in the discussion of the *Canons of Dort*. The Articles are from Schaff, *Creeds*, 3:545–49.

9. "TULIP" is explained in the essay on the *Canons of Dort*.

Regarding perseverance (sometimes called "eternal security") the Remonstrants remained agnostic. They thought more study and thought were necessary.[10]

This refueling of controversy led to a *Counter-Remonstrance of 1611*, and the debate continued for eight more years at which time the *Canons of Dort* were adopted and those in the Remonstrance party were not only labeled as false teachers but were forced to flee the country as heretics.[11]

What a researcher of Arminius and "Arminianism" soon discovers is that many people have formed their opinion of the man and his writings often from what others have said about him and his teachings rather than consulting what he himself has written. J. Matthew Pinson forcefully states this in his criticism of Arminian "scholarship":

> Jacobus Arminius is one of the best known and least studied theologians in the history of Christianity. His writings have been neglected by Calvinists and Arminians alike . . . Arminius scholar Carl Bangs[12] is correct when he says that most modern treatments of Arminius assume a definition of Arminianism that does not come from Arminius. Bangs argues that most interpreters of Arminianism "begin with a preconception of what Arminius should be expected to say, then look in his published works, and do not find exactly what they are looking for. They show impatience and disappointment with his Calvinism, and shift the inquiry into some later period when Arminianism turns out to be what they are looking for—a non-Calvinistic, synergistic, and perhaps semi-Pelagian system."[13]

This is not an unusual assessment,[14] some even concluding that the Synod of Dort did not even consider his writings when they had their deliberation. It is pretty

---

10. Arminius was more specific by saying in response to *Question #7*: "Since God promises eternal life to all who believe in Christ, it is impossible for him who believes, and who knows that he believes, to doubt of his own salvation, unless he doubts of this willingness of God [to perform his promise]" (Arminius, *Works*, 1.3.*Nine Questions*; [283, CCEL edition]). He continues in *Question #8*: "Election to salvation comprehends within its limits not only faith, but likewise perseverance in faith . . . St. Augustine says, 'God has chosen to salvation those who he sees will afterwards believe by the aid of his preventing or preceding grace, and who will persevere by the aid of his subsequent or following grace.'" (Arminius, *Works*, 1.3.*Nine Questions*; [284]).

11. Brandt, in *Life of Arminius*, xvi, says: "Hundreds of clergymen were deposed. Multitudes who refused (though plied with the bribe of a comfortable maintenance) to abstain from preaching, were sent into exile. Even organists of churches were compelled to sign the canons of the Synod of Dort."

12. Bangs, "Arminius and the Reformation," 14.

13. Pinson, "Nature of Atonement," 773.

14. Consider Aloisi, "Jacob Arminius," 183: "The term 'Arminianism' is a very slippery one. Many people who are in basic agreement with Arminius's understanding of predestination, man's condition, and God's role in salvation reject the label 'Arminian.' On the other hand, at times Calvinists have the tendency to apply the term 'Arminianism' to anything short of what Calvin himself taught. Unfortunately, the labels 'Arminian' and 'Arminianism' are used rather inconsistently and at times get thrown around rather carelessly. Perhaps this is the case because few people are familiar with what Arminius actually taught."

much a widely held conclusion that Arminius and what came to be called after him—"Arminianism"—are not the same.[15]

Because of this, it is the purpose of this essay to explore from the primary documents what Arminius taught and believed and then allow the findings to be the "bench mark" against which to measure his conformity or lack of conformity with Calvin and the later *Canons of Dort*.

Although Arminius felt that the issue of predestination was the most important and perhaps a topic about which—as Calvinism in his day defined it—he felt most odious and, therefore, most necessary to respond to and correctly define, a more important issue theologically was his position on original sin and God's grace, which will of necessity be the foundation on which his position on predestination must be seen.

ARMINIUS ON ORIGINAL SIN.

In some of his writings, Arminius seems to contrast his position on original sin with Augustine's total depravity. According to him God had made a covenant with Adam and Eve that if they obeyed their progeny would "receive the gifts conferred on them," but that if they disobeyed, they would not "possess them but should be liable for contrary evils." When the latter occurred, Arminius called the loss to their progeny a "loss of righteousness," that is, the righteousness which Adam and Eve had before they sinned. Too often much is made of this oft quoted comment, but one must not miss what Arminius admitted not only in the same context but immediately following those words: that he was unsure just what this "original sin" caused, but insisted that this loss "alone" [was] sufficient to commit and produce any actual sins whatsoever." In other words, Adam and Eve's sin led their progeny to sin. He explains more as he relates what were the two consequences of Adam and Eve's sin: an "offended" God and "guilt."[16]

What was not fully clear here is found in a fuller account in his *Disputation 11*,[17] which—as Aloisi[18] has noted—shows that Arminius was neither Pelagian nor Semi-Pelagian, as he was accused of being. Indeed, the statements below appear to be very harmonious with what Calvin himself taught. Because this is so important to correct

15. John Mark Hicks, "The Righteous of Saving Faith," 34: "As historians of theology, we owe it to those who have preceded us to carefully understand and categorize their thought. The Arminian tradition is the historical line of Arminius and Wesley. The Remonstrant tradition is the historical line of Grotius, Limborch and Latitudinarianism." Studebaker, "The Theology of Arminius," 15, note 17, commenting on Hicks's words, writes: "Even today, as Wynkoop (*Theology*, 60) observes, 'There are many streams of theology and political ideology called Arminian that lead far afield from Arminius's teaching."

16. All quotations are to be found in Arminius, 2.1.31; [57–58]. This last comment is important. In Arminius's words: "The first and immediate effect of the sin which Adam and Eve committed in eating of the forbidden fruit, was the offending of the Deity, and guilt" (57).

17. Quotations are from Arminius, *Works*, 1.3.Public Disputations,11; [384–87]. The Roman numerals are the paragraph markers in Arminius's original text and are printed here in *italics*.

18. Aloisi, "Jacob Arminius," 196–97.

both confusion and misrepresentation, a rather extensive excerpt from his account of paragraphs 5 through 9 follows, with the author's comment or summary after each of Arminius's statements:

- *In the state of Primitive Innocence, man had a mind endued with a clear under-standing of . . . and powers abundantly qualified of heavenly light and truth concerning God, and his works and will, as far as was sufficient for the salvation of man and the glory of God; he had a heart imbued with "righteousness and true holiness" . . . and powers abundantly qualified or furnished perfectly to fulfill the law which God had imposed on him.*

Adam and Eve (A & E) while in the garden were "innocent" and had the ability both to see "truth" and to respond to God.

- *But man . . . having turned away from the light of his own mind and his chief good, which is God . . . he precipitated himself from that noble and elevated condition into a state of the deepest infelicity, which is Under the Dominion of Sin.*

A & E's sin was a deliberate turn from the truth, and the result was a "state" of bondage to sin.

- *In this state, the free will of man towards the true good is not only wounded, maimed, infirm, bent, and weakened; but it is also imprisoned, destroyed, and lost. And its powers are not only debilitated and useless unless they be assisted by grace.*

The result of A & E's sin was a will that was no longer "free," indeed, not only weakened but "lost." Luther called it the "bondage of the will," a bondage that only could be liberated by God's grace.[19]

- *The mind of man, in this state, is dark, destitute of the saving knowledge of God.*

Further, the result of A & E's sin was that truth could no longer be seen but made people hopeless to find their way back to salvation.

- *To the darkness of the mind succeeds the perverseness of the affections and of the heart, according to which it hates and has an aversion to that which is truly good and pleasing to God; but it loves and pursues what is evil.*

Not only has the mind been darkened, it does not even desire the good, but loves and pursues evil.

- *Exactly correspondent to this darkness of the mind, and perverseness of the heart, is the utter weakness of all the powers to perform that which is truly good . . . The subjoined sayings of Christ serve to describe this impotence. A corrupt tree cannot*

---

19. This comment must not be misunderstood: Arminius did differ from Luther on the nature of grace, not on the result of the fall. (See the previous discussion of Luther in chapter 7.)

bring forth good fruit (Matt 7:18) . . . *To the same purpose are all those passages in which the man existing in this state is said to be under the power of sin and Satan, reduced to the condition of a slave.*

A & E's sin not only brought darkness, but has rendered people incapable of escaping their condition. They are no longer free but slaves to the evil one.

- *To these let the consideration of the whole of the life of man who is placed under sin, be added . . . that nothing can be spoken more truly concerning man in this state, than that he is altogether dead in sin . . . It follows, that our will is not free from the first fall; that is, it is not free to do good, unless it be made free by the Son through his Spirit.*

All of A & E's progeny can only be liberated by Jesus and his Spirit.

To this must be added Arminius's specific discussion of what happened to all the human race because of Adam and Eve's sin:

- *The whole of this sin, however, is not peculiar to our first parents, but is common to the entire race and to all their posterity, who, at the time when this sin was committed, were in their loins, and who have since descended from them by the natural mode of propagation, according to the primitive benediction. For in Adam* all have sinned (Rom 5:12). *Wherefore, whatever punishment was brought down upon our first parents, has likewise pervaded and yet pursues all their posterity. So that* all men *are by nature the children of wrath (Eph 2:3) . . . and to temporal as well as to eternal death; they are also devoid of that original righteousness and holiness (Rom 5:12, 18–19). With these evils they would remain oppressed forever, unless they were liberated by Christ Jesus; to whom be glory forever.*[20]

If this is not consistent with the Augustinian doctrine of original sin and resulting depravity, then, words mean nothing, *despite* some of Arminius's statements in other places that have been understood differently![21]

ARMINIUS ON GRACE AND PREDESTINATION.

Having discussed original sin, a careful look at Arminius's teaching regarding grace and predestination is in order. It is his position on these—more likely than anything

---

20. Arminus, *Works*, 1.3.*Public Disputations*,7; [356]. See in a similar way Arminus, *Works*, 2.1.Letter to Hippolytus, *On Original Sin*; [350].

21. Grace must be shown to Arminius who, because of the attacks on his teaching, became very careful in what he said and wrote so as to avoid being both misunderstood and maligned. Aloisi, "Jacob Arminius," 184, notes the comment of Baptist theologian Augustus Strong who with a little bite in his words wrote: "The expressions of Arminius himself are so guarded that Moses Stuart (*Bib. Repos.*, 1831) found it possible to construct an argument to prove that Arminius was not an Arminian" (Strong, *Systematic Theology*, 3:602). Was this an admission that to be dogmatic about what Arminius taught—as too often has been the case—only shows one's bias?

else—that rattled his opponents. The heart of the issue is his definition of "grace." Arminius made a distinction between (1) the Calvinistic doctrine of "efficacious" grace that God gives only to the elect and (2) the "sufficient" grace which God gives to all.[22] He argues that holding the position of "efficacious" grace held by Calvinists in his day led to a legitimate charge that God was not only a hypocrite but also that he was culpable for the condemnation of some (i.e., those who are not given "efficacious" grace) because such individuals can do nothing to obtain forgiveness. Arminius continues:

> But He [God] further decreed [according to the Calvinists] not to give efficacious grace to the same persons, and this by the decree of reprobation. But their inexcusableness does not depend upon this denial of efficacious grace. If, indeed, sufficient grace should be withheld, they, who do not believe and are not converted, are deservedly excused, for the reason that, without it, they could neither believe nor be converted. But if these things are explained in this way, according to the view of Augustine, and, perhaps also, in accordance with the sense of the Scriptures, *it follows that it cannot be concluded that God admonishes the reprobate to repentance and faith with no other design than that they may be left without excuse.* For according to the decree of providence, by which He gives to them grace sufficient to faith, and exhortation to repentance and faith is addressed and it is to this end, that they may be led to repentance and faith, and that God may satisfy His own goodness and grace, and be clear from the responsibility of their perdition. The exhortation, then, is not made according to the decree of reprobation, therefore, its design is not to be measured by the decree of reprobation.[23]

With these words Arminius is taking the Calvinistic doctrine of "efficacious" grace to its logical end. If God gives this enabling grace only to the elect, how can he justly condemn those who do not and cannot respond to the offer of salvation that Jesus died to make available?[24] If God, as declared by the Calvinists of Arminius's day, is just in damning the "reprobate" (that is, the non-elect) because the gospel is preached to them and they reject the message and Savior, then is not the gospel preached to

---

22. In Arminius's words: "In the decree of reprobation, sufficient grace is not . . . said to be denied, since it is bestowed on many, who are reprobate, namely, on those, who by the external preaching of the gospel, are called to faith and repentance, but *efficacious grace* is denied to them, namely, that grace *by which they not only can believe and be converted*, if they consent, *but by which they also will consent, believe, and be converted*, and certainly and infallibly do so" (Arminius, *Works*, 3.1*Examination of the Treatise*; [239], writer's *emphasis*).

23. Arminius, *Works*, 3.1*Examination of the Treatise*; [240], author's *emphasis*.

24. Arminius, in his answer to *Question #5* (Arminius, *Works*, 1.3.Questions; [281]), says: "God cannot by any right demand from fallen man faith in Christ, which he cannot have of himself, except God has either bestowed, or is ready to bestow, sufficient grace by which he may believe if he will . . . It [his reply] has no alliance with the Pelagian heresy: for Pelagius maintained, that with the exception of the preaching of the Gospel, no internal grace is required to produce faith in the minds of men." Arminius continues in *Question #6* (Arminius, *Works*, 1.3.Questions; [282]): "Faith is the effect of God illuminating the mind and sealing the heart, and it is his mere gift." There is no synergism here.

them an hypocritical offer because they cannot respond? They are not elect, and they are not given "efficacious" grace.

In November of AD 1605 Arminius responded to the requests to answer *Nine Questions* (the answers to which are not always clear because of Aminius's careful responses), but he was very forthright about his denial of an election that unilaterally condemned certain people: "God will be the author of sin if He cause any man to transgress the law. This is done by denying or taking away what is necessary for fulfilling the law, or by impelling men to sin . . . If this 'determination' denote the decree of God by which He resolved that the will should become depraved, and that man should commit sin, then it follows from this that God is the author of sin."[25]

In his *Declaration of Sentiments*—which he wrote after refusing many requests to set forth his position because of his fear that the requests were not out of a spirit of debate but out of antagonism—he clearly sets forth first what beliefs he finds unacceptable (not supported by Scripture) and then follows it with his own position and analysis. His first topic—which he calls most important[26]—is predestination or election. What he sets forth as that with which he is in disagreement is not a "straw man," but "the articles of Predestination which are inculcated in our Churches and in the University of Leyden."[27] With the following he disagrees:

> That God has absolutely and precisely decreed to save certain particular men by his mercy or grace, but to condemn others by his justice . . . That those persons whom God has thus positively willed to save, he has decreed not only to salvation but also to the means which pertain to it; (that is, to conduct and bring them to faith in Christ Jesus, and to perseverance in that faith;) and that He also . . . leads them to these results by a grace and power that are irresistible, so that it is not possible for them to do otherwise than believe, persevere in faith, and be saved. [And] . . . to those whom, by his absolute will, God has fore-ordained to perdition, he has also decreed to deny that grace which is necessary and sufficient for salvation, and does not in reality confer it upon them; so that they are neither placed in a possible condition nor in any capacity of believing or of being saved.[28]

---

25. Arminius, *Works*, 1.3.Questions (*Question #2*); [278].

26. Arminius, *Works*, 1.Declaration of Sentiments, *On Predestination*; [141].

27. Arminius, *Works*, 1.Declaration of Sentiments, *On My Own Sentiments*; [170].

28. Arminius, *Works*, 1.Declaration of Sentiments, *On Predestination*; [145].What Arminius has described is consistent with what the influential Beza taught: "The eternal and immutable decree of God, going before all the causes of salvation and damnation, whereby God has determined to be glorified in some by saving them in Christ by mere grace, but in others by damning them by His rightful judgement in Adam and in themselves. From the use of Scripture we call the former vessels of glory, and elect, that is predestined to salvation from eternity through mercy; the latter are called reprobates and vessels of wrath, that is, those who are predestined likewise to rightful damnation from eternity" (Beza, *A Little Book of Christian Questions and Responses*, A195), quoted in John Aloisi, "Undertanding Arminius."

With this Arminius offers twenty objections, each with subpoints,[29] the essence of which are (1) that the first decree is that Jesus will be the Savior; (2) [and most importantly] that God decrees the eternal destinies of all: "to receive into favour those who repent and believe, and . . . to effect the salvation of such penitents and believers as persevered to the end; but to leave in sin, and under wrath, all impenitent persons and unbelievers, and to damn them as aliens;"[30] (3) that there will be sufficient means for faith and repentance; and (4) that God decrees who will be saved and lost based on God's "foreknowledge . . . by which he knew from all eternity those individuals who would, through his preventing[31] grace, believe, and, through his subsequent grace would persevere . . . and, by which foreknowledge, he likewise knew those who would not believe and persevere."[32]

There is nothing new in these words with the exception of (4) in which he posits God's decree of those who will be saved or damned based on his "foreknowledge from all eternity." Arminius is very careful in his definitions here. In his *Answers to Nine Questions* the Deputies asked (*Question #1*): "Which is first, election, or faith truly foreseen, so that God elected his people according to faith foreseen"?[33] He replied that great precision needs to be made as to the meaning of "election," and therefore distinguishes the election as (1) the decree to save people who believe from election understood as (2) the selection of certain people who then are given the grace to believe, the former of which he feels is biblically correct and the latter to which he disagrees: "If, therefore, 'election' denotes 'the decree which is according to election concerning the justification and salvation of *believers*,' I say election is prior to faith, as being that by which faith is appointed as the means of obtaining salvation. But if it signifies 'the decree by which God determines to bestow salvation on someone,' then faith foreseen is prior to election. For as *believers* alone are saved, so only *believers* are predestinated to salvation."[34]

This focus on believing and believers for Aminius is very important because he understands that grace is given to everyone without distinction, a grace that is sufficient for all to believe, though not all will. Thus, election is the decree based on the foreknowledge of those who will believe.

Arminius set this forth very persistently in his writings. He shudders at the suggestion of what is called "double predestination." Hear his words: "It is a horrible affirmation, that 'God has predestinated whatsoever men he pleased not only

29. Arminius, *Works*, 1.Declaration of Sentiments, *On Predestination*; [145–162].

30. Arminius, *Works*, 1.Declaration of Sentiments, *On Predestination*; [170].

31. *Preventing* is an old English word for "preceding" (See 1 Thes 4:15 in the *KJV*), thus, "preventing" grace is the grace that precedes and makes it possible for a person to believe (though in Arminius's thinking he could resist that grace).

32. Arminius, *Works*, 1.Declaration of Sentiments, *On Predestination*; [170].

33. Arminius, *Works*, 1.3.Questions, *Question #1*; [277]. Many today would distinguish "fore-seen" from "fore-known." See further discussion in chapter 14.

34. Arminius, *Works*, 1.3.Questions, *Question #1*; [277], author's *emphasis*.

to damnation, but likewise to the causes of damnation' (Beza, vol. I, fol. 417). It is a horrible affirmation, that 'men are predestinated to eternal death by the naked will or choice of God, without any demerit on their part' (Calvin, *Inst.* l.1.2–3.). This, also, is a horrible affirmation: 'Some among men have been created unto life eternal, and others unto death eternal.'"[35]

Since predestination is related to foreknowledge, it is important to see how in other writings he fleshes out what he means by God's foreknowledge, distinguishing it from divine determinism: "Prediction sometimes follows this prescience . . . But neither prediction nor any prescience induces a necessity of anything that is afterwards to be, since they are [in the divine mind] posterior in nature and order to the thing that is future. *For a thing does not come to pass because it has been foreknown or foretold; but it is foreknown and foretold because it is yet to come to pass.* Neither does the decree itself, by which the Lord administers providence and its acts, induce any necessity on things future; for, since it, the decree, is an internal act of God, it lays down nothing in the thing itself."[36]

Showing his acquaintance with Augustine's writings, he quotes him: "God, (as St. Augustine says again, book 6) 'does not predestinate all which he foreknows. For He only foreknows evil. He does not predestinate it, but He both foreknows and predestinates good.' God does not will evil, but He wills, and preserves a certain order even in evil. Evil comes from the will of man."[37] Arminius is so very careful to explain—unlike the Calvinism of his day—that God's foreknowledge in no way implicates God as the author of evil. Toward the end of his life he wrote:

> It is, therefore, certain that there is no determinate or definite prescience in reference to culpable evil, unless it has been preceded by a decree to permit sin. For without this, sin will not exist. Prescience has also reference to things future and certainly future; otherwise, either it is not prescience or it is uncertain . . . God, from eternity, knew that it was possible that man, assisted by divine grace, should either receive or reject Christ; also, that God has decreed, either to permit a man to reject Christ, or to co-operate with him that he may accept Christ by faith, then, that God foreknows that one will apprehend Christ by faith, and that another will reject him by unbelief. From this follows the execution of that decree, by which he determined to justify and save believers, and to condemn unbelievers, which is an actual justification of the former, and a condemnation of the latter.[38]

35. Arminius, *Works*, 2.1, *On Predestination to Salvation*; [342].

36. Arminius, *Works*, 2.1, *Disputation #28*; [52], author's *emphasis*. Similarly, he said: "God foreknows future things through the infinity of his essence, and through the pre-eminent perfection of his understanding and prescience, not as he willed or decreed that they should necessarily be done, though he would not foreknow them except as they were future, and they would not be future unless God had decreed either to perform or to permit them" (Arminius, *Works*, 2.1, *On God Considered*; [339]).

37. Arminius, *Works*, 3, *Sixth Proposition*; [39].

38. Arminius, *Works*, 3, *An Examination of the Treatise*; [338–39]. This is possibly one of the

ARMINIUS ON THE "ORDER OF DECREES."

Arminius vigorously resisted any definition of election that included a *special* grace given to some individuals which alone enabled them to believe, while not giving it to others resulting in their damnation. This insistence led him to speak of the decrees with such technicality that it has been a challenge for people both yesterday and today to understand:

> This is the order of the decrees. (1.) [God says:] It is my will to save believers. (2.) On this man I will bestow faith and preserve him in it. (3.) I will save this man. For thus does the first of these decrees prescribe, which must necessarily be placed foremost; because, without this, faith is not necessary to salvation, and therefore no necessity exists to administer the means for faith. But to this is directly opposed the opinion which asserts, that faith is bestowed on him on whom God had previously willed to bestow salvation. For, in this case, it would be his will to save one who did not believe. All that has been said about the difference of the decree and its execution, is futile; as if, in fact, God willed salvation to any one prior to faith, and yet not to bestow salvation on any others than believers. For, beside the consistent agreement of these, [the decree and its execution,] it is certain that God cannot will to bestow that which, on account of his previous decree, He cannot bestow. As therefore faith is, in a general manner, placed before salvation by the first decree; so, it must, specially and particularly, be placed before the salvation of this and that man, even in the special decree which has the subsequent execution.[39]

This sounds obtuse, but basically this was Arminius's reaction to the Calvinists's definition of "unconditional election" and "irresistible grace." Election is of believers, individuals who are able to respond to the gospel because of the common grace given to all.[40]

One could go on and provide far more documentation of Arminius's teachings, because there are three large volumes of his collected writings. But the limits of space and the specific subject at hand prevent more from being included here. And it should be noted that Arminius wrote about many other subjects—e.g., the church and government—but it is the above discussion of Arminius's position on grace, foreknowledge, faith, and free will that is of interest to this writer. Although Stanglin and McCall

---

closest resemblances to Molina's concept of "middle knowledge," that is, the belief that God in his omniscience knew from all eternity all that human beings would do in all circumstances and in his (God's) love and commitment to human freedom "actualized" what he logically foreknew so that both those who will believe and those who will reject or neglect his offer of pardon freely make those choices he (God) foreknew. See further Molina's discussion of middle knowledge in chapter 14. See also a fine discussion of this in Dekker, "Was Arminius a Molinist"?

39. Arminius, *Works*, 1.3.Questions, *Remarks*; [286].

40. Bangs, "Arminius and the Reformation," 168–70, offers an excellent summary at the end of his essay.

may not miss the mark much in concluding that Arminius gave more space to what he disagreed with than what were his own positions,[41] the historian must remember that he was operating in a very adversarial context. What he did write, however, is clear enough to dispel for the careful researcher that he did not teach what many have accused him of believing.

41. Stanglin and McCall, *Jacob Arminius*, 20.

10

A survey of human freedom during the Reformation and post-Reformation periods

The Synod of Dort (13 November 1618 to 9 May 1619)

THE SYNOD OF DORT (Dordt) gets its name from the city of Dordrecht in the Netherlands, where it was held. Rogge highlights the importance of the synod when he says it was the "largest and . . . the most imposing synod (next to the Westminster Assembly) convened by the Reformed churches."[1] Though it was called by the Dutch Reformed Church, it indeed was a large and diverse gathering. There were 102 official delegates including bishops, priests, pastors, elders, chaplains, theologians (academics), and denominational leaders. Certainly, the Dutch were the largest delegation, but delegates also came from Great Britain, Scotland, and Switzerland. French representatives had been invited but prohibited by Louis XIII from attending. The synod was called for a very serious purpose: to address the growing breach in the church which was occurring because of the teaching of Arminius (who had died before the council in AD 1609) and/or his followers, especially because of the document they had published to promote their views: *The Remonstrance of 1610*. Even the length of the synod's deliberations says something about the intensity of the issue and the widespread concerns. It was convened on 13 November 1618, and continued for almost seven months, concluding on 9 May 1619, with the publication of *The Decision of the Synod of Dort on the Five Main Points of Doctrine in Dispute in the Netherlands*, more commonly called the *Canons*[2] *of Dort*.

The events which led up to the synod are an interesting story. Arminius grew up in Holland and was greatly respected, so much so that he was sent and financed to

---

1. Rogge, "Dort," 494.

2. The word "canon" is a word rarely used in contemporary English, but it is the term for "measure, criterion" by which something is judged. Thus, the *Canons* document has become the classic expression and explanation of the "approved" Calvinism (the Five Points commonly represented by the acronym TULIP), even to this day.

study in Geneva under no less than Beza, Calvin's prominent disciple. Upon returning to Amsterdam, where he was a pastor, he was asked to respond to a pamphlet that was circulating among Dutch reformed pastors that was critical of Beza's position on predestination. Since he had studied under Beza, he was a natural scholar to respond to the issues raised. But as he researched the subject, instead of refuting it, he became convinced that the pamphlet had valid and convincing arguments which supported it. Consequently, he not only embraced the position, but furnished additional support to its arguments.[3] He put his conclusions into print (AD 1591), but began lectures in the book of Romans which he felt supported what was being called "Arminianism" or the teachings of Remonstrants.

His teaching stirred up opposition, which became far more vocal when he was being considered for professor of divinity at the University of Leyden. He obtained the position and his teaching continued to influence students and then graduates, many of whom assumed responsibilities as clergymen. The movement was growing. According to Miller, Arminius resisted the increasing opposition to have him defend himself and his anti-Calvinist position before a group of peers.[4] Finally, in AD 1609 he was summoned by the administrative body of the Dutch Reformed Church—States General—to explain his position, but he died before the conference was adjourned. Some say he was so distressed about the conflict his views had caused that the stress led to his sudden death. His close friend Betius reported that Arminius said: "Woe is me, my mother, that thou hast borne me a man of strife, and a man of contention to the whole earth. I have lent to no man on usury, nor have men lent to me on usury; yet everyone doth curse me!"[5]

It is interesting that historians are not consistent in their evaluation of what Arminius believed. Some only charged him with disagreeing with Calvin's absolute decrees, while his followers—on the other hand—were charged with being far more radical. This will be explored in the next section of this essay where the essential teaching of *The Remonstrance of 1610* is summarized.

THE REMONSTRANCE OF 1610

After the *Remonstrance* was published, the controversy grew to the place that England's king—James I, to whom the *KJV* of the Bible was dedicated—requested a council be called to address Arminianism and the growing discord in the churches.[6] A

3. Miller, "Introductory Essay," 8–9.

4. Miller, "Introductory Essay," 15–16.

5. Miller, "Introductory Essay," 18–19.

6. Many efforts were made prior to this council to resolve this issue, to call a truce. Though there was bitterness on both sides, things were made far more complicated by Prince Maurice, who was opposed to peace between the two sides. Politics became intertwined with theological deliberations. Brandt wrote: "The deliberations here referred to were of the very gravest character, and proved the source of that alienation between the ambitious Prince Maurice and the incorruptible Oldenbarneveldt, which

year later the Synod of Dort was convened. There is no consensus on the decorum of the proceedings of the synod: some were saying that a real spirit of free debate was squelched, while others charged that the Remonstrants were grandstanding to get the opportunity to win over as many of the delegates as possible.[7] Even Miller, who was supportive of the decision of the synod, was dismayed at the way discussions were handled. He writes: "The language of the President [Bogerman] in dismissing[8] the Remonstrants was rough, and adapted to give pain. He pointedly charged them with fraudulent proceedings, with disingenuous acts, with falsehood, etc. For this language, however, he alone was responsible. It had not been dictated or authorized by the Synod. And a number of the members, we are assured, heard it with regret, and expressed their disapprobation of it."[9]

He continues: "It is probable that all impartial persons . . . will judge that some of these proceedings were by far too harsh and violent. To suppress the religious assemblies of the Remonstrants, by secular authority, and to banish their leaders from their country, were measures which we cannot, at this day, contemplate but with deep regret, as inconsistent with those rights of conscience, which we must regard as indefeasible."[10]

A sample of Bogerman's leadership is provided by Rogge: "It was decided [that the synod would] proceed without them. They [the Remonstrants] tried to bring about a reconciliation by offering to answer any questions submitted to them in writing, but the president rejected their proposal . . . They were finally asked if they would submit, and [they] answered decidedly, 'No.' Bogerman [the elected president, then] delivered a passionate speech, exclaiming, 'You have begun with lies and you end with lies.'"[11]

---

caused the latter ere long to lose his head. Maurice was opposed to the truce. Oldenbarneveldt, knowing his ulterior designs against the new-born liberties of Holland, promoted it in the face of storms that thickened around him from every side" (Brandt, *The Life of James Arminius*, 294).

7. Rogge, "Dort," 494, reports that "the Remonstrants (as the followers of Arminius were called) had selected sixteen clergymen and the Leyden professor Simon Episcopius to represent their position. It was their hope that they would be able to not only to explain their beliefs and document them with Scripture, but also explain how and why they disagreed with the position of the organizing members of the synod. They wished to specifically show why they felt some of the Calvinistic positions were untenable, especially the plight and destiny of the non-elect. The synod denied this request. Instead they were asked to give a written position of their understanding of the Five Articles and how their position differed from the Belgic Confession. Though they protested against this decision, they provided the synod delegates with both, but insisted they would not be involved in further deliberations without being able to debate and argue against the church's commonly held, Calvinistic doctrines. Their request was denied." (See also the reference below regarding "Bogerman's leadership" reported by Rogge.)

8. Professor Callie Coetze—North-West University mentor—made a helpful comment to the writer: "It is interesting that the decision that the Remonstrants should be dismissed if they continued with their obstructive behavior was taken by the States-General (civil authorities) quite a while before the dismissal really took place."

9. Miller, "Introductory Essay," 39.

10. Miller, "Introductory Essay," 41.

11. Rogge, "Dort," 494.

Despite these bitter interactions and accusations, at the synod's end the delegates unanimously both condemned the Remonstrants's positions and supported the final document, the *Canons of Dort.* Many Remonstrant pastors lost their churches and some were driven into exile.[12] Yet history afterward documents that the council's decision did not end the conflict, nor the persecutions (and martyrs!) on both sides.[13] And labels—like "Calvinism," "Arminianism," "Pelagianism," etc.—tossed around during that day live on, often then as today without careful definition and often as *ad hominem* epitaphs.

COMPARING THE REMONSTRANCE AND THE CANONS.

So, what caused such an uproar? Beyond the label, the following discussion will seek to summarize as accurately as possible both the key statements of both *The Remonstrance of 1610*[14] and the *Canons of Dort,* not only to carefully define the distinct doctrinal beliefs, but the arguments in support of each. One has to admit from the outset of this essay that the *Canons* is an excellently researched document and a remarkably valuable expression of doctrine. Any student of theology would find it a thorough expression of systematic theology. It is comprehensive though brief. This comparison/ contrast of the two would have been far more definitive if the Remonstrants's document had been more nuanced.

Perhaps it is fitting—before detailing the comparisons/contrasts—to say something about the word *Remonstrance.* It is a rather rare term in contemporary English, but it is actually a synonym of the word "Protestant" in the expression "Protestant Reformation." It denotes an expression or communication of opposition—a protestation—and, in the case under discussion, an opposition to the Dutch Calvinism of the late sixteenth century and early seventeenth. Like the "Protestants" who a century earlier were responding to the Roman Catholic Church, the "Remonstrants" felt that the Calvinism of their day was in error. How so? Though their basic concerns expressed as five articles were briefly considered earlier in the essay on Arminius, since they are very brief, they are reproduced in full below. The plan will be to look at what the Remonstrants stated as their position and then examine what they were resisting as seen in the highlights of the *Canons.*

1. **Article 1:** That God, by an eternal, unchangeable purpose in Jesus Christ his Son, before the foundation of the world, hath determined, out of the fallen, sinful race of men, to save in Christ, for Christ's sake, and through Christ, those who, through the grace of the Holy Ghost, shall believe on this his Son Jesus, and shall

12. Aloisi, "Understanding Arminius," 8.

13. Olson, *Arminian Theology,* 14.

14. Sometimes these are called *The Five Articles of Remonstrance* or *The Five Arminian Articles.* The text used comes from Bratcher, editor of *The Five Articles of the Remonstrants* (1610).

persevere in this faith and obedience of faith, through this grace, even to the end; and, on the other hand, to leave the incorrigible and unbelieving in sin and under wrath, and to condemn them as alienated from Christ, according to the word of the gospel in John 3:36: *He that believeth on the Son hath everlasting life: and he that believeth not the Son shall not see life; but wrath of God abideth on him,* and according to other passages of Scripture also.

These words were not hastily chosen. The Remonstrants make it clear that:

A. "Election" (the word is not used but is the meaning of "determined") was made on the basis of God's unchangeable purpose.

b. Election was made before the foundation of the world.

c. Election applies only to the saving of certain sinners.

d. Those saved owe their salvation to the grace of the Holy Spirit.

e. Election results in these certain sinners believing in Jesus.

f. Eternal salvation (perseverance) is based on grace.

G. The "non-elect" are the unbelieving, on whom God's wrath abides.

There are many details which are noted in the *Canons* which are not explicit in the above article. Both theologies note that salvation is by grace; that election occurred before the foundation of the world; that election relates to some sinners out of a corpus of people "equally lost;" and that election was based on God's good pleasure not on human merits. This agreement is apparent in the first fourteen articles of the "First Main point of Doctrine."[15] They differ in what the *Canons* goes on to declare: double election (predestination): "Not all people have been chosen . . . some . . . have been passed by in God's eternal election . . . concerning whom God . . . made the following decision: to leave them in the common misery . . . not to grant them saving faith and the grace of conversion; but finally to condemn and eternally punish them" (1.15). It is the words—*not to grant them saving faith and the grace of conversion*[16]—which the Remonstrants

---

15. The *Canons* document consists of five "Main Points" which correspond to and are a response to the five "Articles" of the Remonstrant document. Under each "Main Point" are numerous "Articles" which state or clarify that main point. Finally, at the end of each main point there is a short section entitled "Rejection of Errors," each section of which is identified with a Roman numeral. Quotations from the *Canons,* then, will be identified by the Main Point (1 = Main Point #1), the Article in that main point (15 = Article 15). For example: (1.15); and the Error as (Error 1).

16. Compare *Canons* 2.8: "It was the entirely free plan and very gracious will and intention of God the Father that the enlivening and saving effectiveness of his Son's costly death should work itself out in all his chosen ones, in order that *he might grant justifying faith to them only* and thereby lead them without fail to salvation. In other words, it was God's will that Christ through the blood of the cross . . . should effectively redeem from every people, tribe, nation, and language all those and *only those who were chosen from eternity to salvation and given to him by the Father*; that he should grant them faith" (author's *emphasis*).

found offensive and errant, because they argued that grace was given to all enabling anyone to believe. Yet they also maintained the ability to reject that grace (or not) and thus God's provision of forgiveness. Because of the *Canons's* statement on election (double predestination), critics often accused Calvinists that with such a belief human accountability was taken away. The accusation might—in the author's words—be put this way: "I cannot be acceptable. I am damned without even trying. How can I be blamed because God has rejected me, for what reason I will never know? I do not understand. Everyone stands self-condemned for his own sins. But God chooses some and rejects others. How can a person not feel he is unfair? And he—by rejecting me—has made me only to sin more and more. In what sense am I free? My destiny has already been determined before I was even born"![17] Perhaps this is the reason why the person(s) who authored the *Canons* added the assertion after the statement of double predestination: "And this is the decision of reprobation, which does not at all make God the author of sin [a blasphemous thought!]" (1.15). The implications this has on human freedom will be discussed in a chapter 12.

Though there may have been some who taught that God's election was based on "foreseen" faith (1. Error 5), this was not taught in the Remonstrants's document, and its conclusion makes it clear that—while election is of believers—their faith is the fruit of God's grace, grace given by the Holy Spirit. Grace stands opposite of human merit. This is even explicitly stated in the *Canons* (2.7): "But all who genuinely believe and are delivered and saved by Christ's death from their sins and from destruction receive this favor solely from God's grace—which he owes to no one—given to them in Christ from eternity."

2. **Article 2:** That, agreeably thereto, Jesus Christ, the Saviour of the world, died for all men and for every man, so that he has obtained for them all, by his death on the cross, redemption and the forgiveness of sins; yet that no one actually enjoys this forgiveness of sins except the believer according to the word of the Gospel of John 3:16: *God so love the world that he gave his only-begotten Son, that whosoever believeth in him should not perish, but have everlasting life.* And in 1 John 2:2: *And he is the propitiation for our sins; and not for ours only, but also for the sins of the whole world.*

These words explicitly state that Jesus's death paid the price for all sinners, not only for the elect, but also for those who ultimately would have as their

---

17. This hypothetical example is consistent with the conclusion to the *Canons*: "This teaching [of the Remonstrants] makes God the author of sin, unjust, a tyrant, and a hypocrite . . . This teaching means that God predestined and created, by the bare and unqualified choice of his will, without the least regard or consideration of any sin, the greatest part of the world to eternal condemnation; that in the same manner in which election is the source and cause of faith and good works, reprobation is the cause of unbelief and ungodliness; that many infant children of believers are snatched in their innocence from their mothers's breasts and cruelly cast into hell so that neither the blood of Christ nor their baptism nor the prayers of the church at their baptism can be of any use to them" (*Canons*, Conclusion).

destiny Hell. The *Canons* deny that Jesus died for *all* men, though they say this in no explicit words. They speak of his death as "of infinite value and worth, more than sufficient to atone for the sins of the whole world" (2.3). With this the "Arminian" article above would agree. To be sure, Jesus's death only effectively applies to believers, but the Remonstrants would insist that there is a difference between "Redemption Accomplished and Redemption Applied," to use the title of John Murray's book. The basic argument of the *Canons* is that to teach that the penalty was paid for all is to waste Jesus's death: "The Synod rejects the errors of those who teach that God the Father appointed his Son to death on the cross without a fixed and definite plan to save anyone by name, so that the necessity, usefulness, and worth of what Christ's death obtained could have stood intact and altogether perfect, complete and whole, even if the redemption that was obtained had never in actual fact been applied to any individual" (*Canons,* 2.Error 1). At best one must conclude that the *Canons* are a bit vague and never directly address this difference.[18]

3. **Article 3:** That man has not saving grace himself, nor of the energy of his free will, inasmuch as he, in the state of apostasy and sin, can of and by himself, neither think, will, nor do anything that is truly good (such as saving Faith eminently is); but that it is needful that he be born again of God in Christ through his Holy Spirit, and renewed in understanding, inclination, or will, and all his powers, in order that he may rightly understand, think, will, and effect what is truly good, according to the Word of Christ, John 15:5: *Without me ye can do nothing.*

4. **Article 4:** That this grace of God is the beginning, continuance, and accomplishment of all good, even to this extent, that the regenerate man himself, without prevenient or assisting, awaking, following and co-operative grace, can neither think, will, nor do good, nor withstand any temptations to evil; so that all good deeds or movements, that can be conceived, must be ascribed to the grace of God in Christ. But as respects the mode of the operation of this grace it is not irresistible, inasmuch as it is written concerning many, that they have resisted the Holy Ghost (Acts 7:51), and elsewhere in many places.

Because this is the or a most important element of the controversy, much more documentation will be given from the *Canons* so that the Calvinist's position can be carefully and accurately framed. Though Adam and Eve possessed libertarian freedom and were good from the hand of their Creator, all persons since then are in bondage and sinners under condemnation. All persons (including unregenerate sinners), however, still have some light: "There is, to be sure, a certain light of nature remaining in man after the fall, by virtue of which

---

18. One must add that the *Canons* in *this* article does not address it, but it is simply stated in Article 3.Error 5: [The Remonstrants teach that] "God, for his part, shows himself ready to reveal Christ to all people, since he provides to all, to a sufficient extent and in an effective manner, the means necessary for the revealing of Christ, for faith, and for repentance."

he retains some notions about God, natural things, and the difference between what is moral and immoral, and demonstrates a certain eagerness for virtue and for good outward behavior" (*Canons* 3.4). This is a very important statement because it implies that people can make some decisions freely for matters other than evil[19]—and thus have (at least) limited libertarian freedom—though this freedom never can lead to salvation: "This light of nature is far from enabling man to come to a saving knowledge of God and conversion to him" (*Canons* 3.4). This does not mean that the invitation (the "call") presented in the Gospel is not given to all men—it could be—but:

> The fact that many who are called through the ministry of the gospel do not come and are not brought to conversion must not be blamed on the gospel, nor on Christ, who is offered through the gospel, nor on God, who calls them through the gospel and even bestows various gifts on them, but on the people themselves who are called . . . The fact that others who are called through the ministry of the gospel do come and are brought to conversion must not be credited to man, as though one distinguishes himself by free choice from others who are furnished with equal or sufficient grace for faith and conversion (as the proud heresy of Pelagius maintains). No, it must be credited to God: just as from eternity he chose his own in Christ, so within time he effectively calls them, grants them faith and repentance, and, having rescued them from the dominion of darkness, brings them into the kingdom of his Son, in order that they may . . . boast not in themselves . . . But this certainly does not happen only by outward teaching, by moral persuasion, or by such a way of working that, after God has done his work, it remains in man's power whether or not to be reborn or converted. Rather, it is an entirely supernatural work . . . Faith is a gift of God, not in the sense that . . . bestows only the potential to believe, but then awaits assent—the act of believing—from man's choice; rather, it is a gift in the sense that he who works both willing and acting and, indeed, works all things in all people produces in man both the will to believe and the belief itself (*Canons* 3.9–14).

In short, according to Dort, faith is not a human-originated action, but is the result of God's work. To say it another way, in the *ordo salutis*, regeneration precedes faith and produces it. Explicitly, this is opposite of (as the Remonstrants put it) the grace that is given to all—the *"equal or sufficient grace for faith and conversion."*[20] In the "Error" section of this main section of the *Canons*, the writer(s) are more explicit. They reject those:

> Who teach that corrupt and natural man can make such good use of common grace (by which they mean the light of nature) or of the gifts remaining after

---

19. See also the section quoted below: "God . . . bestows various gifts on them."

20. See the previous definition and discussion of supralapsarianism and infralapsarianism in footnote #5. p.126.

the fall that he is able thereby gradually to obtain a greater grace—evangelical or saving grace—as well as salvation itself; and that in this way God, for his part, shows himself ready to reveal Christ to all people, since he provides to all, to a sufficient extent and in an effective manner, the means necessary for the revealing of Christ, for faith, and for repentance . . . Who teach . . . that even when God has accomplished all the works of grace which he uses for man's conversion, man nevertheless can, and in actual fact often does, so resist God and the Spirit in their intent and will to regenerate him, that man completely thwarts his own rebirth; and, indeed, that it remains in his own power whether or not to be reborn . . . Who teach that grace and free choice are concurrent partial causes which cooperate to initiate conversion, and that grace does not precede—in the order of causality—the effective influence of the will; that is to say, that God does not effectively help man's will to come to conversion before man's will itself motivates and determines itself (*Canons* 3.Errors 5, 8–9).

It is clearly evident that the *Canons* oppose a view that is not explicit in the Remonstrants's document, though such may have been the teaching which they accused the "Arminians" as holding. What the Remonstrants's document states is that a person cannot "*think, will or do anything*" that would lead to "*faith*." Only Holy Spirit-regeneration ("*born again*") can make such possible. Further, what is explicit in the Remonstrants's document—contrary to the *Canons*—is that such gifting, grace, Holy Spirit-enabling is not irresistible. It is sufficient—yes, a necessary enablement—for all to believe and receive God's pardon, and, thus, this grace—enabled-faith—can only be attributed to God, but this "sufficient" grace can be resisted and rejected (or not), and as a consequence such persons engaged in this eternal resistance are responsible for their own eternal condemnation.

It is important to note that if one possesses the ability to resist or not to resist, then one possesses libertarian freedom. Be that as it may, however, if one does not possess the libertarian freedom to resist or not to resist the Holy Spirit's grace, it does not logically entail that no one ever possesses the libertarian ability to choose among a range of options each of which is compatible with one's nature regarding matters that are not related to soteriological issues.

5. **Article 5:** That those who are incorporated into Christ by a true faith, and have thereby become partakers of his lifegiving Spirit, have thereby full power to strive against Satan, sin, the world, and their own flesh, and to win the victory; it being well understood that it is ever through the assisting grace of the Holy Ghost; and that Jesus Christ assists them through his Spirit in all temptations, extends to them his hand, and if only they are ready for the conflict, and desire his help, and are not inactive, keeps them from falling, so that they, by no craft or power of Satan, can be misled nor plucked out of Christ's hands, according to the Word of Christ, John 10:28: "Neither shall any man pluck them out of my hand." But whether they are capable, through negligence, of forsaking again the first

beginnings of their life in Christ (Heb 3:6, 14; 2 Pet 1:10; Jude 3; 1 Tim 1:19; Heb 11:13), of again returning to this present evil world, of turning away from the holy doctrine which was delivered to them, of losing a good conscience, of becoming void of grace, that must be more particularly determined out of the Holy Scripture, before we ourselves can teach it with full persuasion of our minds.

It is important to note that what is most relevant in this final article is the last sentence. The Remonstrants are on record that they do not have a position on what is called "eternal security" and feel it demands more study on their part *before we ourselves can teach it with full persuasion of our minds.* Undoubtedly, some "Arminians" did conclude that people could later renounce or lose their faith, just as many do today. And one must add, the arguments in the *Canons* on this subject are worthy of careful study. It is possible for a Remonstrant and a Calvinist to be united on this point!

As the above discussion shows, the focus of the Remonstrants's document and the *Canons* was chiefly on election, the provision Jesus's death made for the forgiveness of the world's people, and the nature of the grace that moves a person to faith. The Remonstrants repudiated double predestination, while affirming the election of "those who would believe." Admittedly, these words are ambiguous, an insufficient explanation of Remonstrant understanding, and subject to misunderstanding. Is election based on foreseen faith—as they were accused of teaching—or were they merely saying that the elect would be grace-enabled to believe? Their position on grace seems to imply the second, especially since they emphatically state that God's grace is not merited, and that saving faith is impossible to come from human effort. About these issues the debate continues.

Moreover, and most importantly (with the focus of this essay in mind), notably absent is any clear discussion of the human freedom and the role it plays in the individual's salvation. But as noted earlier, the *Canons* document (3.4) does touch on it as it relates to non-salvific matters. Because the "light of God" remains in fallen man and to him God has given gifts, he can freely make choices among those matters and choices that many would deem "good," because they are consistent with the light of God.[21] As will be seen later, this is quite relevant to the thesis of this book.

Thus, the *Canons of Dort* (like Luther and Calvin) do not oppose the idea of *limited* libertarian freedom—the ability to choose among a range of options each compatible with one's nature—even if one's nature does not provide a "range of options" from which to choose regarding issues pertaining to salvation.

---

21. See Calvin's discussion above of "light."

11

A survey of human freedom during the Reformation and post-Reformation periods

Jonathan Edwards (AD 1703–1758)

JONATHAN EDWARDS, WHO HAS been called "the greatest theologian America has produced,"[1] comes from a family with remarkable academic and professional credentials. His father—Timothy Edwards—graduated with degrees from Harvard (AD 1691 and 1694) and was ordained (1694) as the pastor of the Congregational Church of Windsor Farms and served that same church for sixty-three years! When a person adds that during those years of service there were "four or five outpourings of the Spirit" (his son's words!),[2] one has a greater appreciation of the man and of the impact he had on his son. Jonathan's mother—Esther Edwards—was the daughter of the notable pastor Solomon Stoddard[3] who served the Congregational Church of Northampton, Massachusetts, for fifty-seven years. Jonathan was one of their eleven children. He was "home schooled," and "began the study of Latin at the age of six, and before he was thirteen had acquired a good knowledge of Latin, Greek, and Hebrew . . . When he was about nine, he wrote an interesting letter on materialism and when he was about twelve, he wrote some remarkable papers on questions of natural philosophy. One month before he was thirteen, he entered Yale College and was graduated, with the highest honors of his class, in AD 1720.[4]

---

1. Foster, "Edwards," 80.

2. Marsden, *Jonathan Edwards*, 25.

3. Marsden, *Jonathan Edwards*, 11, calls Stoddard "the most renowned man in the promising valley of the Connecticut River." Jonathan Edwards in a letter to Thomas Gillespie noted that the people of his church "regarded Stoddard 'almost as a sort of deity.'" (Marsden, *Jonathan Edwards*, 114).

4. Foster, "Edwards," 81.

He stayed at Yale three more years and received a degree in divinity.[5] Four years later—after a brief pastorate and being a tutor at Yale—he became an assistant pastor with his grandfather (Stoddard). That same year (AD 1727) he married Sarah Pierpont, the daughter of James Pierpont Sr., who was the founder of Yale. She was the mother of his eleven children. Edwards served his grandfather's church for twenty-three years, both as an assistant and then senior pastor, until he was fired for disagreeing with the church about serving communion to unbelievers.[6] During this time he wrote many books and pamphlets.[7] In AD 1757 he became president of Princeton, but died the following year at the young age of fifty-four due to complications of a small pox vaccination.

Though his life was cut short, Edwards's influence must not be measured alone by his voluminous writings, nor from his impact as a pastor and missionary to the Housatonic Indians, but also by the legacy of the family which followed after him. As Marsden finishes his fine biography of him, he notes that "the Edwards's family . . . produced scores of clergymen, thirteen presidents of institutions of higher learning, sixty-five professors, and many other persons of notable achievements."[8]

EDWARDS ON "DOUBLE PREDESTINATION."

Edwards is accurately described today as a strict Calvinist, but in his growing up years he found its teaching of double predestination a "horrific doctrine." In his *Personal Narrative* (AD 1740)[9] he wrote: "From my childhood up, my mind had been wont to be full of objections against the doctrine of God's sovereignty, in choosing whom he would to eternal life, and rejecting whom he pleased; leaving them eternally to perish, and be everlastingly tormented in hell. It used to appear like a horrible doctrine to me. But I remember the time very well, when I seemed to be convinced, and fully satisfied, as to this sovereignty of God, and his justice in thus eternally disposing of men, according to his sovereign pleasure. But never could give an account, how, or by what means, I was thus convinced."[10]

---

5. Schafer, "Jonathan Edwards."

6. He disagreed with his grandfather's practice, but it should be noted that this disagreement was not what Scripture taught about an unbeliever's partaking of the communion elements in an "unworthy" manner, but about policy. Stoddard felt that it was not the church's responsibility to determine who was regenerate. Instead each person was to make his or her own decision and choose to partake or not to do so (Marsden, *Jonathan Edwards*, 30–32 and 122–23).

7. Most of his writings—which to date number seventy-two volumes!—can be found in digital format at the Edwards Center at Yale University.

8. Marsden, *Jonathan Edwards*, 500–501.

9. This is an approximate date given by Marsden, *Jonathan Edwards*, 517, n. 2: "Edwards's narrative was apparently written for the edification of one of his protégés, perhaps his future son-in-law Aaron Burr."

10. Edwards, "Personal Narrative."

Despite his admission of not knowing what influenced the change, history shows that Edwards's education was occurring during a theologically changing time. Those who held ties both to England and to the Anglican tradition were often associated with Arminian views, which Edwards and his fellow reformed brothers felt was incompatible with Scripture.[11] The issue then has changed little to this day. Calvinists accused Arminians of importing into the gospel "works salvation" because the latter insist on the place a person's decision plays in his salvation instead of declaring that a person's salvation is solely dependent on God's revelation and grace. Whether or not that was the theological controversy that led him back to a strict Calvinism, one may never know. (New insights may arise as more Edwardian research occurs). But it can be said with certainty that the conflict with Arminianism was a significant factor because of the emphasis he gives in arguing against it in his seminal work *The Freedom of the Will* (FOTW), to which attention now turns.

EDWARDS ON THE FREEDOM OF THE WILL (FOTW).

Having said that Arminianism—in name at least—figures prominently in Edwards's argumentation throughout FOTW, it is important to add from the outset that it is not Arminianism in its classical, soteriological sense that is the subject. Rather, Edwards's work is a philosophical treatise on the nature of human freedom. From the broader perspective of theological history—versus the controversy between the Arminian-bent of Anglican pastors or leaders and Edwards and Calvinists in his day—Edwards stood opposite of Aquinas's view of human freedom, or (to take a contemporary) opposite of open theist Clark Pinnock. Since the latter defines—in terms without using philosophical lingo—the sort of libertarian freedom which is the template against which Edwards will spend his book seeking to refute, his definition is worth expressing as a preface to this essay:

> What I call "real freedom" is also called libertarian or contra-causal freedom. It views a free action as one in which a person is free to perform an action or refrain from performing it and is not completely determined in the matter by prior forces—nature, nurture or even God. Libertarian freedom recognizes the power of contrary choice. One acts freely in a situation if, and only if, one could have done otherwise. Free choices are choices that are not causally determined by conditions preceding them. It is the freedom of self-determination, in which the various motives and influences informing the choice are not the sufficient cause of the choice itself. The person makes the choice in a self-determined way. A person has options and there are different factors influencing us in deciding among them but the decision one takes involves making one of the reasons one's own, which is anything but random.[12]

11. Marsden, *Jonathan Edwards*, 86–87; 137–39.
12. Pinnock et al., *Openness*, 127.

Edwards on the definition of the "Will."

With that as a background of the issue which Edwards is addressing, Edwards begins his discussion ("Part One" is devoted to definition) by noting that there would be little misunderstanding about what is the Will (he capitalizes the word) if it were not for philosophers![13] What is the Will? It is "that by which the soul either chooses or refuses . . . So that by whatever names we call the act of the Will, choosing, refusing, approving, disapproving, liking, disliking, embracing, rejecting, determining, directing, commanding, forbidding, inclining, or being averse, being pleased or displeased with; all may be reduced to this of choosing."[14]

Though Locke was one of his favorite writers,[15] Edwards disagreed with his thinking that willing is "preferring" because a person could prefer something which could not even have been an option at the given time. His example is that a person may prefer flying versus walking to a certain destination, but the former is not possible. (There were no airplanes in his day, so flying meant having some sort of wings). Thus, Will and "desire" are not identical for the same reason, but in the end a person wills what he desires, "and he does not will a thing, and desire the contrary, in any particular."[16]

But this definition leaves unaddressed the debate about what "determines" the Will. Therefore, Edwards sets forth his position by stating that it is a person's "motive" which determines the Will's decision, that motive being what "moves, excites, and invites the mind to volition."[17] There may be many motives that are active,[18] but it is the "strongest motive" which determines the decision/action. This "strongest motive" Edwards also calls the "greatest apparent good," that is, what is most "agreeable or pleasing to the mind."[19] The word "apparent" in that definition is an important adjective because it denotes what is immediately before the person, not something which

---

13. All references to this work will be from Edwards, *Freedom of the Will* (1754) and will be denoted with page numbers from the CCEL edition.

14. Edwards, *Freedom of the Will*, 3.

15. Marsden, *Jonathan Edwards*, 62.

16. Edwards, *Freedom of the Will*, 4. Edwards in this discussion appears to reflect a kinship (influence) from Aquinas, who speaks of these influences (motives) as "appetites," and Edwards himself may show this by using that very word (*Freedom of the Will*, 10). Aquinas speaks of the "natural" appetite that is instinctive in animals (including human beings). But unlike the animals, the person's reason weighs all influences outside and inside of him (e.g., his emotions) and works in conjunction with the will, the latter faculty then issuing the choice or decision. Edwards seems to attempt to distinguish the reason from these "motives."

17. Edwards, *Freedom of the Will*, 6.

18. There may be other motives that are relevant to the decision, but the Will acts in a given moment on only the motives which the person is conscious of at the time. See Edwards's discussion (Edwards, *Freedom of the Will*, 6–8).

19. Edwards, *Freedom of the Will*, 7.

at other times or in other circumstances might be deemed by the same person the greatest good.[20] Good or agreeable objects have several characteristics:

1. Beauty

2. Pleasure in obtaining the object or resulting in having obtained it.

3. What is most available at the time versus what is of necessity delayed in its effects. But Edwards also acknowledges that the opposite certainly can be true. For example, infidelity that is presently available can be incredibly strong, but reflecting on the long-term (future) consequences can lead a person to resist the temptation.[21]

4. A pleasure more certain to occur.

5. Thinking that has been influenced by education, custom or the state of mind at the time, that is, a person's mood or loss of sleep.[22]

The strength of these characteristics is shaped by habits,[23] that is, how they have influenced the Will in the past.[24]

Edwards on the definition of the "necessity."

If the term "*Will*" is confusing, Edwards would also say that "*necessity*" and similar terms—*impossible, unable, irresistible*—are also confusing because of the way they are used by philosophers. In common parlance, such terms are relative, that is, they are used in a subjective sense because they denote a person's present or future perceived ("supposed" is Edwards's term)[25] circumstances, which might be inaccurate. When philosophers use these terms—including the word "*contingent*"—they do not use them to refer to a person's subjective perception, but to the necessity which resides in the object itself: "red" cannot be "not red;" 2 + 2 must be 4; etc.[26] Another example is

20. Edwards's example is of the alcoholic who often being drunk knows sobriety is the best choice, but when the bottle is on the table in front of him drinks because it is his compelling desire (Edwards, *Freedom of the Will*, 8). Alternatively, he may find not drinking is the strongest because he remembers the agony of detoxing or the harm he inflicted on his family or others.

21. A question may be raised, "Does a person have the ability to reflect or not reflect on long-term future consequences"? If so, would this not provide elbow room for limited libertarian freedom on Edwards's view?

22. Edwards, *Freedom of the Will*, 9–10. One might think of the alcoholic who has a bottle in front of him when his AA buddy walks in the door. Suddenly, his "strongest" desire changes! That desire then might be not to disappoint his friend or the embarrassment it might bring. But the critic might ask, "Has this changed his 'strongest' desire? Might it not indicate merely that a determiner outside of himself has been introduced to the occasion"? Does this raise questions about Edwards's definition?

23. "Habits" is a word Aquinas also used. See chapter 5.

24. Edwards, *Freedom of the Will*, 6.

25. Edwards, *Freedom of the Will*, 13–14.

26. Edwards, *Freedom of the Will*, 14.

that necessary things are things which have already come to pass, because it cannot be that they have not come to pass.[27] Though Edwards does not use the term "tautology," this might be another example: Red is red.

In the same way one should understand the terms "moral" necessity and "natural" necessity. The former is based on perceived, subjective circumstances, while the latter is most accurately used to denote what absolutely will be done because of the nature of the case. Of course, these two approach equivalency when the morality of the person is strong because of established patterns ("habits") of moral decisions. Edwards explains: "We are said to be naturally unable to do a thing, when we cannot do it if we will, because what is most commonly called nature does not allow of it,[28] or because of some impeding defect or obstacle that is extrinsic to the Will . . . Moral Inability consists not in any of these things; but either in the want of inclination; or the strength of a contrary inclination; or the want of sufficient motives in view, to induce and excite the act of the Will, or the strength of apparent motives to the contrary."[29]

Examples of "moral inability" (according to Edwards) are a virtuous woman prostituting herself, a child who adores her parents killing them,[30] a drunkard unable to resist a drink, etc.[31]

Edwards: What human freedom is not.

All this discussion leads Edwards to define and reject a concept of freedom which he associates with "Arminians, Pelagians, and others who oppose the Calvinists,"[32] whom he says believe that freedom consists of the following:

> These several things belong to their notion of Liberty. 1. That it consists in a self-determining power in the Will, or a certain sovereignty the Will has over itself, and its own acts, whereby it determines its own volitions; so as not to be dependent, in its determinations, on any cause without itself, nor determined by anything prior to its own acts. 2. Indifference belongs to Liberty in their notion of it, or that the mind, previous to the act of volition, be in *equilibrio*. 3. Contingence is another thing that belongs and is essential to it; not in the common acceptation of the word, as that has been already explained, but as opposed to all necessity, or any fixed and certain connexion with some previous ground or reason of its existence. They suppose the essence of Liberty so much to consist in these things, that unless the will of man be free in this

27. Edwards, *Freedom of the Will*, 15.

28. In this book the author often refers to this when the expression "consistent and compatible with one's nature." See a fuller explanation in chapter 12.

29. Edwards, *Freedom of the Will*, 20.

30. Maybe an example otherwise would be a Muslim honor killing, despite familial love.

31. Edwards, *Freedom of the Will*, 21.

32. Edwards, *Freedom of the Will*, 24.

sense, he has no real freedom, how much soever, he may be at Liberty to act according to his will.[33]

Whether Edwards is accurate in his assessment of what these designated parties believe is not the concern here. But what he is arguing *against* is that the will as an independent agent can only be "free" if nothing controls, compels its decision. Such a view of the Will, Edwards says, is "nonsense."[34] The essence of his argument is that there are factors which approximate determinism, that is, which determine a person's choices. The most obvious and prominent one of these "determiners" is "habit." People become who and what they are by the decisions they make and have made. As someone has put it, "We make our decisions and then our decisions turn around and make us."[35] In other words, there are things which "constrain" the will and others which "restrain" it. If so—and Edwards argues the same[36]—then there is no such thing as absolute "freedom of the will" in the sense that is supposedly advocated by Arminians, Pelagians, etc.

"The Will cannot will itself."

Just how strict Edwards is in his concept of "determinism" is fleshed out in Part 2 of his treatise. The Will cannot will (determine) itself because:

1. Reason #1: *It is against the law of cause and effect.*

   Edwards expresses his argument this way:

   > Every free act of choice is determined by a preceding act of choice, choosing that act . . . But if that first volition is not determined by any preceding act of the Will, then that act is not determined by the Will, and so is not free in the Arminian notion of freedom, which consists in the Will's self-determination[37] . . . The Arminian notion of freedom [is] that the Will influences, orders, and determines itself thus to act . . . To say, it is caused, influenced, and determined by something, and yet not determined by anything antecedent, either in order of time or nature, is a contradiction[38] . . . Nothing ever comes to pass without a Cause[39] . . . Whatsoever begins to be, which before was not, must have a Cause why it then begins to exist, seems to be the first dictate of the common and natural sense which God hath implanted in the minds of all mankind, and

---

33. Edwards, *Freedom of the Will,* 24.

34. Edwards, *Freedom of the Will,* 23.

35. These words are from an address at a conference of ministers the writer attended. They are akin to indirect, doxastic voluntarism which will be discussed in chapter 12.

36. Edwards, *Freedom of the Will,* 23–25.

37. Edwards, *Freedom of the Will,* 28.

38. Edwards, *Freedom of the Will,* 32.

39. Edwards, *Freedom of the Will,* 34.

the main foundation of *all our reasonings* about the existence of things, past, present, or to come.[40]

In other words, if the Will is separate from (prior to) what is willed—if there is a distinction between the Cause (willing) and the effect (the choice made)—then there were also influences before the Will made that decision.[41]

2. Reason #2: *The argument is incoherent which suggests that when there are two or more* equal *options, there is no compelling reason/influence that determines one choice or another, and in such a case there is absolute freedom.*

This is an interesting argument, and admittedly it appears to be strong at face value. Edwards quotes from Whitby to illustrate:

> That there are many instances, wherein the Will is determined neither by present uneasiness, nor by the greatest apparent good, nor by the last dictate of the understanding, nor by anything else, but merely by itself, as a sovereign self-determining power of the soul; and that the soul does not will this or that action, in some cases, by any other influence but because it will. Thus, says he, I can turn my face to the south, or the north; I can point with my finger upward, or downward.—And thus, in some cases, the Will determines itself in a very sovereign manner, because it will, without a reason borrowed from the understanding: and hereby it discovers its own perfect power of choice, rising from within itself, and free from all influence or restraint of any kind.[42]

But, Edwards argues, this provides no support for uncaused, human freedom because the choice made among the alternatives is a preference. Therefore, a "preference" cannot be at the same time "not a preference."[43] In Edwards's words: The very act of choosing one thing rather than another, is preferring that thing, and that is setting a higher value on that thing[44] . . . That which the Will prefers, to that, all things considered, it preponderates and inclines[45] . . . If Indifference be essential to liberty, it must be perfect Indifference; and that so far as the Will is destitute of this, so far is it destitute of that freedom by which it is in a capacity of being its own determiner."[46]

To say it simply, if the Will would stay in a state of indifference, it would never act![47]

---

40. Edwards, *Freedom of the Will*, 35, author's *emphasis*.

41. See also Edwards, *Freedom of the Will*, 42–43.

42. Edwards, *Freedom of the Will*, 45.

43. Edwards, *Freedom of the Will*, 45.

44. Edwards, *Freedom of the Will*, 46.

45. Edwards, *Freedom of the Will*, 51.

46. Edwards, *Freedom of the Will*, 52.

47. Edwards, *Freedom of the Will*, 54. This argument is weak at the least, and fallacious at the worst. Consider the illustration which Edwards uses (Edwards, *Freedom of the Will*, 47–52). A person has the opportunity to put his finger on a square on a chessboard. There are sixty-four possible, equal choices. He cares less which he will choose. He's "indifferent" to which one. Of course, he might prefer one which is

3. Reason #3: *Whitby in his Discourses on the Five Points argues unreasonably when he insists that there is no determiner of the will but that decisions—without outside, determining influences—are forged by an internal interaction of the Understanding and the Will.*[48]

In the context, this is an Arminian argument against "irresistible grace."[49] But Edwards again insists that arguing this way overlooks the plain fact that the Understanding does not exist in a vacuum. It is shaped by past decisions which the Understanding and Will have made in conjunction with each other. To deny this is to conclude that "In vain are all instructions, counsels, invitations, expostulations, and all arguments and persuasives whatsoever . . . If, after all, the will must be self-determined, and independent on the Understanding, to what purpose are things thus represented to the Understanding, in order to determine the choice?"[50]

4. Reason #4: *Chubbs in his treatise* Collection of Tracts on Various Subjects, *errs in his proposal that, while the will responds to "Motives" (i.e., influences, inducements, that which excites or invite decisions or actions), it* freely *considers which one it will yield to or reject.*[51]

Edwards quotes Chubbs as saying: "Every man is at liberty to act, or refrain from acting, agreeably with, or contrary to, what each of these motives, considered singly, would excite him to. Man has power, and is as much at liberty, to reject the Motive that does prevail, as he has power, and is at liberty, to reject those Motives that do not . . . In order to constitute a moral agent, it is necessary, that he should have power to act, or to refrain from acting, upon such moral motives, as he pleases."[52]

But, Edwards argues, though a person may reject one motive and then select another, still those decisions are influenced by the motives. To deny this causal connection is an explicit "contradiction": "If the mind, in willing after the manner it does, is excited by no motive or inducement, then it has no end which it proposes to itself, or pursues in so doing; it *aims* at nothing, and seeks nothing. And if it seeks nothing, then it does not go after anything, or exert any inclination or preference towards anything."[53]

---

close to him, or one which does not have a pawn on it. But isn't it also conceivable that he might just close his eyes and put his finger "indifferently," blindly on whatever square it falls on? Moreover, what if the person is equally indifferent between acting and not acting? Now, the person must make a free choice between the alternative options of acting or not acting. Perhaps God provides a great example of considering two "equally good" options: to create or not to create. See more discussion on this in chapters 15 and 16.

48. Whitby, who is referenced by Edwards, seems to agree with how Aquinas argued. See chapter 5.

49. Edwards, *Freedom of the Will*, 62.

50. Edwards, *Freedom of the Will*, 65.

51. Edwards, *Freedom of the Will*, 66–74.

52. Edwards, *Freedom of the Will*, 67. This appears to be or is a good definition of what the writer of this book calls "libertarian free will."

53. Edwards, *Freedom of the Will*, 66. It is interesting to note that Edwards uses the phrase "it aims at nothing." "Aiming" will become problematic for Edwards—if his views are applied universally. See discussion in chapter 12.

Chubbs also denies Edwards's argument that choices are (always?) made based on the "strongest Motive." Perhaps such a theorem is true in the physical world, but not in moral (or rational?) decision-making. But Edwards responds by noting that this still avoids the fact that the decision made—whether it be in response to a stronger motive or weaker one—nevertheless flows from past (free?) decisions and thus is still determined. It is, therefore, inconsistent to speak of free acts that follow from other free acts and not also to conclude that these "free" acts do not influence future "free" acts: "If Motives excite the Will, they move it; and yet he says, it is absurd to say, the Will is moved by motives. And again, if language is of any significance at all, if Motives excite volition, then they are the cause of its being excited; and to cause volition to be excited, is to cause it to be put forth or excited."[54] Edwards seems correct; if decisions and actions always have Motives, the law of cause and effect still prevails. No person is totally free in choosing.

Edwards reinforces his basic argument with a lengthy treatment of God's foreknowledge. More than other philosophical arguments, God's foreknowledge to Edwards shows the absolute determinedness of all of life: "If there be any such thing as a divine Foreknowledge of the volitions of free agents, that Foreknowledge, by the supposition is a thing which already has, and long ago had existence; and so, now its existence is necessary; it is now utterly impossible to be otherwise, than that this Foreknowledge should be or should have been."[55]

The knowledge of human beings can increase with further learning. God, however, does not learn over time.[56] He simply knows everything logically prior to His creative decree and time itself.[57] But Whitby argues for human freedom on the analogy of human foreknowledge: a person may "know" what another person may do, but such knowledge in no way determines what he will do. Likewise, he says, just because God "foreknows" does not mean that a person necessarily will do it. This is a blunder, Edwards rightly argues. Human knowledge is not infallible; a person can err. God's knowledge, however, is not fallible. It is always perfect.[58]

Edwards seals his argument and his book by defining God's sovereignty over the world he created, over all his creatures, and over all that happens:

> The following things belong to the sovereignty of God: viz. (1.) Supreme, universal, and infinite power: whereby he is able to do what he pleases, without control, without any confinement of that power, without any subjection, in the least measure, to any other power; and so without any hindrance or restraint . . . It is the glory and greatness of the Divine Sovereign, that God's will is

54. Edwards, *Freedom of the Will,* 74.

55. Edwards, *Freedom of the Will,* 90.

56. Edwards, *Freedom of the Will,* 93.

57. See Augustine's discussion of foreknowledge (page 42 above) and Craig's discussion on "necessity" (footnote #9, p.50) and foreknowledge (Craig, *Only Wise God,* 72–74).

58. Edwards, *Freedom of the Will,* 94–95.

determined by his own infinite, all-sufficient wisdom in everything; and in nothing at all is either directed by any inferior wisdom, or by no wisdom; whereby it would become senseless arbitrariness, determining and acting without reason, design, or end.[59]

In brief, Edwards's treatise argues philosophically and theologically that there is no sense in which a person's will is totally free. Whatever choices are made are predicated by past decisions and influences, not the least of which is the influence of the Sovereign Lord.

CONCLUSION.

With this discussion of Edwards, the survey of prominent theologians and philosophers concludes, though—of course—others have made contributions to the subject of human freedom. The individuals which have been cited here, however, are adequate to show how diverse are their approaches even in their presentations and interaction of biblical exegesis and theological argumentation. Although there is much disagreement among the theologians surveyed, each of them—except for Edwards—seems to occasionally affirm some level of libertarian freedom limited to some things, some of the time.

This survey also has raised a number of questions: Whose view is most believable? Moreover, do people have a choice as to what and whom they should believe? Can a person choose his/her beliefs—any of them? The discussion which will now follow in the subsequent chapter will reflect the author's dependence on or disagreement with these great thinkers.

---

59. Edwards, *Freedom of the Will*, 179–80. This is an interesting statement that could easily fit with Molina's middle knowledge.

12

Philosophical arguments for libertarian freedom

WHEN ONE USES THE term "human freedom" or "free will," it is important to know in what sense the term is being used. As noted earlier, neither Calvin, Luther nor Edwards liked the term "free will" because they believed it was prone to being misunderstood. Furthermore, as we saw in the brief historical survey of prominent theologians over the centuries from Pelagius to Jonathan Edwards, there is a wide diversity of meaning given to the term:

- **Augustine:** People have freedom of choices in areas that are not related to salvation. However, when it comes to salvation, people are slaves to sin and cannot respond to God apart from the irresistible grace given by God, a grace given to the elect only.

- **Pelagius:** People are free and, therefore, accountable for their choices, and they can come to God without being prompted by him to do so, and some can live without sinning because there is no such thing as "original sin."

- **Aquinas:** There are no external things, such as persons or influences, that compel one to choose something. An individual makes his decisions (to choose or not to choose) through an internal interaction of emotions, thinking and will. But salvation is possible only by God's grace. He affirms a person's ability to choose among a range of options, each compatible with his nature.

- **Erasmus:** People are free and, thus, they are responsible for their choices, both in regard to non-soteriological and soteriological matters.

- **Luther:** A person's will is in bondage to sin and they cannot, without the grace of God, respond to the Gospel. However, apart from salvation-related issues, people can choose freely. Melanchthon held the same views.

- **Calvin:** As Luther believed, people cannot respond to the Gospel without God's grace. However, there are "earthly matters" (i.e., matters not related to salvation) about which people can make free decisions.

- **Arminius:** All people receive grace that enables them to respond to the Gospel. However, this grace does not compel one to accept salvation; one can respond to God's grace or reject it. Those who respond to God's grace are then given regenerating grace.

- **Synod of Dort:** The sovereignty of God over the salvation of man is understood in terms of a strict determinism. Although Dort primarily objects to Arminianism, their approach is essentially focused on soteriological determinism. Thus, limited libertarian freedom is left as an open question.

- **Edwards:** Human free will does not exist; everything, soteriological and otherwise, is directed by, and has a cause and effect under, the hand of God.

DEFINITION OF LIBERTARIAN FREE WILL.

The philosophical use of the term "libertarian free will" is often not distinguished from its soteriological application. If one is not careful, this may (often does) lead to misunderstandings. Therefore, at the outset it is important to define "libertarianism" and/or "libertarian free will," against which other views will be contrasted, compared, and evaluated.

Libertarianism is often described as the view (1) that free will is incompatible with determinism (the view that past events *necessarily* entail subsequent events) and (2) that some of our actions are free. It is important to note that libertarianism does not require that *all* of one's actions be free, nor does it require that *every* human being possess free will as there could be persons who lack free will, at least for some time (such as infants or those in a coma). Libertarianism simply says that some of the actions of some (or most) human beings are free. The term "action" in the phrase "free action," as Stratton and Erasmus[1] note, may refer to either a physical action, such as raising one's hand to vote, and/or a mental action, such as willing or trying to raise one's hand to vote (even if actually raising one's hand is physically impossible). Hence, if a person's hand is tightly chained to an armrest and cannot be raised, and if he wills or tries to raise his hand, then he is still performing a free action (even if the physical act cannot actually be performed).

Libertarianism, as defined above, is a broad view that covers a family of views. Although libertarians agree that at least one person has free will and that this fact is incompatible with exhaustive determinism, they disagree on what free will is and why it is incompatible with determinism. Nevertheless, most libertarians agree (or

1. Stratton and Erasmus, "Mere Molinism," 19.

the most common version of libertarianism affirms) that an agent's action is *free* if the agent is ultimately responsible for the action. This simply means that the agent is not causally determined via an external source (something other than the thing the self refers to as "I") to do what he chooses; the agent is the source.[2] Indeed, if one possesses libertarian freedom, then one seems to possess "self-control" (Prov 25:28; Gal 5:22–23; Tit 1:8; 2:1–12).

However, the version of libertarianism adopted here affirms that an agent possesses libertarian freedom if and only if the agent performs, has performed, or can perform a free action. This implies that a person possesses libertarian freedom if he, at some time, is not causally determined to do what he chooses, and/or has the ability to genuinely choose among a range of alternative options, each of which is consistent and compatible with his nature.[3] Libertarianism, so defined, is most likely what most people think of when they use the term "freedom." Indeed, all of the theologians surveyed in the previous chapters (apart from Edwards[4]) could easily agree on this definition of libertarianism and affirm that humans possess it.

Since the debate about human freedom is typically focused on the debate between compatibilism and libertarianism, the definition of libertarian freedom here allows compatibilists and libertarians to get on the same page and engage in rational discourse. This is the case because both views affirm that choices incompatible with one's nature cannot be chosen. Indeed, given the above definition of libertarianism, both compatibilists and libertarians might affirm that some form of libertarian freedom at least occasionally corresponds to reality. However, it is at this point that the debate moves to the issue about the *degree of freedom* to choose, that is to say, the conversation moves to the issue about how one's range of alternatives from which to choose is, or could be, causally determined to increase or decrease. Nevertheless, a range of genuine choice options remains.

COMPATIBILISM.

Speaking of "compatibilism"—or "compatibilistic freedom"—begs for that term to be defined as well, especially since sixty percent of philosophers accept or lean toward that view.[5] The *Stanford Encyclopedia of Philosophy* defines it this way: "Compatibil-

2. Timpe, "Free Will," discusses the sourcehood model of libertarianism, which implies that the ability to do otherwise is not necessary for libertarian freedom. As long as the agent is not causally determined and the agent is the source of a thought or action, then the agent is free in the libertarian sense. See chapter 8 and footnote #29, p.118, for Timpe's actual words on source incompatibilism.

3. MacGregor, *Luis de Molina*, 50.

4. Edwards might agree with this definition, but he, however, would appear to be the only one consistently affirming exhaustive determinism.

5. According to a poll taken by PhilPapers Surveys, only about fourteen percent of professional philosophers accept or lean toward libertarian concepts of freedom. About twelve percent accept or lean toward exhaustive determinism. Roughly sixty percent seem to accept or lean toward the

ism is the thesis that free will is compatible with determinism. Because free will is typically taken to be a necessary condition of moral responsibility, compatibilism is sometimes expressed as a thesis about the compatibility between moral responsibility and determinism."[6]

This definition stands in contrast to the position defined above as libertarian freedom, which affirms that a person possesses "freedom of moral and rational responsibility"[7] and "that the freedom necessary for responsible action is not compatible with determinism."[8] Perhaps Guillame Bignon, the French philosopher and leading advocate of compatibilism today, can frame the conflict. He is an ardent Calvinist who believes Calvinism entails exhaustive divine determinism (EDD)—that is, that God, in one way or another, causally determines all things. Some Calvinists disagree and simply focus on TULIP in a soteriological context. But with his deterministic views in mind, Bignon faults many of his peers who also affirm EDD: "They respond with embarrassment, start confessing their rational limitations, argue for mystery in the face of the unknown, and some get dangerously close to admitting irrationality."[9] In fact, naming examples, he says that "Edwin Palmer[10]unduly shoots himself in the foot: 'The Calvinist freely admits that his position is illogical, ridiculous, nonsensical, and foolish.'"[11] Bignon continues: "We can appreciate a refreshing Calvinist epistemic humility, but let us not confuse ourselves about the logical problems posed . . . Calvinists must take a deep breath, relax, and deal with the arguments."[12] Yet Bignon concludes that "The burden of proof is still firmly on the shoulders of the incompatibilist [including the libertarian], and we are still looking for an argument to support the incompatibilist thesis."[13]

The remainder of this chapter takes up Bignon's challenge and endeavors to provide multiple arguments against determinism on the one hand and those supporting libertarian freedom on the other. The aim, then, is not merely to argue against the thesis of compatibilism, but to demonstrate that this thesis does not actually correspond to reality, and thus, compatibilism does not always explain the way things are. For the purposes of this chapter, compatibilism will entail the thesis that exhaustive

---

idea that compatibilism (which entails determinism) corresponds to reality. This means that roughly seventy-two percent of professional philosophers think determinism is true. (See further discussion later in chapter 16). Fifteen percent are "other." This is puzzling because either libertarian freedom exists or it does not exist. The law of the excluded middle demands this. See https://philpapers.org/surveys/results.pl.

6. McKenna and Coates, "Compatibilism."

7. Moreland and Craig, *Philosophical Foundations*, 2nd ed., 268.

8. Moreland and Craig, *Philosophical Foundations*, 2nd ed., 303.

9. Bignon, *Excusing Sinners*, 61.

10. Palmer, *Five Points*, 104.

11. Bignon, *Excusing Sinners*, 61.

12. Bignon, *Excusing Sinners*, 61.

13. Bignon, *Excusing Sinners*, 62.

determinism describes reality, at least everything about humanity. That is to say, compatibilism will not simply be referred to as the thesis that freedom and/or responsibility is compatible with determinism; it will be referred to as the thesis that exhaustive determinism is, in fact, true.

The Consequence Argument.

One strong argument against exhaustive determinism, as argued by Edwards and Bignon, is the "*Consequence Argument*" (CA) set forth in Peter Van Inwagen's seminal book *An Essay on Free Will*. In the introductory pages he argues: "If determinism is true, then our acts are the consequences of the laws of nature and events in the remote past. But it is not up to us what went on before we were born; and neither is it up to us what the laws of nature are. Therefore, the consequences of these things (including our own acts) are not up to us."[14]

While this informal version of the CA argues against naturalistic determinism, one can simply replace the "laws of nature" with "God" and "His will" when dealing with a view of exhaustive divine determinism. A modified statement—the author's revision—might be expressed like this: "If determinism is true, then our thoughts, beliefs, and behaviors are ultimately the consequences of God's will and acts of causation. But it is not up to us what God wills or what he has caused. Therefore, the consequences of these things (including our own thoughts, beliefs, and behaviors) are not up to us."

The CA assumes two "rules" that require further examination:

1. *Rule Alpha*: There is nothing anyone can do to change what must be the case (or what is necessarily so).

2. *Rule Beta*: If there is nothing anyone can do to change X, and nothing anyone can do to change the fact that Y is a necessary consequence of X, then there is nothing anyone can do to change Y either.[15]

The second rule seems obvious because, if an event (or thought) necessarily occurs from a necessary entity, then the event (or thought) itself is necessary, and one is powerless to stop its occurrence. This notion has been called the "Transfer of Powerlessness Principle" and, as Kane explains it, "Our powerlessness to change X 'transfers' to anything that necessarily follows from X."[16]

The CA suggests, then, that if determinism is true, humanity is powerless or not responsible, in an "up to us" sense, for their thoughts or actions because (i) thoughts and actions were causally determined by something external to humanity, and (ii)

---

14. Van Inwagen, *An Essay on Free Will*, 16.

15. Kane, *A Contemporary Introduction*, 25.

16. Kane, *A Contemporary Introduction*, 25.

there is no libertarian freedom regarding an ability to think or act otherwise. Bignon, however, argues that Van Inwagen misses the mark: "Traditionally, and in the present work, incompatibilism has been defined as the thesis that determinism is incompatible with moral responsibility. Instead, Van Inwagen's argument aims to establish the thesis that determinism is incompatible with 'free will.'"[17]

However, it seems properly basic to take it to mean that, if some action x is not ultimately "up to us," then, a person cannot genuinely be responsible (morally responsible or otherwise) for x. As Jerry Walls concludes, this is a properly basic belief that needs no supportive argument: "We believe that libertarian free will is intrinsic to the very notion of moral responsibility. That is, a person cannot be held morally responsible for an act unless he or she was free to perform that act and free to refrain from it. This is a basic moral intuition, and we do not believe there are any relevant moral convictions more basic than this one that could serve as premises to prove it."[18]

This is an important point. According to exhaustive determinism, the past entails that an agent has one and only one possible thought, belief, or action compatible with his nature (as opposed to a choice among various options) at a given moment. However, libertarianism, or the ability to choose among a range of alternative options, each of which is consistent or compatible with one's nature, corresponds with the compatibilist's belief that a person's nature determines certain things about the person. The key difference is that the compatibilist often asserts that one's nature determines the *only* thing that will or must happen regarding the person—only one possibility—while the libertarian says that one's nature simply determines a *range of possible options* from which he is free to choose.

For example, perhaps one may contend that an unregenerate sinner does not possess the ability (left to his or her own devices) to do anything that is "spiritually good." However, that does not rule out the unregenerate sinner's ability to choose among a range of bad options that are each consistent with his sinful nature. He is free to rob the bank or to rob the liquor store and free to simply choose to sit on the couch and merely think about robbing the bank, robbing the liquor store, or watching some television instead.

As previously noted, both Luther and Calvin (among others) seemed open to the concept of *limited* libertarian freedom, that is to say, libertarian freedom limited to things apart from soteriological matters. As Kirk MacGregor notes, both Luther and Calvin believed that "unregenerate humans, while possessing the freedom to choose between opposites in the physical realm (in matters below), lack the ability to choose between spiritual good and evil (in matters above) due to original sin."[19]

Strikingly, though Bignon disagrees with Van Inwagen and argues that determinism is true and moral responsibility is compatible with exhaustive determinism, he

17. Bignon, *Excusing Sinners*, 62–63.

18. Walls, "A Philosophical Critique," 105.

19. MacGregor, *Luis de Molina*, 50.

candidly admits and "happily concede[s] . . . that libertarian free will is incompatible with determinism, but falls short of refuting compatibilism."[20] This acknowledgment is quite significant to the argument of this chapter. It means that Calvinists—such as Edwards and Bignon who affirm that the doctrine of EDD always describes reality—are far more extreme on the issue than Luther and Calvin seemed to be. In fact, EDD seems to be more of metaphysical commitment or a philosophical assumption about reality as opposed to a biblically supported theological view.

Therefore, the libertarian should merely (1) provide one sound argument in favor of the view that people possess libertarian freedom (in a limited sense) or (2) show that God does not always causally determine everything about humanity. If the libertarian succeeds at just one of these, then he is justified in claiming that determinism and, consequently, compatibilism (as historically understood) do not always correspond to reality. The question, then, that must be explored is this: "Do libertarians have access to such arguments, or do they simply affirm libertarian freedom because they are determined to do so"? Libertarians do, in fact, have such convincing arguments which demonstrate that not all things are determined and that humans—at least occasionally—possess libertarian freedom.

Limited libertarian freedom.

Many Christians reject libertarian freedom because they assume that, if a person possesses libertarian free will, then he must be free to choose to love and follow God apart from divine aid. This assumption seems to be unnecessary and based on a confusion. Libertarian freedom does not require maximal autonomy. Libertarianism simply requires an ability to freely choose some things some of the time, or the power to choose among a range of alternative options that are each consistent and compatible with one's nature. As the philosopher Angus Menuge declares, "Just as I have the power to jump [or not to jump] doesn't mean I can leap tall buildings (it is a limited power) so my freedom to steal or not steal does not mean I have the unaided power to choose God."[21] The last four words—"power to choose God"—is debated in theological cir-

---

20. Bignon, *Excusing Sinners*, 63. "Frankfurt Examples" are often trotted out at this point to demonstrate that the libertarian freedom to "do otherwise" is not needed for moral responsibility. Although it seems intuitive that one must possess the ability to behave otherwise in order to be held morally responsible for his or her actions, the Frankfurtian counters this intuition by offering some clever thought experiments often featuring a mad scientist interfering with an American election. See chapter 1 for an example written by Craig and discussion there.

But what if this thought experiment is considered another way? Suppose the voter, after deliberating for whom to vote, decides to press the red button casting a vote for "politician Y." The mad scientist has access to the voter's brain and the moment before the voter pushes the red button to vote "Y," the mad scientist sees what is about to happen and activates the electrodes in the voter's brain to make the man's finger hit the blue button to vote for "politician X." The man, although intending to vote for "Y" actually casts a vote for "X."

21 Via personal email conversation with Angus Menuge (31 Jan. 2018). Used with permission.

cles, but the salient point is that libertarian free will does not have to be exhaustive freedom or include soteriological issues. In fact, one merely needs to argue for what is known as "soft libertarian freedom." If this "limited libertarian freedom" is true, then one is ultimately responsible for what he uses his ability to think about or physically act on (at least some of the time).

Contrary to popular opinion, therefore, libertarian freedom is not the ability to do things that are not within one's nature or power. For example, if a human possesses libertarian freedom, he does not necessarily have the freedom to flap his arms and fly like a bird to the top of a skyscraper. However, he does have the freedom to choose among a range of options each consistent or compatible with his nature or power. He can choose, for example, to take the elevator, or the stairs, or to do nothing at all. Libertarian freedom is a limited power. Therefore, possessing this "limited power" does not imply that a person has the ability to choose among options that are inconsistent or incompatible with his nature.

The Free-Thinking Argument.

Libertarianism is criticized, not only by divine determinists, but also by most naturalists (such as Richard Dawkins, Stephen Hawking, Sam Harris, Will Provine, Alex Rosenberg, and Jerry Coyne). These critics often argue that free will is an illusion. Hawking and Mlodinow, for example, write, "It is hard to imagine how free will can operate if our behavior is determined by physical law, so it seems that we are no more than biological machines and that free will is just an illusion . . . Human behavior is indeed determined by the laws of nature and our actions are as determined as the orbits of the planets."[22]

The "New Atheist" philosopher, neuroscientist, and best-selling author, Sam Harris, agrees. In his book, *Free Will*, Harris writes: "Free will is an illusion. Our wills are simply not of our own making. Thoughts and intentions emerge from background causes of which we are unaware and over which we exert no conscious control. We do not have the freedom we think we have . . . Either our wills are determined by prior causes and we are not responsible for them, or they are the product of chance and we are not responsible for them."[23]

Harris (a naturalist) and Bignon (a theological determinist) both seem to agree that things external to humanity govern and control everything about humanity. According to them, this determining would include the wills and *intentions* of humanity. However, if all intentions are casually determined by external factors, then something or someone other than the self (the thing a person refers to as "I") always causally determines exactly *what* a person thinks about, and exactly *how* he thinks about it.

22. Hawking and Mlodinow, *The Grand Design*, 32.

23. Harris, *Free Will*, 5.

Naturalists and divine determinists are indeed odd bedfellows; nevertheless, they offer a united front proclaiming that libertarian freedom is an illusion.

Although libertarian freedom seems to be the kind of freedom worth wanting or having, there are questions which remain: "Do humans actually have this kind of freedom? If so, how does one know? Are some of a person's thoughts, actions, beliefs, and behaviors ultimately decided by the person, or are they always determined by external factors"?

As this author sees it, of all the arguments that have been developed in support of libertarian freedom, there is one that seems to supersede all others. This argument stems from the very *ability* to reason. It appears to be true that one may argue that human beliefs can be rationally affirmed only if humans possess libertarian freedom. This argument shall be referred to as the *Freethinking Argument against Naturalism* and represented as follows:

A1   If naturalism is true, human nature does not include an immaterial soul.

A2   If human nature does not include an immaterial soul, then humans do not possess libertarian freedom.

A3   If humans do not possess libertarian freedom, then humans do not possess the ability to rationally infer and rationally affirm knowledge claims.

A4   Humans do possess the ability to rationally infer and rationally affirm knowledge claims.

A5   Therefore, humans possess libertarian freedom.

A6   Therefore, human nature includes an immaterial soul.

A7   Therefore, naturalism is false.

Although this author affirms the above premises and thinks that one is not being irrational in holding these beliefs, the purpose here is not to fault or accuse anyone who denies any of the premises (perhaps besides the fourth premise). It seems that one person can have justifiable grounds for believing some proposition *p*, while another person can have justifiable grounds for believing not-*p*. The intention, then, is simply to argue that the Christian libertarian is not unjustified or being unreasonable or irresponsible in believing the above premises. One may offer good reasons in support of the premises.

The first three steps of the argument are rather straightforward. In summary, (A1) is synonymous with "If naturalism is true, nature is all that exists." (A2) is tantamount to "If all that exists is nature, then everything about humanity is causally determined by the forces of nature, the initial conditions of the big bang, and perhaps some quantum events, all of which are outside of human control." (A3) communicates the fact that "if something outside of human control causally determines you to affirm a false belief, then it would be impossible for you to infer or affirm a better belief—let alone the truth!"

If all things are outside of human control, then this includes exactly what every human thinks of and about and exactly how each human thinks of and about it. That is to say, "If all things are causally determined by something other than humanity, then that includes all thoughts and beliefs held by humanity." If a person's thoughts and beliefs are forced upon him, and he could not have chosen better thoughts and beliefs, then he is simply left assuming that his determined thoughts and beliefs are good (and that his beliefs are true). Therefore, one could never rationally affirm or argue that his beliefs really are the inference to the best explanation; this can only be assumed, and this assumption would likewise be causally determined and forced upon him. This, then, is the paramount concern for the atheistic naturalist who affirms exhaustive determinism. If determinism is true, then atheists—or anyone else for that matter— cannot possess justification for their beliefs. To make matters worse, if justification is required for knowledge, then knowledge becomes illusory.

Epistemologists often define knowledge, in the simplest terms, as justified true belief.[24] One may happen to possess true beliefs; however, if he does not possess a proper justification for a specific belief and his true beliefs are simply based on "luck," his belief does not qualify as a knowledge claim (even if it happens to be true). If one cannot freely think and infer the *best* explanation (among a range of alternative options each compatible with one's nature), then there can be no justification that that specific belief really is the best explanation. Without justification, rationally inferred and affirmed knowledge goes down the drain. All that remains is question-begging assumptions. Moreover, further argumentation is rendered a series of logical fallacies based upon these question-begging assumptions. This is the case because any argument based on a logical fallacy is no argument at all.

If (A3) is true, then the above conclusion seems to become inarguable, since to argue against it one must appeal to rationality and assume he has knowledge and/or some degree of justification about why the third premise is faulty. Consequently, the act of objecting to (A3) appears to inadvertently presuppose the truth of (A3). Given naturalistic determinism, how could anyone freely choose to engage in the process of rationality? The *process of rationality*, or simply *reasoning*, does not imply that one has a certain set of beliefs. Rather, unlike belief or knowledge, the process of rationality denotes the mental steps one takes when trying to decide what *he should* believe or which propositions *he ought* to affirm.

Determinism implies that a human being's thoughts and beliefs are causally determined by external factors. It is easy to see, then, why some determinists (like Harris

---

24. If one denies that knowledge requires justification, then premise (3) can be revised: "If humans do not possess libertarian freedom, then humans do not possess justification for their beliefs." A good discussion regarding epistemology and related issues (What is knowledge? What is justification? Internalism vs. externalism, etc.) can be found in Steup, "Epistemology."

and Bignon) claim that human choices are illusory. This illusion would include, of course, the choice to follow (or not to follow) epistemic rules and to think rationally. However, the implication of this is that determinists (if correct) would not have come to their conclusion about determinism based on their intelligence or by choosing to examine the evidence to infer the best explanation. Rather, their very conclusion about determinism would simply be determined by external factors (perhaps chemistry and physics) that are not aimed at truth and have nothing to do with rationality, the process of acquiring reason-based knowledge, or critical thinking and logic. If exhaustive determinism is true, as Smith put it, "there is no free will involved either in assessing whether one thought is better than another."[25] Agreeing with Smith, William Lane Craig notes:

> There is a sort of dizzying, self-defeating character to determinism. For if one comes to believe that determinism is true, one has to believe that the reason he has come to believe it is simply that he was determined to do so. One has not in fact been able to weigh the arguments pro and con and freely make up one's mind on that basis. The difference between the person who weighs the arguments for determinism and rejects them and the person who weighs them and accepts them is wholly that one was determined by causal factors outside himself to believe and the other not to believe. When you come to realize that your decision to believe in determinism was itself determined and that even your present realization of that fact right now is likewise determined, a sort of vertigo sets in, for everything that you think, even this very thought itself, is outside your control. Determinism could be true; but it is very hard to see how it could ever be rationally affirmed, since its affirmation undermines the rationality of its affirmation.[26]

While it seems intuitively obvious that humans possess libertarian freedom and make real choices after deliberating among a range of genuinely available options (at least occasionally), the person who denies this ultimately must reject rationality and the knowledge (justified, true belief) gained via the process of rational inference and deliberation. Therefore, a naturalist affirming that determinism is true has no grounds to rationally conclude his affirmation. In fact, it is an utterly non-rational statement. If the determinist just so happens to be correct about determinism—that libertarian free will does not exist—it would seem to follow that the ability to rationally affirm his beliefs is lost as well. This is a major problem for the determinist because he cannot conclude a model of reality that destroys the method he used to reach the conclusion.

Another supporting argument can be added. As a syllogism—it might be called *"The Deliberation and Liberation Argument"*—and it is as follows:

B1   Rationality requires deliberation.

25. R. Scott Smith, in personal correspondence with author.
26. Craig, "Molinism vs. Calvinism."

B2   Deliberation requires libertarian freedom (liberation).

B3   Therefore, rationality requires libertarian freedom (liberation).

B4   Some humans are rational.

B5   Therefore, some humans possess libertarian freedom.

Obviously, this argument hinges on the meaning of the word "deliberate." Webster defines it this way: "To weigh in the mind; to consider and examine the reasons for and against a measure; to estimate the weight of force of arguments, or the probable consequences of a measure, in order to a choice or decision; to pause and consider."[27] The question, then, that *The Deliberation and Liberation Argument* raises is this: "Is it possible to truly deliberate without libertarian freedom"? A person can readily see how this creates a difficult dilemma for those who believe in exhaustive determinism, because their philosophy compels them to reply that the non-rational laws of nature and past events, or God, always exhaustively determine a person's considerations, examinations, and estimations. In other words, the evaluative thoughts a person may *feel* are governing his deliberations are actually caused and determined by things (or persons) external to him. He is making no decision; it was made for him! And if that is the case, then the person cannot rationally affirm, justify, or provide any warrant that his beliefs are in fact true (including his belief that determinism is true). It would seem, then, that libertarian freedom is necessary if one genuinely is to possess the ability to evaluate his thoughts/beliefs and to deliberate in the truest sense. And it would follow, then, that a person is (at least occasionally) free to choose what he ultimately believes by way of his self-controlled, free thinking. In philosophical discussions, this is referred to as "doxastic voluntarism."[28]

Philosophers have sought to distinguish two different varieties of doxastic voluntarism: direct and indirect. Those who hold to direct doxastic voluntarism believe that a person has immediate control over all his beliefs or propositional attitudes. In contrast, those who argue for indirect doxastic voluntarism insist that a person is free to do certain things to move himself to a position to change his beliefs—or not to do those things. A simple illustration will show why direct doxastic voluntarism appears to be completely absurd. If a person—who sincerely believes in historical events and that God exists—were offered a billion dollars to genuinely choose to believe at this moment that there is no such thing as the reality of the past or that God does not exist, he would—despite the offer—have no ability to simply choose to believe that or any proposition (or not) at that given moment, because he cannot simply decide not to believe what he knows to be true.

However, if indirect doxastic voluntarism is true, a person is truly responsible for (at least some of) his beliefs or propositional attitudes in the sense that he can

---

27. Webster, "Deliberate."

28. Moreland and Craig, *Philosophical Foundations*. 87.

exercise libertarian freedom at various points in life. For instance, he can freely think and choose (1) what he will or will not consider, (2) how a particular subject is to be viewed, (3) if he is open to a particular line of argumentation or not, and so forth. Moreover, one can freely choose to be open-minded, or to be closed-minded, to focus or not to focus. Joshua Rasmussen is clear: "To illustrate, you have the power to choose whether to focus on these words or to release your focus. This power is within the options available to you."[29] Accordingly, then, even if a belief cannot be otherwise at a certain moment, "little things" along the way to your current belief were within your power and seemingly could have been otherwise. Thus, you are responsible for said current belief. Moreland and Craig put it well when they wrote: "Libertarians claim that we hold people responsible for what they believe (and the New Testament would seem to command people to believe certain things and hold them accountable for their choice to believe or not to believe), and this requires some form of doxastic voluntarism to be true."[30]

All who hold to exhaustive determinism (natural or divine) reject the idea of indirect doxastic voluntarism because it implies libertarian freedom to indirectly freely choose among a range of options consistent with a person's nature. In this case, that range of options consists of what one will or will not believe by way of free thinking. By denying indirect doxastic voluntarism, however, they are tacitly admitting that they are in effect doing so without good reason (or any reason at all). At the least, determinists of any stripe must affirm that they have not freely chosen to believe indirect doxastic voluntarism is false.

In short, if deliberation is impossible to those who hold exhaustive determinism, then so is rationality. This can be most clearly expressed in a *Revised Freethinking Argument*:

C1   If naturalistic or divine determinism is true, then libertarian free will does not exist.

C2   If libertarian free will does not exist, then libertarian free thinking does not exist.

C3   If libertarian free thinking does not exist, then the process of rationality is illusory.

C4   If the process of rationality is illusory, then knowledge gained via the process of rationality is impossible.

C5   Knowledge can be gained via the process of rationality.

C6   Therefore, libertarian free thinking exists.

C7   Therefore, libertarian free will exists.

---

29. Rasmussen, *How Reason Can Lead to God*, 90.

30. Moreland and Craig, *Philosophical Foundations*. 87.

C8   Therefore, both naturalistic and divine determinism are false.

The argument begins with the simple premise that the forces of nature are non-thinking and arational (non-rational) phenomena which are not intentionally aimed at truth. If any stripe of exhaustive determinism is true, then the evaluative thoughts a person may *feel* he is responsible for are actually caused and determined by factors external to him. Given naturalism, then, can a person sensibly think that his cognitive faculties are reliable? This is similar to what Alvin Plantinga has demonstrated when he argues that if naturalism is true (the view that God or nothing like God exists), then one's cognitive faculties are merely a product of blind evolution which is not concerned with truth value, but merely survivability.[31]

But the syllogism above is different in that it contends a deeper truth than Plantinga's argument. A person's beliefs are not merely the result of survivability on a deterministic paradigm. The deterministic process of physics and chemistry and the events of nature—which are non-thinking things outside of human control—determine all thoughts and beliefs. If naturalistic determinism is true, then a person's cognitive faculties are not reliable since they are not intentionally aimed at truth. Hence, a person cannot reliably reason since belief-forming faculties are not reliable. Thus, there is an intrinsic defeater to the *belief* that this view of naturalism is true.

However, these problems are also burdensome for the Calvinist who—aligning himself with the naturalist—affirms that *all* things are exhaustively, causally determined, though, not by the forces of nature, but by God. Notable Calvinist, Matthew J. Hart, agreeing with Bignon, not only identifies himself with this exact position but admits that there is a greater body of scholars who agree with him. Hart writes: "Calvinists, I shall assume, are theological determinists. They hold that God causes every contingent event, either directly or indirectly."[32] In other words, all of a person's thoughts and beliefs are "caused" by God. The implications of this are alarming. When there is disagreement amongst individuals, does this imply that God is forcing (causing) some/many people to believe false propositions? Surely, if God determines the manner in which a person feels—that is, as if he is making judgments about his own beliefs (and the beliefs of others)—then how is one to know if God is causally determining him to think and believe correctly or not? One is left only with question-begging assumptions (which would not be under his control either).

---

31. Plantinga, *Where the Conflict Really Lies*, 307–10.

32. Hart, "Calvinism and the Problem of Hell," 248. Hart notes that Paul Helm—the leading Calvinistic philosopher today—is a theological determinist. One must add, however, that there are some Calvinists who affirm all five points of TULIP and still affirm the libertarian freedom to choose among a range of options consistent with one's nature. Greg Koukl, *Tactics*, 128–29, takes this position and Oliver Crisp, *Deviant Calvinism*, 17, seems to affirm this possibility. Muller, *Divine Will*, 30, quotes Crisp, *Deviant Calvinism*, 17, and notes that Reformed Theology is "not necessarily committed to hard determinism" and allows for "free will in some sense." He continues and says that a "libertarian Calvinist" will affirm that God "ordains whatever comes to pass but does not either determine or cause all things: some human acts are merely foreseen and permitted."

Ultimately, if naturalistic determinism is true, the thoughts and beliefs of humanity are not intentionally "aimed" at anything since physics and chemistry are running the show. Hence, since the thoughts and beliefs of humanity are not aimed at truth, our thoughts and beliefs are not reliable. Alternatively, if God is exhaustively running the show via causal determinism, then the thoughts and beliefs of humanity are not necessarily aimed at truth either. Rather, the thoughts and beliefs of humanity are always perfectly aimed at the will of God—and God causally determines the majority of humanity to possess and affirm false theological beliefs. Hence, if EDD is true, then human theological beliefs are not reliable (including those discussed here).

A similar area in which human freedom becomes an issue is in discussions of intentional states of consciousness. Many atheistic naturalists[33] deny the existence of the "self," what most people refer to as "I." Though the Christian determinist has access to explain intentional states of consciousness via the soul created in God's image, for the sake of argument suppose intentionality exists on naturalistic determinism just as it would on a divine deterministic view. Although a human would possess mental states *of* and *about* things, he would not possess any ability as to the what he will choose to think *of* and *about*, and, perhaps more importantly, *how* he will choose to think *of* and *about* things. These thoughts are not up to that which one refers to as the "I" but to things other than the self, that is, to the forces of nature or God. Thus, the thing called "I" is left with no epistemic grounds to rationally affirm a current mental state. At best, the self on any deterministic view is reduced to a mere bag of beliefs—none of which are up to the bag!

This point can be made clear by way of a thought experiment. Suppose a mad scientist exhaustively controls (causally determines) all of Smith's thoughts and beliefs all the time, including Smith's thoughts about his own beliefs and Smith's beliefs about his thoughts. The mad scientist causally determines exactly what Smith thinks of and exactly how Smith thinks about it. This also would include the next words that will come from Smith's mouth.

Now consider this rhetorical question: "How could Smith (not the mad scientist) rationally affirm the current beliefs in his head as good, bad, better, the best, true or probably true without begging the question"? This is an impossible task because any answer Smith might give would not be "up to him" but up to the mad scientist. This again illustrates a good reason to believe that causal determinism is incompatible with rational inference or reason-based knowledge. This is the case because if the mad scientist is replaced with "physics and chemistry," "God," or anything else, then, one has the exact same rationality problems but for different reasons. After all, if something

---

33. E.g., Rosenberg, *The Atheist's Guide*, 214, 217, 238: "The illusion that there is someone inside that has thoughts about stuff is certainly as old as the illusion that there are thoughts about stuff . . . If the physical facts fix all the facts, there can't be a me or you inside our bodies with a special point of view . . . Scientism must firmly deny [the self's] existence. The self, as conveyed to us by introspection, is a fiction. It doesn't exist . . . Now that we see that the self is an illusion, it should be easier to give up the notion that the self is free."

or someone other than Smith causally determines Smith to affirm a false belief, then it would be impossible for Smith to infer or affirm a better or true belief. As epistemologist Kelly Fitzsimmons Burton aptly notes: "Proper function of our cognitive faculties must first rule out the [deterministic] influences of outsiders such as Alpha Centurion, cognitive scientists, Cartesian evil demons, and also internal influences such as a brain lesion or even the influence of mind-altering substances. All of these influences may cause one's faculties to fail to function properly."[34]

Perhaps it is helpful once again to express this in a syllogism which is simple and easy to remember. Consider the *Free Thinking Argument's* "core":

D1   If libertarian freedom is not possessed by humans, then humans cannot rationally affirm knowledge claims.

D2   Some humans can rationally affirm knowledge claims.

D3   Therefore, some humans possess libertarian freedom.

The second premise is one that all wish to affirm (lest they affirm their own lack of rationality), thus, the first step of the syllogism must be attacked by those who are determined to avoid the conclusion. Premise D1, however, seems true because, if everything about a person (the thing one refers to as "I") is exhaustively causally determined by something other than oneself, then that includes every thought and belief. And, if all thoughts and beliefs are forced upon a person—*and he could not have chosen better thoughts and beliefs*—then he is simply left assuming that his determined thoughts and beliefs are good or the best, as well as whether or not they are true. Therefore, to reiterate, one could never rationally affirm that his beliefs really are the inference to the best explanation; he could only assume it (and that assumption is out of his control as well).

This is the crux for any exhaustive determinist. If exhaustive determinism is true, and the forces of nature, God, or mad scientists cause and determine one to affirm false beliefs, then it is impossible for one to infer or affirm better beliefs. From this it follows that if exhaustive determinism is true, then no one can possess inferential knowledge or rationally affirmed knowledge. That is to say, no one can rationally affirm that he or she has inferred the *best* explanation since they were causally determined to think and believe by something other than themselves. Recall, that at minimum (and for the purpose of this book), reason-based knowledge is defined as "justified true belief." One can happen to hold true beliefs; however, if one does not possess justification for a specific belief, his belief does not qualify as a knowledge claim. And if a person cannot freely infer the *best* explanation (from within a range of multiple possible competing explanations), then he has no justification that his belief really *is* the best explanation. Without justification, reason-based knowledge goes down the drain. All that remains is fallacious, question-begging assumptions.

34. Burton, *Reason and Proper Function*, 23.

This becomes quite apparent by the answers given to one simple question: "Does a person possess the ability to reject irrational thoughts and beliefs in favor of rational thoughts and beliefs"? What is interesting about this question is that it assumes that the one who is asked has the ability to choose among a limited range of options which are consistent with his or her nature. So, simply taking part in this exercise supports the concept of libertarian freedom. Further, if a person answers "Yes" to the above question, then he simultaneously, tacitly affirms libertarian freedom and affirms his ability to choose between options consistent and compatible with his nature. But, if he answers "No," then it appears that his noetic structure has been damaged and his cognitive faculties are not functioning properly. This is made clear via the following syllogism:

E1   For any human x, x's cognitive faculties are designed to function properly in an appropriate environment.

E2   For any human x, if x's cognitive faculties are designed to function properly in an appropriate environment, then, through a mature, conscious process of properly functioning faculties, x can reject irrational thinking in favor of rational thinking.

E3   Therefore, for any human x, x can, through a mature, conscious process of properly functioning faculties, reject irrational thinking in favor of rational thinking (entails libertarian freedom).

To quickly fly over this syllogism, it seems properly basic to affirm that if one does not possess the ability to reject incoherent thinking in favor of coherent thinking, then something has gone terribly wrong with his or her cognitive faculties. And if one asserts that this ability is not necessary to gain reason-based knowledge, they seem to be affirming that they, themselves, do not possess the ability to judge and evaluate this premise as good, bad, better, worse, the best, true, or false. If one does not possess this ability, then he or she stands in no position to know if he or she should disagree with this premise or not.

Be that as it may, it is a properly basic belief that at least some humans do possess the ability to make these evaluative and rational judgments. In fact, if one objects to this premise, he or she seems to actually be affirming the same premise. That is to say, it is self-defeating to affirm determinism. Robert Lockie concludes that if one affirms determinism, then one "cannot be epistemically justified in her embrace (adoption, articulation, and defense) of determinism."[35] It follows that if one's noetic structure is functioning properly, then libertarian freedom is a vital ingredient in the rationality mix. It stands to reason that if the ability to be a "free thinker" has been lost—and one is not free to employ the use of reason (in appropriate circumstances)—then something seems to have damaged one's thinking faculties.

35. Lockie, *Free Will and Epistemology*, 231.

Moreover, if one affirms that he does not possess the ability to reject irrational thoughts and beliefs in favor of rational thoughts and beliefs, then, several problems arise:

1. Why should he trust his answer?

2. Why should anyone listen to his opinions about anything (including those on this topic)?

3. Libertarian freedom exists anyway—at least if he affirmed his ability to reject "yes" (in favor of "no"), and, thus, tacitly affirmed "yes."

As libertarian, Five-point Calvinist Greg Koukl has pointed out: "The problem with [determinism] is that without freedom, rationality would have no room to operate. Arguments would not matter, since no one would be able to base beliefs on adequate reasons. One could never judge between a good idea and a bad one. One would only hold beliefs because he had been predetermined to do so . . . Although it is theoretically possible that determinism is true—there is no internal contradiction, as far as I can tell—no one could ever know it if it were. Every one of our thoughts, dispositions, and opinions would have been decided for us by factors completely out of our control. Therefore, in practice, arguments for determinism are self-defeating."[36]

Koukl is exactly right. Consider the *FreeThinking Argument's* "core" once again. It is self-defeating to argue for determinism. If one is still determined to object to the final conclusion, he is free to reject (D2). A person will have major problems by offering that rejection because it is equivalent to proclaiming to others that he is not a rational agent. Thus, the entire "rational objection" is defeated via the objection made. The eminent philosopher of the mind, John Searle sums up the conundrum nicely: "[A]ctions are rationally assessable if and only if the actions are free. The reason for the connection is this: *rationality must be able to make a difference.* Rationality is possible only where there is a genuine choice between various rational and irrational courses of action. If the act is completely determined, then rationality can make no difference. It doesn't even come into play."[37]

Although Searle refers to an act being "completely determined" as opposed to saying that it "cannot be otherwise," he clearly affirms a range of options from which one can choose and the essentiality of the principle of alternative possibilities (PAP) for rationality: "Rationality is only possible where irrationality is possible. But the possibility of each requires freedom. So, in order to behave rationally, I can do so only if I am free to make any of a number of possible choices and have open the possibility of behaving irrationally . . . When we perform conscious voluntary actions, we typically have a sense of alternative possibilities."[38]

36. Koukl, *Tactics*, 28–29.

37. Searle, *Rationality*, 202, author's *emphasis*.

38. Searle, *Rationality*, 66–67.

Angus Menuge argues the same way: "Rationality presupposes an entity with libertarian free will that can act on some reasons rather than others."[39] Menuge and Searle seem to be correct, and if so, even if one asserts that libertarian freedom exists but the ability to think otherwise does not, then nothing ever really "makes a difference" because no one can really think other than the way he does think—even if he is not causally determined via an external source.

Regarding this view, Moreland and Craig write: "If one is to have justified beliefs . . . then one must be free to obey or disobey epistemic rules. Otherwise, one could not be held responsible for his intellectual behavior."[40] The phrase "to obey or disobey" implies the principle of alternative possibilities (PAP) and a range of options available from which one may choose when it comes to thinking, rationality, and "intellectual behavior." Evan Fales supports the case that the PAP is vital for rational deliberation:

> The analysis of free choice which I shall propose derives, in part, from Aristotle's conception of practical reasoning. According to it, acting freely consists in acting as a result of rational deliberation over what act to perform. To choose is to deliberate: it is not to perform some superadded "act of will." This conception of freedom makes obvious the connection between being free and having the capacity to engage in rational deliberation. It also makes it clear why PA [PAP] is so central to the possession of a free will: to have a free will is to have the capacity to act as a result of engaging in efficacious deliberation; but in order for my deliberation to have any point, I must at least believe that I have before me two or more genuinely possible alternative courses of action. Of course, I can take my deliberation seriously even if this belief is false; but in that case, my supposition that I am free to choose is a delusion. So, freedom consists in efficacious deliberation, i.e., in the performance of deliberation-guided actions; and efficacious deliberation presupposes genuine alternatives, each possible given antecedent conditions.[41]

Also, Koons and Pickavance support this position with force:

> It might be argued that rational deliberation requires only the epistemic possibility of alternate futures. All we must assume is that we do not know with certainty how the future is fated to unfold. However, this is simply false. Whenever we find out, after the fact, that we were wrong in thinking that the future was really open with respect to certain alternatives, we conclude that our deliberation about which alternative to bring about was empty and pointless. For example, suppose that one believes that one has two alternatives open to one: to leave or to stay in one's living room. If it turns out that one is locked in one's living room in such a way that one cannot possibly leave, then one's deliberation about whether or not to leave is, objectively speaking, pointless.

39. Menuge, "Neuroscience," 95.
40. Moreland and Craig, *Philosophical Foundations*, 2nd ed., 66.
41. Fales, "Divine Freedom," 83.

This is so even if it is, subjectively speaking, a reasonable thing for one to deliberate. A metaphysical fatalist must believe that there are never real alternatives open to anyone. Thus, she must believe that all deliberation is objectively pointless. Believing this, she cannot rationally engage in deliberation at all.[42]

Finally, John Polkinghorne, physicist and Christian explains:

In the opinion of many thinkers, human freedom is closely connected with human rationality. If we were deterministic beings, what would validate the claim that our utterance constituted rational discourse? Would not the sounds issuing from mouths, or the marks we made on paper, be simply the actions of automata? All proponents of deterministic theories, whether social and economic (Marx), or sexual (Freud), or genetic (Dawkins and E. O. Wilson), need a covert disclaimer on their own behalf, accepting their own contribution from reductive dismissal.

The point is that causal determinism cannot even be meaningfully affirmed, since if it were true then the affirmation itself would be determined, and so would not be a belief freely formed on the basis of weighing the evidence for and against. The affirmation is therefore irrational. Furthermore, it is common for determinists to try to convince non-determinists to convert to determinism. But that assumes that the non-determinists are free to convert, and therefore their non-determinism is not determined in the first place. The cost of holding human free will to be an illusion would appear to be impossibly high, as it entails the invalidity not only of human morality but also of human rationality.[43]

Obviously, humans possess the ability to rationally infer and affirm knowledge claims. To argue this would affirm it, as one would have to offer *knowledge* to the contrary. Moreover, if a person rejects knowledge, why should anyone listen to his arguments or what he claims to know? Ultimately, if one rejects this premise, then it follows that he affirms that he cannot rationally affirm that this premise is false. Since it is ultimately self-refuting to reject either premise in the argument, the following conclusion is deductive: *Therefore, some humans possess libertarian freedom.*

The salient point is this: If one does not possess any ability to think otherwise (at least some of the time), then he has no choice but to affirm that a current thought cannot be otherwise—even if it should be otherwise. Moreover, if all thoughts cannot be otherwise, then this includes the evaluative thoughts and beliefs a person has regarding his *own* thoughts and beliefs—all of them! Rational deliberation becomes illusory, and thus, any so-called "knowledge" a person supposedly gains via this illusion of rational deliberation is also illusory.[44]

42. Koons and Pickavance, *Atlas*, 320.

43. Polkinghorne, *Quantum Physics*, 58, quoted in Lennox, *Determined to Believe*, 59–60.

44. Interestingly, Randolph Clarke, *Libertarian Accounts*, 114, makes a similar claim when he writes, "Thus, if determinism is true, and if either variety of incompatibilism is correct, then at least

If exhaustive causal determinism of any flavor is true—if something other than or external to the self is causally determining all thoughts—then as Craig pointed out above *"a sort of vertigo sets in, for everything that you think, even this very thought itself, is outside your control."*[45] So much for "free thinking."

To summarize, if free thinking does not exist, then a person does not possess any epistemic ability to assess or evaluate his or her thoughts and beliefs. Further, if an agent is not the source and originator of his own thoughts (and something external to the person is causally determining the person's thoughts), or if he does not ever possess the ability to think otherwise regarding anything, then he is merely left assuming his or her determined thoughts are good—let alone true! However, when one keeps in mind the "vertigo" to which Craig refers, he would not even be free to make that assumption (or not) if he cannot think otherwise.

This leads to the fallacy of question-begging assumptions. Yet determinists presuppose that they have rationally inferred the best or true beliefs. Can they rationally affirm their thoughts and beliefs are the best when an external causal force has determined them to have no ability to think otherwise? If not, then, all that remains for the committed determinist is fallacious reasoning. Any argument based on a logical fallacy is no argument at all.

The *FreeThinking Arguments,* then, provide metaphysical reasons based on logical deduction to reject exhaustive determinism of any stripe (natural or divine). Since compatibilism entails determinism, the *FreeThinking Arguments* have demonstrated the failure of compatibilism (applied universally) as well.

generally when we deliberate, we presume that alternatives are open when they are not. We are, then, generally, subject to an illusion. The illusion is sometimes avoidable. But it is practically impossible for us to avoid it on a consistent basis. And since it is practically impossible for us not ever to deliberate, if determinism is true, then we are routinely subject to a practically unavoidable illusion."

45. Craig, "Molinism vs. Calvinism."

13

Theological arguments for libertarian freedom

ALTHOUGH THE *FREETHINKING ARGUMENTS* provide philosophical reasons for all people to reject determinism, theists—and Christians specifically—have other reasons to reject determinism: theological and biblical data. Chapter 2 documented that there seems to be ample Scriptural support for libertarian freedom: the ability to choose among a range of alternative options each compatible with one's nature. The Apostle Paul makes many claims suggesting that his audience possesses this type of freedom. For example, Gal 5:13 (*NLT*): *For you have been called to live in freedom, my brothers and sisters. But don't use your freedom to satisfy your sinful nature. Instead, use your freedom to serve one another in love.* Burton, in his classic commentary on Galatians, highlights the "voluntary" choice of using human freedom wisely in a sort of "slavery" shown by loving actions/decisions in relationships especially among believers: "To men who have been accustomed to think of law as the only obstacle to free self-indulgence . . . such language is . . . easily taken to mean that for the Christian there is nothing to stand in the way of the unrestrained indulgence of his own impulses . . . The thought is . . . convert not this freedom into . . . Having urgently dissuaded the Galatians who were formerly enslaved to gods that are not really gods . . . [he] bids them serve one another, yet clearly not in the sense of subjection to the will, but of voluntary devotion to the welfare, of one another . . . The present tense of δουλεύετε [serve] reflects the fact that what Paul enjoins is not a single act of service, nor an entrance into service, but a continuous attitude and activity."[1]

Paul is clear that those to whom he is writing possess the freedom—an ability—to choose among a range of options each of which is compatible with their *sinful natures*, namely, a choice to satisfy selfish desires, or to serve others in love. However, one of the most significant arguments is based on Paul's teachings in 1 Cor 10:13. There he writes: *No temptation has overtaken you that is not common to man. God is*

---

1. Burton, *Galatians*, 292–93.

faithful, and he will not let you be tempted beyond your ability, but with the temptation he will also provide the way of escape, that you may be able to endure it. There is an obvious contrast in this brief sentence. On the one hand the Christian's temptations are not "super-human" in strength, but the normal experiences of all people, yet in them a "super-human" God is faithful so that each individual can *bear* them and their seduction to sin . . . and *escape*. It is important not to overlook the emphasis on the Christian not succumbing but choosing *the way of escape*. Robertson and Plummer note that the translation of "*a way to escape (AV)* ignores the article before ἔκβασιν [*way of escape*], 'the necessary way of escape,' the one suitable for such a difficulty. The σὺν [*together*] and the articles imply that temptations and possibilities of escape always go in pairs: there is no πειρασμῷ [*temptation*] without its proper ἔκβασιν, for these pairs are arranged by God, who permits no unfairness. He knows the powers with which He has endowed us, and how much pressure they can withstand. He will not leave us to become the victims of circumstances which He has Himself ordered for us . . . The power to endure is given σὺν τῷ πειρασμῷ [*together with the temptation*], *the endurance is not given; that depends on ourselves.*"[2]

In brief, every temptation calls for a personal response: to choose among a range of options, each compatible with a person's nature, to endure and resist temptations or not. A syllogism based on this text might be stated this way:

F1   If Christians possess the ability to choose among a range of options consistent and compatible with their nature, then they possess libertarian freedom.

F2   Christians possess the ability to choose between giving into temptation or to take the way of escape God promises to provide (1 Cor 10:13).

F3   Therefore, Christians possess libertarian freedom.

The first premise simply defines what is meant by libertarian freedom and thus, the only premise in which the determined determinist is left to attack is the second. However, this puts the divine determinist in an awkward and uncomfortable position if he also claims to be a Bible-believing Christian. Indeed, the Christian who rejects premise F2 opposes a plain and common-sense interpretation of the Apostle Paul's words.

Since God has provided (at least some) people—Christians—with an "ability" not to sin, Christians, therefore, are able to not fall into temptation. It logically follows, then, that whenever a Christian commits a sin, he did not have to "miss the mark" because there was a genuine ability for him to do otherwise (*a way of escape*). This is exactly what is meant by libertarian freedom. The Christian possesses the ability to choose among a range of options (in this case, to sin or not to sin), both of which are consistent and compatible with his regenerated nature. Therefore, when a Christian

---

2. Robertson and Plummer, *1 Corinthians*, 209–10, author's *emphasis*.

freely chooses to sin and he was able not to sin, it follows that he is genuinely responsible for his sin.

Since premise F1 is true by definition and F2 is supported by the inspired Word of God, Christians have good reason—biblical reason—to affirm limited libertarian freedom. That is to say, the Bible is clear that at least some people possess the ability to choose among a range of options consistent and compatible with their natures even if their natures are determined by God. To say it another way, by God's grace, Christians can choose to sin or take the way of escape promised by God.

THE PROBLEM FOR COMPATIBILISM.

This raises severe problems for those who contend that compatibilism—and thus, determinism—always describes reality. Since compatibilism (as commonly, historically, and traditionally understood) entails determinism, and thus, there is never a genuine range of options each of which is compatible with a human's nature, and since two arguments have been offered in response to Bignon's challenge demonstrating that humans actually possess a categorical ability to occasionally choose among a limited range of alternative options, hereafter, the terms "libertarian free will" and "free will" can be used synonymously and in the sense previously described.

Compatibilism, if understood to actually correspond universally to reality, entails the thesis that exhaustive determinism is true, that is, something other than the person himself causally determines *everything* about the person. Despite affirming that, the compatibilist declares that a person can still be free and/or responsible for thoughts, actions, beliefs, and behaviors. Perhaps what Searle, who has no theological axe to grind, has said cannot be improved upon: "I think compatibilism simply misses the point about the problem of free will . . . To repeat, the determinist says, 'Every action is preceded by causally sufficient conditions that determine that action.' And the libertarian asserts the negation of that: 'For some actions the antecedent causal conditions are not sufficient to determine the action' . . . I cannot think of any interesting philosophical problem of free will to which compatibilism provides a substantive answer."[3]

With the above arguments and Searle's words in mind, consider the following argument against compatibilism:

G1   If compatibilism is true, then determinism is true.[4]

G2   If determinism is true, then no human possesses the libertarian freedom to ever think otherwise.

---

3. Searle, *Rationality*, 278.

4. The word "true" refers to the correspondence theory of truth. Thus, by "if compatibilism is true" means, if the thesis of compatibilism actually describes the way things are.

G3   If one does not ever possess the libertarian freedom to think otherwise, then he cannot rationally affirm knowledge claims.

G4   Some Calvinists have rationally affirmed that compatibilism is true.

G5   Therefore, it is possible to rationally affirm knowledge claims.

G6   Therefore, some Calvinists possess the libertarian freedom to think otherwise.

G7   Therefore, determinism and compatibilism are false.

This logical argument provides good reason for a rational thinker to reject compatibilism. Yet compatibilists continue to claim that a person can still be free and/or responsible even though everything about him is *ultimately* always causally determined by God, and he never could have *actually* chosen to think, believe, or behave otherwise. For example, Jonathan Edwards writes: "The plain and obvious meaning of the words Freedom and Liberty . . . is the power, opportunity, or advantage, that any one has, to do as he pleases . . . for one to do and conduct as he will, or according to his choice, is all that is meant by it."[5] Wayne Grudem argues similarly: "We are free in the greatest sense that any creature of God could be free—we make *willing* choices, choices that have *real effects*. We are aware of no restraints on our will from God when we make decisions."[6]

These views are troublesome for several reasons. First, Grudem seems to be dealing with epistemology, when the salient issue is ontology. But the bigger problem with Grudem's statement—for example—is that he is essentially stating that God does not possess the power to create a being with an ability to ever choose among a range of options, each of which is consistent and compatible with the creature's God-given nature. This is problematic for anyone who affirms the omnipotence of God.[7]

There are also flaws in Edwards's argument. He implies that a person *always* and only chooses based on his *"greatest desire"* at a given time. But, if a person believes that if he is free to act on his greatest desire, then he *must* act on his greatest desire and never has the ability to choose against his greatest desire—even if it is the rational or moral thing to do. It follows that he *could never choose otherwise.* The Edwardsian compatibilist, then, even though he is not genuinely free to ever choose among a range of options which are *each* consistent or compatible with his nature—or choose otherwise—has really always only one option available to him at any given time. However, if a person is free to act on his greatest desire at a given time, then he as an Edwardsian compatibilist asserts that this "choice" (that cannot be otherwise) is "free" since it was "voluntary" (based upon a "nature" ultimately causally determined by God).

---

5. Edwards, *Freedom of the Will*, 24.

6. Grudem, *Systematic Theology*, 331.

7. See the *MMA* in chapter 15.

This view, however, runs into rationality problems once again—but for slightly different reasons. Choices based on "greatest desires" are not choices based on logic and reason. In fact, if the compatibilist claims that he can "exercise his reason," what he really means is that his "reason" is simply his "greatest desire." But if choices are always—and only—aimed at the target of a person's "greatest desire," they are never aimed at the target of truth. Sure, some stray "bullets" may accidentally—or luckily—hit the target of truth, but they were never aimed at truth in the first place. On this Edwardsian view, even if a person happens to hold a true belief, it is not a *rationally inferred* belief; it is simply his greatest desire.

Accordingly, the compatibilist cannot rationally affirm or justify any of his beliefs as objectively better or worse than a competing belief—for even the evaluations of his own thoughts and beliefs will also be determined by his greatest desires! Therefore, the Edwardsian compatibilist cannot ever possess knowledge that a specific belief is good, bad, better, or worse (let alone true) than a competing belief. His belief (even if true) is not justified and thus, does not count as a knowledge claim. It follows that if the compatibilist really has rationally inferred that compatibilism is a *better* explanation than libertarianism, then his view of Edwardsian compatibilism must be false. As a result, the compatibilist has inadvertently defeated his project by way of his project. Ultimately, according to the Edwardsian compatibilist, the only reason he has chosen to reject libertarian freedom is because he has a "greatest desire" for exhaustive divine determinism (EDD) to be true. That is not a good (rational) reason to believe anything. Subjective personal preference is vastly different than selecting a view based on objective truth.

Why can it not be the case that human nature is based on the fact that human persons are the kind of "things" which are designed to be neutral (at least occasionally) with an ability to make decisions—not based on "preferences" or "desires," but rather, based on rationality and truth? Even unregenerate sinners, although they might not be able to rationally infer the truth of Christianity, can still be rational or logical in "external matters" (Calvin and Luther would agree). The regenerate Christian, on this Reformed view, would simply have an expanded range of options from which to logically consider.

The salient point is this: If *all* choices are *always* based on mere "preferences" or "desires," then the Edwardsian compatibilist's so-called "choice" to reject free will is not based on objective truth. Rather, the only reason he rejects the idea of libertarian freedom is because of the fact that he simply possesses a subjective desire for determinism based on "the way he is" (just as he might subjectively prefer chocolate over vanilla) which was ultimately determined via an external force; namely, God.

To reiterate, if the only reason the Edwardsian compatibilist affirms his beliefs are true is that he possesses a nature which desires these specific beliefs to be true, then the compatibilist stands in no epistemic position to know if his determined desire corresponds to reality—or not. This is the case because his beliefs are not aimed at truth, but rather, his desires (which are causally determined by his nature which is ultimately causally determined by something or someone else). It follows that the compatibilist cannot rationally affirm that his "preferred beliefs" are true, and thus, he stands in no position to justify his claims. If one cannot provide justification for a claim, then his or her claim is not a claim of reason-based knowledge. Indeed, it is nothing but a question-begging assumption. With this in mind, it is vital to remember that any argument based on a logical fallacy is no argument at all. This provides a significant defeater against exhaustive determinism and compatibilism, which is a good reason to reject compatibilism altogether. In fact, it is self-defeating to argue for determinism and/or compatibilism and thus, one ought to reject it (at least if he is free to reject irrational beliefs in favor of rational beliefs—but that would require libertarian freedom).

There are more arguments which demonstrate the absurdity of compatibilism. For example, if compatibilism is true, then, ultimately, humans are just as necessary as God. Consider the following deductive syllogism:

H1   If compatibilism is true, for any person P and action A, necessarily, if P desires to perform A and nothing prevents P from performing A, then P performs A.

H2   For any person P and action A, if P necessarily desires to perform A and nothing prevents P from performing A, then P necessarily performs A.

H3   Therefore, if God necessarily desires to create humans and nothing prevents God from creating humans, then God necessarily creates humans.

H4   God necessarily desires to create humans and nothing prevents God from creating humans.

H5   Therefore, God necessarily creates humans.

H6   Therefore, if compatibilism is true, then it is impossible for God not to create humans.

H7   Humans do not exist necessarily.

H8   Therefore, compatibilism is false.[8]

If compatibilism is not always true for God, then it stands to reason that God could create humans in his likeness who also have the categorical ability to genuinely choose among a range of options which are each compatible with human nature.[9] Theists, especially Christian theists, have no reason to assume that compatibilistic determinism should be applied universally.

---

8. The author's friend and ministry colleague, John Limanto, developed this syllogism, and it has been included here with his permission.

9. This will be discussed further in chapter 15.

It is not without significance that many naturalists like John Searle and Evan Fales concede that rationality presupposes a strong libertarian view of free will, while many theologians continue to favor compatibilism. It is unfortunate—when atheists realize the deterministic compatibilism, they have argued for in the past is now a sinking ship, while many Christians, nevertheless, decide to drown with their theological presuppositions.

This theological deterministic view of compatibilism cannot rationally be defended. One should, however, affirm what this author refers to as "biblical compatibilism." Biblical compatibilism entails the thesis that God *predestines* all things, and humans are genuinely free and responsible for some things. This might seem like a contradiction at face value (note the *all* vs. the *some*), but, if people have reason to believe that predestination is not equivalent with causal determinism, then perhaps there can be some "elbow room" for libertarian freedom—a particular question answered later (chapter 15).

The remainder of this chapter examines an argument that is more controversial than the previous arguments. Indeed, although many Calvinists might affirm the aforementioned arguments for libertarian freedom, they will probably offer resistance to the next. This is because the following argument against EDD seems to delve into soteriological issues.

THE OMNI ARGUMENT VS. EXHAUSTIVE DIVINE DETERMINISM (EDD).

The third theological reason to believe in human freedom is based on the definition of God as the greatest conceivable being.[10] Not only can God be conceived as a Maximally Great Being, the Bible seems to affirm that God is the epitome of perfection (Psa 18:30). God—as an omnipotent, omniscient, and omnibenevolent being—is the focus of the following discussion.

The omnipotence of God.

Omnipotence is easy to define if one uses only the etymology of the word. It simply means "all powerful," or "all potential." God is the perfection of power. But one must move beyond etymology. Does "all powerful" mean that God can do anything and everything? Even that question goes against what many people in the church today think is the case. But, in fact, God cannot do *all* things! For example, can God create a married bachelor? Can God create a triangle with four sides? Can God create a stone that is so big that even he cannot lift it? Can God create something that is not contingent

---

10. Anselm's definition in *Proslogium*, chapter 2: "Lord . . . we believe that you are a being than which nothing greater can be conceived."

upon him? Can God sin? Even the Bible gives examples of certain acts which God cannot do. For example, he cannot repent (Num 23:19), nor can he lie (Tit 1:2).

A question of great importance to the subject of human freedom is: "Can God *force* someone to *freely* choose to love him"? Of course, not; that is logically impossible. Therefore, if there are clearly things that God cannot do, then the "omnipotence" of God must be carefully defined. A good definition of omnipotence might be: *God can do all things that are* logically *possible.*[11] Therefore, if a being can do all things that are *logically* possible, that would include many things that are considered *scientifically* impossible (these are different categories) like creating a universe from nothing or raising a man from the dead, acts which are simply referred to as "miracles."

The Bible teaches that God is All-Mighty: *Oh, Lord God, it is you who made the heavens and the Earth by your great power! Nothing is too hard for you* (Jer 32:17). But when a person contemplates and reflects on "triangles with four sides" and "married bachelors," such expressions are not really *things* at all. As Craig states, "They are nothing but an inconsistent combination of words."[12] Thus, it is important to understand *all* in the context of his ability to do all things that are not logically impossible.

This has practical applications to the Christian's everyday life. If a person has a personal relationship with Christ, then God's omnipotence lives also within him. This means a person practically has super-powers! As the author's parents used to teach: *"The same power that created the universe and raised Jesus from the dead is the same power that lives in you through the Holy Spirit! That is the ultimate force."* And with God's power working in and through a person, he also can do *all things* that are logically possible (Phil 4:13). Though this passage is often taken out of context, the truth remains: If an omnipotent God chooses to use a person—though he might allow a person to resist his will—then God can do through him and in him *all things* that are logically possible. Of course, one must add that this is only in regard to the things that God wants him to accomplish. For example, a person cannot choose to use God's power to rob a bank, but if God desired him to walk on water or to simply love an unlovable neighbor, then God's power is available for him. He wants a person to choose wisely.

The omniscience of God.

Another "omni" word is God's omniscience, that is, he is all-knowing. Philosophers and theologians have sought to clarify exactly what this means. It might be defined this way: For every proposition that could be uttered or thought of, God knows whether any and all propositions are true or false, and he is never wrong. Therefore, if God is

11. Some might offer an alternative definition such as, "God can do anything that is in accordance with his being." This essentially means the same thing as the definition provided above. After all, God can do anything that is in "logical" accordance with his being.

12. Craig, *On Guard,* 155.

omniscient as the Bible seems to teach, then he knows all that *could* happen; all that *would* happen, if something else were to occur (even if he knows it will not occur); and all that *will* happen with perfect certainty. God does not make probability judgments. The weatherman might say that there is a thirty percent chance of rain tomorrow, but God knows with perfect certainty if it will rain tomorrow or not.

Moreover, it is impossible to keep a secret from God. David in Psa 139:1–4 put it this way: *O, Lord, you have searched me and known me! You know when I sit down and when I get up . . . and know all about what I do. Even before I say a word, O, Lord, you know all about it.* Since limited libertarian freedom has been demonstrated to be possessed by humans, it seems to follow that an omniscient and maximally great being even knows what free agents could, would, and will *freely* choose to do. For example, God knows with perfect certainty what a person will freely choose to drink the next time he is in a restaurant. When the waiter offers Pepsi, Mountain Dew, or Dr. Pepper, even if a person is not completely sure what to drink and needs to think about it a bit longer, God still knows with absolute certainty what he will eventually—and freely(!)—choose to drink! Even if a person were to change his mind at the last possible moment, God would have still have known that he would—and will—freely choose Mountain Dew over Pepsi at the last second. God simply knows (even if a person does not know *how* he knows).

Some critics might argue that since God perfectly knows what a person is going to freely choose to do, then he does not really have free choices at all. But drawing this hasty conclusion is a terrible mistake and a logical blunder. First, it is vital to remember definitions. Libertarian freedom is not defined as "the ability to choose what God does not know," or "the ability to trick God." Libertarian freedom is minimally concerned with source agency or the ability to choose among a range of alternative options each of which are compatible with one's nature. Second, the weatherman referenced above, whose primary tool called a weather barometer, provides an excellent illustration for the above argument. Weather barometers help the weatherman predict the weather with high degrees of certainty, though they obviously are not infallible and are sometimes wrong. Imagine, then, a fictional device—an "infallible weather barometer"—one that is never wrong! Suppose that a person could type in the date and coordinates into this infallible weather barometer for any place and time into the infinite future, and it would always yield a perfect weather forecast. Further, suppose a date chosen for Spain's weather ten years from the present were entered into the remarkable device, and it predicted it would rain. When the decade passed, on that exact day it did rain in Spain.

People would be impressed. But philosophers—though equally impressed—would be thinking about a different question: Because the infallible weather barometer "knew" that it was going to rain in Spain with perfect certainty, did it *cause* the rain to fall in Spain? Of course not. But the philosophers would continue thinking and conclude that knowledge does not stand in causal relation to what actually happens.

And the philosophically minded theologian would apply the same thinking to God's omniscient knowledge. Just because God knows what will happen, it does not necessarily follow that God caused it, or forced it to happen. His knowledge includes free choices. God does not cause a person's choices. He simply knows (as per the discussion of 1 Cor 10:13 discussed above) if a person will freely choose to sin or if he will freely choose the means of escape which God (in his grace) has provided. God knows with absolute certainty what a person will *freely* choose to do, and this is why people are held responsible for their actions.[13]

God knows the truth-value to all propositions. His perfect and limitless knowledge encompasses all that has happened in the past, all that is occurring right now, and all that will happen in the future. Moreover, God knows all that could, would, and will happen. God knows everything—including what a person is thinking right now. This is why a believer can pray to God in his mind without using his voice box. Since God knows all things, it is impossible for him to learn things the way humans do. He does not have to "think things through" to come to conclusions. He simply *knows* the truth perfectly. Moreover, he does not have to "look" into the future to see what will happen. He simply *knows* what will happen from eternity past (without beginning).

Perhaps this sounds too "academic," but the implications to the life of the Christian are profound. Because believers have a Heavenly Father who has perfect knowledge, they have access to the most intelligent being (a perfectly intelligent being). This is why Christians should be the most intelligent, reasonable, and logical thinkers on the planet. The Bible instructs readers to go to the Ultimate Intelligence (God) to ask for wisdom: *Now if any of you lacks wisdom, he should ask God, who gives to all generously and without criticizing, and it will be given to him* (Jas 1:5). Further, Paul adds: [God] *desires all people to be saved and to possess knowledge of the truth* (1 Tim 2:4).[14] The heavenly Father wants to teach his children about reality. The question is this: Are they willing to learn from him?

The Omnibenevolence of God

The last of the "Big Three" attributes of God is his perfect love. He is Omnibenevolent. Simply put, God is all-loving. Erickson expressed this well when he wrote: "God's love is an unselfish interest in us for our sake . . . Jesus laid down his life not only for his friends . . . but also for his enemies, who despised and rejected him . . . He is concerned with our good for our own sake, not for what he can get from us."[15] Not only does the Bible make this clear (e.g., Psa 100:5; 145:17; John 3:16; etc.), but philosophers have

13. Consider also Craig's discussion of foreknowledge and necessity in chapter 3, footnote #19, p.50, based on Craig, *Only Wise God*, 72–74.

14. This latter text from 1 Timothy is a crucial text and will be examined in great detail later in this chapter.

15. Erickson, *Christian Theology*, 263.

also argued for this conclusion apart from the Bible through both the *Moral Argument* and the *Ontological Argument* (both of which will be addressed in the final chapter). The importance of this attribute cannot be over-emphasized. If God were simply omnipotent (all-powerful) and omniscient (all-knowing), but not all-loving, he might rightly be feared. In fact, this is how Muslims seem to view their god, Allah. The god of Islam does not seem to be all-loving, and whatever he does is simply called "good," even if it is really hateful. As a result, Muslims have no assurance of salvation (unless they die in Jihad).[16]

Some Christians fall into a similar trap and incorrectly think of their God this way. Indeed, the church has been infected with a low view of God for ages. Tozer, in his book *The Knowledge of the Holy*, says, "What comes into our minds when we think about God is the most important thing about us."[17] In the preface of the same book Tozer writes: "The Church has surrendered her once lofty concept of God and has substituted for it one so low, so ignoble, as to be utterly unworthy of thinking, worshipping men . . . The low view of God entertained almost universally among Christians is the cause of a hundred lesser evils everywhere among us."[18]

This low view of God has infected the minds of many Christians today, but its roots can be found in the beginning. The original sin in its essence does not seem to be eating of a forbidden fruit, but rather, doubting the omnibenevolence of God. This was the trap Satan lured Eve into in the Garden of Eden (Gen 3): *Did God really say*? Satan convinces Eve to consider the idea that God is not really interested in her ultimate flourishing, and she doubted that God was omnibenevolent and desired the best for herself. This doubt led to the fall of man, and terrible suffering has followed in its wake. True is the counterfactual: "*If* Adam and Eve would have kept God's commands (and all of their offspring followed suit), then every single human *would* eternally flourish and never experience any suffering." Despite Adam and Eve's decision, the fact of the matter is that God does desire the ultimate flourishing for each and every

16. Siddiqi, "Salvation," 41, quotes affirmatively Ismail al-Faniqi as saying, "In the Islamic view, human beings are no more 'fallen' than they are 'saved.' Because they are not 'fallen,' they have no need of a saviour. But because they are not 'saved' either, they need to do good works—and do them ethically—which alone will earn them the desired 'salvation.' Indeed, salvation is an improper term, since, to need 'salvation,' one must be in a predicament beyond the hope of ever escaping it. But men and women are not in that predicament. Humans are not ethically powerless. They are not helpless puppets capable of neither good nor evil. They are capable of both. To 'save' themselves by deeds and works is their pride and glory." According to the *Koran, Sura* 22:58–59 "Those who have left their homes, or been driven out therefrom, or suffered harm in My Cause, or fought or been slain,- verily, I will blot out from them their iniquities, and admit them into Gardens with rivers flowing beneath;- A reward from the presence of Allah, and from His presence is the best of rewards." A similar promise is *Sura* 3:195: "Those who have left their homes, or been driven out therefrom, or suffered harm in My Cause, or fought, or been slain, verily, I will blot out from them their iniquities, and admit then into Gardens with rivers flowing beneath; a reward from the Presence of God, and from His Presence is the best of rewards." Compare also the conclusion of David A. Noebel, *Understanding the Times*, 224.

17. Tozer, *The Knowledge of the Holy*, 4.

18. Tozer, *The Knowledge of the Holy*, 2.

human being. This is taught throughout the Bible: (e.g., John 3:16; 1 Tim 2:4; 4:10; 2 Pet 3:9; etc.). God did create a world in which it was logically possible for all people to flourish.

Many people continue to doubt God's perfect goodness and love. Some divine determinists (like Arthur Pink[19]) actually teach that God does not love all people or desire the best for all people. This is a horrible mistake—perhaps even a sin—that leads to weak faith. Other "divine determinists" may not be so forthright as Pink, but if—as they affirm—God controls all thoughts and beliefs all the time, then does it not raise damning questions such as: Does God causally determine (directly or indirectly) people to believe lies? Does God force some to believe truth and others to affirm false beliefs? And does this not make God a "divine deceiver," a "god of mischief," or anything less than a maximally great being? This low view of God has led many in the church to doubt their salvation just as Muslims do (both views of God are incorrect). Indeed, this low view of God is reflected in the *Dogmatic Canons and Decrees* of the Council of Trent (AD 1563): "No one, moreover, so long as he is in this mortal life, ought so far to presume as regards the secret mystery of divine predestination, as to determine for certain that he is assuredly in the number of the predestinate; as if it were true, that he that is justified, either cannot sin any more, or, if he does sin, that he ought to promise himself an assured repentance; for except by special revelation, it cannot be known whom God hath chosen unto himself."[20] When one doubts or rejects the fact that God is omnibenevolent, he not only is incorrect in his low view of God, but major problems arise, and he follows in the footsteps of Adam and Eve.

Because *God is love* (1 John 4:8), God created humans to love Him and all people for eternity. Indeed, central to Jesus's teaching is that love is the objective purpose of

---

19. Pink has a long discussion in his book *The Sovereignty of God*: "To say that God the Father has purposed the salvation of all mankind, that God the Son died with the express intention of saving the whole human race, and that God the Holy Spirit is now seeking to win the world to Christ; when, as a matter of common observation, it is apparent that the great majority of our fellowmen are dying in sin, and passing into a hopeless eternity; is to say that God the Father is *disappointed,* that God the Son is *dissatisfied,* and that God the Holy Spirit is *defeated.* We have stated the issue baldly, but there is no escaping the conclusion. To argue that God is 'trying His best' to save all mankind, but that the majority of men will not let Him save them, is to insist that the will of the Creator is impotent, and that the will of the creature is omnipotent. To throw the blame, as many do, upon the Devil, does not remove the difficulty, for if Satan is defeating the purpose of God, then, Satan is Almighty and God is no longer the Supreme Being.

To declare that the Creator's original plan has been frustrated by sin, is to *dethrone* God. To suggest that God was taken by surprise in Eden and that He is now attempting to remedy an unforeseen calamity, is to *degrade* the Most High to the level of a finite, erring mortal.

To argue that man is a free moral agent and the determiner of his own destiny, and that therefore he has the power to checkmate his Maker, is to *strip* God of the attribute of Omnipotence" (Pink, *Sovereignty,* 16).

Later Pink (*Sovereignty,* 17, 19) writes: "God bestows His mercies on whom He pleases and withholds them as seemeth good unto Himself . . . When we say that God is Sovereign in the exercise of His love, we mean that He loves whom He chooses. *God does not love everybody*" (author's *emphasis*).

20. *Dogmatic Canons,* 39.

human existence. For example, Matthew (5:44) records his words: *But I say to you, "Love your enemies and pray for those who persecute you."* His account continues (Matt 22:37): *And he said to him, "You shall love the Lord your God with all your heart and with all your soul and with all your mind.* [38] *This is the great and first commandment.* [39] *And a second is like it: You shall love your neighbor as yourself."*

Jesus's teachings in the Gospel of Matthew could be summarized in the following manner:

1. People should love God first.

2. Everybody should love everybody (from his neighbors to those who consider him to be an enemy).

Therefore, when humans freely choose to do loving things, they approximate the perfect standard of God, and they are "good." Loving God is good. Loving a person's neighbor is good. Loving one's enemy is good. In short, Christians ought to be the most loving people on the face of the planet.

No person is perfect, but Christians should make every effort to approximate the One who is. God himself said this to his Old Testament people (Lev 19:1–2): *You shall be holy; for I the Lord your God am holy.* Since God is the standard of love, people can always trust the commands he has given to be perfectly in line with the purpose for which he created us—love. Moreover, since God is perfectly intelligent, it follows that his commands are always the most intelligent things to do (even when it might not make sense to a person at the time). Therefore, it is simply unintelligent, wrong, and sinful to not obey the commands of God.

God's perfect love and what it means to be all-loving are part of his omnibenevolence. If God *is* love,[21] then God's very nature is loving. This is so simple that children can comprehend this truth.

God is the perfect Father. To briefly speak in the first person: I am not a perfect dad by any means and do not require my son, Ethan, to be perfect either. I know he will make mistakes; he will sin; he will disappoint me; and he will be anything other than perfect. But even though I know these things about Ethan, it does not mean that I do not love him with all of my heart. I am still willing to die for my imperfect son! If that is how imperfect dads are, imagine what a perfectly intelligent, and loving Heavenly Father is like. God does not love people based on their actions; he just loves them and desires their love.

---

21. This precise statement is mentioned twice in 1 John 4:8, 16. Westcott in his extended note on the meaning of *"God is love"* writes: "And this love is original, and not occasioned (1 John 4:10). It corresponds to the innermost nature of God, and finds its source in Him and not in man (1 John 4:19; 3:1). It is not like the love which is called out in the finite by the sense of imperfection (*eros*, Plat. *Sympos.* 201ff.), but is the expression of perfect benevolence. The only earthly image which answers to it is the love of parents for children (Eph 3:15), while that of Christ for the Church is compared to the love of husband for wife (Eph 5:25)" (Westcott, *John*, 168).

That is what a saving relationship is: since *love never fails* (1 Cor 13:8), it follows that when a human is in a true love relationship with God, he is simultaneously in an eternal saving relationship with God.

It could be argued that since God first loved humankind, when a person does not resist his love, he is saved. This seems to be demonstrated by Jesus in his Parable of the Prodigal Son found in Luke 15:11–32. Jesus is telling this fictional story of a dad—a great dad—who loves his son the way God loves humanity (e.g., John 3:16; 1 Tim 2:4;[22] 2 Pet 3:9; etc.). In fact, the purpose of Jesus's story is to provide an analogy of the great and loving Heavenly Father so that those listening to this parable could begin to understand the way God loves everyone. His love was always available to his son, and it never decreased or disappeared. The son, however, made some choices—free choices—that separated him from the love of his father. It was not until the son made the choice to return to his father's love, that their relationship was restored. Plummer says it well:

> The Parable of the Prodigal Son . . . completes the trilogy of these parables of grace . . . The first two parables give the divine side of grace; the seeking love of God. *The third gives the human side; the rise and growth of repentance in the heart of the sinner* . . . Like the Lost Coin, it is peculiar to Lk., who would take special delight in recording a discourse, which teaches so plainly that God's all-embracing love is independent of privileges of birth and legal observances . . . This *coming to himself* is manifested in the thought of home and the longing for it. Want rekindles what his revelry had extinguished . . . The *repentance is as real and decided as the fall. He prepares full confession,* but no excuse; and, having made a good resolution, he acts upon it without delay . . . He had not counted on his father's love and forgiveness when *he decided* to make this request.[23]

This brings forth another counterfactual: If the son would have never made the choice to return to his father, then their relationship would have never been restored. This is representative of God's love for all people. God loves all people unconditionally, just as the father in the parable, and his love is always available. Indeed, God is omnibenevolent.

Peter Van Inwagen nicely describes the maximally great nature of God: "God is love as he is Goodness and Knowledge and Power: all these things are perfectly realized in him . . . We may equally well say that God is Goodness or that God is Knowledge or that God is Power . . . all these 'God is' statements are really the same statement."[24]

---

22. This important text will be discussed somewhat lengthily later in this chapter.

23. Plummer, *Luke*, 371–79, author's *emphasis*.

24. Van Inwagen, "The Vision of the Hazelnut," 192.

Divine Desire vs. Divine Determinism Argument.

One final argument against EDD might be called the *Divine Desire* vs. *Divine Determinism Argument*. In syllogistic form it would go like this:

I1   If divine determinism is true, then, if God desires all people to go to heaven, then all people go to heaven.

I2   Not all people go to heaven.

I3   Therefore, if God desires all people to go to heaven, then divine determinism is false.

I4   If God is all-loving, then God desires all people to go to heaven.

I5   God is all-loving.

I6   Therefore, God desires all people to go to heaven.

I7   Therefore, divine determinism is false.

There are implied premises hidden in this argument as well: namely that if God is omnipotent, omniscient, and omnibenevolent—a Maximally Great Being—then God would have the power and ability to save all people, he would know exactly how to accomplish this feat, and he would desire the ultimate best for all people. The key premises stated in this argument are (I1), (I2), (I4), and (I5). As noted above, divine determinism is the view that God determines all things exhaustively and according to his will. This includes every person's thoughts, actions, beliefs, and behaviors. This implies (I1) because, if God desires all people to go to heaven (or to be saved), then God will causally determine that they repent, turn from their sins, and place their faith in Christ.[25] This is a conversion process that guarantees salvation (Acts 3:19; 16:31). According to divine determinism, if it is God's desire that all people turn to him, then all people must turn to him. Moreover, premise (I5) is uncontroversial among Christians; as it seems that the majority of determinists and non-determinists agree that God is all-loving. This leaves the two controversial premises—(I2) and (I4)—to be defended.

Premise (I2) states that not all people go to heaven. That is to say, some people reject Christ and go to hell. And it is self-evident that many people do not convert to Christianity in this life. Beyond the fact that there are numerous non-Christians in the world is Jesus's remark that many people will not enter by the *narrow gate* of salvation (Matt 7:13–14; Luke 13:22–30). Some, because of this, have adopted universalism[26]

---

25. See especially the extended discussion of 1 Tim 2:4 which follows later in this chapter.

26. Knight makes note of universalism in the early church: "Among Christians and those associated with the Church, the first advocates of Universalism were some Gnostics (Valetinians, Carpocratians, and Basalidians, about AD 130), although their doctrine as to individualism is not entirely clear. At the same time or later, certain orthodox Christians who were the authors of the forged Sibylline Oracles . . . were undoubtedly Universalists. The earliest system of Universalistic theology was by

as a solution.[27] In their view, although many do not accept Christ in this life, God's love will continue to draw those people in hell to Christ until they all repent and go to heaven. Skinner, in a series of sermons, wrote: "It is not part of mainline Christian doctrine either Catholic or Protestant. Repentance is a means by which all men are brought into the enjoyment of religion, and we do not expect any man will be saved while he continues in sin. However, Unitarian Universalism holds a universal salvation, because we expect all men will repent."[28]

Of course, this view seems to be at odds with the teachings of Jesus just mentioned. But this does not solve the problem for divine determinists either, because—even if universalism were consistent with Scripture—affirming universalism does not explain why God does not simply determine that everyone would turn to Christ in this life (an omnipotent God would have the power to do so).

But there are serious weaknesses in the universalists's use of Scripture. Several examples of their appeal to Scriptures demonstrate this problem. A first example comes from their use of Eph 1:9–10: [God made] *known to us the mystery of his will, according to his purpose, which he set forth in Christ as a plan for the fullness of time, to unite all things in him, things in heaven and things on earth.* Universalists give as support for their position the phrase *to unite all things in him,* which they (e.g., Beecher as noted above) assert suggests that even those people in hell will be united with Christ and eventually go to heaven. As Stratton and Erasmus have argued, the problem with this interpretation is that the Greek word for *unite* (ἀνακεφαλαιώσασθαι) more precisely should be translated "to bring together under one head."[29] This is why the *NLT* translates this phrase: *At the right time he will bring everything together under the authority of Christ.* Hodge writes: "The Scriptures speak of the whole universe, material and rational, as being placed under Jesus Christ; as they speak especially of all orders of intelligent creatures being subject to him; as they teach the union of the long disjected members of the human family, the Jews and Gentiles, in one body in Christ, of which union this epistle says so much and in such exalted strains; and as finally they speak

---

Clement of Alexandria . . . who was the head of the theological school in that city until AD 202. His successor in the school was the great Origen . . . the most distinguished advocate of this doctrine in all time" (Knight, *Pastoral Epistles*, 96). Interestingly, universalists espoused the Calvinist doctrine of irresistible grace, which they said applied to all (in contradiction to the Calvinist use of the term) and called it "death and glory" theology (Knight, *Pastoral Epistles*, 97).

27. See "Excursus on 1 Timothy 2:4" later in this chapter for documentation. H. W. Beecher (*Heaven and Hell*)—who was a key proponent of universalism in the past—said, "I believe that punishment exists, both here and hereafter; but it will not continue after it ceases to do good. With a God who could give pain for pain's sake, this world would go out like a candle" (quoted in Strong, *Systematic Theology*, 1047). See also Crockett, ed., *Four Views on Hell*, and Sprinkle et al., eds., *Four Views on Hell*, 2nd ed., for the current debate. Rob Bell—as reflected in his recent book *Love Wins*—is an example of a prominent proponent of universalism: "No one can resist God's pursuit forever, because God's love will eventually melt even the hardest of hearts" (Rob Bell, *Love Wins*, 108).

28. Skinner, *A Series of Sermons,* 209.

29. Stratton and Erasmus, "Divine Determinism," 7.

of the union of the saints of all ages and nations, of those now in heaven and of those now on earth, in one great family above."[30]

While one could argue that the word could be translated as meaning that all will be saved—though that is denied by and is not harmonious with the rest of Scripture—the more likely interpretation, is that even those condemned to hell are by their judgment *under the authority of Christ*. Ellicott is emphatic: "Any reference to the redemption or restoration of those spirits (Crellius), for whom our Lord Himself said τὸ πῦρ τὸ αἰώνιον [*the eternal fire*] (Matt 25:41) was prepared, must be pronounced fundamentally impossible."[31] Meyer, after surveying passages of Scripture where such thinking is firmly rejected, concluded:

> The doctrine of Restoration, according to which those who have continued unbelieving and the demons shall still ultimately attain to salvation, altogether opposed as it is to the N.T., finds no support, in our passage, where (in opposition to Origen, Samuel Crell, and others), on the contrary . . . there is obviously implied, from the general point of view occupied by Christian faith, the separation of unbelievers and of the demoniac powers, and their banishment into Gehenna; so that the ἀνακεφαλαιώσασθαι [*uniting*] is not meant of every single individual, but of the whole aggregate of heavenly and earthly things, which, after the antichristian individuals have been separated and consigned to hell, shall again in the renewed world be combined into unity under God, as once, before the entrance of sin, all things in heaven and on earth were combined into such unity.[32]

A second passage commonly used to support universalism is Phil 2:10–11: *At the name of Jesus every knee should bow, in heaven and on earth and under the earth, and every tongue confess that Jesus Christ is Lord, to the glory of God the Father*. Universalists interpret this passage as meaning that every person will eventually repent and turn to Christ. Lightfoot draws on the passage's association with Psalm 148 and concludes: "Any limitation to intelligent beings, while it detracts from the universality of the homage, is not required by the expressions. The personification of universal nature offering its praise and homage to its Creator in the 148th Psalm will serve to illustrate St. Paul's meaning here. If this view be correct, all endeavours to explain the three words of different classes of intelligent beings; as Christians, Jews, heathens; angels, men, devils; the angels, the living, the dead; souls of the blessed, men on earth, souls in purgatory, etc., are out of place."[33]

Again, while the phrases *to bow* and *to confess* may mean "to worship" or "to repent" respectively, they more likely mean "to acknowledge," that is, to acknowledge

30. Hodge, *Ephesians*, 30.

31. Ellicott, *Ephesians*, 15.

32. Meyer, *Ephesians*, 325.

33. Lightfoot, *Ephesians*, 113.

as Lord. Consequently, a more plausible interpretation of this passage is that the unrighteous will *resentfully* acknowledge that Christ is Lord, similar to how James (2:19) speaks of the demons fearfully acknowledging God. Commenting on these two passages, Millard Erickson declares: "The reconciliation, the uniting of all things [in Eph 1:9–10], is not a restoration of fallen humanity to fellowship with God, but a restoration of harmony within the creation by, among other actions, putting sin into subjection to the Lord. It is not a matter of humans's accepting God, but of his quelling their rebellion. And while it is indeed true that every knee will bow and every tongue confess Christ as Lord, we must picture the wicked not as eagerly joining forces with the Lord, but as surrendering to a conquering army, so to speak. There will be an acquiescence in defeat, not a joyful commitment."[34]

Therefore—despite the universalists's arguments to the contrary—there are good grounds to believe, with the majority of scholars, that not all people will go to heaven.

The second key premise is (I4): If God is all-loving, then God desires all people to go to heaven. Does he? In addition to the biblical passages noted earlier, there are several other texts which plainly teach this divine desire. The prophet Ezekiel (18:23), quoting God himself, records: *"As I live," declares the Lord God, "I have no pleasure in the death of the wicked, but that the wicked turn from his way and live; turn back, turn back from your evil ways, for why will you die, O house of Israel"?* The clause *I have no pleasure in the death of the wicked* makes a sweeping claim that applies to all wicked people, and it thereby rules out the possibility that this passage is only, as per Calvin, meant "to give the hope of pardon to them who repent."[35] There is no reason to suggest that God through Ezekiel was saying anything other than that he desires no person to face spiritual death and desires all people to be saved.

The familiar verse—John 3:16—is another supportive text: *God so loved the world, that he gave his only Son, that whoever believes in him should not perish but have eternal life.* It is difficult to see how the word *world* (κόσμος) could mean anything other than "the inhabitants of earth" or "all people." Godet says *world* denotes the world as a whole: "The world, that fallen humanity the greater part of which God had left during the O.T. outside of His theocratic government, and which the Pharisees devoted to wrath and judgment, Jesus presents to the eyes of Nicodemus as the object of the most boundless love . . . The closing words of verse 15, repeated here almost word for word, have the effect of a refrain. It is the triumphal shout of the conqueror of sin and death and of the giver of life. The *universality of salvation (whosoever)*; the easiness of the means (*believeth*); the greatness of the evil prevented (*should not perish*); the infinity, both in excellence and duration, of the blessing bestowed (*everlasting life*)."[36]

There is simply no hint in John 3 that *world* could mean "only the elect." Indeed, when verse seventeen is read along with verse sixteen it is clear that—as Westcott put

---

34. Erickson, *Christian Theology*, 1134–35.

35. Calvin, *Institutes*, 818.

36. Godet, *John*, 67–68.

it, "The love of God is without limit on His part (verse 17, note), but to appropriate the blessing of love, man must fulfil the necessary condition of faith."[37] He also says that "potentially the work of Christ extends to the whole world (6:33; 1 John 2:2)."[38]

Further, John uses the same term (κόσμος) in the subsequent verse to refer to humanity: *For God did not send his Son into the world to condemn the world, but in order that the world might be saved through him* (John 3:17). The first occurrence of the word *world* in this verse refers to the planet, and the second refers to the people who populate the planet. If one restricts *world* to only "the elect" in John 3:16, one must do the same in John 3:17 and interpret the latter as claiming that God sent his Son into "the society of the elect," which would be an obvious twisting of the natural sense of the text. John 3:16, then, implies that God desires everyone to be saved.

One additional passage supportive of Premise (14) is 1 Tim 2:1–6: *First of all, then, I urge that supplications, prayers, intercessions, and thanksgivings be made for all people, for kings and all who are in high positions, that we may lead a peaceful and quiet life, godly and dignified in every way. This is good, and it is pleasing in the sight of God our Savior, who desires all people to be saved and to come to the knowledge of the truth. For there is one God, and there is one mediator between God and men, the man Christ Jesus, who gave himself as a ransom for all, which is the testimony given at the proper time* (emphasis added).

Excursus on 1 Tim 2:4.

This text has been debated for centuries, from the earliest of times right down to the present day. To be sure it was a key issue between Arminians[39] and Calvinists[40] in the seventeenth century,[41] but it was an issue back in the time of the church fathers (e.g., Tertullian, Chrysostom, Theodore of Mopsuetia, and John Damascene).[42] The debate has surrounded how to reconcile, on the one hand, that Christ's *desire* is for all to be *saved* and yet some end up going to hell and, on the other hand, that God has predestined only some to eternal life. Arguments usually have focused on three words/segment and their definition: (1) *All*, (2) *Desires*, and (3) *Saved . . . knowledge of the truth*. Each of these is worthy of careful research and must be weighed for their relevance to any discussion of the text's meaning.

37. Westcott, *John, Greek Text*, 120.

38. Westcott, *John, Greek Text*, 41.

39. See chapter 10 and the discussion of Article 2 of the *Five Articles*.

40. See chapter 10 and the discussion of Article 1 of the *Canons of Dort*.

41. Guthrie, *Pastoral Epistles*, 81.

42. Kelly, *Pastoral Epistles*, 62.

The usage of the word "all."

Marshall states that this word is defined in three[43] different ways in theological discussion:

1. All people, without exception.

    A. Position #1: That God's design is that everyone will be saved regardless of the beliefs which they hold.[44] But this "universalism" is repudiated throughout the New Testament. For example, John 3:16–18 makes it clear that all people stand *condemned* and only by *believing* do they receive eternal life. Mounce notes that in the Pastoral Epistles repeatedly salvation is by grace to those who believe (e.g., 2 Tim 2:9; 3:15; Tit 3:5; etc.).[45]

    B. Position #2: That God desires everyone to share in the forgiveness made possible by his Son's death on the cross, whether they ultimately do or not. This is Guthrie's[46] and Marshall's[47] view. Mounce says that "although God is the Christian's savior, he wishes that the benefits of his salvific work be enjoyed by all, even by the 'worst of sinners' (1:15)."[48]

2. All the elect, those predestined to be his children.

    For example, Tertullian said it referred to "All the adopted" and Augustine "all the predestined," both of which Kelly feels are "out-of-place" and "remote to the Apostle's mind."[49] Mounce argues that election is absent from the context of the "historical situation," which is Paul urging his readers to not withhold the proclamation of the Gospel to all.[50]

3. All "kinds" of people, briefly illustrated in verse 1.

    Calvin argued this way: that the words *all people* do not mean "every individual person" but, rather "all orders or types of people."[51] Usually this position is held in conjunction with those who think "all" relates only to the elect.[52]

---

43. Marshall, *Pastoral Epistles*, 426, actually lists four, adding "All people, except the worst," which he considers rightly as "untenable."
44. E.g., Hanson, *Pastoral Epistles*, according to Guthrie, *Pastoral Epistles*, 81.
45. Mounce, *Pastoral Epistles*, cxxxii.
46. Guthrie, *Pastoral Epistles*, 81.
47. Marshall, *Pastoral Epistles*, 426.
48. Mounce, *Pastoral Epistles*, 84.
49. Kelly, *Pastoral Epistles*, 62.
50. Mounce, *Pastoral Epistles*, 85–86.
51. Calvin, *Institutes*, 819.
52. See also Hendriksen, *Pastoral Epistles*, 9–10.

The usage of the word "desire"

The attempt by some—Bernard[53] and Kent[54]—to distinguish the Greek words θέλειν and Βούλομαι—the former meaning "to wish" and the latter "to intend"—and thus to suggest that here the meaning is preference not absolute will is more likely theologically motivated than the conclusion of a rigorous word study. Mounce says that "although there are examples where these original meanings are still present, and while there is much to be said for distinguishing between God's preference and what he wills to accomplish, it is the context that determines meaning and not the choice of words."[55]

The meaning of the words "saved . . . come to the knowledge of the truth."

Hendrickson says these words mean "more than intellectual knowledge . . . [It] is that they may be saved, and may come to 'full knowledge,' a knowledge in which not only the mind but also the heart partakes."[56] So also Kelly[57] and Knight, the latter who says it is a "technical term for conversion."[58] Therefore, there appears to be little debate about the meaning of the words *"saved . . . come to the knowledge of the truth,"* and there is little linguistic basis for distinguishing qélein and boúlesqai. This makes the salient issue a theological matter, that has been framed—as noted above—as a clash between Arminianism and Calvinism. Without rehashing that issue, this leaves as the defining question what Marshall asked at the beginning of his discussion: "Why does Paul bring up this discussion"?[59] He considers several reasons,[60] but he concludes that the likely reason is that the "Jewish or Judaizing ostracism of the uncircumcised led to the exclusion of Gentiles from the church in certain circles . . . [which] Paul addressed . . . in Galatians and Romans, and maintained that all had equal access to God."[61] He finds support not only in those epistles, but also in 2:7 which appears to be a conclusion (*for this*) of Paul's argument begun in 2:1–6: "The context shows that the inclusion of Gentiles alongside of Jews in salvation is the primary issue here, and the best solution is to adopt (a) [that is, Position #2 of the discussion of *all* above] with the recognition that the point of stressing God's desire to save all people is to indicate that his desire includes Gentiles as well as Jews. The emphasis is thus on

53. Bernard, *Pastoral Epistles*, 40–41.

54. Kent, *Pastoral Epistles*, 98–99.

55. Mounce, *Pastoral Epistles*, 86.

56. Hendriksen, *Pastoral Epistles*, 96–9.

57. Kelly, *Pastoral Epistles*, 62.

58. Knight, *Pastoral Epistles,* 120.

59. Marshall, *Pastoral Epistles*, 425–26.

60. Marshall, *Pastoral Epistles,* 426. The two other possibilities which he disallowed were the "exclusivism" of the Qumran community and Gnostic doctrine of salvation of only the "elect."

61. Marshall, *Pastoral Epistles*, 426. So also Knight, *Pastoral Epistles*, 119, 124–25.

universal accessibility to God's salvation on the basis of a faith open to all and a gospel preached to all."[62]

To argue that the word *all* is a reference only to the "elect" appears to be an example of a person's theological philosophy shaping his/her exegesis. Is it not more natural to think that Paul is using the phrase *kings and all who are in high positions* as illustrations for whom a person ought to pray? Is it not more natural to conclude that Paul is stressing to his readers that they should not neglect those in high positions? Indeed, it is obvious that the phrase *kings and all who are in high positions* is not synonymous with the phrase "all types of people," since there are many other types of people than kings and the elite. Furthermore, if one thinks that Paul makes this restriction to *all people* in 1 Tim 2:1, then he accordingly should interpret Paul in 1 Tim 2:4 to mean that God only wants kings and all who are in high positions to be saved. Such an interpretation is clearly unintelligible. Therefore, the best interpretation of 1 Tim 2:4 is that God desires no one go to Hell.[63]

Apart from Scripture, there is another reason to affirm Premise (I4): it is intuitively obvious. Would not the majority of people, including this writer, have enough love in their hearts honestly to say that they sincerely desire all people to go to heaven? If this would be how imperfect persons feel about humanity, it seems intuitive that God—a perfect, morally good, and all-loving being—would at least desire the same thing.

Perhaps a more concrete, personal way to put the issue is to take a moment to think about the loved ones in our lives, people whom we love so much that we are willing to die for them. Would we not want what is best for them? Would we not want them to experience eternal paradise in heaven? If our answer is "No," can we truly say we love them? Certainly not.

If a man declared his love for his wife, but in his heart did not really care if she suffered in hell for all eternity, then his wife would have good reason to think they needed marriage counseling! If a mother told her daughter how much she loved her, but then added, "but I hope you don't make it to heaven," this child will probably need therapy and have trust issues for the rest of her life! It is utterly absurd to even entertain the notion that a person can really love another person and still not desire the eternal best for that person.

In brief, if an imperfect human desires heaven for those he loves—yes, for those whom he does not even know, and even for those who hate him—it seems obvious that an all-loving being (God)—who is the ground of love (1 John 4:8)—would at the least desire that every human created in his image would go to heaven.

Perhaps someone might object, saying that, although God loves everyone, he does not desire the ultimate best for everyone. He might contend—on the basis of Matt 5:45—that, although God demonstrates some degree of love for everyone (common

62. Marshall, *Pastoral Epistles,* 427.

63. Stratton and Erasmus, "Divine Determinism," 3–15.

grace), he need not desire heaven for everyone. The problem with this thinking, however, is that, even if God only loved certain people to some extent, he would still want them to be saved. How can anyone forget about the nature of hell, which is an eternal separation from God and all that is good for eternity? There is nothing good about hell, and this lack of goodness is a state of affairs which is infinite into the future; there is no end to suffering. Indeed, hell makes Hitler's holocaust look like a summer picnic! At least in the Nazi concentration camps there were occasionally a few "goods." There were some friendships, while others received some limited food and water. Some survived and eventually were set free. No one was forced to stay in Hitler's concentration camps forever—in fact, these camps lasted from 1933 to 1945, and everyone in them eventually died or was set free. Hell, however, is far worse than Hitler's concentration camps because hell is an eternal holocaust with no good and no escape. Why would God want anyone to end up there—especially those who had no ability to make a choice to follow or not follow him? Surely, as Scripture makes clear, God really does desire all people to be saved. So, why are some people damned?

Some Christians might reply (contra divine determinists) that humans have free will. In contrast, many divine determinists affirm that God desires the salvation of all people (as the Bible does teach), but that he also desires (and chooses) some to be damned for eternity. In other words, one might say God has "competing desires." Those words may seem peculiar and puzzling, but this is what John Piper contends: God has "competing desires" between (i) all persons going to heaven and (ii) the greater desire of "the manifestation of the full range of God's glory in wrath and mercy and the humbling of man so that he enjoys giving all credit to God for his salvation."[64] What Piper is proposing is that God is like limited, weak, and finite humans who have "competing desires." For example, a person can have a desire to be physically fit and also have a desire to eat pizza daily. The desire to stay in good physical condition may be greater than the desire to eat pizza daily, influencing one to choose not to eat pizza often. So, one shudders to think of God possessing "competing desires" regarding the salvation or denial of salvation to human beings. How can such thinking be harmonious with 1 Tim 2:4 and John 3:16 quoted above? Even more vexing to such a position are the words of Paul in 2 Cor 5:14–15: Christ *died for all*. How can it be consistent, on the one hand, to affirm with Scripture that Christ *died for all* but at the same time say that some of the *all* were causally determined by God to spend eternity in hell? Does not "providing salvation for all," while also affirming that "only those who accept it are saved,"[65] imply that God not only desires all but offers to all his free gift of forgiveness?

Furthermore, a philosophical analysis of the nature of a maximally great being would reach this same conclusion: he would (at least) desire all people to "flourish" and avoid eternal hell.[66] Thus, there is good reason to believe that God desires all people

---

64. Piper, "Are There Two Wills"?

65. Earle, *1,2 Timothy*, 358.

66. Walls, "What's Wrong with Calvinism"?, 46:20. See also Walls, *Purgatory*, 95.

to go to heaven. Some advocates of determinism, however, in order to address the issue as to why God's desire for universal salvation is not achieved, argue that God has a greater desire than his smaller desire for universal salvation, to use Piper's words. And what is this "greater, competing desire"? These determinists reply: "God's own glory, a desire that dwarfs God's lesser desire for universal salvation."[67] More precisely, the full range of God's glory can only be displayed through his attributes of wrath and mercy, which requires that God send some people to hell while saving others.

This view, however, faces several difficulties. First, if it is true, then it seems that God's glory is incompatible with maximal human flourishing. Even worse, creation then becomes necessary for God's glory, since God must punish some people in hell for eternity to receive glory. If one affirms such things, one tacitly affirms that God is dependent upon the existence of mankind and the eternal punishment of the many.

A second difficulty is that it does not address the crucial issue of why God would even have a desire for something (such as universal salvation) that would detract from or negate his glory. Anything that does not bring glory to God is evil. It seems those holding this "competing desires" view inadvertently contend that God has a desire (albeit a lesser one) for evil.

Third, if God cannot have both of his desires, then it seems that he is not omnipotent, unless God's glory and universal salvation are logically incompatible. This is like stating that God's glory and his desire for all to be saved is on the same logically fallacious level as triangles with four corners and married bachelors. However, the idea that God's glory and universal salvation are logically contradictory is far from obvious. Surely God could be glorified if universal salvation were attained. After all, it seems that God would receive more glory if all humanity praised, worshiped, and loved him as opposed to only a few. Indeed, even if God can only be glorified through his wrath by sending someone to hell, he could have created unconscious, soulless "persons" and sent them to hell instead of sending conscious persons to hell. In the latter case, God's wrath is demonstrated on the soulless person. However, if for some unknown reason, God can be glorified only by damning a conscious person to hell, then there is still no need for God to condemn all human persons, as he could simply condemn Satan alone to hell. In this last case God's desire for glory and his desire for human universal salvation are both attained. Therefore, since these two desires are not logically incompatible, it seems the divine determinist inadvertently dethrones God from the status of being omnipotent.

Perhaps the most serious theological problem with this view is that, if it is logically impossible for God to have both his desire of glory and his desire of universal salvation, then the atonement of Christ was simply not enough. Piper's position entails that Jesus merely picked up part of the check and left the unconditionally hated "non-elect" to pick up the rest of the tab and suffer the holocaust of hell into the infinite

---

67. Piper, "Are There Two Wills"?

future so that those in heaven might "enjoy giving all credit to God."[68] In other words, the cross of Christ—together with the damned in hell—is what it takes to secure salvation for a few. Thus, Jesus's atonement is only a necessary condition but not a sufficient condition to make salvation possible for the elect. To the above discussion, Piper adds: "The difference between Calvinists and Arminians [notice the assumption of a false dichotomy] lies not in whether there are two wills in God, but in what they say this higher commitment is."[69] In other words, Piper argues that the Arminian claims that humans freely choosing to love God is more valuable to God than universal salvation. Unfortunately, he fails to recognize that the former is exactly what salvation is. There are no competing desires here but, rather, one desire, namely, for all people to freely choose to love God. Salvation is only found in a true love relationship with God.

The marriage covenant furnishes a valuable analogy. True love is attained when two people freely enter into a covenantal relationship. If a person is kidnapped against her will and forced into a relationship, then true love is not a part of that relationship. One is left with something akin to what Patrick Carnes called the "Stockholm Syndrome,"[70] a psychological trauma, not true love. Since it is logically impossible to force someone freely to do something, God cannot force someone freely to love him in a real and genuine sense. However, when one does not resist God's love and amazing grace (since God loved him first), he will be saved. This eternal flourishing and love relationship with God is the ultimate "good" a human can experience, and simultaneously brings God ultimate glory.

Divine determinism—coupled with the claim that God must damn some humans in order to save others (if one argues logically from such a statement)—implies that Christians should not be angry at the damned; rather, Christians ought to be extremely grateful that these "others" would suffer eternal hell for their benefit and in their place. In fact—without being irreverent—when divine determinists praise Jesus for all he has done, should they not also take a moment to thank the damned in hell as well since they could not have been saved without them? Obviously, this is utterly absurd and preposterous—the answer is "no"—but it highlights the point that the cross was both necessary and sufficient to secure the possibility of salvation for all humanity. The cross was enough. Jesus paid it all. God does not need anyone to suffer hell into the infinite future to receive his glory.

If one remains committed to divine determinism, then, as Walls[71] has said, it is better for him to simply "bite the bullet" (as Arthur Pink has done[72]) and be honest and admit that, according to his philosophy, God does not love all people. If he believes that God really does love all people, then he ought to reject any view stating

68. Piper, "Does God Get More Glory"?
69. Piper, "Does God Get More Glory"?
70. Carnes, *The Betrayal Bond*, 34.
71. Walls, "What's Wrong with Calvinism"?, 46:20.
72. See the Pink, *Sovereignty*, 16–19.

that God causally determines the eternal destinies of all humans (this is not to be confused or conflated with the statement that God predestines the eternal destinies of all humans.[73]

Humans are genuinely responsible for their choices. Although heaven and hell are real states of affairs, it might be better to think of them not only as places but also as statuses of relationship. Heaven is an eternal love relationship with the Creator. Hell is an eternal divorce or separation from God. *Since God first loved us* (1 John 4:19), it rationally follows that God desires all humans made in his image to love him in return. But God is also an "ultimate gentleman," and he will not force anyone into a relationship with him. Because God so loved the world (every person) and because the atonement of Christ made salvation possible for everyone, each person has a choice to resist God's grace or not. He or she, in a sense, can either say "Yes" to God's spiritual marriage proposal or reject it and say, "No thanks."

The answer, then, to the question raised in Premise (I4)—"Is it true that if God were all-loving, he would desire all people to be in heaven"?—seems obvious: "Yes." If God genuinely loves each and every human, then God desires each and every human to freely choose to love him in return for all eternity. This makes the best sense of the biblical and philosophical data. Since each premise of the deductive syllogism seems to be true, it is quite rational to affirm the final conclusion: "Therefore, divine determinism is false."

CONCLUSION.

The arguments of the last two chapters demonstrate that humans at least occasionally possess limited libertarian freedom, a freedom which—at minimum—only requires a limited power to choose among a range of options (two or more), each of which is compatible with a person's nature at a certain time. Three essential arguments have been offered: The first argument was based on metaphysics, the second on biblical data, and the third and final argument on systematic theology/perfect being theology. Even if one rejects the final argument due to previously held soteriological commitments, the first appears impossible to rationally deny, and the second is biblical. For these reasons, a rational mind ought to reject any form of exhaustive determinism—and its cousin compatibilism—in favor of some level of libertarian freedom.

---

73. More on this distinction later in chapter 15.

14

A Spaniard named Luis de Molina
(AD 1535–1600)

THUS FAR THIS STUDY of the nature of human freedom has had three foci. It began with a study of specific statements or narrative accounts drawn from both the Old and New Testaments, which provided documentation that appears to support both human freedom and divine sovereignty (that is, that God was and is behind the scenes carrying out his eternal plan). Although it seems contradictory to simultaneously affirm that humans are responsible for *some* things and that God is responsible for *all* things, no attempt was made to set the seemingly opposite positions against each other. There was only an attempt to illustrate why readers of the Bible could come to different conclusions about the dilemma found there.

The next chapters briefly summarized the writings of selected, important theologians covering approximately fifteen hundred years from St. Augustine to the conclusion of the Synod of Dort's delegates (called the *Canons of Dort*). The objective was to sample the historical efforts—sometimes antagonistic toward one another—and to understand how they ought to (a) explain and argue for one or another side of the debate or to (b) attempt a harmonization of the two. These writings provide the broad shoulders—the foundations—on which the argument here is constructed.

In the previous chapter a new focus—a new direction—began with a discussion and analysis of philosophical/logical considerations that provided a trifecta of deductive arguments that support the proposition that humans possess libertarian freedom.

With the current chapter the argumentation becomes far more focused. Building on past discussions, there is an introduction of a model or system which is prominent in theological or philosophical circles today, a model which the writer thinks best explains the diverse data and provides a logical harmonization of the dilemma that the previous chapters illustrated.

Many important topics are written and discussed by scholars or experts in their fields who have their "own" vocabulary, and thus the terms one encounters in reading their tomes, while they may be understood by others in their field, are a foreign language to the student or an uninitiated reader. Certainly, this is true of the writings of Luis de Molina for at least three reasons:

1. To understand Molinism—the philosophy and theology named after Luis de Molina—the reader is introduced to some giants in theology: St. Augustine (AD 354–430), Thomas Aquinas (AD 1225–1274), Martin Luther (AD 1483–1546), and John Calvin (AD 1509–1564), to name a few. Acquaintance with them and also the philosophical traditions of Plato (428–348 BC) and Aristotle (384–322 BC) as their writings are introduced or alluded to in discussions of Molinism can be a bit intimidating (perplexing) to the typical reader.

2. Only one of Molina's seven-volume tomes—(vol. 4) *Liberi arbitrii cum gratiae donis, divina praescientia, providentia, praedestinatione et reprobatione Concordia* (A Reconciliation of Free Choice with the Gifts of Grace, Divine Foreknowledge, Providence, Predestination and Reprobation), commonly called *Concordia*—has been translated from Latin into English.[1] Further, the *Concordia* is based on Molina's three-volume commentary on Aquinas's *magnum opus, Summa Theologiae: Commentaria in primam divi Thomae partem* (AD 1592). Although Aquinas's work is available in English, Molina's commentary is available only in Latin.

3. And the *Concordia* itself is no light, after-supper reading. One reviewer put it this way: "As to style, the work has little to recommend it. The Latinity is heavy, the sentences are long and involved, and the prolix exposition and frequent repetition of the same ideas are fatiguing; in short, *Concordia* is neither easy nor agreeable reading."[2]

Having listed these difficulties with and limited availability of Molina's writings, however, is not to suggest that Molina's writings are unimportant. Just the opposite is the case. Indeed, it is—as William Lane Craig's often quoted evaluation of Molina states—[Molinism is] "one of the most fruitful theological ideas ever conceived."[3] Such an evaluation should peak the attention of anyone who is interested in theology and biblical studies.

But Molina's work is not for philosophical and theological venues alone. The purpose that motivated Molina to write *Concordia* was to address an issue with which students have struggled in their study of philosophy and theology for centuries, before

---

1. MacDonald, "Review of *On Divine Foreknowledge*," 177.
2. Pohle, "Luis de Molina."
3. Craig, "God Directs All Things," 84.

and after Molina's writings, namely, "How can the view that 'all things are fixed' be harmonized with 'human freedom'? Is life merely fatalism—being caught on the wheel of fortune—or do people have the freedom and categorical ability of choosing one way or the opposite or making no choice at all"? Therefore, there is great relevance to the subject under consideration here.

One footnote should be added: the following discussion will be limited to Molina's *Concordia* (and some references to his commentary on Aquinas's *Summa Theologica*) but not to his writings *On Justice and the Law*.

LUIS DE MOLINA AND THE HISTORICAL CONTEXT IN WHICH HE WROTE.

Luis de Molina became a Jesuit priest when only eighteen years old.[4] A year later he began studies in theology and philosophy at the University of Coimbra in Portugal (AD 1554–1562) and upon graduation taught philosophy at his alma mater and then became chair of the theology department at Évora College also in Portugal.[5] Especially significant and well-received was his class on Aquinas's *Summa Theologica*, a class he taught for twenty years.[6] Retiring in AD 1583, he spent the remainder of his life writing. His chief works were the seven-volume *Concordia* published in AD 1588; the three-volume *Commentary* on Aquinas's *Summa Theologica* published in AD 1592; and the five-volume *De Justitia et Jure* (On Justice and Law) published posthumously in AD 1614. Of these three, the first two are the seminal sources for the movement that has been named after him: *Molinism*.

Prior to Molina's publications there was a debate especially among the Jesuits that raised questions about Augustinian deterministic theology and the Dominicans, Thomas Aquinas in particular.[7] Molina also was a participant in this debate, and it was his desire to clarify the Bible's teaching on grace and to especially address the conflict of causal determinism and human freedom.[8] His views—especially in *Concordia*—brought the debate to a higher intensity within the Catholic Church, so much so that those who opposed Molina's position requested that the Vatican get involved.[9] As time passed Molina published other editions of the *Concordia* in which he replied to many of the criticisms. Alfred J. Freddoso, who translated Book 4 of the *Concordia*, described the controversies that ensued this way:

4. Freddoso, "Molina, Luis de."

5. Pohle, "Luis de Molina."

6. Pohle, "Luis de Molina."

7. Freddoso, "Molina, Luis de."

8. MacGregor, *Luis de Molina*, 16–24.

9. Pohle, "Luis de Molina."

When the dispute began to jeopardize civil as well as ecclesiastical harmony, political and religious leaders in Iberia implored the Vatican to intervene. In 1597 Pope Clement VIII established the *Congregatio de Auxiliis* (Commission on Grace) in Rome, thus initiating a ten-year period of intense investigation—including eighty-five hearings and forty-seven debates—that rendered the *Concordia* one of the most carefully scrutinized books in Western intellectual history. At first, things did not go well for the Jesuits; Molina died in Madrid amid rumors that he was being burned in effigy in Rome. However, due to the efforts of Cardinals Robert Bellarmine and Jacques du Perron, Molina's views emerged unscathed in the end. In 1607 Pope Paul V issued a decree allowing both parties to defend their own positions but enjoining them not to call one another's views heretical.[10]

Though the controversy was muted in the Roman Catholic Church by the pope's decree, Molina's writings were mistakenly understood in Protestant circles (where the focus was not even on Molina or his writings) as equivalent to what another individual taught, who like Molina was concerned about human freedom: Jacobus Arminius.[11] As discussed above in chapter 9, Arminius published a book entitled *Disputationes,* which set forth his understanding of free will in contrast to the sovereignty and determinism that were associated with Calvin and "Calvinists" of his day. A year after Arminius's death in 1609, those who were influenced by his teaching published *Remonstrantiae (Remonstrance)* defining his views,[12] the essential points of which were election based on foreseen faith, universal atonement, partial depravity, resistible grace, and the possibility of a lapse from grace. Calvinists, in response to his teachings which they considered heresy, published the *Canons of Dort,* a document which was fruit of Calvinists from a number of countries who met at the Synod of Dort.[13] The five pillars of this document—directly addressing Arminianism's points—have been rearranged with the familiar acronym TULIP: Total depravity, Unconditional election, Limited atonement, Irresistible grace, and Perseverance of the saints.[14]

Although Molinism, as noted above, sometimes has been associated with Arminius's teachings, such was not the case, as the following descriptions of Molina's teaching will demonstrate. This and the fact that he was a Jesuit priest[15] may account for the neglect of translations and study of his works. But according to Kirk MacGregor,[16] there

10. Freddoso, "Molina, Luis de."

11. MacGregor, *Luis de Molina,* 18–24.

12. Aloisi, "Understanding Arminius," 7. Since the *Remonstrance* was published after Arminius's death, it may or may not have been what Arminius himself taught.

13. Details and documentation can be found in chapter 10, specifically under the discussion of Arminius and the Synod of Dort.

14. See chapter 10 for documentation of these details.

15. Though Molina never "left" the Roman Catholic Church as Luther did, he agreed with many of the reformer's criticisms of the church. For more, see MacGregor, *Luis de Molina,* 16–18.

16. MacGregor, *Luis de Molina,* 11–13.

has been a revival of interest in the last forty years, especially being promoted by William Lane Craig, under whom MacGregor (and this author) studied at Biola University. Craig's books *The Only Wise God* published in 1999; "The Middle-Knowledge View," the chapter in *Divine Foreknowledge: Four Views* (2001); and "God Directs All Things," the chapter in *Four Views on Divine Providence* (2011); and MacGregor's books—*A Molinist-Anabaptist Systematic Theology* (2007) and especially *Luis de Molina* published in 2015—are valuable sources on the teachings of Molinism. Of course, Molina's *Concordia* is the primary source, but both of the writers mentioned have extensive bibliography and references on Molinism for those who wish to explore the subject in a more exhaustive way. And to them some of the exposition which follows is indebted.

THE DRIVING ISSUE: THE BIBLE AND HUMAN FREEDOM.

Those who have sought to describe and explain Molinism have often begun with the three logical moments[17] of God's knowledge so ably summarized by William Lane Craig:

1. God's *natural* knowledge.

2. God's *middle* knowledge.

3. God's *free* knowledge.[18]

Important as these categories are in any discussion of Molinism, it is not the place to begin to understand Molina and his writings. Instead, the first step is to consider where Molina began: with his view of the problem of human freedom and determinism, both of which he saw clearly articulated in the Scriptures. What he wrote was not a response to Jacobus Arminius (AD 1560–1609)—another strong proponent of human freedom, though a Protestant Reformer—who was writing at the same time as Molina. Though both were interacting with Calvin and Luther, Molina worked from the framework of a more Roman Catholic audience and was interacting particularly with the writings of Thomas Aquinas. Although the philosophical question of human

17. "Logical" is an important concept in theology and philosophy and must be understood if one is to understand Molina's *Middle* knowledge. It is to be contrasted with "temporal" or "chronological," terms which suggest periods of time: centuries, years, days, hours, etc. A person is using *temporal* terms when he or she speaks of time before and after. It is difficult for most people to think differently than in a temporal sequence. But it is important to understand how *logical* is different. *Logical* is not defined by time but *order*. Logically, something or thinking (which is the subject of the three moments of God's knowledge) has an order—first, second, etc. Craig put it this way: "Logical priority means that something serves to explain something else. The one provides the grounds or basis for the other" (*Only Wise God,* 127). Perhaps an illustration will help. Take an explosion. Investigators may say that the explosion was caused by an electrical short. But the short and explosion occurred at the same time. Yet *logically* the short preceded the explosion. That is why Craig speaks of God's knowledge as having three *moments*. God knows all that he knows simultaneously. He does not learn, nor forget. Thus, all he knows is timeless, but there are logical sequences. This will become more clear when the subject of God's knowledge is later discussed.

18. Craig, *Only Wise God,* 129–31.

freedom and determinism is wider than its application to soteriology, Molina was particularly addressing these two seemingly polar opposites in that specific context. This is implicit in the title of the *Concordia*: "A Reconciliation of Free Choice with the Gifts of *Grace*, Divine *Foreknowledge*, *Providence*, *Predestination* and *Reprobation*" (the author's *emphasis*). Each of these *italicized* topics is a subject of soteriology, and Molina compared and/or contrasted them with Aquinas's view in *Summa Theologica* and with the writings of the reformers. Of special significance was the subject of grace.[19] It was then and remains so today.

Molina, who was an expert on Aquinas and especially on his *Summa Theologica*, did not agree with him on his solution to the problem of God's role in condemning some men to Hell. In fact, Aquinas himself appeared to struggle with the issue.[20] He acknowledged that God "predestined" the "reprobate,"[21] but he also wanted to insist that such did not destroy the individual's free choice.[22] Aquinas had difficulty resolving this issue because he could not justify from Scripture (especially Rom 9:11–12 and 2 Cor 3:5) a belief that God predestined the "elect" because of their own works or choices.[23] Nor did he feel fully comfortable with "others who claimed that the merits which follow upon the effect of predestination are an explanation for predestination. The idea is that God gives grace to someone, and preordained that He would give it, because He foreknew that this person would make good use of the grace—in the way that a king might give a horse to some soldier whom he knows will make good use of it."[24]

---

19. See also MacGregor, *Luis de Molina*, 50–73.

20. Roger Olson, *The Story of Christian Theology*, 336–39 helps with understanding Aquinas's thinking by noting that Aquinas was deeply influenced by Aristotle. Aquinas proposed that there were two worlds: a lower world (the world in which people live) in which much about God can be discerned [this is the world of Aristotelean philosophy], and a higher realm of grace and special revelation. Man, by his reason, can understand God's general revelation, but such knowledge is insufficient for a person to know God and obtain his pardon. That demands a work of God's grace, which must come down from the upper story. In theological studies, *general* revelation is what can be known about God in nature and conscience, while *special* revelation is what is known about God that he *additionally* reveals to mankind through Scripture, visions, prophets, etc.).

21. The word *reprobate* is not a derogatory reference to a person's character. In theology it essentially has no reference to how a person is living, has lived, or will live. Instead, the *reprobate* is a person(s)who is not elect to salvation and, therefore, condemned to hell.

22. Aquinas shows this in his affirmation of "free choice" but also of God's "predestination:" "Just as predestination is the part of providence that has to do with those who are divinely ordered toward eternal salvation, so reprobation is the part of providence that has to do with those who fall short of this end . . . God's reprobation does not take away any power at all from the one who is reprobated. Hence, when it is claimed that one who is reprobated cannot obtain grace, this should be understood to mean a relative impossibility rather than an absolute impossibility—in the same way that, as was explained above (q. 19, a. 3), one who is predestined is necessarily saved, but with a relative necessity that does not destroy free choice. Hence, even if someone who is reprobated by God cannot obtain grace, nonetheless, the fact that he falls into this or that sin happens because of his free choice. Hence, he is rightly held to be guilty of his sin" (Aquinas, *Summa Theologica*, 193–94).

23. Aquinas, *Summa Theologica*, 195–96.

24. Aquinas, *Summa Theologica*, 196.

Though uncomfortable with this, Aquinas seems to have accepted this explanation: God predestines and gives his effectual grace based on his foreknowledge.[25] With this Molina dissented on two counts. First, God's grace is based solely on his love, not on any man or woman's personal merit, even that which is "foreseen." In fact, the selections of Scripture that Aquinas held (mentioned above) Molina felt could not be understood in any other way other than that grace alone was the cause of a person's salvation.[26] To these he added Rom 3:23–24; 11:5–6; and Eph 2:8–9.

Second, Molina argued that God's grace is given to all without discrimination. Though he agreed with the reformers (against his understanding of Aquinas) that grace is totally unmerited, he disagreed with Calvinism's "irresistible grace," which to Calvinists refers to that the grace given only to the elect and is different from the grace given to all, elect and non-elect.[27] The Calvinists's use of grace is a grace given to the elect is called "irresistible" or "effectual" because, when the elect receive it, they are "enabled" to put their *faith* in Christ—and do (must)—and thus, are *justified* (Rom

25. Aquinas's words: "However, these thinkers seem to have distinguished what comes from free choice and what comes from grace in such a way that the same effect could not come from both of them at once . . . Therefore, one should claim that the effect of predestination can be thought of in two ways: (a) One way is in particular, and in this sense nothing prevents one effect of predestination from being a cause of, and explanation for, another effect of predestination—where a later effect is a final cause of a prior effect, and a prior effect is a meritorious cause (which is traced back to a material disposition) of a later effect. For instance, we might say that God preordained that He would give glory to some individual because of his merits, and that He preordained that He would give him grace in order that he might merit glory" (Aquinas, *Summa Theologica*, 196). Thus, God's "preordination" is *because of the individual's* [foreknown] *merits*, and at the same time the preordination gives grace so that he might have that *merit*. See also the following footnote, quoting Roger Olson.

26. In a recent article in *Christianity Today*, Roger Olson expresses a sentiment similar to Molina's: "Bishop Barron [who had written an article published in the same issue of *Christianity Today*] quotes church father Irenaeus: 'The glory of God is a human being fully alive.' Protestants agree, but like to point out that the Bishop of Lyon did not say anything there about the glory of the creature; the glory is all God's. If a human being is made "fully alive," it is solely due to God's grace, even if the creature "contributed" assent through grace-enabled repentance and faith. For Protestants, both followers of Luther and of Wesley, *gratia prima* ["grace first"] is not strong enough to prevent human boasting. Grace is not only primary; grace is all and everything [*gracia sola*], even if it is a gift to be freely received" (Barron and Olson, "Grace First," 46).

27. Calvinists distinguish "prevenient grace" (the grace given to all) from "irresistible grace" (the grace given only to the elect). The word "prevenient" is archaic terminology which came out of an Arminian context and persists in theological circles. It literally meant/means the grace that "went before," that is, the grace given prior to a decision to put one's faith in Christ, though it is grace that can be "resisted." It is sometimes called "common grace," i.e., grace given to all ("common"). Molina agreed with Calvin that every person because of Adam's sin is unable to respond to God with a faith that results in salvation. Left to himself, human beings do not turn to God. But unlike Calvin, Molina felt common grace enabled a person to respond to God and thus be saved. (Molina, *Commentaria*, 14.13.7; 43.3.1). All quotations from Molina's *Commentaria* and volumes of *Concordia* other than volume 4 (which has been translated into English) are translations from the Latin by MacGregor. For the above discussion, see MacGregor, *Luis de Molina*, 50, 60–62). William Combs defines prevenient grace, as used by Arminians, as "[the] grace that enables depraved man to believe and be saved, but it does not guarantee such since it may be rejected. Prevenient grace is sufficient for salvation but not efficacious (irresistible)" (Combs, "Does the Bible Teach"?, 5).

8:29–30). In contrast, Molina insisted that there is no difference in the grace God gives to both. It is the same for all and enables *all* to respond to God and receive forgiveness, despite the fact that some will and do reject it. Thus, the giving of God's grace does not destroy their free choice to reject or not. Nevertheless, Molina would strongly affirm with Calvinists that a person's eternal salvation is solely due to the grace of God, not the result of any merit of his/her own.[28]

This complementary relationship between human decision and divine grace (enablement) appears often in Jesus's teaching recorded in John's gospel. Jesus—in John 1:12–13; 3:1–18—speaks of the "new" birth as being *of the Spirit* (John 3:5–8). Yet at the same time he repeatedly taught the role of the person in believing (John 1:12–13; 3:5–19).[29]

Molina argued that the explicit statements in Scripture that God was not *willing that any should perish* (2 Pet 3:9), that *he wants all to come to repentance* (1 Tim 2:4), and that he *does not take pleasure in the death of the wicked* (Ezek 18:23) showed that God's grace—the *drawing* and "enabling by the Spirit"—was given to all. To posit that only some received the grace necessary for securing salvation in Molina's eyes cast doubt on the sincerity of God's desire, because in the final analysis it implied that a sinner's condemnation had to be traced to a God who was "unwilling" to give the assistance needed.[30]

This rather lengthy discussion of Molina's understanding of grace may appear at first not particularly relevant to the discussion at hand, but the association of his teachings with Arminianism in the immediate years after Arminius's death—though an erroneous association (as demonstrated in scholarly writings)[31]—has persisted. Critics may not use that label, but they see Molina's emphasis on human freedom as inconsistent with human depravity and a person's inability to respond to God, and thus they incorrectly view Molina's insistence that a person can freely choose to respond to Christ's work on the cross as contradictory. One writer who identified himself as a "Calvinist" recently put it this way: "This [Molinism] isn't really different from Arminius's doctrine of prevenient grace. In other words, God's grace brings us up to a point where we can choose God . . . I understand that most Arminians and Molinists

---

28. Molina says this explicitly in *Commentaria*, 22:1–2 (quoted by MacGregor, *Luis de Molina*, 65, and footnote 88–89). Arminius's followers (Arminius too?) were agnostic to eternal salvation (security). See the discussion of this in chapters 9 and 10.

29. There is a false believing (John 2:23–25), people who *believed because of his miracles* (verse 23 and John 6, especially 6:26–30, 60–66).

30. In Molina's own words: "God wills for all humans to be saved. Of the same truth God even affirms under oath . . . that he does not will the death of the wicked but wills that the wicked should be converted and live. And all humans are under the same state and without exception are invited by God to eternal life. In addition, Christ is given for the redemption of all so that all, if such does not stand opposed by the persons themselves, arrive at eternal life" (Molina, *Commentaria*, 12.6.4, quoting MacGregor's translation [*Luis de Molina*, 64, note 85]).

31. For example, Olson, *Arminian Theology*, 196. For further documentation, see MacGregor, *Luis de Molina*, 18–24, and note 20).

agree that we need God's grace to embrace Christ. However, the Calvinist maintains that if even the slightest part of us works autonomously from God's grace, we are so depraved that we would choose hell."[32] Molina would shutter at such an accusation and misunderstanding! A careful reading of the above explanation shows how unfair is this charge and that it is a misrepresentation.

This discussion of grace, then, is a necessary foundation and introduction to Molina's greatest contribution to the human freedom and determinism debate (middle knowledge), which again is explained in the context of soteriology. To a discussion of this attention is now turned.

GOD'S KNOWLEDGE.

Craig's outline of the three moments in God's knowledge, though touched on before, has been well outlined in the chart found in his book *The Only Wise God*. Before inserting that chart (which follows below), Craig uses three words to describe the three moments of knowledge that are helpful in understanding what he is describing:

1. Natural knowledge: What *could* be.

2. Middle knowledge: What *would* be.

3. Free knowledge: What *will* be.[33]

These words in *italics* may be confusing now, but they will become clarified and quite helpful after the discussion which follows.

The Three Logical Moments of God's Knowledge

1. *Natural Knowledge:* God's knowledge of all possible worlds. The content of this knowledge is essential to God.

2. *Middle Knowledge:* God's knowledge of what every possible free creature would do under any possible set of circumstances and, hence, knowledge of those possible worlds which God can make actual. The content of this knowledge is not essential to God.

God's Free Decision to Create a World

3. *Free Knowledge:* God's knowledge of the actual world. The content of this knowledge is not essential to God.

---

32. These words come from the author's blog and his interaction with a Calvinist (Stratton, "Molinism is Biblical").

33. Craig, *Only Wise God*, 131.

The three terms in Craig's table (*natural*, *middle*, and *free* knowledge) are unfamiliar to most people (it does not help that they are a translation of Latin terms and different ones for Aquinas and Molina),[34] but they are essential for an understanding of Molina's system. Therefore, it is worth the intellectual work needed to understand them. Maybe the best way is to work from the known to the unknown by using a term that is far more familiar. That term is an attribute of God: His omniscience.

Understanding "omniscience."

Obviously, "omniscience" is a compound word from the Latin: *omni* = "all," plus *scientia* = "knowledge." But the great Baptist theologian Augustus Strong defines God's omniscience with much more precision: "By this we mean God's perfect and eternal knowledge of all things which are subjects of knowledge, whether they be actual or possible, past, present or future."[35] God is unlike human beings who, for example, will never master everything which can be known even in a given field. Indeed, some studies have shown that knowledge is doubling every thirteen months, and then—with the Internet considered—every twelve hours![36] But a maximally great God, from eternity past without beginning, knows all there is to know, will be known, or can be known about everything. Omniscience may in this way be defined, but its immensity is beyond our comprehension. Perhaps the best way to define omniscience is regarding propositional knowledge. That is, God knows the truth-value (whether a statement is true or false) to any and all propositions that could be thought of or uttered, and he is never wrong.

Also, unlike human kind, God does not learn or discover anything new, nor does he forget. He not only has infinite knowledge but has an awareness and understanding of everything he knows or is knowable. He knows everything he as Creator could do and all that is within his power to create (this includes all that he could have created but never did create). God knows all the kinds of creatures he could create and everything a person within his power to create could and would do. God also knows everything that could and would incidentally or randomly occur.[37] But the word in Strong's definition above that relates to God's *natural* knowledge and is key is the word *possible*. Logically prior ("before") to God's creating the world, he knew

---

34. Molina's Latin terms for Craig's English words are as follows: (1) God's natural knowledge (*scientia naturalis*) or as Aquinas called it (*scientia simplicis intelligentiae*: knowledge of simple intelligence). This is "knowledge of what may be—of the possible;" (2) God's middle knowledge (*scientia media*). This is a new term coined by Molina and will be defined later; and (3) God's free knowledge (*scientia libera*) or as Aquinas called it (*scientia visionis*: visionary knowledge)." The brief explanations in the quotes following the Latin are from Strong, *Systematic Theology*, 358.

35. Strong, *Systematic Theology*, 282.

36. See http://www.industrytap.com/knowledge-doubling-every-12-months-soon-to-be-every-12-hours/3950

37. Such "incidentals" or "random" occurrences are called in philosophy "stochastic processes."

everything that could be in all possible worlds. Craig put it comprehensively and succinctly: "God's natural knowledge includes knowledge of all possibilities. He knows all the possible individuals he could create, all the possible circumstances he could place them in, all their possible actions and reactions, and all the possible worlds or orders which he could create. God could not lack this knowledge and still be God."[38] In other words, God knew exactly what was in his power to make actual. Logically prior to creation, God possessed knowledge of all the possibilities which could have been the actual world, but that are different from the actual world. God could have created different beings (human and otherwise), different conditions or circumstances—which he never brought into existence, in contrast to the world that actually exists.

Given his omnipotence, God could have chosen to bring into existence any of these possibilities, but—as Aquinas put it—some of these possibilities "do not actually exist and have never actually existed and will never actually exist."[39] God knows[40] all possibilities—everything within his power to create and make actual, even if he never does actualize these possibilities. Human beings (sans philosophers and theologians) usually never think of God having such knowledge because they have a propensity to merely think of his knowledge as pertaining only to this world. Perhaps a better way to distinguish God's *natural* knowledge from what is known as his *free* knowledge is to consider the former as his knowledge of all the *possibilities in God's mind* which he could create in contrast to the total (*free*) knowledge of what he has created and which has become the *actual world*.[41]

Usually the word "omniscience" is associated with God's knowledge of everything in the actual world (seen and unseen, past, present, and future), but this is not comprehensive enough. Omniscience does include this particular type of knowledge, but it also applies to the wider scope of *possible* worlds described above (at least if "all" knowledge really means all knowledge). This also includes what Molina called "God's middle knowledge," which now must be considered.

Because people have less difficulty understanding both God's knowledge of possible worlds (God's *natural* knowledge) and how that would logically precede his knowledge of the particular world he created—the actual world (God's *free* knowledge)—they need insight into Molina's suggestion of God's *middle* knowledge because it challenges people's thinking. Better, it has outright baffled people's thinking; it has been ignored or rejected[42] because of being misunderstood; it has been confused with

---

38. Craig, *Only Wise God*, 129.

39. Aquinas, *Summa Theologica*, 118.

40. Though the reader may have expected the writer to use a different word "knew" (the past tense), but with God a person must speak of his knowledge not as a matter of the past but as timeless. He always knows all things.

41. In philosophical terminology, the action of God's choosing and creating certain of the infinite *possibilities* in his mind into the *actual* world, which we know and live in, is called "actualizing" or "instantiating."

42. In Protestant circles it did not get much attention because it was a "Roman Catholic" issue,

Arminianism (or "simple foreknowledge"); it has been dismissed because it is merely a "philosophical" construct and not a theological or biblical one (indeed, it is all of these!); and it has been opposed because it argues against the determinism of many deterministic expressions of Calvinism. Therefore, the discussion which follows seeks (1) to clarify what Molina taught, (2) to contrast it with other theological or philosophical positions, and (3) to seek to illumine it via charts and other visual media.

God's middle knowledge.

Before discussing the following chart, which summarizes the key ideas of the three *logical* moments in God's knowledge, perhaps it would be helpful to define what Molina meant by "middle" knowledge and why he chose that term. God's *natural* knowledge and his *free* knowledge were concepts which were used in ancient Latin writings, though—as noted above—their names were changed by Molina. *Middle* knowledge, however, was a term Molina himself coined. And, while the other two terms have careful definitions from usage by past philosophers and theologians, *middle* knowledge simply speaks of the knowledge of God which Molina proposed as lying logically in between (in the "middle" of) the other two. The word itself tells little about the content or process of *middle* knowledge. Consequently, its meaning must be found in Molina's explanation of it and be further understood by comparing and contrasting it with the other two moments of divine knowledge.

One last comment needs to be made about the following chart. Each column takes the reader deeper in understanding Molina's use of terminology and introduces more technical information about the meaning of *middle* knowledge. New terminology also is added progressively, because without the mastery of this terminology further study of Molinism will be limited. Of singular importance is the term "counterfactuals," or as they sometimes are called "counterfactual conditionals."[43] While philosophers typically use the single word "counterfactuals," the student, however, will find that "counterfactual conditionals"—because of the emphasis of the second word—helps to make the concept more readily understood. "Counterfactuals" are statements about "conditions." They are expressions of God's hypothetical knowledge which are conditioned on certain factors: "If this were the case (conditional phrase), then this *would* be the case." Because they are conditional, they are expressed in the subjunctive mood.[44]

---

especially among the Dominicans in Molina's day, who vigorously opposed Molina, even getting the pope involved. Current examples of diverse views may be found in Beilby and Eddy, *Divine Foreknowledge,* and outright denial of middle knowledge in Baptist theologian Strong (*Systematic Theology,* 358). See also chapter 9 and the association of Molinism and the teaching of Arminius, though the conflict then focused mostly on soteriological issues and especially on the question of grace given to all *versus* "irresistible" grace (*Canons of Dort*). There is also further discussion of different views later in this chapter.

43. Starr, "Counterfactuals."

44. The subjunctive mood is not a tense: past, present or future. For example, these three tenses

God's omniscience			
God's **Natural** Knowledge	Infinite possibilities Total (All)	**COULD BE** Neutral to divine evaluation *All the worlds and kinds of creatures that God could create and make actual.*	Possible worlds
God's **Middle** Knowledge	Feasible worlds All the "possibilities" delimited	**WOULD BE** True and false counterfactuals known *All that would happen if God created a world in which he does—or does not—causally determine all things.*	"Weighed" (evaluation) Feasible worlds Possible Criteria: 1. Human freedom; thus, not God-controlled 2. God's love 3. God's plan 4. God's freedom

God's Free Decision to Create a World

God's **Free** Knowledge	Actual world	**WILL BE** True counterfactuals actualized *All that will happen in the world God chose to actualize.*	God's providence Predestination

Perhaps a good introduction to the above chart—and an analysis of it—is Craig's helpful explanation of "counterfactuals" that can be seen in one of the most well-known Christmas narratives outside the Gospels: Charles Dickens, *The Christmas Carol*. Ebenezer Scrooge on that dreadful night is enabled by the ghost to see into the future, his possible future. After being visited by the ghost, Scrooge asks, "Are

---

could be expressed this way: "I *did*, I *am doing*, I *will do*." In contrast, the subjunctive mood typically has the conditional "*if*:" "*If I did* this . . . then . . ." It expresses a possibility in the mind of the person. For more information on the term "counterfactuals," see Starr, "Counterfactuals."

these the shadows of the things that will be, or are they shadows of things that may be only"? Craig says that Scrooge asks the wrong question. The ghost was offering Scrooge specific knowledge of what *would* happen, *if* Scrooge kept living his selfish and inconsiderate lifestyle. If Scrooge did not change his life, the ghost warned him of all of the horrible things that would happen. Scrooge is quick to change his life, and therefore, these terrible things the ghost warned Scrooge would happen, do not actually happen. The kind of knowledge the ghost possessed is called *counterfactual knowledge*, and Molina's concept of middle knowledge operates in a similar way.[45]

As a basic first-principle of understanding Molina's *middle* knowledge, one should note in the second column in the chart above that there is a dotted line that encompasses (1) all the box of infinite "possible" worlds, (2) part of the box of feasible worlds, and (3) a smaller part of the box representing the actual world. Though the percentages of space in the boxes below the first are totally hypothetical, the point is to indicate that God's *free* knowledge of the actual world assumes his knowledge (*middle*) of feasible worlds, which assumes his knowledge (*natural*) of all possible worlds.[46] All three moments in God's knowledge are included in God's omniscience. He knows all that *could* happen, all that *will* happen, and all that *would* have happened had he chosen to create differently. All are illustrated in the third column.

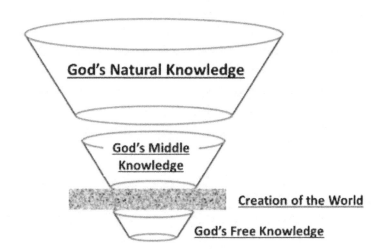

God's Natural Knowledge

God's Middle Knowledge

Creation of the World

God's Free Knowledge

45. Craig, *Time and Eternity*, 118–19. Later in this essay a biblical illustration (1 Sam 23:9–13) of "counterfactual knowledge" is given when David asked God for information about what would happen if he were inside the city Keilah and Saul attacked.

46. Molina's words: "*Middle* knowledge partly has the character of natural *knowledge* [the first box in the chart above], since it was prior to the free act of the divine will . . . and partly has the character of *free* knowledge [the box at the bottom of the first column]." (Molina, *Concordia*, 169. [Bracketed] comments are the author's).

Another way to visualize this is to think of the logical progressions in God's knowledge as a funnel. In other words, from the logical moment of God's *natural* knowledge to his decree to create our world and his comprehensive knowledge of that world (God's *free* knowledge) there is a delimiting[47] of "possibilities," that is, from what *could* be, to what *would* be, to what *will* be.[48]

To understand the precise difference between God's *natural* knowledge and his *middle* knowledge, a person must remember these are logical sequences, not chronological.[49] The former is God's knowledge of an infinite range of possibilities: of worlds, of circumstances in which a person could be found, of random occurrences. *Middle* knowledge is what God knows—logically prior to his decision to create the world—of what would happen in any possible scenario he could create. In God's natural knowledge and given his omnipotence, God knows that he possesses the power to create a being with an ability to choose among a range of options each compatible with that being's nature (libertarian freedom). In God's *middle* knowledge he discerns how each creature with libertarian freedom, within his power to create, *would* freely respond in every possible circumstance and in context of any random occurrences ("stochastic circumstances") if he were to actualize this potential creature in those possible circumstances. To use the word often employed in science, God's *middle* knowledge is perfect knowledge of "hypotheticals." "Hypotheticals" are possibilities. In God's *middle* knowledge an infinite number of possibilities are considered, possibilities that are expressed in conditional sentences: "If this were the case, then this *would* be the case." As in science there can be any number of epistemic hypotheses, some of which may prove inaccurate when they are tested or after more data have been obtained. However, to say this is not to suggest that God is a "scientist" who makes hypotheses which are mistakes. It is rather that among all hypotheticals in God's *middle* knowledge, many will never occur in the world he will create. But he knew these hypotheticals, and they were ontological possibilities. These possibilities are called "counterfactuals." *True*

47. Craig, *Only Wise God*, 130–31: "His middle knowledge serves, so to speak, to *delimit* the range of possible worlds to those he could create, given the free choices which creatures would make in them. God's middle knowledge . . . consists in his selecting to become actual one of the possible worlds known to him in the second moment."

48. MacGregor, *Luis de Molina*, 91: "Molina . . . fit counterfactual knowledge into the basic structure of omniscience inherited from Aquinas . . . Since what *would* happen in particular circumstances (counterfactual knowledge) is logically subsequent to what *could* happen in particular circumstances (knowledge of simple intelligence) [God's natural knowledge], Molina placed counterfactual knowledge after God's knowledge of simple intelligence, thereby positioning it between God's knowledge of simple intelligence and the divine creative decree. So, while on Aquinas's view there were two moments of divine knowledge, one on either side of the creative decree, on Molina's view there were three moments of divine knowledge, two before the creative decree and one after."

49. Stratton and Erasmus, "Mere Molinism," 25: "For example, the words in a sentence are logically, but not temporally, prior to the meaning of the sentence; and the left-hand of an equation (e.g. '2 + 4') is logically, but not temporally, prior to the answer or right-hand of the equation (e.g., '6'). In a similar way, the stages of God's knowledge are logically, not temporally, prior or posterior to each other, since God has these stages eternally without beginning or timelessly."

counterfactuals are those possible circumstances which are feasible and which God could choose to actualize. There are some counterfactuals which are true but which God nevertheless did not choose to actualize. In contrast, there are false counterfactuals which are not feasible to be a part of his created world.[50] These two sentences are written in *italics* because this is an important concept in Molina's view of God's *middle* knowledge.[51]

MacGregor has been helpful in his explanation of true versus false counterfactuals:

> The counterfactual "If I had $2 million, then I would buy a yellow Lamborghini" is true because it correctly describes what I would do under various circumstances. However, God chose for those circumstances not to be a part of his created world. So, the difference between true and false counterfactuals is that true counterfactuals correctly describe what would obtain under various circumstances (regardless of whether or not God decides to create them), and false counterfactuals incorrectly describe what would obtain under various circumstances. Hence God doesn't control whether counterfactuals are true or false, and God can only choose between true counterfactuals in his divine creative decree.[52]

The illustration of Peter.

This still can be quite confusing to the student of Molinism, so an illustration of what this would mean using Peter as the example is insightful. Note in the example the use of what *could* occur (God's *natural* knowledge) and what *would* occur in specific

---

50. Craig, *Only Wise God*, 134: "Statements about how creatures would decide to act if placed in certain circumstances are true or false; since God is omniscient, he knows all truth; therefore, God simply knows all true statements about how creatures would act in certain circumstances." Molina put it this way: "It is clear from Sacred Scripture that the supreme God has certain cognition of some future contingents that depend on human free choice, but that neither have existed nor ever will exist in reality and that hence do not exist in eternity either; therefore, it is not simply because future contingents exist outside their causes in eternity that God knows them with certainty" (Molina, *Concordia*, 116).

51. This whole paragraph is the essence of Molina's discussion *Disputation 49*, especially in paragraph 11: "Through His natural knowledge God comprehends Himself, and in Himself He comprehends all the things that exist pre-eminently in Him and thus the free choice of any creature whom He is able to make through His omnipotence . . . He discerns what the free choice of any creature would do by its own innate freedom . . . It would be insulting to the depth and perfection of the divine knowledge . . . to assert that God is ignorant of what I would have done by my freedom of choice (i) if He created me in some other order of things, or (ii) if, in this very order of things which He has created me, He had decided to confer on me more or fewer aids than He in fact decided to give me, or (iii) if He had granted me a longer life or handed me over to more serious temptations. From this it follows that by the very fact that He freely chose the order of things which He in fact chose, He knew absolutely and with certainty which contingent things were going to be or not going to be . . . Therefore, God does not need the existence of those things in His eternity in order to know them with certainty. We have been forced to touch upon the whole foundation on the basis of which we believe that God knows all future contingents with certainty, and . . . reconcile freedom of choice and the contingency of things with divine foreknowledge" (Molina, *Concordia*, 119–20).

52. MacGregor in a private correspondence (8 February 2019) with the author.

circumstances (God's *middle* knowledge): "To illustrate the distinction between the first two moments of divine omniscience, God knew in his natural knowledge that Peter, if placed in the courtyard of the Sanhedrin, could freely affirm or deny Christ, but God discerned in his middle knowledge that Peter would freely deny Jesus under those circumstances. As previously indicated, that is not because the circumstances compelled him to deny Jesus—for Molina all sets of circumstances are necessarily freedom-preserving in character—but rather that God knew which way Peter would freely choose."[53]

MacGregor continues:

> There are logically possible worlds where Peter freely affirms Jesus, flees from the courtyard, or does any of a number of things other than denying Jesus in precisely the same circumstances where Peter in fact denied Jesus, along with a logically possible world where Peter denies Jesus in those circumstances. But in light of the counterfactual truth that if Peter were in those circumstances, then he would freely deny Jesus, none of the logically possible worlds on our list except for the last is possible for God to create. Now this does not mean that God could not prevent Peter from denying Jesus, for he could easily do this by putting Peter in different circumstances or not making Peter at all.[54]

God's Middle Knowledge

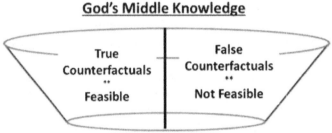

53. MacGregor, *Luis de Molina*, 92–93. MacGregor's quote (in this context) does not emphasize enough that God not only—in his middle knowledge—knew what Peter, given his sinful nature, would freely do, but what in the actualized world he will *freely* do. Indeed, as will be noted below, one of the principles or bases of God's middle knowledge is human freedom. MacGregor's illustration is not his own. It is Molina's (Molina, *Concordia*, 145–46). Molina stated it this way: "If you excluded the free choice of . . . human beings . . . with respect to those acts wherein there is found a trace of freedom, and if you posited the universe with its present constitution and assumed that God did nothing over and beyond the common course and order imposed on things, then contingency would be taken away from all the effects of secondary causes, and everything would have to happen by a kind of fatalistic necessity" (Molina, *Concordia*, 93).

54. MacGregor, *Luis de Molina*, 94. Compare also Craig, "The Difference between Possible and Feasible Worlds": "For example, logically prior to His creative decree, God knew that *if Peter were in circumstances C, he would freely deny Christ three times* . . . There is an intrinsically possible world in which Peter freely affirms Christ in precisely the same circumstances in which he in fact denied him; but given the counterfactual truth that if Peter were in precisely those circumstances he would freely deny Christ, then the possible world in which Peter freely affirms Christ in those circumstances is not feasible for God. God could force Peter to affirm Christ in those circumstances, but then his confession would not be free."

All this has been to say that—while God's *natural* knowledge has infinite possibilities—God in his *middle* knowledge "weighs"[55] or simply knows what every person would freely do in every possible set of circumstances, every possible world, and sovereignly chooses which world he will create. This "weighing" (discernment) results in removing many possibilities (false counterfactuals) which are logically not possible.[56] The term given to those which are logically possible is simply "possible worlds." The term given to the set of logically possible worlds in which indeterminism is true (and where libertarian freedom pertains) is "feasible worlds."[57]

Criteria for the "weighing" in God's middle knowledge.

What has been said in the last few paragraphs raises important questions: "Against what standard does God choose what will be the true counterfactuals (what world he will create) and what will be false (what world he chooses not to create)? Against what criteria does he weigh the possibilities from which he will actualize one world? Moreover, if God chooses a world to actualize among those worlds which are feasible, does this not lend itself to belief in a form of exhaustive divine determinism that makes God responsible for what a person does"?

HUMAN FREEDOM AS A WEIGHING FACTOR.

If the reader has followed the chart above, he/she will realize that this discussion has introduced key words found in the final column. In Molina's writings, there are at least four criteria on which God bases his decision of what "feasible" world he chooses to actualize (create).[58] The set of feasible worlds is not "constituted" by God, nor is it up to God (essential to God). God simply knows what he has power to create. The actual world is chosen from the set of feasible worlds. All these are factored into God's thinking, but a key criterion—not to the exclusion of the others—is the first: human

---

55. The use of "weighing" is not meant in any way to suggest that God is weighing the merits of the person(s) involved. No one merits God's forgiveness and salvation. God pardons on the basis of his mercy and grace alone. Weighing is meant to denote that God is not arbitrary in the process of what world he will create but employs criteria by which he weighs all "possible" options, some of which he chose to actualize (create).

56. Molina, *Concordia*, 131: [God knows] "both future and contingent possibles that will never exist and future things that will exist in some interval of time."

57. "So, there are worlds which are intrinsically possible but which God, given the counterfactuals that happen to be true, is not capable of actualizing and which are therefore, in Flint's terminology, infeasible for God . . . It all depends on how creatures would freely behave in various circumstances, which is beyond God's control" (Craig, "The Difference between Possible and Feasible Worlds."). The role of human freedom which Craig refers to in this quotation is explained in the discussion which follows.

58. Each of these criteria will be discussed giving appropriate documentation. Also, see note #54, p.222 and Molina, *Concordia*, 121, quoted in the following footnote.

freedom. This was the issue that prompted Molina's quest for answers: How could the God—whom the Bible reveals is sovereign over all he creates and further knows all that will occur in his creation—yet be the one who the Bible says gives people the freedom to choose? Molina argued as a solution to this dilemma that God did not determine arbitrarily what a person would do, but—knowing in his *middle* knowledge what persons would *freely* choose to do in whatever circumstances they would be in—he decided to create the world in which those persons would freely—and thus will freely—make those choices among a range of alternative options each compatible with those persons's natures.[59]

Two examples are prominent:[60]

- *The* Lord said to Cain, *"*Why are you angry, and why has your face fallen? [7] If you do well, will you not be accepted? And if you do not do well, sin is crouching at the door. Its desire is contrary to you, but you must rule over it." (Gen 4:6–7)

- *Therefore, I will judge you, O house of Israel, every one according to his ways, declares the Lord God.* Repent and turn from all your transgressions, lest iniquity be your ruin. *[31] Cast away from you all the transgressions that you have committed, and make yourselves a new heart and a new spirit! Why will you die, O house of Israel? [32] For I have no pleasure in the death of anyone, declares the Lord* God; so turn, and live. *(Ezek 18:30–32)*

Both examples—from God himself—affirm that human beings have the ability to make choices among a range of options each compatible with their nature (libertarian freedom). Cain is told *if you do well.* He has the power in his own hands, and opposition to making the choice is not from God but from the powerful influence of evil. In the second example, Israel is urged to take action—*Repent, Cast away, make*

---

59. Molina says this explicitly also in *Disputation 49*, section 13: "There is a precognition by which He [God] foreknows with certainty, before anything exists, what is or is not going to be on the hypothesis and condition that He should grant this or that assistance or means, or arrange things in this way or some other way. If this is not so, then how did He preordain and arrange things by His providence, intending good contingent effects via both natural and free causes while permitting evil contingent effects in order that He might draw forth from them greater goods? Likewise, in what sense was there a predestining of various freely acting causes in order that they might achieve contingent effects and goals by these or those means"? (Molina, *Concordia*, 121). See also footnote #678 and Flint's note later in chapter 15.

60. Both of the following texts—both still untranslated from the Latin of *Concordia* (1.14.13.23.2.1)—are noted by MacGregor (*Luis de Molina*, 75) along with noting eighteen others that Molina thought relevant: Deut 30:11–19; Josh 24:13–15; Psa 119:108–9; Prov 1:24–33; Isa 5:4; Jer 8:3–5; 26:2–3; Ezek 18:21–22; Zech 1:2–4; Matt 19:17; 23:37; Mark 13:34; John 1:12; Acts 5:4; 1 Cor 7:37; 1 Tim 2:4; Rev 2:21; 3:18–20. Another comprehensive list can be found in D. A. Carson, *Divine Sovereignty,* 18–22, where he annotates texts which show human freedom "under nine heads: (1) people face a multitude of divine exhortations and commands; (2) people are said to obey, believe, and choose God; (3) people sin and rebel against God; (4) their sins are judged by God; (5) people are tested by God; (6) people receive divine rewards; (7) the elect are responsible to respond to God's initiative; (8) prayers are not mere showpieces scripted by God; and (9) God literally a pleads with sinners to repent and be saved" (quoted in Craig, *Only Wise God,* 46).

yourselves a new heart . . . Why will you [choose] *to die?*—and God affirms he does not want to do what their choices dictate.

Relating this freedom to God's *middle* knowledge, Craig explains: "If it be asked how God has middle knowledge of free decisions by creatures, proponents of middle knowledge usually respond . . . [that] God by his infinite understanding knows each creature so completely that he discerns even the creature's free decisions under any conceivable circumstance. Since the moment of middle knowledge is logically prior to God's creation, no actual creatures exist at that moment, but God *comprehends them as they exist in his mind as possible creatures. He knows them so well that he knows what they would freely do in any situation.*"[61]

By this human freedom is maintained. God does not causally determine, force, or compel people to think, act, believe, or behave in a certain way (God's way or repudiation of it). This would be fatalism. Instead, there are no causal strings (or chains) attached and people are free, in a libertarian sense, to make their own choices.[62] These choices often do not reflect God's "will,"[63] because God has given them such freedom, but God's plans in the actual world never fail. Creaturely choices, then—and God's knowledge of them—are logically prior to God's determination of what they would and will do in the world he eventually chooses to create. Molina insisted, then, that human freedom was an essential ingredient in "God's *middle* knowledge."[64]

The implication of such freedom—if Molina is correct and the idea of middle knowledge is applied to soteriological issues—should have a sobering impact on every person's thinking. On this model, God's grace is given to all. No one needs to spend eternity separate from God! But in each person's hands is the libertarian freedom—the choice—to reject the forgiveness and grace God has provided in the death of his beloved son or not.[65] As Aquinas, Molina, the reformers and those who endorse Ar-

61. Craig, *Only Wise God*, 133–34.

62. Molina put it this way: "Freedom can be understood in the first place insofar as it is opposed to coercion . . . But freedom can also be understood insofar as it is opposed to necessity. Thus an agent is called free who, with all the prerequisites for action taken into account, is able to act and able not to act, or is able to do something in such a way that s/he is also able to do some contrary thing" (Molina, *Concordia*, 1.14.13.2.2–3, translated and quoted by MacGregor, *Luis de Molina*, 49). Also in the *Concordia* Molina says, "Through His natural knowledge, God comprehends Himself and in Himself, He comprehends all the things that exist eminently in Him and thus the free choice of any creature whom He is able to make though His omnipotence" (Molina, *Concordia*, 119).

63. God's will, that is, what he would desire: (1) *not willing that any should perish* and (2) God's will in the sense of thinking, decisions and behaviors consistent with Scriptural principles. Sometimes "God's will" is used by determinists as a reference what God will necessarily do. It is not used in this way in the above example. For instance, Gordon Clark, *Religion, Reason and Revelation*, 221, quoted by Erickson, *Christian Theology*, 442, draws "a distinction between preceptive and the decretive will of God. The preceptive will is what God commands, such as the Ten Commandments. This is what *ought* to be done. God's creative will, however, causes every event. It causes what *is* done." The author uses "will of God" in the preceptive sense.

64. See Craig, *Only Wise God*, 134.

65. This does not necessarily entail synergism. An excellent treatment of this may be found in

minian theology all would insist: If a person's final destiny is Hell, he has no one to blame but himself. As someone put it, "We make our choices, and then our choices turn around and make us."[66]

God's love as a weighing factor,

But there are other criteria which are included in God's weighing/selection process which must be understood. God's middle knowledge must be seen in the context of God's character so pervasively expressed in the scriptures: his love.[67] Beyond the explicit expressions of John (John 3:16: *God so loved the world* and 1 John 4:8: *God is love.*) and the ultimate illustration of Jesus's death for sinners (Rom 5:9–10) on the cross, the Bible affirms and repeatedly illustrates God's character: e.g., Deut 7:9; 1 Kgs 8:23; 10:9; Psa 36:7; etc. Surely the heart of God is seen in Jesus's response to the antagonism and persistent hardness on the part of religious leaders: *O Jerusalem, Jerusalem, the city that kills the prophets and stones those who are sent to it! How often would I have gathered your children together as a hen gathers her brood under her wings, and you were not willing! 35 Behold, your house is forsaken* (Luke 13:34–35).

Interestingly when Moses asked God to "show" himself to him, God's revelation of himself to Moses was: *The Lord passed before him and proclaimed, "The Lord, the Lord, a God merciful and gracious, slow to anger, and abounding in steadfast love and faithfulness."*[68] As noted above, Molina assumed that this was the sort of love God had for all persons because God was not *willing that any should perish* (2 Pet 3:9), that *he wants all to come to repentance* (1 Tim 2:4),[69] and that he *does not take pleasure in the death of the wicked* (Ezek 18:23).[70]

God's eternal plan as a weighing factor.

Another criterion in God's sifting process was his eternal plan. The Scriptures are filled with both statements and prophecies of God having a plan for his kingdom and history and its conclusion. It is a plan that is not being formulated "on the go," but one established from eternity past in the mind of God. Twice the book of Acts alludes to this eternal plan:

MacGregor, *Luis de Molina*, 77–92.

66. This is not a published saying, but one which was heard at a pastors's meeting.

67. See Penner, "Francisco Suarez."

68. Such expressions—*God is gracious, slow to anger*, etc.—are found in at least eight other places in Scripture! (Num 14:18; Neh 9:17; Psa 86:15; 103:8; 145:8; Joel 2:13; Jonah 4:2; and Nah 1:3).

69. See chapter 13 for a discussion of this very important text.

70. God because he is not "a manipulative tyrant [but] loves his creatures . . . wants the best for them. We may trust in the wisdom of his decision concerning which world to create" (Craig, *Only Wise God*, 134).

- *This Jesus, delivered up according to the definite plan and foreknowledge of God, you crucified and killed by the hands of lawless men.* (Acts 2:23)

- *Truly in this city there were gathered together against your holy servant Jesus, whom you anointed, both Herod and Pontius Pilate, along with the Gentiles and the peoples of Israel, [28] to do whatever your hand and your plan had predestined to take place.* (Acts 4:27–28)

Molina posits the implementation of this plan in the logical moment of God's *middle* knowledge. As God "weighs" all the issues that result in identifying the feasible world he will create—e.g., human freedom, his profound love for his creation and creatures—he selects a world which will fulfill his eternal plan, yet he accomplishes it with the libertarian freedom of each creature who plays a vital role in it.[71]

God's freedom as a weighing factor.

Another factor in God's "sifting process" is implicit in the previous discussion of God's eternal plan, but it is worth noting. Not only do human beings possess the ability to choose among a range of options each compatible with their natures, but God himself also—in determining what world he would create as the sovereign Lord—has freedom to choose the sort of world (conditions and circumstances), what kind of creatures, and all random events.[72]

"Best of possible worlds" as a weighing factor.

A fitting summary of this discussion on the *logical* process in the mind of God that Molina called God's *middle* knowledge is what one of his later disciples referred to as "the best of all possible worlds." The world which God would choose to bring into existence would be one which in his wisdom and love would be best when all things are considered (especially with eternity in mind). This term was coined by the German,

71. Molina, *Concordia*, 119–20; 139–40. Craig writes: "Since God knows what any free creature would do in any situation, he can, by creating the appropriate situations, bring it about that creatures will achieve his ends and purposes and that they will do so *freely*. When one considers that these situations are themselves the results of earlier free decisions by creatures, free decisions which God had to bring about, one begins to see that providence over a world of free creatures could only be the work of omniscience. Only an infinite Mind could calculate the unimaginably complex and numerous factors that would need to be combined in order to bring about through the free decisions of creatures a single human event such as, say, the enactment of the lend-lease policy prior to America's entry into the Second World War. Think then of God's planning the entire course of world history so as to achieve his purposes! Given middle knowledge, the apparent contradiction between God's sovereignty which seems to crush human freedom, and human freedom, which seems to break God's sovereignty, is resolved. In his infinite intelligence, God is able to plan a world in which his designs are achieved by creatures acting freely" (Craig, *Only Wise God,* 135).

72. The concept that God has a plan and freely chooses the world he will create (and all that goes on in it) in theology is called God's "sovereignty." See further discussion of this in chapter 15.

Christian philosopher Gottfried Wilhelm Leibniz (AD 1646–1716) in a book entitled *Theodicy*.[73] Though Leibniz writes almost a century after Molina's death, his concept of "best possible worlds"[74] certainly is a further development of Molina's thinking because one of Leibniz's key mentors was Francisco Suarez (AD 1548–1617), who like Molina was a Jesuit from Spain. Suarez also was known for his adoption of Molina's position.[75] Leibniz's argument may be summarized as follows:

1. God has the idea of infinitely many universes. ("Idea," that is, in his mind)

2. Only one of these universes can actually exist.

3. God's choices are subject to the principle of sufficient reason, that is, God has reason to choose one thing or another. ["This reason can be found only in the *fitness*, or the degrees of perfection, that these worlds contain."]

4. God is good. ["God knows through his wisdom, chooses through his goodness, and produces through his power."]

5. Therefore, the universe that God chose to exist is the best of all possible worlds.[76]

Molina's appeal to Scripture for evidence of middle knowledge.

It might be tempting for the beginner to dismiss the discussions above of Molina's *middle* knowledge as mere philosophical sophistry, but before drawing such an erroneous conclusion, it is wise to survey several examples Molina gave from Scripture which demonstrate that the concept of *middle* knowledge has merit for consideration. For simplicity of examining his biblical foundation, three biblical texts provided by Molina are given below:

1. Example #1: 1 Sam 23:9–13: *David knew that Saul was plotting harm against him. And he said to Abiathar the priest, "Bring the ephod here."* [10] *Then David said,*

---

73. Kempf, "Theodicy."

74. It is important to note that "possible worlds" could seemingly, infinitely increase in greatness. If this were the case, it would be impossible for there to be a best of all possible worlds that God could choose to actuate. It is better to note that with libertarian freedom in mind, there could be, however, a best of all feasible worlds—or at least a "tied for the best" range of feasible worlds. See footnote #703 for documentation from Leibniz's own writing.

75. See Penner, "Francisco Suarez."

76. This list and the [quoted] section are a summary of what is found in Leibniz, *The Monadology*, 53–55. There Leibniz said it in a fuller way: "Now, as there is an infinity of possible universes in the ideas of God, and as only one of them can exist, there must be a sufficient reason for God's choice, which determines him toward one rather than another" (Leibniz, *The Monadology*, 53). "And this reason can be found only in the *fitness*, or the degrees of perfection, that these worlds contain, since each possible thing has the right to claim existence in proportion to the perfection it involves" (Leibniz, *The Monadology*, 54). "And this is the cause of the existence of the best, which God knows through his wisdom, chooses through his goodness, and produces through his power" (Leibniz, *The Monadology*, 55). See Leibniz, *The Monadology*, for the location and further discussions in Leibniz, *Theodicy*.

"O Lord, the God of Israel, your servant has surely heard that Saul seeks to come to Keilah, to destroy the city on my account. ¹¹ Will the men of Keilah surrender me into his hand? Will Saul come down, as your servant has heard? O Lord, the God of Israel, please tell your servant." And the Lord said, "He will come down." ¹² Then David said, "Will the men of Keilah surrender me and my men into the hand of Saul"? And the Lord said, "They will surrender you." ¹³ Then David and his men, who were about six hundred, arose and departed from Keilah, and they went wherever they could go. When Saul was told that David had escaped from Keilah, he gave up the expedition.

What is significant about this example is that God tells David what in fact the people of Keilah *would* do if Saul threatened to destroy the city because David was inside its walls. Though God tells David this in real time, it shows that it was one of the possible circumstances that God knew would occur. MacGregor draws out the significance of this example by saying "The knowledge mediated here did not constitute predictions of the future (foreknowledge), for Saul did not actually come to Keilah and the citizens of Keilah never actually handed over David to Saul."[77] The critic might reply, "This merely is a possibility, not unlike any person who would offer his counsel." Not so! People at best can give a conjecture—an uncertain possibility—but in the text the God of truth declares what would certainly happen. Thus, this was a possible scenario in God's middle knowledge (at least if God possessed this knowledge from eternity past without beginning). If David would have freely chosen not to heed God's warning, and have instead chosen to stay within the walls of Keilah, then this was an option that God could have decided to have actually happen ("actualize") but did not.[78]

2. Example #2: Jer 38:17–18: *Then Jeremiah said to Zedekiah, "Thus says the Lord, the God of hosts, the God of Israel: If you will surrender to the officials of the king of Babylon, then your life shall be spared, and this city shall not be burned with fire, and you and your house shall live. 18 But if you do not surrender to the officials of the king of Babylon, then this city shall be given into the hand of the Chaldeans."*

Again, God declares what would truly happen if the residents of Jerusalem would *surrender to the king of Babylon.* If the people were to make that choice, they would live. An omniscient God knows this possibility from eternity past without beginning, and thus, knows—if they chose rightly—their destiny would be their well-being. Knowing they would freely choose to disregard Jeremiah's message, that choice and its consequences were decreed to happen (was "actualized").

3. Example #3: Matt 11:20–24: *Then he began to denounce the cities where most of his mighty works had been done, because they did not repent. 21 "Woe to you,*

---

77. MacGregor, *Luis de Molina*, 81–82.

78. Though not included in Molina's examples, the writer feels that Genesis 20:7–8 is a similar example.

Chorazin! Woe to you, Bethsaida! For if the mighty works done in you had been done in Tyre and Sidon, they would have repented long ago in sackcloth and ashes. 22 But I tell you, it will be more bearable on the day of judgment for Tyre and Sidon than for you. 23 And you, Capernaum, will you be exalted to heaven? You will be brought down to Hades. For if the mighty works done in you had been done in Sodom, it would have remained until this day. 24 But I tell you that it will be more tolerable on the day of judgment for the land of Sodom than for you."

Jesus's words are remarkable for several reasons: (1) In God's *middle* knowledge he knows not only every world, every possible creature, every possible circumstance, and all random processes that *could* occur, but also what *would* happen in every circumstance and situation should he create them. Here Jesus cites one such situation, one scenario: If Tyre, Sidon, and Sodom had had the privilege of observing the miracles he had been performing before his first century audience. If God had chosen to create the world of these cities and afforded them the opportunity of seeing Jesus's miraculous signs, they would have repented. Human beings might conjecture about what would happen under certain circumstances, but when God the Son declares what would have happened, he speaks of a reality (counterfactual) that would have occurred, but—as history shows—a reality he chose not to create/actualize (a false counterfactual).

(2) Jesus's words also are remarkable because of what they convey about the people of these cities who have already experienced (will experience) God's judgment on their sinful deeds. They declare explicitly that there were possible circumstances under which even those who are the reprobate in this world (the world that has been actualized)—reprobate because of their sin—who *would have* believed had they lived in Jesus's day! Under different circumstances—circumstances known in God's *middle* knowledge—their choices/decisions would have been different and thus also their destinies.[79]

---

79. See MacGregor: "While never stated in these terms by Molina, various comments of Molina imply that God also commits himself, out of his goodness, to consider for creation only those feasible worlds that obtain an optimal balance between salvation and damnation, containing no more of the lost than are necessary to achieve the greatest salvation. According to Molina, within the range of those feasible worlds in which God gives prevenient grace to all and that obtain to the optimal salvific balance—a range that is infinite—God perceives from his middle knowledge that there is at least one feasible world where each possible individual exists and would freely receive salvation. And God likewise middle-knows that there is at least one feasible world where each possible individual exists and would freely spurn salvation, so being lost. And God likewise middle-knows that there is at least one feasible world where each possible individual does not exist at all . . . On the one hand, Molina was claiming that no possible individual, made in the image of God, is depraved enough so that, given prevenient grace, she or he would freely spurn God's offer of salvation in all available circumstances. On the other hand, Molina was also claiming that no possible individual, prone to sin, is good enough so that, given prevenient grace, she or he would freely accept God's offer of salvation in all available circumstances" (MacGregor, *Luis de Molina*, 145–46). Craig, "New Questions from Facebook," has noted that he does not think this is an example of counterfactual knowledge, but simply a remark about "how bad" these individuals were.

There are other examples Molina gives[80] which—since God or Jesus is making the statement—would certainly have occurred otherwise if different conditions had been met. MacGregor says it well: "If these statements were assertions of foreknowledge, they would self-contradictorily be mistakes on the part of a God who cannot err, since the consequent or 'then' clause of these statements did not come to pass. On the other hand, these statements cannot be stating mere possibilities, since they affirm what *would* happen, not what *could* happen, under certain conditions different than those which in fact materialized. Therefore, Molina declared it was indisputable that the God of the Bible possesses counterfactual knowledge."[81]

CONCLUSION

In this chapter Luis de Molina and his innovative approach to the knowledge of God have been introduced. Though his concept of *middle* knowledge was framed nearly five hundred years ago and was a debate in Roman Catholic theology at the time and hardly discussed outside of that context, it has become a more widely known and a viable concept in the last fifty years, both in Catholic and Protestant circles. Though it influenced Spanish theology (Suarez) and likely Arminius, it was Arminianism that became the focus in the debate in Protestant circles in contrast to Calvinism. This no longer is so. There are now Calvinistic Molinists, Arminian Molinists, and Mere Molinists. (See the following chapter). This discussion, however, has not been to defend or evaluate Luis de Molina's position so much as to understand its essence. In the chapter which follows there is a defense and argumentation that this Spanish monk speaks powerfully and convincingly to the question of libertarian freedom and God's sovereignty in all things.

80. Other examples/texts to which Molina appealed included: John 15:22–24; 18:36; and 1 Cor 2:8 (MacGregor, *Luis de Molina*, 83–84). This writer thinks these are not decisive evidence for God's *counterfactual* (or *middle*) knowledge, but certainly can be understood as illustrations of such knowledge. MacGregor also notes that Craig, *Time and Eternity View*, sees counterfactual knowledge in prophecies which are made and then rescinded by God because of prayer (Isa 38:1–5; Amos 7:1–6) or repentance (Jonah 1–3) of the people (MacGregor, *Luis de Molina*, 84, note 13). To this writer this may be less evidence *for* than it is hindsight to the already convinced.

81. MacGregor, *Luis de Molina*, 84.

15

Arguments for middle knowledge
and mere Molinism

IN CHAPTERS 2–11, BIBLICAL data and the history of Christian thought have been surveyed. Most of these writers—from the authors of Scripture to those involved in the Reformation—have offered support for what this author refers to as limited "libertarian freedom" (libertarian freedom in some things some of the time). In addition, chapters 12 and 13 offered several logic-based arguments, each concluding that these important Christian thinkers of history were exactly right in their assessment—that humans at least occasionally possess a categorical ability to choose among a range of alternative options each of which is compatible with their nature.

Chapter 14 addressed the following conundrum: Although there is biblical data supporting a limited libertarian view of human freedom, there is also scriptural warrant that God predestines and controls all things all of the time. To say it another way, the Bible seems to teach two truths: (i) God is sovereign over *all* things, and (ii), humans are responsible for *some* things. At face value, it might seem as if the Bible contains a major contradiction weaving its way throughout its sixty-six books.

Of course, this dilemma is not new. What rather recently is being examined by theologians and scholars is the proposal made centuries ago by the Spanish Jesuit scholar Luis de Molina. His life, writings and thinking—especially his concept of middle knowledge—were also briefly introduced in chapter 14.

Building on that foundation, this chapter moves beyond Molina's argument for counterfactuals to consider the crucial question: "*When* does God possess counterfactual knowledge? Does he have this knowledge before, that is, logically prior to his creative decree, or does God create the world, and then gain knowledge of it"? If God owns this counterfactual knowledge eternally and causally before his creative decree in which he actualized this world, then God possesses middle knowledge. That is to say, if God is eternally omniscient, then God possesses middle knowledge.

Because Scripture is silent regarding *when* God has this knowledge, appeal must be made to philosophical and theological argumentation to infer the best explanation. If a theologian wants to deny that God has middle knowledge, it seems he/she must hold that God only possesses counterfactual knowledge *after* his divine decree. But would this not logically entail that there was a "time" or state of affairs in which God existed, yet was not omniscient? This, of course, should make many theologians uncomfortable. The alternative is to affirm that God must have eternally possessed this knowledge. If it is true that this knowledge is possessed eternally (without beginning), then it seems that God must have had it logically prior to the creative decree. Thus, God possesses middle knowledge.

To be sure, this is a bold conclusion and thus merits careful analysis. In the discussion which follows, then, several arguments are marshalled to support not just counterfactual knowledge, but the *when* of middle knowledge, i.e., that God possessed this knowledge logically prior to actualizing the world.

MAXIMAL GREATNESS AND MIDDLE KNOWLEDGE ARGUMENT.

This argument demonstrates that a being who has middle knowledge is greater than a being who lacks middle knowledge. The argument Stratton and Erasmus offer is phrased as follows:[1]

J1   If God lacks middle knowledge, then God is not a maximally great being.

J2   God is a maximally great being.

J3   Therefore, God has middle knowledge.[2]

The Molinist and the divine determinist both typically affirm (K2) and, thus, the crucial premise here is (J1). But why think (J1) is true? It seems clear, that a being whose knowledge of counterfactuals *does not* depend on the being's prior will, decisions, or actions is greater than a being whose knowledge of counterfactuals *does* depend on these. To illustrate this, consider the following thought experiment.

Suppose that both Sally and Jones know that: (a) "If Smith were to run for president, Smith would win and become president." Suppose further that Smith will eventually run for president and win (and thus (a) is true), and that Sally and Jones know (a) before Smith runs for president. Furthermore, suppose that Sally knows (a) only because she has rigged the election in such a way that Smith would win if he runs for president. In this case, Sally's knowledge of (a) is neither extraordinary

---

1. For simplicity the argument begun in chapter 12 used statements "A" through "I." Thus, the argument here picks up and continues those statements, the next being "J."

2. Stratton and Erasmus, "Mere Molinism," 26.

nor remarkable. No one would be impressed by the fact that Sally knows (a), since it is known that she intentionally performed actions that would guarantee (a). Sally's knowledge of (a) depends on her prior knowledge of the rigged election. However, suppose that, unlike Sally, Jones has not rigged the election and he knows (a) simply by virtue of his nature. Hence, Jones's knowledge of (a) does not depend on his prior knowledge or actions. In this case, Jones's knowledge of (a) is truly remarkable. Indeed, a person should be impressed by the fact that Jones has the ability to know (a) without having to do anything. Thus, it seems clear that Jones's knowledge of (a) is *greater* than Sally's knowledge of (a) precisely because Jones's knowledge does not depend on his prior will, decisions, or actions, whereas Sally's knowledge does depend on her prior will, decisions, or actions.

The above thought experiment illustrates that a being whose knowledge of counterfactuals does not depend on the being's prior will, decisions, or actions is greater than a being whose knowledge of counterfactuals does depend on one or more of these. Now, since a maximally great being is omniscient, this being will know all counterfactuals either prior to its will (thus possessing middle knowledge) or posterior to its will (thus lacking middle knowledge). However, as the Sally and Jones's illustration has shown, it is greater to know all counterfactuals prior to one's will and, thus, a maximally great being must have middle knowledge. Since God is a maximally great being, it follows that God has middle knowledge.

In order to avoid this conclusion, some have appealed to the so-called *grounding objection*, according to which middle knowledge is impossible because there is nothing that grounds counterfactuals of creaturely freedom (CCFs). The alleged problem is that, if CCFs are independent of God's will, then nothing makes them true (or there is nothing in virtue of which they are true). Consequently, CCFs either lack truth-values or they are all false. Either way, the grounding objection asserts that God cannot possess such counterfactual knowledge.[3]

---

3. In a response to Plantinga's dismantling of the logical problem of evil (Plantinga, *Nature of Necessity*), Adams may have been the first to hint at the grounding objection (Adams, "Middle Knowledge," 109–17). It was later taken up by Hasker in a series of papers: Hasker, *God, Time and Knowledge*, 39–52; Hasker, "Middle Knowledge," 223–36; and Hasker, "Explanatory Priority," 389–93; and Hasker, "The (Non-) Existence of Molinist Counterfactuals," 25–36. Preceding the Haskerian period, Freddoso had translated *Concordia IV* (Molina, *Concordia*, 68–75) while pre-empting the modern grounding objection with a much-discussed parallel between future contingents and CCFs. Freddoso's piece responded to the earliest modern formulation of the grounding objection as can be found in Garrigou-Lagrange, *The One God*, 465, and Adams, "Middle Knowledge," 109–17.

Hasker's grounding objection sparked many discussions. In a series of exchanges, Thomas P. Flint's writings (*Divine Providence*, 138–58, and "Whence and Whither, 37–39) emerged as formidable interlocutors. Flint takes an offensive stance by unravelling the implausibility of Hasker's "bringing about" thesis. His work—*Divine Providence*, 152—advanced the debate by undercutting twelve possible routes in which Hasker could clarify his stipulations. Under Flint, Jensen, *The Grounding Objection*, made significant contributions bifurcating between the two types of grounding objection: causal-style and truth-maker-style. In responding to the truth-maker-style, Jensen took cues from Craig, "God Directs All Things," in which Craig scathingly argues against the hypothetical "grounding objection."

This author wishes to thank John Limanto in personal correspondence for the above list of the key

Unfortunately, it is difficult to see what, exactly, the problem is. Perhaps the objector means that:

1   *A true contingent proposition is true in virtue of the existence of some concrete object(s).*

Accordingly, for example, if the proposition "Jones is eating eggs" is true, it is true in virtue of the existence of Jones and his action of eating eggs. However, (1) implies that contingent propositions about objects that no longer exist are false. The proposition "Socrates no longer exists today," for example, is false because there exists no concrete object that renders the proposition true. The objector will have to adjust (1) as follows:

2   *A true contingent proposition is true in virtue of the existence or past existence of some concrete object(s).*

But what about future contingent propositions, such as the proposition "It will rain in Spain in exactly ten years from today"? If a person asserted this proposition ten years ago, and it does, in fact, rain in Spain exactly a decade later, then surely it is correct to say that he asserted a *true* proposition ten years ago. Thus, to account for future contingent propositions, the objector should adjust (2) as follows:

3   *A true contingent proposition is true in virtue of the existence, past existence, or future existence of some concrete object(s).*

This (3), however, does not account for certain negative existential propositions, such as the proposition "Unicorns have not, do not, and will not exist." Such a proposition is surely true even though the past, present, or future existence of one or more concrete objects does not render it true. Hence, (3) will have to be adjusted further as follows:

4   *A true contingent proposition is true in virtue of the existence, past existence, future existence, or non-existence of some concrete object(s).*

It is apparent now that it is really facts (or obtaining states of affairs), and not the existence of some concrete object(s), that ground true contingent propositions. Thus, "Socrates is dead" is grounded by the fact that *Socrates is dead*; "It will rain in Spain tomorrow" is grounded by the fact that *it will rain in Spain tomorrow*; and "Unicorns do not exist" is grounded by the fact that *unicorns do not exist*. Consequently, if the objector insists that CCFs must be grounded or have truth-makers, then the Molinist may simply respond that CCFs are grounded by counterfactual facts. For example, the CCF "If Jones grew up in Germany, then he would learn to speak French" is grounded by the fact that *if Jones grew up in Germany, then he would learn to speak French*. Thus, the Molinist may simply adjust (4) as follows:

contributors to the grounding objection and the specific documentation.

> 5   *A true contingent proposition is true in virtue of the fact that some concrete objects exist, or did exist, or will exist, or do not exist, or would exist under specific conditions.*

This adjustment (5) seems to be as reasonable as (4) and, thus, if the grounding objection were to succeed, a person must show why (5) is implausible while (4) is plausible. This challenge, to this author's knowledge, has not yet been met. Therefore, it is rational to believe that the grounding objection is unsuccessful and middle knowledge is possible. There are, therefore, good reasons to believe that God, as a maximally great being, has middle knowledge.

THE SELF-IMPOSED LIMITS OF GOD ARGUMENT.

One of the primary objections raised against Molinism is based on a misunderstanding of what it entails. The typical objection is that Molinism somehow entails that God is "dependent upon" or "limited" by the libertarian freedom of man.[4] This is simply not a view that a Molinist must affirm, and thus a poor (irrational) reason to object to Molinism. Indeed, this is the case because Molinists affirm that man's existence—whether a person has libertarian freedom or not—is completely dependent and contingent upon God. Moreover, God did not have to create humanity at all. God is omnipotent; he had the power and ability to choose otherwise and not create mankind. Obviously, he freely chose to create humanity in his image.

What can God do?

Here is where it gets interesting: If God is omnipotent, then he has the power and ability to refrain from creation, or to create human beings in his image. Thus, God possesses a range of options from which to choose, each of which is consistent and compatible with his nature. To argue otherwise is to affirm the necessary existence of mankind. Since God possesses this ability (libertarian freedom), he can create mankind with the same ability to choose among a range of options consistent and compatible with human nature (limited libertarian freedom). Thus, God has the power to create humans with limited libertarian freedom—even if he never does such a thing. To deny this is to reject the omnipotence of God. Thus, if (and only if) God freely chooses to be limited by creatures with limited libertarian freedom, then (and only then) can he be "limited" by human free choices in that contingent sense.

---

4. See Craig's interaction with other bloggers (Craig, "Is Molinism Biblical"?) and Tom Barnes's recently authored book (Barnes, *Divine Sovereignty*, 144–46). Both focus on this issue.

Why would God want to?

The question is raised: Why would God want to do a crazy thing like that? Could it not be that it is God's greatest desire to limit himself by creating limited libertarian humans? As previously argued in Chapter 11, God could desire such limitations because it allows for true love, rationality, and real responsibility. These seem to be essentials for maximal personal relationships.

This "God-desired limitation" is similar to the fact that he is not limited by space, unless he chooses to be limited by space. The second person of the Trinity (Jesus) provides a perfect example. Although God is not limited by spatial coordinates, Jesus—the incarnate Son of God—chose to be "limited" by spatial coordinates, that is to say, God chose to create the space-time universe and also chose to enter into—*became flesh*—and live—*lived among us*—in it.

This omnipotent God, then, can also choose to create human beings *in his image* who possess the ability to freely choose from a limited range of options, each of which is consistent and compatible with their human nature. Since God is omniscient, he can create this world knowing that libertarian choices—made by free humanity—would/will line up with his perfect plan and bring him ultimate glory. In short, just as God does not *have* to be limited by space, but *can* be limited by space if he so chooses—as the incarnated Son of God did[5]—he can also be "limited" by the choices he knew man would freely make if he were to use his maximal power to create mankind with limited libertarian freedom. After all, Jesus—the God manifested—*was tempted as we are.*

OMNISCIENCE, OMNIPOTENCE, AND MIDDLE KNOWLEDGE ARGUMENT.

A summary of the above can be offered via a syllogism presented this way:

K1   *If God is omnipotent, he possesses the ability to create a world including humans who possess limited libertarian freedom, even if he never does.*

---

5. The incarnation of the Son of God is a fascinating study! Matthew speaks of his conception in a woman's womb and birth in the natural way, which if Joseph had not been informed otherwise, would have led him to divorce Mary for adultery (Matt 1:18–26). Luke speaks of his circumcision and growing up in Joseph and Mary's home, learning carpentry (Luke 2). John is the most theological. He speaks of the Son of God as being the *Word*, and the *Word taking on flesh and dwelling among us* in space time (John 1:1–2, 14, 18). Paul speaks of the Son *emptying himself, taking the form of a servant* and being crucified (Phil 2:5–8). Especially interesting is the writer of Hebrews: He speaks of the Son *being for a little while lower than the angels* (2:9), being *perfected through suffering* (2:10), sharing the humanity of mankind (2:14), and having the experiences of every human being (2:17–18; 4:14–16).

Of course, the incarnation of the Son of God is the preeminent example of God putting himself into space time, but there are scholars who note that there are other "theophanies" or "Christophanies." Kautzsch, ("Theophany," 304) says that theophany has the sense of "every extraordinary manifestation of God reported by the Biblical authors, apprehensible by the human senses . . . Theophany in reality presupposes that somehow the person of God enters into relation with man in terms of space." Good examples of them in the Old Testament are Gen 16:10–13, 19:1; etc.

> K2   *If God is omniscient, he possesses perfect knowledge of how humans who possess libertarian freedom would choose if he were to create them, and even if he never creates them (this is referred to as middle knowledge).*
>
> K3   *God is omnipotent and omniscient.*
>
> K4   *Therefore, God possesses middle knowledge.*

If it is even possible for God to create humanity in his image with libertarian freedom (even if he never does), then a maximally great and omniscient God knows how these potential creatures would freely choose if he were to create them. If this is the case, then some "flavor" of Molinism seems to be true.

Because God is omnipotent and omniscient, he can use his libertarian freedom to choose, or not to choose, to be limited by space, by time, and also by the libertarian freedom possessed by humanity to make genuine choices. Since God perfectly knows how humans would freely choose if he were to create humans with libertarian freedom, it follows that he knows how humans with libertarian freedom would freely choose even if he never chose to create libertarian beings. It also follows that God's perfect knowledge is logically prior to his creative decree (his choice to create this world).

Thus, if God chooses to be "limited" by libertarian creatures, he does it for perfectly good reasons and perfectly knows exactly what he is "getting himself into." If so, can this really be referred to as a "limitation" (at least in a negative sense)? Ultimately, God is not limited by or contingent upon anything—or anyone—he may or may not choose to create. It might be said, "It is up to God and his good pleasure."

The bottom line is this: if a person objects to Molinism because he believes it makes God dependent upon his creatures, then he needs to either get a new objection or join "Team Molina."

THE "MERE MOLINISM" ARGUMENT.

In-house "fights" behind the doors of the church are nothing new. Since Paul and Barnabas split over differences some two thousand years ago, Christians have disagreed on many theological issues.[6] Likewise, passionate disagreements regarding God's sovereignty/determinism and human freedom/responsibility have been debated in centuries past (as noted in chapters 3–11) and continue today (as illustrated and documented in chapters 1 and 12–13). Although these heated disputes are not usually physically violent, these debates often occur with the same ferocity of a mixed martial arts title fight.

---

6. This is evident, not only on the basis of the diversity of published books which treat one or the other side, but especially in the plethora "four views" books on many theological issues. For example, Beilby and Eddy, *Divine Foreknowledge: Four Views*; Jowers, *Four Views on Divine Providence*; Crocket, *Four Views on Hell*; etc.

Despite these "in house debates," something typically keeps Christians who disagree united. What has kept brothers and sisters in Christ united over all this time is what C. S. Lewis referred to as "Mere Christianity."[7] Keeping it "mere" means focusing on one simple proposition: "God raised Jesus from the dead." If this one statement is true, then two sub-propositions are also true: (i) God exists and (ii) Jesus rose from the dead. There is evidence for both of these propositions being true.[8]

If God really did raise Jesus from the dead, then *Mere Christianity* is true. The affirmation of this single statement unites many Christians who otherwise are divided on other peripheral theological issues. Keeping it "mere" allows most Christians to lay down their non-essential disagreements and come together as brothers and sisters in Christ to worship and minister together.

Keeping it "mere" brings unity. That is the goal in suggesting the *"Mere Molinism" Argument*. This argument can help both Calvinists and Arminians find—in the process—common ground and can put an end to the "no holds barred" fights between Christians over exactly *how* God is sovereign and *if* humans are really responsible agents. "Mere Molinism" simply affirms two essential propositions, which might be called the "Two Pillars of Molinism." They are the following: (i) Humans sometimes have limited libertarian freedom and (ii) God has middle knowledge.[9]

The *"Mere Molinism" Argument* (MMA): can be expressed in a series of statements leading to several deductive conclusions:

L1   *If God possesses the ability to choose among alternatives consistent with his nature, then he possesses libertarian freedom.*

L2   *God possessed the ability to create or not create the universe and chose to create the universe.*

L3   *Therefore, God possesses libertarian freedom.*

L4   *God possesses the ability to create humans in his image/likeness.*

L5   *Therefore, God possesses the ability to create humans who possess limited libertarian freedom—even if he never does.*

L6   *If God possesses perfect knowledge of how humans with libertarian freedom would choose if he would create them (and even if he never does create them), then he possesses middle knowledge.*

L7   *Since God is omniscient, he knows how humans who possess libertarian freedom would choose—even if he never creates them.*

L8   *Therefore, God possesses middle knowledge.*

7. Lewis, *Mere Christianity*, vii–xvi. John Stott meant something similar when he entitled his well-known book *Basic Christianity*.

8. Many arguments comprising the cumulative case of evidence pointing to the truth of Christian theism will be found in chapter 16 which focuses on apologetics.

9. Stratton and Erasmus, "Two Pillars of Molinism," 17–29.

L9 *If libertarian freedom is not possessed by humans, then humans cannot rationally affirm knowledge claims.*

L10 *Some humans can rationally affirm knowledge claims.*

L11 *Therefore, some humans possess libertarian freedom.*[10]

L12 *Therefore, God, given his middle knowledge, knows how these humans who possess libertarian freedom would freely choose.*

L13 *If God possesses middle knowledge and some humans possess libertarian freedom, then "Mere Molinism" is true.*

L14 *Therefore, given (L8) and (L11), "Mere Molinism" is true.*

Premise (L1), states, *"If God possesses the ability to choose among alternatives consistent with his nature, then he possesses libertarian freedom."* The vast majority of Christians probably will not dispute this premise. Be that as it may, a small handful of committed divine determinists[11] assert that the concept of libertarian freedom is nonsensical and that no one has this power—not even God!

However, if a person rejects this first premise, he must reject the second as well. Premise (L2) states: *"God possessed the ability to create or not create the universe and chose to create the universe."* If one is committed to the impossibility of libertarian freedom, then two big problems arise: (a) fatalism entails and (b) humans are necessary.

Why are these problematic? If fatalism is true, then God is *not* omnipotent as he simply does not have the ability to choose among a range of options consistent with his nature. On this view, God can only do one thing. He is not really omni-potent, but rather, merely uni-potent. So, if one is going to maintain orthodoxy and affirm that God is omnipotent, then he must affirm the first two premises.

What might be worse, although God is still necessary with no beginning on this "uni-potent view," humanity ultimately becomes as necessary as God (albeit with beginnings) if the first two premises are rejected. After all, if God does not have a choice to create or not to create—and he *must* create and create exactly as he did create—then humanity exists necessarily. It could not have been otherwise. Assuming the objective reality of evil, this sort of fatalism makes evil necessary as well. John D. Laing makes this clear: "If [God] had to create, then in some ways he is dependent upon the creation. Under theological fatalism, we all become necessary beings of sorts. Second, theological fatalism is based on the false idea that God's obligation to do the best

---

10. One is free to choose an alternate version of the MMA and replace steps 9–11 with the following: (*L9) *If Christians possess the ability to choose among options consistent with their nature, then these humans possess libertarian free will.* (*L10) *Christians possess the ability to choose between falling into temptation or to take the way of escape God promises to provide* (1 Cor 10:13). (*L11) *Therefore, Christians possess libertarian free will.*

11. For example, Sproul, Hendryx and Edwards. These are discussed in some detail in chapter 16. Documentation is provided there in the footnotes.

limits him to only one option . . . There could be several equally good options which are the best way for God to achieve his desired ends."[12]

Fatalism seems both absurd and heretical. This is why the vast majority of Christians affirm the first two premises and the following deductive conclusion: "*Therefore, God possesses libertarian freedom.*" The salient point here is that the concept of libertarian freedom is logically coherent.

The fourth step (L4) is also non-controversial: "*God possesses the ability to create humans in his image/likeness.*" It is hard to foresee any orthodox Christian objecting to this statement. After all, a God with limitless power and knowledge has the ability to create humans with limited power and knowledge. However, if this is true, then the conclusion (L5) follows logically: "*Therefore, God possesses the ability to create humans who possess limited libertarian freedom—even if he never does.*"

At this point, the argument says nothing about humans actually possessing limited libertarian freedom. It simply concludes that an omnipotent God possesses the power to create beings in his image/likeness, and thus, it is possible for him to create humans with limited libertarian freedom.[13]

The sixth step (L6) is key and true by definition: "*If God possesses perfect knowledge of how humans with libertarian freedom would choose if he creates them (and even if he never does create them), then he possesses middle knowledge.*" Why is (L6) true by definition? Because if God has the power (given omnipotence) to create a free creature and knows (given omniscience) how the free creature would freely choose (among the range of options each consistent with the creature's nature), if he were to create this being, then it logically follows that he possesses this perfect knowledge logically prior to his decision to bring this free agent into existence. This follows even if God chooses *not* to create this being.

Step (L7) states: "*Since God is omniscient, he knows how humans who possess libertarian freedom would choose—even if he never created them.*" Some might contend that God does not possess the ability to know future tense propositions or counterfactuals of creaturely freedom. Indeed, some (e.g., open theists) assert that these types of propositions are impossible to know. If that were the case, however, then there would be propositions which God does not know if they are true or false. And if that were the case, then—by definition—God is not omniscient. So, if one affirms that God is eternally omniscient without beginning and does not "learn" or become "surprised" by new information, then the conclusion (L8) deductively follows: "*Therefore, God possesses middle knowledge.*"

---

12. Laing, *Middle Knowedge*, 32.

13. The fall did not eliminate or destroy the ability of human beings to make choices among a range of options compatible with their nature, but it did greatly damage their ability to make wise/good choices. Despite this damage, both Calvin and Luther affirm that there is freedom (not bondage) to make choices in "earthly matters," but acknowledging that *without God's grace* all are in bondage to sin. See chapters 7–8 for documentation from both of these theologians. More discussion is also to be found later in this chapter.

The next three steps of the syllogism refer to the "core" of the *Freethinking Argument* (discussed in chapter 12). The ninth step (L9) of the syllogism goes as follows: "*If libertarian freedom is not possessed by humans, then humans cannot rationally affirm knowledge claims.*" As argued earlier, this is true because if all things about a person (the thing one refers to as "I") are exhaustively causally determined by something other than him, then that includes all of his thoughts and beliefs. If all a person's thoughts and beliefs are forced upon him—and he could not have chosen better beliefs—then that person is simply left *assuming* that his determined beliefs are good (let alone true). Therefore, he could never rationally affirm that his beliefs really are the inference to the best explanation—he could only assume it (and that assumption is out of his control as well). Ultimately, if something or someone outside of human control causally determines a human to affirm a false belief, then it is impossible for the human to infer or affirm a better or true belief.

This presents a huge problem for the determinist: if determinism is true, then no one can possess justified beliefs. At minimum, as discussed in chapter 12, knowledge is defined as "justified true belief." One can happen to hold true beliefs. However, if one does not possess justification for a specific belief, his belief does not qualify as a knowledge claim. If one cannot freely infer the best explanation (from within a range of multiple possible explanations), then he has no justification that his belief really is the inference to the best explanation. Without justification, "rationally inferred knowledge" goes down the drain. All that remains is fallacious question-begging assumptions.

As explained in chapter 12, it is self-defeating to *argue* for determinism. This leads to the tenth step (L10) of the argument: "*Some humans can rationally affirm knowledge claims.*" It would be difficult to deny this premise. Obviously, humans possess the ability to rationally infer and affirm knowledge claims. To argue against this would actually affirm it because one would have to affirm knowledge claims to the contrary. Furthermore, if one rejects the ability to affirm claims of knowledge, why should anyone listen to him? Ultimately, if one rejects this premise, it would follow that he is affirming that he cannot rationally affirm that this premise is false. Since it is ultimately self-refuting to reject (L9) and (L10), the following conclusion (L11) is deductive: "*Therefore, some humans possess libertarian freedom.*"

Since it has already been deductively established that God possesses middle knowledge, another deductive conclusion (L12) follows: "*Therefore, God, given his middle knowledge, knows how these humans who possess libertarian freedom would freely choose,*" that is to say, an omniscient God simply knows how humans with libertarian freedom would freely choose if he were to create them. If that is the case, then God possessed this knowledge logically prior to his choice to create these libertarian agents.

Step (L13) simply states the obvious: "*If God possesses middle knowledge and some humans possess libertarian freedom, then 'Mere Molinism' is true.*"[14] With each step of

14. In chapter 2 documentation was provided for biblical support for human freedom and for

the argument in place, the final conclusion (L14) deductively follows: "*Therefore, given* (M8) and (L11), '*Mere Molinism*' is true."

It is important to note that the *"Mere Molinism Argument"* says nothing regarding issues related to salvation. In fact, soteriology is not even implied in the argument. This allows a Five-Point TULIP Calvinist to also be a Molinist. "Mere Molinism" makes it possible to resolve the centuries-old conflict between fellow Christians fighting over God's sovereignty and human freedom.[15]

The Omni Argument and middle knowledge.

One further argument for Molinism is offered by elaborating on a previous argument from chapter 12, where it was deductively concluded that exhaustive divine determinism is false. From this syllogism, two more premises are added which abductively conclude that Molinism is the best explanation of all the data.

The "Big Three" of God's omni attributes (omnipotence, omniscience, and omnibenevolence) are all subtly implied in this argument. The argument now will primarily focus on what logically follows from God's perfect love and the reality of an eternal hell. The syllogism runs as follows:

M1   *Divine determinism is false.*

M2   *God is completely sovereign and predestines all things.*

M3   *Therefore, divine predestination and divine determinism are not to be conflated.*

M4   *The best explanation of the data is Molinism.*

The Omni Argument expanded.

One should notice that (M1) is deductively concluded in (I7) found in chapter 12. With this in mind an expanded syllogism would go like as follows:

N1   *If divine determinism is true, then, if God wants all people to go to heaven, then all people go to heaven.*

---

determinism. Chapter 14 also gave a number of biblical illustrations that led Molina to argue for human freedom. The above discussion—which also argues for freedom—not only assumes the biblical evidence, but is also based on the logically deductive conclusion found in chapter 12. If one does not agree with a conclusion (that is, he believes it is not true), then he must demonstrate either that the structure of the syllogism is faulty, or show that at least one premise ("step") is false or more probably false than true. It is the author's position that the syllogism above is both valid and sound.

15. It cannot be denied that middle knowledge can be and has been applied in a soteriological context (Luis de Molina himself does this in his *Concordia*, which is evident from terms for salvation in the very title he gave to volume 4). But the above discussion has sought to show that human freedom can be divorced from soteriological applications and apply to "earthly matters," to use Calvin's words.

N2   *Not all people go to heaven.*

N3   *Therefore, if God wants all people to go to heaven, then divine determinism is false.*

N4   *If God is all-loving, then God wants all people to go to heaven.*

N5   *God is all-loving.*

N6   *Therefore, God wants all people to go to heaven.*

N7   *Therefore, divine determinism is false.*

N8   *God is completely sovereign and predestines all things.*

N9   *Therefore, divine predestination and divine determinism are not to be conflated.*

N10   *The best explanation of the data is Molinism.*[16]

If it is true that God loves all humans and that he desires all humanity to be saved and come to the knowledge of the truth (1 Tim 2:4)[17]—as argued above—then this state of affairs is ultimately inconsistent with divine determinism. But the Bible is clear that God exhaustively predestines all things (Rom 8:29–30; Eph 1:5, 11). Unfortunately, many Christians wrongly assume that, if God predestines all things, then God causally determines all things. However, it has been demonstrated that this is an incoherent conflation that Christians ought to reject.

So, why should one think the final abductive conclusion (N10) of the above syllogism is true? Because Molinism is the inference to the best explanation because it affirms two essential ingredients, namely, (1) human libertarian free will (God does not causally determine all things), and (2) God's possession of eternal middle knowledge. If God has eternal middle knowledge, then God can create a world in which he knows logically prior to his creative act how every human could, would, and will freely choose. Thus, God can predestine all that will occur without causally determining all that will occur.

Not only does the doctrine of God's middle knowledge answer many of these tough questions, it also explains how God is sovereign and how humanity simultaneously possesses libertarian freedom and genuine responsibility. Moreland and Craig point out that: "If our actions are freely performed, then it lies within our power to determine causally what the course of future events will be."[18] One might add, however, that God in his omniscience simply knows with perfect certainty how humans will freely choose. Therefore, he knows the future, but human beings are logically free

16. This is an expansion of the argument which was originally published by Stratton and Erasmus, "Divine Determinism," 3–15.

17. In chapter 12, note is made of Calvin and Piper's interpretation and several pages are devoted to a counter-argument, showing that this text (along with 2 Pet 3:9) is not referencing only the elect, but every single human being.

18. Moreland and Craig, *Philosophical Foundations*, 2nd ed., 526.

in the source sense and also seem to possess the ability to think or act otherwise. There are no "causal strings" attached, even though he knows people *will not* act otherwise. Although they could freely choose to act otherwise, they simply will not freely choose to act otherwise. If people had freely "acted otherwise," that is what God would have middle-known and foreknown.[19]

It is important, therefore, to remember that God's knowledge does not stand in causal relation to human action. If God knows with certainty how a person will freely choose, then if God's knowledge is removed, the person would still freely make the same choice. This means a person can logically affirm the future is predestined by God, while at the same time affirming that people are still free to determine the future. At first glance, this might seem confusing, but logically speaking, predestination and human freedom need not be mutually exclusive.[20]

The views that deny God's middle knowledge, yet affirm his foreknowledge, do so because of his foreordination. However, this seems to make God the author of evil, or as Craig concludes, "[Such a] view seems, in effect, to turn God into the devil."[21] This is so because, if God only has counterfactual knowledge after his creative decree, then it is God who causally determines the actions of humans—including evil actions. Therefore, humans are not really responsible for evil; God is! The middle knowledge view escapes this problem by logically affirming trust in an all good and sovereign God. Moreover, Molinism logically affirms a person's moral responsibility as genuine free agents.

Craig concludes his essay by stating that while: "Not explicitly taught in the biblical text, the doctrine of divine middle knowledge is certainly compatible with it, which cannot be said for at least some of its competitors. Middle-knowledge redounds to the glory of God and illuminates biblical truth in a dazzling way."[22]

After examining all of the biblical data and considering it logically, competing views fall short. Further, it appears that Molinism is the only view which can logically explain all of the data.

PRACTICAL RATIONALITY ARGUMENT (ELLIOTT CROZAT).

Elliott Crozat recently published an article entitled *Does the Purpose Theory of the Meaning of Life Entail an Irrational God?* in which he was responding to an objection

---

19. See Craig, *Only Wise God,* 72–74, and comments on foreknowledge and necessity in chapter 3.

20. (O9) is a conclusion which follows deductively from the preceding steps. This logically deductive conclusion demonstrates the harmonious association of these two seeming "opposites." The *Omni Argument*, however, differs from the *Mere Molinism Argument* (MMA). One can reject the *Omni-Argument*, while still affirming the MMA. The MMA has nothing to do with soteriological matters, while salvation-related issues might be inferred from the *Omni-Argument*.

21. Craig, "God Directs All Things," 91.

22. Craig, "Middle Knowledge View," 143.

to Thaddeus Metz's Purpose Theory (PT).[23] Metz defined PT as the view that (i) God created human beings for a purpose; (ii) fulfilling this purpose is a necessary condition for human life to have objective meaning; and (iii) human beings must have libertarian free will to freely choose to appropriate God's purpose. Metz concluded that some might reject PT, noting that people are "undependable" in their choices, and thus reason this way: If God has no control over a person's free (undependable) choices, his *practical* plan may not be fulfilled, which would demonstrate that PT is false.[24] To use Crozat's words, such would lead one to conclude that God is *practically* "irrational," that is, his plan had no means associated with it to make it happen. In contrast, practical "rationality" denotes that the God who purposely created human beings also determined the means by which they would accomplish his purpose. Broome, in his fine article on "Rationality" says, "It is commonly recognized that rationality requires you to intend what you believe is a necessary means to an end that you intend."[25] An illustration provided by Crozat is helpful: "If I intend to squat four hundred pounds but lack and never intend the means to do so, such as exercising and eating appropriately and patiently increasing my leg strength over time, then I am practically irrational regarding my goal. My practically irrational effort to squat four hundred pounds would likely bring harm to human persons, namely, myself and anyone who needs me to be healthy, such as my family, my students, and my employers."[26]

Divine determinists would respond that God determines the choices people make and thus his plan will be fulfilled. But such a position denies a key premise of PT: that people have LFW. But, if one insists that people have LFW, how could God fulfill his plan because "he does not know the free choices of his would-be human creatures"?[27] What does this two-forked dilemma, then, do with PT? Crozat replies: "It seems, then, that if PT is true, God actualizes the world without an adequate plan. He might have a goal, but he is unable to know whether he would succeed or fail to accomplish it. If God has a purpose logically prior to creation, it is an irrational one."[28]

But this is where Molina's proposal of middle knowledge has not only great relevance but it also offers a solution. Crozat says that from a Molinism perspective PT is true and that God in his middle knowledge is seen to be practically rational: humans have purpose, they have LFW, and at the same time God's eternal plan is being fulfilled. "Based on his natural and middle knowledge, God can perfectly plan world *W* by arranging the precise circumstances of *W* and hypothetically placing his

23. Crozat, "Does the Purpose Theory"?, 401–13.

24. Metz, *Meaning in Life*, 209. See also Metz, "Could God's Purpose"?, 200–18.

25. Broome, "Rationality," 289, noted by Crozat. See also Wallace, "Practical Reason": "Instrumental rationality, in its most basic form, instructs agents to take those means that are necessary in relation to their given ends. In the modern era, this form of rationality has widely been viewed as the single unproblematic requirement of practical reason."

26. Crozat, "Practical Rationality."

27. Crozat, "Does the Purpose Theory"?, 404.

28. Crozat, "Does the Purpose Theory"?, 404.

would-be free creatures in those situations so that, if he were to actualize *W*, he would know whether they will freely accept his purpose. The creaturely choices would not be causally determined; rather, they would be libertarianly free . . . God's free decision to actualize *W* then guarantees his foreknowledge of the choices of his human creatures. Given his natural knowledge, middle knowledge, and free decision to create *W* (the actual world), God foreknows what will happen in *W*, including all future free choices. God's knowledge of what will happen in *W* is called *free knowledge*. This knowledge is logically posterior to God's free decision to create *W*."[29]

The following year Crozat wrote again about PT but this time he defended Molinism by holding that God's practical rationality is evidence for God's having middle knowledge.[30] In other words, if Molinism is practically rational and thus PT is true, then God has middle knowledge. Therefore, if one can provide a good reason for accepting PT, then there is a *modus ponens* argument for Molinism.

Crozat's practical rationality and middle knowledge syllogism.

Crozat's syllogism—a *reductio ad absurdum* argument—consists of seven steps:

O1   *God lacks middle knowledge.*

O2   *If God lacks middle knowledge, then God is practically irrational.*

O3   *Thus, God is practically irrational.*

O4   *God is not practically irrational.*

O5   *Thus, God is practically irrational and God is not practically irrational.*

O6   *Thus, God does not lack middle knowledge.*

O7   *Thus, God possesses middle knowledge.*

Support for the syllogism.

The first premise (O1) is an assumption for the sake of argumentation. But behind the argument are Metz's three assumptions: (a) God created this world with purpose (on purpose and for a specific purpose), (b) that human life, therefore, is objectively meaningful, and (c) people have libertarian free will. Few theists would disagree with the first two, but concerning the last one there is much disagreement. It is fitting, then, to provide support for this assumption before progressing to offering support for the next premises.

---

29. Crozat, "Does the Purpose Theory"?, 404–5.
30. Crozat, "Practial Rationality."

Further support for libertarian freedom.

Several arguments in support of libertarian freedom—including what is referred to as the *"Free Thinking Arguments"*—are found in chapter 12. But further support is offered by considering competing options which provide possible explanations for how God determined what world he would create. There seem to be four approaches:

1. Middle knowledge.
2. Exhaustive divine causal determinism.
3. Simple foreknowledge.
4. Open theism.

The second approach has already been discussed in a previous chapter. The third option raises the question how God could have "foreknowledge" without "middle" knowledge. Since nothing has been created and no creatures exist, how is it possible for God to "foreknow" but not have middle knowledge? Does this push those who hold to a "simple foreknowledge" explanation to become determinists or middle knowledge Molinists? As for open theists, how much must God "limit" his sovereignty over mankind's "free choices" before the world is no longer in his control? Flint's arguments are pertinent here:

> The Molinist God is not a risk taker. He never has to deal with acting in situations where he knows only what *probably* would result from his actions. Rather, he knows *precisely* how his free creatures would react to any action on his part . . . If he were to put Libby in situation *A*, she would freely do *X*; if he were to put her in situation *B*, she would do *Y*; and so on. God can then decide which situation to put her in (say, *A* or *B*) depending on which result (*X* or *Y*) can more readily be woven into a world that satisfies his creative intentions. God need not worry about things heading off in an unintended direction—about his being surprised by unexpected actions on the part of his creatures. With middle knowledge, he truly does know what he is about. By exercising his providential control through the free actions of his creatures, he (and we) are assured that the world that results will fully manifest his wisdom and love.[31]

More could be said here about how middle knowledge provides the best explanation about how God could create the best world with maximal benefit to his creatures. But to do so here would be only repeating the arguments more fully stated in chapter 14.

31. Flint, "Molinism."

Understanding "practical rationality."

That God is a thinking (rational) being is intuitive to his having created mankind (rational beings) in his image. Further, God is "practically" rational since he both created human beings with and for a purpose and included the means to carry that purpose(s) out. That is possible if God has middle knowledge. Crozat explains: "If God lacks middle knowledge (MK), then logically prior to creation God intended an end (namely, a world with a sufficient number of libertarianly free humans who freely choose to know and love him forever) but he lacked the means (MK) to plan out the accomplishment of this end. Such practically irrational behavior could lead to serious and everlasting harm to human persons. Suppose, for example, that in the actual world every libertarianly free human person freely chooses to reject God's purpose. If God lacks MK, then logically prior to creating the actual world he was unable to know that this universal and free rejection would happen. In the logically prior state, God knew it *could* happen. But he needs MK to know that it *would* happen and to plan accordingly. Arguably, without MK, God's decision to create is practically irrational and reckless, which is absurd."[32]

Support for premise (O4).

Since "God is the greatest conceivable being, he possesses every perfection and has no imperfection. Practical rationality is a perfection. Practical irrationality is an imperfection. Hence, God is practically rational and not practically irrational in any way."[33] In other words, when Jesus asked Peter to "walk on the water," he also included the means to do so. He was "practically rational." To not make it possible to walk on the water's surface would have only made impossible Peter's step of faith. Thus, God is practically rational when Jesus invited Peter to step out of the boat and come to him.

Conclusion.

Crozat summarizes his argument in the following manner: "If God lacks middle knowledge, then God is practically irrational. But it is absurd to hold that God is practically irrational. Thus, God does not lack middle knowledge. Thus, God possesses middle knowledge."[34]

32. Crozat, "Practical Rationality."
33. Crozat, "Practical Rationality."
34. Crozat, "Practical Rationality."

KIRK MACGREGOR'S ARGUMENT.

MacGregor has devoted much of his academic career to studying and understanding Molina's work—reading it and making his own translation from the original Latin. He is arguably one of the world's leading authorities (if not the authority) regarding Luis de Molina and is the author of several scholarly works, including *Luis de Molina.* Recently this writer had the opportunity to discuss Molinism and middle knowledge with him, and he shared an argument that he teaches to his students at McPherson College in Kansas. It is a new argument (not previously published) for God's middle knowledge, and he has given permission to share it here. It consists of three premises reaching a deductive conclusion.

MacGregor's syllogism.

P1   *God either possesses his counterfactual knowledge logically prior or logically posterior to his creative decree.*

P2   *If humans possess soft [limited] libertarian freedom, then God possesses his counterfactual knowledge logically prior to his creative decree.*

P3   *Humans possess soft libertarian freedom (they sometimes have a range of options from which they can choose, even if that range consists of all bad options, all good options, some bad and some good, etc.).*

P4   *Therefore, God possesses his counterfactual knowledge logically prior to his creative decree.* [This is middle knowledge].

Defense for MacGregor's syllogism.

The Bible is clear that God possesses counterfactual knowledge: (e.g., 1 Sam 23:6–14; Jer 38:17–18; Deut 18:22; Isa 38:1–5; Amos 7:1–6; Jonah 3: 1–10; John 15:22, 24; 18:36; Matt 26:24; Mark 4:10–12; etc.) Further, based on the logical law of the excluded middle, God either possesses omniscient knowledge of counterfactuals prior to his creative decree or God gains this knowledge after his creative decree. Therefore, (P1) is intuitively true. There are no other options.[35]

But this raises a question which provides support for the second premise (P2): If one affirms that God is truly omniscient and possesses perfect counterfactual knowledge, then one is faced with the question: "Is God *eternally* omniscient or does he gain knowledge"? It has to be either one or the other. God's omniscience by definition means that he does not learn (God does not gain knowledge regarding the truth-value

---

35. The creative decree is not to be confused with a "logical moment." Rather, it is an action or decision.

of certain propositions). What he knows, he has always known. What is knowable, he simply always knows.

Another argument for the truthfulness of (P2) is achieved by showing the impossibility of the opposite. After all, if God only possesses his knowledge of counterfactuals after (logically posterior) his creative decree, then God decrees what every possible individual would do in any possible circumstances. In that case, no possible individual possesses a categorical ability to choose among a range of alternative options each compatible with his or her nature. They would not possess soft or limited libertarian freedom. MacGregor clarifies what follows if God does not possess counterfactual knowledge before (logically prior) to his decree in this way: "For any circumstance, God has locked them into one course of action. From these considerations (P2) follows."[36]

Support for (P3) can be illustrated from the following scenario: If humanity does not possess (at the least) limited or soft-libertarian free will, then it would be impossible for an unregenerate sinner to ever choose among sinful options (for example, choosing between robbing a bank or robbing a liquor store). And it would be impossible even for a Christian to choose to *take his thoughts captive* (2 Cor 10:5) before bad thinking takes him captive (Col 2:8), or for a person to choose to resist temptation to sin when he is tempted to sin (1 Cor 10:13). If no one possesses limited or soft-libertarian free will, then even regenerate believers do not possess an ability to choose between reading a red Bible or a blue Bible. That is to say, if John Piper reads a red Bible, he could not have chosen otherwise to read a blue Bible. Because Piper is causally determined to read the red Bible, it was impossible for him to read the blue Bible.

Further, if Christians do not possess limited or soft-libertarian freedom, then they do not possess the libertarian freedom to deliberate and rationally think things through to reach conclusions like, "Calvinism is probably true," or "Molinism is the inference to the best explanation." Indeed, all of a Christian's thoughts—whatever they are—are not up to the Christian person, and they could not be otherwise. Even the Christian's thoughts about that last sentence are causally determined if soft-libertarian freedom does not exist.

As reasonable as this is, (P3) is supported by the entirety of arguments offered in chapters 12–13, as well as the host of biblical data implying libertarian freedom surveyed in Chapter 2. Included in that list are the following: Gen 4:6–7; Deut 30:11–20; Josh 24:14–15, 22; Psa 119:108–9; Isa 5:3–4; Prov 1:23, 28; Jer 26:2–4; 36:3, 7, 17–20; Ezek 18:21–24, 30–32; 33:11; Zech 1:2–4; Matt 23:37–39; Acts 5:4; 1 Cor 7:37; 10:13; Rev 2:21; etc.

Given the biblical data for limited or soft libertarian free will, a Christian who denies that humans possess the ability to choose among a range of alternative options each consistent or compatible with his nature must reject the evidence of the above data. To the degree that these examples are valid understandings of the biblical text, a

---

36. This is not a published comment, but one the writer had with MacGregor during a recent visit.

Christian—if he affirms the authority of God's Word, as well as the logic-based arguments surveyed in chapter 12—must also affirm (P3) of MacGregor's syllogism.

If the Bible is true, if limited or soft-libertarian freedom is possessed by humans, then these free choices are not causally determined by God. For example, then, it follows that God would possess counterfactual knowledge of what *would* have happened if an agent would have freely chosen to eat at McDonalds instead of Burger King (or vice versa) prior to his creative decree. If God does not possess this eternal omniscience (prior to creation), then the person who eats a Big Mac simply was determined to do so and could not have done otherwise, that is, to have eaten a Whopper. Thus, God's so-called counterfactual knowledge would be based upon what he (God) could have chosen to do—not based on the counterfactual of the creature's freedom to choose.

As MacGregor has explained to this author: "Since the decree is not a logical moment of knowledge but an intervening act of will, nothing can be logically (i.e., explanatorily) simultaneous with it. In other words, some element of knowledge is either prior to the act of will or a result of the act of will. Indeed, some have asserted that God, as part of his creative decree, freely assigned truth values to all counterfactual statements. This, however, does not mean that counterfactual knowledge is logically simultaneous with his decree. It means that God's decree explains his counterfactual knowledge and that the counterfactual knowledge is therefore logically posterior to his decree on this view."

With this in mind, (P4) logically follows as a deductive conclusion from the previous premises: "God possesses his counterfactual knowledge logically prior to his creative decree." This is middle knowledge! Therefore, multiple arguments have been offered demonstrating the truth of Mere Molinism.

THE CALVINIST QUIZ AND UNITING THE BODY OF CHRIST.

Mere Molinism affirms and explains how God predestines *all things,* while humans are genuinely free and responsible for *some things.* This point was affirmed after engaging in a conversation with a well-known Reformed theologian who had been publicly adamant in his condemnation against Molinism after taking what is referred to as the "Calvinist Quiz." With the definition of libertarian freedom in mind—the "ability to choose between or among a range of alternative options each of which is compatible with one's nature"—the questions asked were the following:

The quiz.

1. *Did Satan possess the categorical ability to rebel or not rebel against God?* (This question can be rephrased: *Did God causally determine Satan to rebel?*)

2. *Did Adam and Eve possess the categorical ability to eat or not eat of the forbidden fruit? (This question can be rephrased: Did God causally determine Adam and Eve to eat of the forbidden fruit?)*

3. *Do unregenerate sinners have the categorical ability to choose among a range of sinful thoughts and actions? (This question can be rephrased: Does God causally determine each specific sin?)*

4. *Do Christians possess the categorical ability to choose to either sin or to resist temptation in thought and action as per 1 Cor 10:13? (This question can be rephrased: Does God causally determine Christians to sin?)*

5. *Do Christians have the categorical ability to choose between reading a red Bible or a blue Bible? (If John Piper were to choose to read a red Bible, could he have genuinely chosen otherwise and read the blue Bible?)*

6. *Do Christians possess the categorical ability to deliberate and rationally infer and affirm claims of knowledge such as, "Calvinism is a better explanation than Molinism," or "Molinism is the inference to the best explanation"? (This question can be rephrased: Does God causally determine some Christians to affirm false beliefs?)*

The dialogue.

After completing the quiz, the Calvinist noted that he had answered in the affirmative *all* of the questions (affirming only one is sufficient). The dialogue that followed went as follows:

- **Stratton:** *So, with this quiz in mind, you do believe creatures possess limited libertarian free will at least in some issues not pertaining to salvation, right?*

- **Calvinist:** *Yes! I do believe that humans have limited libertarian free will—just not when it comes to salvation.*

- **Stratton:** *Great! Now, let's bracket soteriological issues for a moment. Since you affirm that some humans possess libertarian free will at least some of the time, how would you answer the following: "When did God know how humans would freely choose? Did God gain this knowledge or has God always possessed this knowledge without beginning"? (I also asked: "How is God sovereign over these libertarian free choices"?).*

- **Calvinist:** *God is necessarily omniscient; he always knows all things perfectly.*

- **Stratton:** *Exactly—I thought you would respond that way! So, God knew how you would freely choose in these circumstances (not related to salvation) logically prior to his creative decree?*

- **Calvinist:** *Yes.*

- **Stratton:** *Then you are a Molinist!*

- **Calvinist:** *How did you reach that conclusion?*

- **Stratton:** *Well, Molinism is not necessarily a soteriological view. It simply offers a model as to how some human thoughts and actions can be free in a libertarian sense—so responsibility entails—and also how God can be sovereign over these free thoughts and actions by choosing to create a world in which he knew how people would freely choose. You just affirmed the two essential pillars of "Mere Molinism":* (1) *Humans occasionally possess libertarian freedom and* (2) *God possesses middle knowledge* (knowledge of how humans would freely choose logically prior to his creative decree). This theologian paused for a few moments and then offered a response that this author will never forget:

- **Calvinist:** *Well, if that's what it means to be a Molinist, then I guess I'm a Molinist!*

- **Stratton:** *I already knew you were!*

The Calvinist seemed to feel rather liberated after seeing how he could affirm all Five Points of *TULIP* and simultaneously reject the exhaustive divine determinism of all human thoughts, actions, beliefs, and behaviors. Conclusion: The Five Points of Calvinism are not mutually exclusive with the two essential pillars of *Mere Molinism*.

Building bridges?

These tactics begin to build bridges between theologians on both sides of the determinism/freedom debate. In fact, the more one studies these issues, the closer Molina's views seem to align with some of Calvin's. Moreover, as MacGregor has pointed out, the Molinistic framework can be completely monergistic as opposed to synergistic, that is to say, both Calvin and Molina would affirm that God does *all* the work in the salvation process.[37]

It appears that the only major thing about which Calvin and Molina would disagree is whether God's grace is *resistible* or not. Be that as it may, a Reformed theologian can continue to affirm the irresistible grace of *TULIP*, and also logically affirm limited libertarian freedom in issues unrelated to soteriological matters and thus, consistently affirm both the Five Points of Calvinism and Mere Molinism.

CONCLUSION.

This chapter has addressed theological and philosophical issues that are central in the argument for middle knowledge. Though the concept of counterfactuals was made prominent by Molina—a concept in itself not controversial—the central question is how they figure in the omniscience of God, or more precisely, *when* God possesses

37. MacGregor, "Monergistic Molinism," 77–92.

that knowledge: Did God "know" all counterfactuals logically before his decree to create a particular world (middle knowledge) or afterward (a concept that Latin theologians and philosophers called "free knowledge")?

The arguments used were basically five-fold: (1) that God "knew" all counterfactuals of the world he could create; (2) that, since God with libertarian freedom possessed a range of options from which to choose, each of which is consistent with his nature, he also could create creatures after his image/likeness who like him would possess a similar freedom to choose among a range of alternative options, each compatible with their natures; (3) that humans possess at least limited libertarian freedom (vs. exhaustive determinism), which is apparent in their ability to think about and weigh choices and decisions consistent with their natures; and (4) that, if God knew what people would freely do if he chose to actualize them and their circumstances in the world he would create, he also had to plan the means logically prior to actualizing it and also plan it in such a way as to achieve his purpose via the "libertarianly" free choices of his creatures.

Finally (5), MacGregor brought all these arguments together and returned full circle by showing that God had counterfactual knowledge logically prior to his decree to create the world. Thus, theologians have multiple reasons to affirm the middle knowledge of God and some form of Molinism.

16

The apologetic significance of Molinism

It may be difficult to see how the biblical, theological, and philosophical data in the previous chapters have any real relevance to Christian apologetics. How do these arguments help people in the church or in the public square give a defense to the Christian faith? Indeed, a pastor wondered why he should not conclude that all the research and writing regarding Molinism (specifically by this writer) should be considered anything but a "colossal waste of time." After all, if the mission of an apologist is to argue for the truth of Christianity, why should he spend so much time promoting a specific Christian theology, especially when it is over such a seemingly peripheral and non-essential issue? Would it not be wiser to spend the majority of one's time as a Christian apologist arguing, for example, against atheism alone? What he did not understand is that, to the contrary, Molinism may be one of the greatest threats to the atheistic worldview.

One may rightly wonder why an atheist should care what view of divine sovereignty and human responsibility Christians hold, but some atheists[1] are beginning to recognize that Molinism—its view of divine middle knowledge and human freedom in particular—addresses one very obvious area of vulnerability of their argument about how God (and a *good* God at that) could/would allow evil in the world. To be sure, Christians adhering to other views of God's sovereignty have proposed responses to atheism, but the thesis of this chapter is that Molinism offers *logically consistent access* to far more apologetics-based arguments for the existence of God and the truth of Christianity, than those holding to a competing view of divine sovereignty. While this does not deductively prove that Molinism is true, it does seem to render Molinism a preferable view. Before looking at some examples of the Molinist approach to apologetics, it is prudent to define briefly the two essential ingredients of "Mere Molinism":

1. See Craig, "Arguing Successfully." The article is a review of prominent atheist philosopher Graham Oppy, who has raised objections to Molinism.

1. Logically prior to God's decision to create the world, God knew everything that *would* happen in any possible scenario he *could* create (this entails God's middle knowledge).

2. As beings created in the image of God, humans, like God, possess libertarian freedom (the ability to choose between a range of options each compatible with human nature).

One can move beyond mere Molinism and apply these two essentials to soteriological issues (which is not necessary), and become a "soteriological Molinist" by affirming a third ingredient:

3. God is a maximally great being who loves and desires the best for all people.

A soteriological view of Molinism entails each of these three key ingredients. Competing views, however, will deny at least one of these vital points. For example, open theists deny that God possesses middle knowledge of possible worlds within his power to create.[2] Calvinists and other divine determinists regularly reject the notion of human libertarian freedom and often dismiss the omnibenevolence of God.[3]

At least one of the three key aspects of Molinism is connected with each of the following apologetics-based arguments.

MOLINISM AND THE PROBLEM OF EVIL.

Molinism and the problem of moral evil.

Some atheists[4] assume that the idea of a perfectly loving God is logically incompatible with moral evil. For example, their conclusion has an affinity with deterministic Calvinists, that is, people who believe that God causally determines *all things*. If so, would it not follow that God causally determined *all* of Hitler's thoughts and actions? Do not atheists have an arguable point and can they not rationally infer that (1) while Hitler is in a sense responsible for the Holocaust, (2) God is *ultimately* to blame; one way or another. After all, did he not *causally determine* all of Hitler's thoughts and actions? Moreover, atheists might rightly infer that God is further guilty of additional evil because he *could not*, *would not*, or *did not* do anything to stop Hitler. Therefore, atheists conclude that God is either not worthy of worship or simply does not exist.

Molinism, however, may be used to solve the problem of moral evil by shifting from a free will defense and offering a traditional theodicy. By affirming a Molinistic

---

2. Beilby and Eddy, *Divine Foreknowledge: Four Views*, 13–47.

3. Walls, "What's Wrong with Calvinism"?, 40:26. See also Pink, *Sovereignty*, 16–19.

4. See, for example, Tyson, "Does Neil deGrasse Tyson Believe"? and the discussion which follows in this chapter. See also Beebe, "Logical Problem of Evil," and his excellent bibliography; Hume, *Dialogues Concerning Natural Religion*; Mackie, "Evil and Omnipotence," 200–2); Peterson, "The Problem of Evil," 71–88, and the bibliography he provides; and Tooley, "The Problem of Evil."

framework, it is plausible for one to conclude that an all-powerful, all-knowing, and perfectly loving God exists. Since God is all-loving, he desires an authentic and eternal loving relationship with each and every human being he has ever created.[5]

Since God desires an authentic love relationship with each individual human being, he had to give humanity the genuine freedom to choose to reject Him—or not (this point is not compatible with *TULIP* or any deterministic view of divine sovereignty, sans a specific and unique view of universalism).[6] With mankind's rejection of God and his law came sin, and these transgressions have infected this world with evil, pain, and terrible suffering. God also allows suffering caused by moral choices and uses suffering to bring people to himself, to both shape believers and bring them closer to him, which is the greatest good a human being could ever experience.

After reflecting upon God's perfect love, the only way God could eradicate the possibility of moral evil is to eradicate libertarian freedom.[7] That would then eradicate the possibility of each person freely entering into a "true love" relationship with his or her creator (making the essence of salvation impossible). Eradicating evil, then, would be evil! Thus, keeping eternity in mind, a person can see that it is good and loving that evil, pain, and suffering—at least temporarily—were made possible and allowed by God.

This line of reasoning, called the *Free Will Argument against the Problem of Moral Evil*, might be expressed this way:

Q1   If a Maximally Great Being (God) exists, he is perfectly good and all loving (this is the property of omnibenevolence).

Q2   If God is all-loving, he desires a true love relationship with all mankind (John 3:16; 1 Tim 2:4; 2 Pet 3:9).

5. Stratton and Erasmus, "Divine Determinism."

6. See also Stratton, "True Love."

7. God might not have the ability to do otherwise when it comes to love, however, it does not follow that God does not possess libertarian freedom regarding love. This is the case because nothing external to or other than God causally determines God's nature. Moreover, nothing other than the Father causally determines his love for the Son and the Spirit. It is vital to remember that there are basically two definitions of libertarian freedom: (i) the PAP/"ability to do otherwise" version, and (ii) the source-hood version (which simply means that a person is not causally determined by something other than the person). When it comes to love, God possesses the source-hood version of libertarian freedom. God is not causally determined by something other than him to love. As 1 John 4:8 makes clear: "God *is* love." With this in mind, love requires libertarian freedom to be possessed by each person in the relationship. The best kind of love is when persons are not causally determined to love the other. In fact, it is simply oxymoronic to refer to a relationship where at least one person in the relationship is causally determined to enter into the relationship as a "love relationship." It is not love at all, rather, it is simply an incoherent combination of words at best, or evil at worst. Since it would be impossible for God to create a contingent being whose nature is necessarily loving (like God is), without causally determining the nature of the creature, God creates humans with the "ability to do otherwise" kind of libertarian freedom so that a true love relationship with humanity can be attained. Humans, then, unlike God, possess both the source-hood and "ability to do otherwise" versions of the libertarian freedom to love. God only has the source-hood version.

Q3   If true love is to be attained with all mankind, all mankind must possess libertarian freedom.[8]

Q4   If mankind possesses libertarian freedom, then mankind can freely choose to do evil.

Q5   If a Maximally Great Being (God) exists, he is all-powerful (this is the property of omnipotence).

Q6   Therefore, God could prevent the possibility of evil actions by eradicating human libertarian freedom (he would have the power).

Q7   If God eradicates libertarian freedom, then he eradicates the possibility of true love with humanity.

Q8   Eternal love with God is the ultimate good humans can experience and humans freely choosing to respond to God's love brings him ultimate glory.

Q9   Therefore, preventing love would be evil.

Q10   Therefore, it would be evil to eradicate libertarian freedom.

Q11   Therefore, it would be evil for God to eradicate the possibility of evil.

Q12   Therefore, since God is perfectly good and all loving, he allows the possibility of evil.

It is vital to understand that Molinism provides the foundation upon which this argument against the "problem of moral evil" is built, as libertarian freedom is one of its essential components. Since this problem of evil seems to be the greatest "reason" for atheism (at least based upon the years of apologetic encounters of this author), it follows that Molinism—if true—takes this so-called "reason" off the table for atheists. Franks, in his survey of different views of the problem of evil, also notes this conclusion: "Establishing that there is evil [in the world] is easy; determining why there is evil is a much more difficult task. Those familiar with the literature on the problem of evil will know that this has been a focus of Christian theists for centuries and with good reason . . . Presumably, an omnipotent being would be able to prevent evil, an omniscient being would know how to prevent evil, and a perfectly good being would want to prevent evil. So why, then, is there evil? In most contemporary discussions . . . [the problem of evil tends] to amount to an argument for atheism since, it is alleged, one is incapable of justifying the belief that God exists given the evil we find in the world."[9] Mere Molinism, however, provides this justification for theists while simultaneously demonstrating that the problem of evil is not justification for atheistic affirmations or a "lack of belief" when it comes to the existence of God.

---

8. See comments in chapter 13 supporting this premise.

9. Franks, *Examining Evil*, 1–2.

If atheists have no good reason for their atheism (and continue to hold to atheistic beliefs anyway), then they clutch their atheistic beliefs with a blind faith apart from reason. Again, this is why the committed atheist will vigorously fight against Molinism and desperately try to find something wrong with this argument.

Christians, on the other hand, who deny human libertarian freedom or God's perfect love (omnibenevolence) do not have access to this argument and are left with a significant problem of carrying an extremely heavy burden of evil. That is to say, the problem of evil cannot be adequately explained by one who affirms that God causally determines *all* things.

Molinism and the problem of natural evil.

Molinism also offers a powerful solution to another version of the "problem of evil" (a.k.a., the "problem of *natural* evil"). Neil deGrasse Tyson, a world-renowned astrophysicist and science popularizer, spends much of his time popularizing an argument against the Christian view of God. He often makes claims such as the following: "Every description of God that I have heard, holds God to be all-powerful and all-good. And then I look around and I see a tsunami that killed a quarter million people in Indonesia—an earthquake that killed a quarter million people in Haiti. And I see earthquakes, tornadoes, and disease, childhood leukemia. And I see all of this and I say I do not see evidence of both of those being true simultaneously . . . If there is a God, the God is either not all-powerful, or not all good. It can't be both."[10]

If Tyson were aware of Molinism, then he would not make such claims and perhaps even consider Christianity. Even the well-known, atheist philosopher Paul Draper argues against Tyson's reasoning: "Logical arguments from evil are a dying (dead?) breed . . . Even an omnipotent and omniscient being might be forced to allow E[vil] for the sake of obtaining some important good."[11]

C. S. Lewis weighs in on this in his great book *Mere Christianity*:

> God created things which had free will. That means creatures which can go wrong or right. Some people think they can imagine a creature which was free but had no possibility of going wrong, but I can't. If a thing is free to be good it's also free to be bad. And free will is what has made evil possible. Why, then, did God give them free will? Because free will, though it makes evil possible, is also the only thing that makes possible any love or goodness or joy worth having. A world of automata—of creatures that worked like machines—would hardly be worth creating. The happiness which God designs for His higher creatures is the happiness of being freely, voluntarily united to Him and to each other in an ecstasy of love and delight compared with which the most

10. Tyson, "Does Neil deGrasse Tyson Believe"?

11. Draper, "The Skeptical Theist," 176–77.

rapturous love between a man and a woman on this earth is mere milk and water. And for that they've got to be free.

Of course, God knew what would happen if they used their freedom the wrong way: apparently, He thought it worth the risk . . . If God thinks this state of war in the universe a price worth paying for free will—that is, for making a real world in which creatures can do real good or harm and something of real importance can happen, instead of a toy world which only moves when He pulls the strings—then we may take it is worth paying."[12]

Molinism explains exactly what this "good" or "important good" is to which Draper refers. At least one of these "important goods" is that this temporary suffering-filled world allows humans the ability to *freely* love for eternity and teaches us not to take a perfect state of affairs for granted as Adam, Eve, Satan, and a third of all the angels seemed to do. With this in mind, it is much easier to answer the following question: "Why did God call this world, *very good*" (Gen 1:31)? Because God *knew* (which implies God's middle knowledge if possessed logically prior to the creative decree), it *would* lead to an *eternal weight of glory beyond all comparison* (2 Cor 4:17). Because God has eternity in mind, people—created in his image—ought to think that way as well.

A broad structure of the argument can be summarized via deduction in the following manner:[13]

R1   *If God is omnibenevolent, then he desires genuine eternal love relations with humans.*

R2   *If God desires genuine eternal love relations with humans, then he creates humans with libertarian freedom.*

R3   *If God creates humans with libertarian freedom, then he allows humans to experience suffering.*[14]

---

12. Lewis, *Mere Christianity*, 47–48. Plantinga, *God, Freedom and Evil*, 30, addresses this in more philosophical terms: "A world containing creatures who are significantly free (and freely perform more good than evil actions) is more valuable, all else being equal, than a world containing no free creatures at all. Now God can create free creatures, but He can't *cause* or *determine* them to do only what is right. For if He does so, then they aren't significantly free after all; they do not do what is right *freely*. To create creatures capable of *moral* good, therefore, He must create creatures capable of moral evil; and He can't give these creatures the freedom to perform evil and at the same time prevent them from doing so. As it turned out, sadly enough, some of the free creatures God created went wrong in the exercise of their freedom; this is the source of moral evil. The fact that free creatures sometimes go wrong, however, counts neither against God's omnipotence nor against His goodness; for He could have forestalled the occurrence of moral evil only by removing the possibility of moral good."

13. The author expresses gratefulness to Matt Fig and Jacobus Erasmus for fine tuning these premises.

14. One's experience of suffering can include both a direct and personal experience as well as an awareness and knowledge of the suffering other sentient beings experience. This assumes that human freedom would not prevent disobedience—which did occur—and such disobedience brought suffering into the world. See the discussion above in chapter 13: "The Omnibenevolence of God."

R4   *God is omnibenevolent.*

R5   *Therefore, God allows humans to experience suffering.*

These premises may be supported by the further sub-premises or reasons:

R1   *If God is omnibenevolent, then he desires genuine eternal love relations with humans.*

R2   *If God desires genuine eternal love relations with humans, then he creates humans with libertarian freedom (because): R2a- A genuine eternal love relationship between God and humans necessarily requires that humans possess libertarian freedom.*

R3   *If God creates humans with libertarian freedom, then he allows humans to experience suffering (because): R3a- Suffering can result from libertarian free humans. And R3b- God created a world in which he knew that unless he permitted moral, natural, and all kinds of evil, some would not freely choose to* eternally preserve *the suffering-free state of affairs in the new heavens and new earth (2 Cor 4:17).*[15]

R4   God is omnibenevolent.

R5   Therefore, God allows humans to experience suffering, resulting from all kinds of evil.[16]

The above syllogism makes use of all three of the essential ingredients of the *soteriological view* of Molinism. In fact, no competing views of God's sovereignty have logical access to this specific argument.

With God's eternal intent in mind, it is easy to see that God is not a "morally guilty mind." That is to say, the concept of *Mens rea* does not apply to God if Molinism is true.[17] This is a knockdown argument against Tyson's assertion above that if God

---

15. Not only does this apply to moral and natural evil, but it also seems to make sense of what is often considered to be gratuitous evil/suffering. The following thought experiment seeks to make the point: Would a person prefer to live in a world free from any and all suffering, a world where even the lower animals never suffer? If he awoke tomorrow in that world, would he freely choose to "keep the rules" to make sure no being capable of suffering ever suffers again? If so, it seems as if Paul was onto something in 2 Cor 4:17. If not, then he simply will not be allowed to hang out with those who have learned to "keep the rules" for the rest of eternity so that suffering of any kind is never experienced again (at least by those who have learned).

16. "All kinds of evil" could also pertain to the "problem of divine hiddenness." After all, Adam, Eve, Satan, and a third of all the angels each took a state of affairs where God was anything but "hidden" for granted. In fact, they rebelled against an "unhidden" God. Perhaps the suffering we experience today, including the times we feel that God ought not be hidden, prepares us to savor the full glory and presence of God into the infinite future—the same or similar state of affairs that Adam, Eve, Satan, and a third of all the angels rejected. Thus, it could be the case that when a skeptic complains about the "hiddenness of God," they are actually assuming the "pre-fall" state or the "eternal weight of glory beyond all comparison" (2 Cor 4:17) as "the way things ought to be."

17. *Mens rea* refers to the legal philosophy of the "guilty mind" and criminal intent.

is all-powerful, then he cannot be all-good or all loving. In fact, when a person keeps eternity in mind, they should clearly see that this world suffused with suffering is the most loving kind of world God could have created.

Molinism takes the teeth out of the bite of Tyson's objection raised against the knowledge of God. Tyson seems to be completely unaware of the work that theologians and philosophers have done in this field which leads to his ignorant claims. Peter Van Inwagen made this clear when he wrote: "It used to be widely held that evil was incompatible with the existence of God: that no possible world contained both God and evil. So far as I am able to tell, this thesis is no longer defended."[18]

This thesis may no longer be defended in the ivory towers of academia, but the majority of today's culture is unaware of these scholarly achievements. This is why it is vital for the church at large—from pastors to the layman—to become aware of the apologetic power of Molinism when engaged in evangelism or influencing the culture for God's glory in any form or fashion. The so-called "problem of evil," when viewed via a Molinistic lens, melts away.

The Calvinist and theological determinist, Guillame Bignon summarizes the issue well: "Arminianism [which Bignon conflates with Molinism] is better-off than Calvinism to answer the atheist argument from evil against God's existence. I do affirm that . . . the libertarian has a resource against the problem of evil that the compatibilist cannot use. That, of course, doesn't mean that Arminianism is overall better, only that it's more useful at rejecting the problem of evil. It's a strength of Arminianism [Molinism] I recognize."[19]

MOLINISM AND THE FREETHINKING ARGUMENT AGAINST NATURALISM.

Not only is the "problem of evil" no problem at all if Molinism is true, Molina's view also provides a foundation for powerful arguments against naturalism—the most common view of atheists. Simply put, naturalism is the belief that physical reality is all that exists. It follows that if nature is *all* that exists, then all that exists *could* ultimately be discovered via the study of nature (physics, chemistry, and biology, for example). Thus, if only scientifically testable and discoverable things exist, then, things like God or anything like God (such as human souls) do not exist. One argument that defeats this naturalistic view is what this writer has called the *Freethinking Argument against Naturalism*:[20]

A1   *If naturalism is true, human nature does not include an immaterial soul.*

---

18. Van Inwagen, "The Problem of Evil," 135.

19. Bignon, "A Response to Kevin Timpe."

20. This syllogism begins with "A" because it was used in chapter 12.

A2   *If human nature does not include an immaterial soul, then humans do not possess libertarian freedom.*

A3   *If humans do not possess libertarian freedom, then humans do not possess the ability to rationally infer and rationally affirm knowledge claims.*

A4   *Humans do possess the ability to rationally infer and rationally affirm knowledge claims.*

A5   *Therefore, humans possess libertarian freedom.*

A6   *Therefore, human nature includes an immaterial soul.*

A7   *Therefore, naturalism is false.*

A8   *The best explanation for the existence of the immaterial soul and/or libertarian freedom is God.*

This writer has defended this argument at length elsewhere,[21] but the point here is that this argument against naturalistic atheism makes perfect sense on Molinism—but it is at odds with exhaustive divine determinism because it deductively concludes: *"Therefore, humans possess libertarian freedom."*

In fact, this argument from rationality is often attacked from both atheists who assume naturalism is true and Christians who assume exhaustive divine determinism to be true. Needless to say, Christian determinists cannot appeal to this apologetic argument for the existence of the human soul created in God's image because it simultaneously destroys their divine determinism.

Because of problems like these, what seems to be a minority of reformed thinkers—such as Crisp,[22] Timpe,[23] Plantinga,[24] Muller,[25] and Koukl[26] freely choose to reject *exhaustive* divine determinism. Greg Koukl stated his position this way: "The problem with [determinism] is that without freedom, rationality would have no room to operate. Arguments would not matter, since no one would be able to base beliefs on adequate reasons. One could never judge between a good idea and a bad one. One

---

21. Stratton and Erasmus, "Mere Molinism," 21, and above in chapter 12.

22. Crisp, *Deviant Calvinism*.

23. Timpe in a personal conversation with the author made it clear: "I am willing (in contexts where I think it'll be righty understood) to affirm the label 'Reformed,' but I think that's a much broader term than 'Calvinist.'"

24. Plantinga, *The Nature of Necessity*. He is known for advancing "Reformed Epistemology" in a three-volume series *Warrant: The Current Debate*, *Warrant and Proper Function*, and *Warranted Christian Belief*. He is also known to be a Molinist because of his books such as *God, Freedom and Evil* (1989). His free will defense specifically hinges upon libertarian freedom. He once wrote: "I hope to continue thinking about 'Reformed' or 'Calvinist' epistemology, a set of views at the heart of which is the claim that belief in God is properly basic . . . and I expect to defend the Molinist contention that some counterfactuals of freedom are true and all counterfactuals of freedom are known by God" (Plantinga, in Tomberlin and Van Inwagen, eds., *Profiles*, 93–94).

25. Muller, *Divine Will*.

26. Koukl, *Tactics*.

would only hold beliefs because he had been predetermined to do so . . . Every one of our thoughts, dispositions, and opinions would have been decided for us by factors completely out of our control. Therefore, in practice, arguments for determinism are self-defeating."[27]

Molinism arguably is the best, most defensible framework by which to understand libertarian freedom, and libertarian freedom is a necessary ingredient for the *Freethinking Argument against Naturalism.* This is another example of how Molinism relates to apologetics.

Braxton Hunter uses one of the deductive conclusions in the *Freethinking Argument*—surveyed in chapter 12—as a premise in an easy-to-remember three-step syllogism which deductively concludes that God exists. It goes as follows:

S1   *If God does not exist, then libertarian freedom does not exist.*

S2   *Libertarian freedom does exist.*

S3   *Therefore, God exists.*[28]

Hunter has noted that he realizes many Calvinists reject the concept of libertarian freedom. Nonetheless, he believes that Calvinists can support the argument if only as a philosophical defeater against atheism. Although he addresses the fact that some Calvinists (not all) reject the idea of libertarian freedom, he offers the following satirical syllogism for context and to make his point:

T1   *If God does not exist, then talking bullfrogs do not exist.*

T2   *Talking bullfrogs do exist.*

T3   *Therefore, God exists.*[29]

While Hunter obviously rejects premise (T2), he notes that if talking bullfrogs do exist, then God would seem to be the best explanation of talking frogs (or to appeal to Old Testament examples, snakes or donkeys). Similarly, he believes that (at least some) fair-minded divine determinists would agree.

MOLINISM AND THE KALAM COSMOLOGICAL ARGUMENT.

Molinism provides additional firepower in the battle of apologetics. One of the most powerful arguments for the existence of God is the *Kalam Cosmological Argument.* The syllogism runs as follows:

U1   *Whatever begins to exist has a cause.*

---

27. Koukl, *Tactics,* 128–29. See also chapter 12.

28. Hunter, "Matt Dillahunty vs. Braxton Hunter."

29. Hunter, "Debating Determinism," discussed this syllogism with the author during a personal conversation in Feb. 2019.

U2   *The universe began to exist.*

U3   *Therefore, the universe has a cause.*

Although the word "God" is not found in the premises or the conclusion, the *Kalam* is one of the most popular arguments for God's existence because theism is rationally inferred from the deductive conclusion (U3), once the word "universe" is properly defined. However, the rational inferences derived from the deductive conclusion not only cause problems for atheists, they also cause problems for Christians who believe libertarian freedom is impossible.

The apologist needs to consider the rational inferences that logically follow from the deductive conclusion of the *Kalam*: The cause of all space, time, and nature must be space-less, timeless, and other than nature (supernatural). Moreover, the cause of the universe must be enormously powerful to create an entire universe from nothing. Could anything require more power?

Additionally, not only did the cause of the universe have to have been apart from time and space, it also must have had the ability—the power—to spontaneously bring the world into existence without anything *causing* it to do so—because then, whatever the cause of the cause was would *be* the cause. But since this cause exists outside of anything physical, temporal, or material, none of these things could logically cause or force this ultimate *cause* to do anything. Therefore, this ultimate cause seems to have its own volition or libertarian freedom to create or not to create the universe. Apart from anything abstract (which would be causally impotent anyway),[30] only an unembodied *mind* (or soul) could logically transcend space-time and all nature.

If this line of thinking were taken further, then would it not lead to concluding that persons are the only type of *things* that could possibly possess immaterial minds with free will (which is supported by the *Freethinking Argument* previously offered)? Therefore, a person can decipher that the cause of the universe was a personal being. If the cause of the universe is personal, then it is at least possible that "It" can have a personal relationship with other personal beings. Humans are personal beings. Therefore, it is *possible* that humans can have a personal relationship with the cause of the universe. No special revelation or biblical data required!

To say it briefly: Some deterministic Calvinists have argued that the idea of libertarian freedom—the categorical ability to choose among a range of options each of which is compatible with one's nature—is incoherent[31] and that even God cannot possess this kind of volition.[32] If that is the case, then these Calvinists cannot appeal

30. Craig, "Middle Knowledge, Truth-Makers": "It is virtually universally agreed that abstract objects, if they exist, are causally impotent."

31. Kenneth Keathley, *Salvation and Sovereignty*, 83, points out, for example, that R. C. Sproul Jr. "does not hesitate to say that in any given situation only one choice is truly available to God, and that decision is determined by His greatest inclination. If God's choices are determined, then this means that He does all things by necessity, a point Jonathan Edwards acknowledged (*Freedom of the Will*, 4.7)."

32. Hendryx, in "Eleven (11) Reasons" says: "God always makes choices according to His holy

to all of the rational inferences provided by the *Kalam*, and humanity—in a sense—becomes just as "necessary" as God Himself. This was the conclusion of Jay Wesley Richards: "[I]f choice and alternatives must be positively barred from our understanding of God's creation of the world, one should conclude that God is not even as free as we are in many situations . . . The better course seems to be to retain the claim that God is free, at least with respect to some things, in the libertarian sense. God could have created a world different from the one he actually did create, or he could have created none at all."[33]

If God does possess libertarian freedom, however, then it stands to reason that if humans are indeed created *in his image* (Gen 1:26–27), then humans could possess the limited, but genuine ability to choose among a range of options *each* consistent with their nature as well. This is exactly what is meant by libertarian freedom.

The *Kalam* also helps us understand even more about Molinism. The rational inferences provided by the *Kalam* show that God exists in a "static state of aseity" in which the universe (time and space) did not exist. That is to say, logically prior to the beginning of the existence of the universe God exists—"and then" (to use temporal language)—God creates the universe. When considering this "static state of aseity," the question is raised: "Is God maximally great in this state"?

What the writer has called "The Cosmological Quiz" can help answer this question:

1. Question 1: *Is it true that God exists in a state of aseity logically prior to creating the universe (and thus without the universe)?*

2. Question 2: *In this state of aseity, is God omnipotent? If so, does he possess the power to create creatures with libertarian freedom (even if he never does create them)?*

3. Question 3: *In this state of aseity, is God omniscient? If so, does he possess the knowledge of what these libertarian free creatures—within his power to create (even if he never does create them)—would freely do?*

If a person answers "no" to any of these questions, he might be a heretic! If one answers "yes" to all of the above, then he needs to be congratulated because he is a Molinist! This is because if one affirms that God is both omnipotent and omniscient in the state of affairs logically prior to the creation of the universe, then *some flavor of Molinism* must be true. God would possess the power to create libertarian free

---

nature. All members of the Trinity have acted in sinless perfection. God cannot even desire an unholy act, nor can He lie, for He would no longer be God if He did. In fact, His choices are so wrapped up in His nature and essence that He could not do otherwise." There is no argument against God acting in accord with his nature, but his actions are not limited to one absolute choice; his moral nature allows for more than one option, indeed, a range of options each compatible with his nature. This is the epitome of libertarian freedom.

33. Richards, *The Untamed God*, 239.

creatures (even if he never creates them), and God would "middle know" exactly how these free creatures *would* freely think, act, believe, and behave logically prior to his creative decree.

It is amazing to see how apologetic arguments for the existence of God can also clarify exactly how a person should think about his sovereignty too.

If humans possess the libertarian ability to choose among a range of alternative options *each* compatible with human nature, then another powerful argument for the existence of God becomes available.

MOLINISM AND THE MORAL ARGUMENT.

The *Moral Argument* might be the most attention-getting of all the arguments in the arsenal of the apologist. This is because virtually every single human makes moral judgments every single day. The *Moral Argument* can be summarized in a three-step syllogism:

V1   *If God does not exist, then objective moral values and duties do not exist.*

V2   *Objective moral values and duties exist.*

V3   *Therefore, God exists.*

There are several reasons as to why the *Moral Argument* is problematic for the naturalist. For instance, the atheist typically affirms that humanity was not created on purpose or for an objective purpose. If humanity was not created on purpose or for a specific purpose, then there seems to be no objective purpose to human life in which one is objectively obligated to approximate.[34]

The Christian theist, on the other hand, has no such problem. The following syllogism clarifies:

W1   *If a truth corresponds to reality, it is objectively true* [apart from human opinion].

W2   *If God created humanity for a purpose, then this purpose is a truth that corresponds to reality.*

W3   *Therefore, if God created humanity for a purpose, then this purpose is objectively true.*

W4   *God created humanity for a purpose.*

W5   *Therefore, God's purpose for creating humanity is objectively true* [apart from human opinion].

God's intent and purpose for creating humanity seems to provide the ontological grounding of objective morality. This is the case because if God created humanity on

34. This also is a key argument in "Purpose Theory." See chapter 15.

purpose and for a specific purpose, then there would be something objectively true about humanity irrespective of the subjective opinions from humanity. After all, if God created humanity for the specific purpose of loving him and all others (Matt 5:44; 22:37–39) and one misses that mark, then one has failed morally in an objective sense.

Not only does the atheist or naturalist have the hard (impossible?) task of providing an objective/ontological grounding for morality, another glaring issue is that naturalists *typically* reject libertarian freedom. Consider the well-known atheist and neuroscientist, Sam Harris. As a naturalist, Harris holds to "scientific determinism," which means he believes that *all* of our thoughts and actions are causally determined by natural forces like physics, chemistry, and the initial conditions of the big bang. All of these things are outside human control. Harris concludes that "Free will is an illusion . . . We do not have the freedom we think we have . . . Either our wills are determined by prior causes and we are not responsible for them, or they are the product of *chance* and we are not responsible for them."[35]

The *chance* Harris refers to seems to be a reference to one possible interpretation of quantum mechanics. Physicists Bruce Rosenblum and Fred Kuttner agree with Harris on this score: "To the extent that we are part of this physical universe, classical physics rules out free will. Because the uncertainty principle denies this Newtonian determinism, it has entered philosophical discussions of determinism and free will. Uncertainty can *allow* free will by denying determinism, but randomness, quantum or otherwise, is not free choice. Quantum uncertainty cannot *establish* free will."[36]

If Harris is correct, then it logically follows that humans could never freely *choose* any action, including actions with so-called moral properties. If Molinism is true, however, then (1) humans can freely think and freely act (at least occasionally) and (2) humans can be held morally responsible for their thoughts and actions because they are not causally determined by anything external to the human, and the human genuinely could have chosen otherwise. But this raises a major problem for the deterministic Calvinist because many of them affirm that God exhaustively causally determines *all* things. Some may consider this a "straw man," but the French, Calvinistic philosopher Guillaume Bignon makes his views on the matter clear: "Do the five points of Calvinism or the *Westminster Confession* necessitate the thesis of theological determinism? I assert that they do . . . It [in his book] will be so as a matter of definition: theological determinism will be referred to as 'the Calvinist view,' or simply 'Calvinism.'"[37]

Matthew J. Hart—another notable Calvinist—affirms this exact position: "Calvinists, I shall assume, are theological determinists. They hold that God causes every contingent event, either directly or indirectly."[38] In a footnote of this quote, he points

---

35. Harris, *Free Will*, 5, author's *emphasis*.

36. Rosenblum and Kuttner, *Quantum Enigma*, 134.

37. Bignon, *Excusing Sinners*, 7.

38. Hart, "Calvinism and the Problem of Hell," 248.

out that some might wish to break ranks and affirm a flavor of Calvinism while denying this exhaustive divine deterministic view that is typically associated with Calvinism [e.g., Muller[39] and Koukl.[40] Hart notes that Paul Helm—whom he considers the leading Calvinistic philosopher today—is a theological determinist.[41] With deterministic Calvinism in mind, one should consider *The Oughts and Thoughts Argument*):

X1　　*If naturalistic or divine determinism is true, then libertarian free will (LFW) does not exist.*

X2　　*If LFW does not exist, then libertarian free thinking (LFT) does not exist (the ability to think otherwise).*

X3　　*If LFT does not exist, then moral oughts about our thoughts (and following actions) are illusory (as it would be impossible to ever think otherwise about anything).*

X4　　*Moral oughts about our thoughts (and following actions) are not illusory.*

X5　　*Therefore, LFT exists.*

X6　　*Therefore, LFW exists.*

X7　　*Therefore, both naturalistic and divine determinism are false.*

If all thoughts are ultimately caused and determined by something or someone beyond human control, then humanity is not responsible for their thoughts or any action that is as a result of a certain thought. This is a problem, however, since human action—at least the actions for which a person is deemed morally responsible—seem to follow from his thoughts. As Christopher Yuan writes, "Thoughts precede action. Good theology, right action. Bad theology, wrong action."[42]

J. P. Moreland provides additional insight regarding the fact that "ought implies can" (an ability): "Now, when it comes to morality, it is hard to make sense of moral obligation and responsibility if determinism is true. They seem to presuppose freedom of the will. If I ought to do something, it seems to be necessary to suppose that I can do it, that I could have done otherwise, and that I am in control of my actions. No one would say that I ought to jump to the top of a fifty-floor building and save a baby, or that I ought to stop the American Civil War in this present year, because I do not have the ability to do either."[43]

If one ought to think one way, instead of another, then it seems the thinker is free in a libertarian sense to choose among a range of alternative thoughts, each of which is compatible with the agent's nature. This seems to make sense of the Apostle Paul's

39. Muller, *Divine Will.*

40. Koukl, "Do Humans Really Have Free Will"?

41. Hart, "Calvinism and the Problem of Hell," 248.

42. Yuan, *Holy Sexuality,* 5.

43. Moreland, *The Soul,* 129.

commands to believers to take their thoughts captive to obey Christ (2 Cor 10:5), before bad thinking takes them captive (Col 2:8).

Here is the point: if a Christian rejects human libertarian freedom to choose or not to choose, then how can he be held morally or rationally responsible for behaving the *only way* he was created to think, act, believe, or behave? Deterministic Calvinism cannot sufficiently answer this question. Molinism, however, provides a sufficient foundation for the Moral Argument to argue in favor of the existence of God. Since libertarian free will is necessary for the moral argument to work, the dedicated apologist ought to be a Molinist.

Molinism's Moral Argument and the Euthyphro Dilemma.

Some atheists have objected to the *Moral Argument* by offering rather sophisticated arguments appealing to the Euthyphro Dilemma. For example, one atheist argued this way:

> If God is the standard of "good," then whatever God does is by definition good. By that argument then hatefulness would by definition be "good." What makes benevolence inherently "good" if you're getting the standard of "good" from God? By that argument, if God is benevolent then benevolence is good, but if it turns out God is hateful then one has to call "hatefulness" good rather than benevolence. Unless you're saying that benevolence is inherently good, apart from God, and therefore benevolence is a necessary trait of an "all-good" God. But that would mean God has these traits because he is good, and their goodness stands apart from his possession of them; they'd be good irrespective even of God's existence.[44]

However, a Molinist might counter this objection with the following: God is all-loving *by nature*. It is irrelevant to argue if love is "good" or "bad." A Molinist may simply state "God is love" without having to label loving all people as "good" or "bad" and thus avoid Euthyphro's horns.

God is "good" in the sense that he always freely acts consistently with his perfectly loving plan for humanity. And he also sets the standard that humans strive for as "the goal." Humans are "good" when they freely choose to approximate to the objective purpose for which they were created. In contrast, they are "bad" or morally sinful when they freely choose to "miss the mark" or fail to miss the goal for which they were created to attain. Whether they are "good" or "bad," is their free choice.

Consistent Calvinists, however, do not seem to have access to this apologetic-based response for at least two reasons:

---

44. The writer is indebted to an unnamed friend who shared this. The substance is a paraphrase of the atheist's position.

1. *It is hard to make sense of God being omnibenevolent or "all-loving" and hold to a deterministic Calvinism (See chapter 13). In fact, notable Calvinist scholar Arthur Pink[45] affirms that God does not love all people.*

2. *The choice is not "up to us" on deterministic Calvinism. God causally determines what "choices" will be made or not made on this deterministic view.*

This is the point: Molinism has logically consistent access to the omnibenevolence of God and to the libertarian freedom of mankind to make genuine choices. Thus, Molinism succeeds again in offering a coherent defeater against the atheist's objections raised against the knowledge of God. Deterministic versions of Calvinism, however, seem to fall short.

MOLINISM AND THE FINE-TUNING ARGUMENT.

By the *Fine-Tuning Argument* reference is being made to certain constants and quantities found in the universe, which—if they were to have only the slightest deviation—would make both the existing universe and life itself impossible. Craig, who has championed this argument, provides the following examples:

- Speed of Light: $c=299,792,458$ m s-1

- Gravitational Constant: $G=6.673$ x $10-11$ m3 kg-1 s-2

- Planck's Constant: 1.05457148 x $10-34$ m2 kg s-2

- Planck Mass-Energy: 1.2209 x 1022 MeV

- Mass of Electron, Proton, Neutron: 0.511; 938.3; 939.6 MeV

- Mass of Up, Down, Strange Quark: 2.4; 4.8; 104 MeV (Approx.)

- Ratio of Electron to Proton Mass: $(1836.15)-1$

- Gravitational Coupling Constant: 5.9 x $10-39$

- Cosmological Constant: $(2.3$ x $10-3$ eV)

- Hubble Constant: 71 km/s/Mpc (today)

- Higgs Vacuum Expectation Value: 246.2 GeV[46]

Craig, speaking of the significance of these special numbers and what would entail if these numbers were not so "special" and slightly altered, concludes: "These are the fundamental constants and quantities of the universe. Scientists have come to the shocking realization that each of these numbers have been carefully dialed to an astonishingly precise value—a value that falls within an exceedingly narrow, life-permitting range. If any one of these numbers were altered by even a hair's breadth,

45. Pink, *Sovereignty*, 16-19.
46. Craig, "God and Abstract Objects."

no physical, interactive life of any kind could exist anywhere. There'd be no stars, no life, no planets, no chemistry."[47]

The *Fine-Tuning Argument*, if put into a syllogism, might go like this:

Y1   *The fine-tuning of the universe is due to either physical necessity, chance, or design.*

Y2   *The fine-tuning is not due to physical necessity or chance.*

Y3   *Therefore, the fine-tuning of the universe is due to intelligent design.*

This has great significance and relevance to Molinism, which explains that God possesses certain knowledge of what *would* occur in possible worlds *if* he were to fine-tune the initial conditions of the early universe with all the "special numbers" referenced (and more) and actualize *this* certain possible world. This also entails that God would possess perfect counterfactual knowledge—not *grounded* in anything that *actually* exists—about what kind of non-life permitting universes would have come into existence if any of those numbers were slightly altered (a different possible world would have been the actual world).

If God possessed knowledge of what *would* follow from a certain fine-tuned point of singularity logically prior to his creative decree to actualize this universe—and God *could* have adjusted these initial conditions otherwise to bring a different kind of universe (or none at all) into existence—then God possesses knowledge of what he *could* accomplish. Moreover, given this knowledge, God also knows what *would* happen *if* the initial conditions of the big bang were not so finely-tuned or tuned otherwise.

Therefore, if God possesses the power to create worlds other than the world that actually exists (or none at all), and if God knows all that *would* happen in all these other worlds if the initial conditions of these other worlds (universes) would have been different and actualized instead, then this seems to strongly suggest that God possesses the middle knowledge advocated by Luis de Molina. "Middle knowledge is God's knowledge of all things that would happen in every possible set of circumstances, both things that are determined to occur by those circumstances and things that are not determined to occur by those circumstances."[48]

To reiterate and clarify: Since God has natural knowledge, he knows what initial conditions of the big bang *could* produce. Since God has middle knowledge, he knows what specific initial conditions *would* produce (this is especially evident once one considers quantum indeterminacy).[49]

47. Craig, "God and Abstract Objects."

48. MacGregor, *Luis de Molina*, 11.

49. Physicist David Newquist in a personal conversation admitted that "Physicists are still arguing about what quantum mechanics means. Indeterminacy is such a basic part of it, I don't think it can be referred to as just a possibility. It is so basic that it would be a challenge to point to any one reference on the subject." Polkinghorne (*Quantum Physics*, 94) seems to agree and put it this way: "For two centuries, Isaac Newton's mathematisation of physical thinking, expressed in equations whose solutions

Because of this, this author contends that if one is an advocate of the *Fine-tuning Argument* for the existence of God, then he or she should also be a Molinist. At the very least, the Molinist has no problem incorporating this argument from intelligent design into his apologetics repertoire.

Molinism and evolution.

There would be little disagreement that the question of the evolutionary origin of man and the universe has occupied much of the apologist's energy and time. Molinism—and specifically God's middle knowledge—has introduced not only a new approach to this debate but mutes many of the arguments against belief in a Creator. For example, if a student (or anyone) should claim to have become an atheist because of believing in evolution, a response could be crafted as follows: *Evolution really is not a reason not to believe in God. If God is omnipotent and omniscient (logically prior to his creative decree), then creating the world and man via evolution is no problem for God. Could it not be that what appears to be "random" or by "chance" to humans is actually precisely the perfect plan of God's intelligently designed and finely-tuned initial conditions of the big bang?*

Might a response such as this take the "problem of evolution" *off the table* so that the apologist/evangelist could then discuss the evidence for the existence of God and the historical data demonstrating the resurrection of Jesus Christ? This approach to reasoning is not to suggest that theistic evolution is, in fact, true. But, if God is omnipotent and possesses full knowledge of what *could* and *will* happen and knows what *would* happen in all other scenarios (middle knowledge), then creating via evolutionary means is simply no problem at all for a maximally great being. The God who knew what a "finely-tuned" universe would require, could have brought it about in any number of ways, even in a "biblical, evolutionary model" as follows:[50]

1. God exists and possesses both natural and middle knowledge.

2. Fine-tuned initial conditions of the Big Bang (God chooses and actualizes this world and all that will happen in it).

---

are uniquely determined by the specification of appropriate initial conditions, had suggested to many people the picture of a clockwork universe of tightly determined process. However, twentieth century physics saw the death of this kind of merely mechanical view of the world, a consequence brought about by the discovery of intrinsic unpredictabilities present in nature, first at the level of atomic phenomenon (quantum theory)."

50. The reader should reflect upon this syllogism with the comments made immediately after statement #15 below. The author is not suggesting that this was the actual process, nor that it is his own position, but it could be a *possible* way to understand the biblical data. The model which follows, then, is the author's construct and assumes the hermeneutical approach known as the "Framework View" (Irons and Kline, "Framework View"). To say it again: the purpose of this model is not to state it as the author's view, nor even that it—in fact—corresponds to reality, but in the world of debate it is a possible way to do apologetics among those who have different views on creation.

3. The universe unfolds as planned over time.

4. Our solar system and earth eventually come into existence as planned.

5. Life evolves over time exactly the way God knew it would via his intelligent design of the finely-tuned initial conditions of the Big Bang.

6. *Hominids* evolve as planned (not by accident).

7. God *breathes his image* (soul) into a male *hominid* making the first human in another act of special creation. (Or God literally creates a physically identical human from the dirt.)

8. God does the same thing with a female *hominid* and then *breathes his image* into her making the first female human. (Or God literally creates Eve from the rib of Adam.)

9. God separates Adam and Eve from the other "soul-less" *hominids* (who are physically identical, but not spiritually), and places them in the Garden of Eden with the Tree of Life (as long as they eat of this tree, they will never experience a physical death).

10. After the fall, Adam and Eve are expelled from the paradise of the Garden of Eden and the Tree of Life (now they will eventually die).

11. After Adam and Eve's son, Cain, kills their other son, Abel, Cain is expelled from the world's only "human tribe." Cain is scared of the other soul-less *hominids* who may kill him (Gen 4:13–4).

12. Cain finds a physically identical but soul-less *homonid* female as a wife (Gen 4:17). The human soul is always passed on to offspring (avoids "bottle-necking" problems).

13. The human soul is a trait preferred via natural selection as it allows for rationality (see the *Freethinking Argument against Naturalism*).

14. Soon, all *hominids* have souls created in the *image of God*. Therefore, now all *hominids* are human (All humans are *hominids*, but not all *hominids* have been human).

15. This is exactly the way God planned and designed life to unfold. It all started with the fine-tuned initial condition of the Big Bang.

It is vital to understand that this author is not stating that this model is true. He, rather, is merely offering a model that is *possibly* true.[51] Further, this is not an argument for or against evolution. This is but a possible case that if one sincerely believes that human beings actually came from a single-celled common ancestor, then it does absolutely nothing to substantiate that God does not exist, nor to negate the truth of

51. A special thanks to evolutionary biologist Dawn Simon for proofing the "science part" of this model.

Christianity. Evolution and biblical Christianity are not necessarily mutually exclusive views, and they *can* both be true simultaneously. Therefore, if one really thinks evolution is true, he can still be a Christian, and as a follower of Jesus still be free to examine the arguments for (and against) evolution.

Such an application of Molinism allows one to bypass the emotionally charged argument of evolution and not be distracted by non-essential matters and then be free to present the life-changing gospel of Jesus Christ—the only thing that *really* matters (1 Cor 15:14–17).

This allows Christians to engage the culture and removes this stumbling block with those in academic circles (or otherwise) who are convinced that evolution is true. As a ministry colleague, Scott Olson, likes to say, "Sprinkle a little Molinism on the issue and problems melt away."[52] Molinism and middle knowledge allows the apologist to show the thinking person that there are models which demonstrate that evolution (and all science) is not incompatible with biblical Christianity.

Further, having removed this obstacle, one can use other arguments—using evolution—as evidence of the existence of God. Alvin Plantinga is well-known for his *Evolutionary Argument against Naturalism*, which concludes that evolution is in deep conflict with atheism/naturalism, but it is not in conflict with theism.[53] William Lane Craig has also brought a similar case against atheists. In his famous debate against Christopher Hitchens, Craig explained how physicists John Barrow and Frank Tipler show that there are ten steps in the course of human evolution which must occur. Each step is so improbable that before it could occur the sun would have ceased to be a main sequence star, and would have incinerated the Earth. Craig notes that these physicists go on to calculate the probability of the evolution of the human genome by chance and arrive at an astronomical figure: "4 to the negative 180th power to the 110,000th power and 4 to the negative 360th power to the 110,000th power."[54] Such a number is unfathomable, but this equation demonstrates that Darwinian evolution is mathematically impossible if naturalism is also true. Craig concludes: "If evolution did occur on this planet, it was literally a miracle . . . and therefore evidence of the existence of God"![55] He goes on to explain that for the atheist [that] "evolution is the only game in town. No matter how fantastic the odds, no matter how improbable, no matter what the fossil record reveals, or what the evidence that a person can empirically investigate via the scientific method can show, evolution has to be true for atheists because it is their only option. Unlike the atheist, Christians are free to follow the scientific evidence wherever it leads."[56]

---

52. Scott Olson is the host of the FreeThinking Podcast. He uses this term often in many settings which are not officially documented. The above can be found in Olson, "The Problem of Evil."

53. Plantinga, *Where the Conflict*, 307–12.

54. Barrow and Tipler, *The Anthropic Cosmological Principle*, 561–69.

55. Craig, "William Lane Craig vs. Christopher Hitchens."

56. Craig, "William Lane Craig vs. Christopher Hitchens."

Beyond the issue of probability, another argument can be raised about belief in evolution as a theory of origin and development to complexity over time. Evolution, by definition (at minimum) simply means *change over time*. Most evolutionists and even young earth creationists will agree that some things do genuinely change over time (even if they disagree on how much some things change over time). In fact, in the world in which humanity currently exists things are constantly changing right in front of everyone's eyes. That is to say, humans exist in an evolving state of affairs (change happens). What is important to note is that Darwinian evolution requires a genuine change over dynamic time—at least if one is hoping to explain primate complexity while avoiding "intelligent design" inferences.

The problem with this, however, is that it is logically impossible for a changing state of affairs to be extrapolated into past infinity. If people currently exist in a changing state of affairs and things are really happening one event after another, then it is impossible for things to happen chronologically in this manner without a first change. A constantly changing state of affairs is impossible to go on and on forever into the past. Logically, there must have been a beginning or a first change. If there never was a first change, then the present moment—"right now"—would not exist. To help illustrate why the concept of past infinity is incoherent, two thought experiments will prove helpful:

Molinism and evolution: Infinite Jumpers and Steppers.

For this first thought experiment, the question may be raised: "Is it possible for someone—say a superhero with infinite jumping powers—to jump out of an infinitely tall bottomless-pit"? Of course not, for there would be no launching pad or foundation from which to jump. When it comes to things changing over time (evolution), if the hole at ground level represents the present moment and the idea of past infinity means there is no foundation to jump from (a first change over time), then the present moment of change could never be reached. The jumper could never get out of the hole because there is no starting point for him to progress upward. Because the present moment does exist and things do change over time (evolution), it logically follows that a foundation must exist for the first change to occur leading to the evolution (change over time) which is apparent today.

Another illustration argues to the same conclusion. A man walks up the steps to a philosopher's front porch and rings the doorbell. He answers the door and asks if he can help his visitor. The philosopher's new friend replies, "I have just walked an infinite number of steps and finally completed them right here on your front porch." Though the home owner does not believe him, the visitor insists that he has accomplished this feat. The only proof he offers is an invitation to join him on a journey to retrace his infinite number of steps, after which—he affirms—it will be clear that the path indeed leads back to the philosopher's door. Obviously if the home owner were to retrace an infinite number of steps he would never get back home, nor even turn around to begin the journey home! Every step he would take, would be followed by one more, and one more, and one more . . . and he would never reach the final step of reaching actual infinity. Just as it would be logically impossible for one to retrace all the steps this pedestrian claims to have made, so it would be just as impossible for the pedestrian to have traversed an actual infinite number of steps ending on the philosopher's front porch. A rational person would know that anyone who makes such a claim is either delusional or deceptive. The "stepper" must have taken a first step.

Change over time (evolution) has the same problem. If a first change occurred, then it logically follows that a first change resulted from an unchanging, eternal, and beginning-less state of affairs. It is like a frozen/static state where nothing happens and nothing has ever happened logically prior to the first change. (This is hard to imagine). This might not seem like a "big deal" but the implications are enormous. This is the case because if things are not changing in a frozen/static state, then nothing would ever happen, because if things are not evolving, emerging, decaying, growing, or becoming unstable (which are all words implying change over time), then these things would never be able to cause the first change. Change over time cannot account for things *starting* to change over time. That is to say, if nothing is happening, then nothing can describe or account for the first change that resulted from a static, frozen, and unchanging state, *unless* . . . a volitional agent possessing libertarian freedom existed in this static state who had the power to act, or not to act. Other than a volitional agent, what else could cause a change from an unchanging state of affairs? At the least, a volitional agent with the power to act (or not to act) *could* exist in a static state and then cause something to happen. If so, that volitional agent with libertarian free will could freely choose to act and cause the first change. This seems to be what Aristotle meant by the "Unmoved Mover."[57]

The argument can be pushed further. Since "volitional agents" are personal types of "things" or rather, "beings," then (1) this being is the kind of "thing" with which a person can have a personal relationship and (2) it is at least *possible* that human persons can have a personal relationship with this unmoved mover.

Molinism and evolution: An Argument from Change Over Time.

This entire argument can be summarized as follows:

Z1   *Things change over time (evolution).*

Z2   *A changing state of affairs cannot be past infinite.*

Z3   *Therefore, a first change resulted from an unchanging state of affairs.*

---

57. Aristotle, *Metaphysics*, 12.

Z4   *Only a volitional agent can cause a change from an unchanging state of affairs.*

Z5   *Volitional agents are personal.*

Z6   *Therefore, this personal agent existed in an unchanging state of affairs.*

Z7   *Anything existing in an unchanging state of affairs never began to exist and is eternal with no beginning.*

Z8   *Therefore, the cause of the first change (and ultimately the change of affairs in the current world) is a personal agent who is eternal with no beginning and was in a changeless state of affairs logically prior to causing the first change.*

This final deductive conclusion should be eye-opening. Why should this get one's attention? Because this volitional personal agent, who caused things to start evolving and changing over time, is what is meant by "God." As noted above, the Bible does not just note the possibility of having a personal relationship with the Unmoved Mover— God—it explains exactly how people can know God personally through Jesus Christ.

The bottom line: If a person believes that things actually do evolve and change over time, then he should seriously consider rejecting atheism.

MOLINISM AND THE ARGUMENT FROM TIME.

The *Change over Time Argument* combined with Molinism also defeats other arguments raised against the knowledge of God. Many philosophers and theologians (including this author) love to spend much of their time thinking about time. This has led to some fantastic conversations with both philosophers and physicists. In a recent interaction, a physics and philosophy grad student asserted that the idea of the Christian view of God was incompatible with the concept of time. Responding to the *Kalam Cosmological Argument*, he argued that God could not have created the universe. His argument went as follows:

1. Premise #1: *The word "choice" must imply a progression from a state of multiple possibilities to a state of single actuality.*

2. Premise #2: *The word "time" must imply a progression from one state to another.*

3. Premise #3: *Since a choice is one such progression between states, time must exist in order for choice to be possible.*

4. Premise #4: *Since there was no time before the creation of the universe, the creation of the universe could not have been a choice.*

5. Conclusion: *Therefore, God either did not create the universe or had no control over how it was created.*[58]

This argument might be problematic for some theists, but not for the Christian who affirms Molinism. To refute a structurally valid deductive argument, all that is required is to disprove (or provide reason to doubt) only one of the premises leading to the conclusion. In this case, there are reasons to doubt or reject at least two of the premises in this particular argument. This is a step-by-step review of his argument:

Analysis of Premise 1: "The word 'choice' must imply a progression from a state of multiple possibilities to a state of single actuality."

Certainly, it is true to state that when a person makes a choice, he must have existed in a state of affairs in which he was aware of multiple possibilities from which to choose. When the choice is actually made, however, the chooser then exists in a different state of affairs from the one in which a choice as of yet had not been actualized. Following actualization, the chooser exists in a state of affairs in which a choice has been made.

Applying this to God and the universe, one could conclude that God existed in a state of affairs in which he existed alone in a static state of aseity. Since God is omniscient (perfectly knowing) without beginning and omnipotent (perfectly powerful), he is eternally aware of everything he has the power to accomplish (if he chooses to do anything at all). This means that God is eternally aware of all his options—he never gains this knowledge; rather, he possesses it infallibly, eternally, and without beginning. And, since God is omniscient, he does not have to "think things through" similar to humans. He simply knows and thus does not have to literally examine his options before coming to a conclusion. He simply knows all of his options eternally and also knows exactly what he will do (even though God is free, nothing is forcing God to act or create—the choice is up to him).

Analysis of Premise 2: "The word 'time' must imply a progression from one state to another."

Many B-theorists of time would disagree. On a B-theory of time, there are not genuine "progressions" from one state to the next, but merely "one static state" with the mere illusion of progressions. Craig writes: "According to this view of time, often called the 'tenseless' or 'static' view of time, the past and future are just as real as the present. The difference between past, present, and future is usually explained as just a subjective illusion of human consciousness. For the people located in 1868, for example, the events of 1868 are present, and we are future; but the same token, for the people living in 2050 it is the events of 2050 that are present, and we are past . . . Time is akin to a

58. Stratton, "A Choice apart from Time."

spatial line, and all the points of the line are equally real. On such a view of time, if something has a finite lifetime, it does not come into being at a certain point and go out of being at a later point."[59]

So, the word "time" *must*, argues the B-theorist, render this premise false. However, in light of treating one's argument with charity, the assumption made here is that the author of the syllogism is assuming the common-sense view of time—the A-theory of time, otherwise known as the tensed or dynamic view of time.[60]

Based on the A-theory of time, this premise may be considered true. In this scenario, it implies a timeless and static state of affairs where nothing ever happens "and then" the first thing happened. As this writer's colleague, Jacobus Erasmus has explained, the static state of affairs is the "first moment" in the history of the world, and then the change between the first moment and the second moment denotes the first event in the sequence of temporal events.[61]

Applying this to God and the universe, one could consider the static state of God's aseity as the first "moment" of time and God's first act as the event of change for the first to the second "moment" or, in other words, the first thing that happened. Consequently, there are no logical problems for God's creating time.

Analysis of Premise 3: "Since a choice is one such progression between states, time must exist in order for choice to be possible."

This premise is false, if Molinism is true. Although it might be true regarding human choices, one must be careful when discussing a being who is no mere human, lest he error and anthropomorphize. If a person thinks properly regarding God's omni-attributes, this premise is mistaken. For example, when one reflects on the omniscience of God, he understands that God exists in a static state of aseity and knows the truth-value to any and all propositions. He simply knows everything ("all at once" with no beginning). Time is not "flowing" in this all-knowing static state. Things are not happening nor are thoughts occurring "one after another." God exists, knows everything, and knows all of his options (the things he has the power to do) and knows all that would happen based on all of his options—if he actualized a possible option.

God also knows that he can create many specific and different worlds. Since he is omnipotent, he has the power to create any logically possible world or none at all, and since he is omniscient, he knows all things about all of these possibly actualizable (feasible) worlds logically prior to creating any world. He also knows counterfactual truths about how free creatures would freely choose if they were to exist in a certain state of affairs. This is the epitome of God's middle knowledge. He knows it all! That

---

59. Craig, *Time and Eternity View*, 68–69.

60. Craig, *Time and Eternity View*, 115.

61. Erasmus, *The Kalam Cosmological Argument*. He is currently working on a journal article regarding this topic. This author is indebted to him for sharing his thoughts in personal correspondence.

is to say, he knows all things about each world that he has the option—the power—to create. (Obviously, this would lead to consideration of logically possible and feasible world semantics, but this is beyond the scope of the present discussion.)

In God's case, his choice to create one of all the possible worlds which he could have created was not made chronologically after something akin to human deliberation or "thinking things through one at a time." Indeed, an omniscient being simply does not behave in this manner. Therefore, this premise is false since it states that "*a choice is one such progression between states.*" This might be true for humans or any being limited in knowledge, but this is not the case for an omniscient being possessing middle knowledge.

Moreover, dynamic time began to exist along with the second moment of "all-time" or the first thing that happened. But in a sense, one could say that time did exist prior to the beginning of dynamic time, at least if one affirms that the first moment of time existed as a static state.

Analysis of Premise 4: "Since there was no time before the creation of the universe, the creation of the universe could not have been a choice."

This premise is based on an assumption that is probably false, and if it happens to be true, it is irrelevant anyway. While it is true, that if the space-time universe is *all* that exists, then the big bang marks the beginning of the space-time universe. Thus, if there is nothing else existing (including God), then the big bang plausibly marks the beginning of dynamic time. It is worth noting, however, that even on an atheistic view, there would still have been a static state of nothingness where nothing happens, "and then" a state of affairs in which something happened.

Therefore, even with atheism, the first moment of dynamic time derives from a static state of affairs. On a theistic view, the first moment of time is grounded in God's static state of aseity. Because God is omniscient, he does not have to "think things through" the way humans do. Thus, in this static state, God knows full well all the options at his disposal. He also knows exactly what world he will create. Simultaneous with the first change of affairs, dynamic time comes into being. To use the Kalam's nomenclature: dynamic time began to exist.

One should note that it is quite possible that dynamic time did exist chronologically prior to the big bang. For example, God could have created the angelic realms prior to creating the space-time universe of human beings. He could also earlier have created other physical universes (perhaps the multi-verse). Perhaps the second person of the Trinity uttered a sentence in Hebrew to the Holy Spirit (not that an omniscient being must do such a thing to another omniscient being). Perhaps God counted down prior to his creative act: "3 . . . 2 . . . 1 . . . *Let there be light*"!

All of these logically possible examples provide states of affairs in which this premise is false and dynamic time (things happening one after another) exists prior to the beginning of our space-time universe.

Might there not be a better ("best") explanation? When considering the beginning of dynamic time, in a sense, both the atheist and the Christian are in the same boat. That is to say, since an infinite regress of things happening in the past is logically impossible—if the present moment really does exist—both the atheist and the Christian agree that a static state of affairs existed logically prior to the first thing that happened. The atheist believes the original static state was absolutely nothing . . . "and then" something happened. The theist affirms that the original static state was absolutely nothing physical or material, but that God exists . . . "and then," God actualizes—and intelligently designs/fine-tunes—the universe into existence . . . BANG! This is no problem for a God who is both omnipotent and omniscient with middle knowledge.

Therefore, Premise 4 seems to be the controversial step of the *Time Proves God Argument*. However, upon further examination, it stands strong. It is virtually synonymous with the following: "apart from dynamic time things do not happen *unless* the cause of dynamic time is a volitional agent."

A further consideration is this: dynamic time itself cannot begin to exist in a timeless and changeless state. This is the case because, as the theoretical physicist Fotini Markopoulou has stated, "if there is no [dynamic] time, then things do not happen."[62] Things do not become unstable, decay, or begin to emerge if dynamic time does not exist. If dynamic time does not exist, all things that *happen to exist* would exist eternally with no genuine beginning and exist in a "frozen" and static state. Therefore, dynamic time could not even begin to exist in a frozen and eternally static state, *unless* at least one of these eternally existing "things" is a volitional agent who can freely choose to act and bring about change. If the cause of dynamic time exists timelessly in a static state, but can also freely choose to act, then simultaneously with the first free action (whatever it is) dynamic time begins and the "clock starts ticking."

Returning to the atheist's original argument, his final conclusion reads:

Analysis of Conclusion: "Therefore, God either didn't create the universe or had no control over how it was created."

It is apparent that the atheist who designed this argument has failed to take God's middle knowledge into account. When one considers and keeps in mind Molinism and God's full knowledge of what *could* and *will* happen and what *would* happen in different possible worlds, the following response to his conclusion is: This statement is false because it fails to account for God's omni-attributes; namely, God's omniscience

---

62. Markopoulou, "Creating Spacetime."

and omnipotence. This is a serious mistake because it has led to faulty premises which, in turn have led to the demise of the conclusion. With God's omniscience in mind, one can see that God can exist in a static state of aseity (where nothing happens) and know all of the things he can or could do, and all of the possible worlds that are available for him to create. Moreover, with God's omnipotence in mind, it becomes apparent that he has the power to choose/actualize one of these possible worlds. This is no problem for a maximally great being.

This is another example of how Molinism has much to offer the field of apologetics. The middle knowledge foundation provided by Molinism dismantles many arguments raised against God's existence and what he can or cannot know.

MOLINISM AND BIBLICAL INSPIRATION.

As pastors and Christian leaders know, many people struggle with how the Bible can be both written by God and man simultaneously. Some may reason that, if "every word is God-breathed" (2 Tim 3:16), then how can any word in the Scriptures *really* also have a human author? At face value, this seems to be a logical contradiction. Many theologians, however, will note that Paul's text basically relates only that God is the source of Scripture[63] without any explanation as to how that interacts with the human writer. Plummer says it this way: "But while this declaration of the Apostle assures us that there is no passage in Holy Writ, which . . . does not yield divine instruction for the guidance of our minds, and hearts, and wills, yet it gives no encouragement to hard and fast theories as to the manner in which the Spirit of God operated upon the authors of the sacred writings. Inspiration is no mechanical process. It is altogether misleading to speak of it as divine dictation, which would reduce inspired writers to mere machines."[64]

Humphreys notes that "inspiration" is: "One word in the original, a passive verbal, occurring only here in N.T., and meaning 'filled with the breath of God' so as to be 'living oracles,' Acts 7:38,"[65] and thus identifies God as the source behind *all Scripture*.

A more difficult text that does address the "how" is 2 Pet 1:16, 19–21: *For we did not follow cleverly devised myths . . . 19 And we have the prophetic word more fully confirmed, to which you will do well to pay attention as to a lamp shining in a dark place, until the day dawns and the morning star rises in your hearts, 20 knowing this first of all, that no prophecy of Scripture comes from someone's own interpretation. 21 For no prophecy was ever produced by the will of man, but men spoke from God as they were*

63. Marshall, *Pastoral Epistles*, 794–95, says that "the point of the adjective here is surely to emphasize the authority of the Scriptures as coming from God and to indicate that they have a divinely-intended purpose related to his plan of salvation." Knight, *Pastoral Epistles*, 447, after a linguistic treatise, concludes that "Paul appears to be saying . . . that all Scripture has as it source God's breath and that this is its essential characteristic. This is another way of saying that Scripture is God's word."

64. Plummer, *Pastoral Epistles*, 393.

65. Humphreys, *Epistles of Timothy and Titus*, 189.

carried along by the Holy Spirit. Much could be said about this text,[66] but the key words are the words in verse 21: *men spoke . . . carried along by the Holy Spirit.* The word *"carried"* is passive—*men* were *carried along*—and is used for a boat "carried" by the wind (Acts 27:17),[67] and thus the idea is that God not only was the source of Scripture but what he wanted to communicate was related accurately by the Holy Spirit so that what the *"prophet"* wrote were his (God's) words. Calvin's comments are in a similar vein: "Another sense seems to me more simple, that Peter says that Scripture came not from man, or through the suggestions of man . . . To the same purpose is what immediately follows: *but holy men of God spake* as they were *moved by the Holy Ghost.* They did not of themselves, or according to their own will, foolishly deliver their own inventions . . . They . . . obediently followed the Spirit as their guide."[68]

Though this affirms that God via the Holy Spirit is responsible for the product—the truth of Scripture—it still does not tell "how" the message accurately sent from God becomes truth through admittedly fallible, human authors. Of course, the law of Moses was inscribed on stone by God himself. But it does not follow that all of Scripture was dictated because it would not account for the variation of writing styles and vocabulary of the various authors of Scripture. Even a beginner New Testament Greek student knows the difference, for example, of the Apostle John's Greek and that of Luke. But exactly how God inspired the Bible (as he wanted it) through fallible human authors remains an enigma for the vast majority of Christians.

Molinism, however, speaks to this issue and offers a solution. Though the traditional doctrine of verbal inspiration of Scripture is accepted by conservative scholars

---

66. For example, "prophecy" does not relate to prediction of some future event as the word is used in contemporary language; prophecy is the proclamation of a message from God, whether that be about the future or the present. Calvin, *Catholic Epistles,* 352, writes: "Understand by *prophecy of Scripture* that which is contained in the holy Scriptures." Plumptre, *General Epistles,* 175, says: "Nor again is there much room for doubt as to the meaning of *prophecy of Scripture.* The words can only point to a 'prophetic word' embodied in a writing and recognised as Scripture."

Further, "interpretation" does not refer to an explanation of the meaning of Scripture, but the syllogistic conclusion drawn from premises of human research. In other words, the text means that data were not gathered leading to Scripture as a human deduction; it was/is God's product. Again, Plumptre, *General Epistles,* 175–76, explains: "The Apostle calls on men to give heed to the prophetic word on the ground that no prophecy, authenticated as such by being recognised as part of Scripture, whether that Scripture belongs to the Old, or the New Covenant, comes by the prophet's own interpretation of the facts with which he has to deal, whether those facts concern the outer history of the world, or the unfolding of the eternal truths of God's Kingdom. It is borne to him, as he proceeds to shew in the next verse, from a higher source, from that which is, in the truest sense of the word, an inspiration. The views held by some commentators, (i) that St. Peter is protesting against the application of private judgment to the interpretation of prophecy, and (ii) that he is contending that no single prophecy can be interpreted apart from the whole body of prophetic teaching contained in Scripture, are, it is believed, less satisfactory explanations of the Apostle's meaning."

67. Bigg (*Peter and Jude,* 270) writes: "'Carried along by the Holy Ghost,' as a ship by the wind (Acts 28:15, 17). Here the Spirit is the wind (Acts 2:2; John 3:8). Similar metaphors are used of inspiration by the heathen writers."

68. Calvin, *Catholic Epistles,* 351.

as something an omnipotent God can do—though about how he did it, they remain uncertain—a logically coherent explanation is found in God's omniscient, middle knowledge and omnipotence. Since he knew with omniscient certainty that Paul, for example, given his circumstances, would freely write epistles, God was able to create a world placing Paul in these specific scenarios where he knew with certainty what Paul would freely write. As Craig notes God created "a world containing just those circumstances and persons such that the authors of Scripture would freely compose their respective writings, which God intended to be His gracious Word to us."[69]

Therefore, with a middle knowledge view of God's providence in mind, Christians can rationally believe the Bible is the verbal and plenary word of God written freely by men. Molinism seems to be the only view that can make logical sense of this theological truth.

Some may object to this conclusion by arguing that God's mere knowledge of what the biblical author would write does not assure it accuracy. To put this in a question format: "What makes the words in the Bible written freely by human authors any different from the words God knew Richard Dawkins would freely write in *The God Delusion*"? The answer is found in the resurrection of Jesus. If God (the Father) raised Jesus from the dead, then, he seems to have given a "divine" stamp of approval regarding who Jesus claimed to be: God in the flesh. Therefore, what Jesus said about the Old and New Testaments is vitally important to one's belief about the truthfulness/ reliability of the Scriptures. He affirmed the validity of the Old Testament by declaring that *not one jot nor tittle would pass away until it was fulfilled* (Matt 5:17–18).[70] He said that the *Scriptures could not be broken* (John 10:35). And he described the corpus of the Old Testament as consisting of *the Law of Moses and the Prophets and the Psalms* (Matt 5:17; Luke 24:25–27, 44), the same divisions of the Hebrew Bible of today. His use of and description of the Old Testament Scriptures puts—as it were—an "imprimatur" on the current Old Testament.[71]

Though the current New Testament was not written in Jesus's day, it is viewed as the reliable source of what he taught because he commissioned his disciples as "apostles," his representatives, as the trustees of his teachings and message (Luke 6:12–6; Acts 9:15). Jesus's miraculous resurrection seems to confirm his choice of apostles to pass along his teachings. Moreover, if the resurrected Jesus possessed counterfactual

---

69. Craig, "Men Moved."

70 A "jot" is the smallest letter in Hebrew/Aramaic, while "tittle" is the appendage to a letter that distinguishes a "k" from a "b."

71. This conclusion is all the more valid because of the amazing twentieth century discovery of the Dead Sea Scrolls. Comparing the text of the current Hebrew Old Testament to it reveals that it is all but identical to the Hebrew text of the Old Testament in Jesus's day. (E.g., the Isaiah Scroll). The assessment of the Biblical Archeological Society ("The Masoretic Text and the Dead Sea Scrolls") is that "the scrolls did not utterly transform our image of the original Hebrew Bible text. Indeed, one of the most important contributions of the scrolls is that they have demonstrated the relative stability of the Masoretic text."

knowledge, then it is no problem for Jesus—the second person of the Trinity—to have given his divine stamp of approval on what he knew the apostle Paul, for example, would/will freely write in the circumstances in which he had been placed.

Given the abundance of multiple and early attestation of the Gospels, people today have a high degree of historical certainty when it comes to knowing what Jesus taught. Therefore, one has good reason to affirm that the New Testament, which is based on thousands of early copies of the original Greek manuscripts,[72] is not only trustworthy, but the authoritative Word of God. A possible way to express this as a syllogism is as follows:

AA1 *Jesus's resurrection validates the teachings of Christ and his hand-picked apostles who would freely author the New Testament.*

AA2 *The New Testament was freely written by Jesus's hand-picked apostles or those who knew them.*

AA3 *The text of the Bible is pure enough.*

AA4 *In the New Testament, Jesus gave His stamp of approval on the Old Testament.*

AA5 *Given 1–3, we have good reason to regard the New Testament as trustworthy and authoritative and, given 4, we have a good reason for regarding the Old Testament as trustworthy and authoritative.*

Therefore, Molinism provides a powerful foundation to affirm the New Testament (and thus, the entire Bible) as the inspired and authoritative Word of God. This is the case because this model appeals to both the libertarian freedom of human authors and God's counterfactual knowledge of what free human authors *would* freely write.

MOLINISM AND THE ONTOLOGICAL ARGUMENT.

When one speaks of possible worlds, there is an excellent argument which makes use of possible worlds semantics—the *Ontological Argument*. The goal of the *Ontological Argument* is to demonstrate that, if the concept of a maximally great being is logically possible, then a maximally great being (God) is necessary and must exist. To counter this argument, as seen above, atheists go to great lengths to demonstrate that the idea of a perfectly good and loving, all-powerful, and all-knowing being is logically incoherent. The problem of evil is the most popular attempt at accomplishing this task. As noted above, Molinism defangs this objection by appealing to the omnibenevolence of God and the libertarian freedom of man. Therefore, if one is going to debunk the *Ontological Argument*, it must be done by other means that take the explanatory power of Molinism into account. There are several forms of the *Ontological Argument*, and they

72. A good discussion of this may be found in Licona, ("The Basis"), and further documentation can be found in Bruce (*New Testament Documents*), Blomberg ("Can We Believe"?), etc.

usually focus on the idea of the possible existence of a "maximally great being" (what many call "God"). The argument typically looks something like this:

BB1 *It is possible that God—a Maximally Great Being (MGB)—exists.*

BB2 *If it is possible that God (MGB) exists, then he (MGB) exists in some possible worlds.*

BB3 *If God (MGB) exists in some possible worlds, then he (MGB) exists in all possible worlds.*

BB4 *If God (MGB) exists in all possible worlds, then he (MGB) exists in the actual world.*

BB5 *If God (MGB) exists in the actual world, then he exists.*

The purpose here is not to argue for or defend the *Ontological Argument*, but to ask the relevant question: "What does the *Ontological Argument* have to do with Molinism"? The answer is twofold and can be found in the fact that Molinism affirms the maximal greatness of God and thus, assumes the first and third essential pillars of the soteriological view of Molinism.[73] Since God is eternally "maximally knowledge-able," he possesses middle knowledge of all the possible worlds in which he possesses the ability—the power—to actualize. While the *Ontological Argument* does not prove Molinism to be true, it is definitely consistent and compatible with it. Moreover, when one properly understands Molinism, the "possible worlds" involved in the *Ontological Argument* become much easier to grasp as well.

MOLINISM AND PASTORAL ISSUES.

God's love for his people.

Molinism is also beneficial in a pastoral sense because it allows one to see that God is a maximally great being who is perfectly powerful, perfectly knowledgeable, and perfectly loving. Because God is perfectly loving, then his children can have assurance that this omnipotent and omniscient being loves *them* perfectly as well. If that is the case, then they can know that God can be trusted since true love always desires the ultimate best for the other (the third essential ingredient of soteriological Molinism).

Although TULIP Calvinism and the practice of Reformed theology are often thought of as one-in-the-same, the Reformed theologian is dedicated to the "practice of theology as a science." Thus, as North-West University makes clear, "This is the basis on which all paradigms (*including our own*) are subjected to constant critical and reformative study."[74] One particular point of the TULIP acronym that Reformed theologians must reexamine is the "I" of the acronym: "irresistible grace."

73. On the "third pillar," see the section—God's love for his people—which follows (288-290).

74. See North-West University's website: http://theology.nwu.ac.za/theology-reformational-foundation.

Advocates of divine determinism and TULIP Calvinism may be painting a picture of a God who cannot be trusted because they inadvertently (and unconsciously) reject at least one (if not more) of God's omni attributes. Building on an argument offered in chapters 13 and 15—called the *Omni Argument*—a syllogism might be constructed that addresses the Calvinist doctrine of irresistible grace:

CC1 *If irresistible grace is true, then for any person x, if God desires to, has the power to, and knows how to cause x to go to Heaven and not suffer eternally in Hell, then x will go to Heaven and not suffer eternally in Hell.*

CC2 *If God is omnibenevolent, omnipotent, and omniscient, then for any person x, God desires to, has the power to, and knows how to cause x to go to Heaven and not suffer eternally in Hell.*

CC3 *There is at least one person who will not go to Heaven and will suffer eternally in Hell.*

CC4 *Therefore, one cannot affirm both (i) that irresistible grace is true and (ii) that God is omnibenevolent, omnipotent, and omniscient (a maximally great being).*

CC5 *God is a maximally great being.*

CC6 *Therefore, irresistible grace is false.*

CC7 *Therefore, divine determinism is false (God does not causally determine all things).*

CC8 *God is completely sovereign and does predestine all things* (Rom 8:29–30; Eph 1:5, 11).

CC9 Therefore, predestination and determinism are not to be conflated.

CC10 The best explanation of the data is a soteriological view of Molinism.[75]

Based on the *Omni Argument*, one can rationally conclude that God is a maximally great being just as the Bible implies. Molinism allows for exhaustive predestination of all things all the time, election, and God's complete sovereignty over all creation (which is arguably the primary goal of what the "I" of TULIP seeks to affirm[76]), all while allowing in a logically broad sense God's love and grace to be "resistible." This conclusion demonstrates how God is a maximally great being who possesses each of his vital omni attributes. Therefore, God can—and should be—trusted.

It is the author's *emphasis* above. See also chapter 1 and "Methodology."

75. The Calvinist does not have to personally affirm this syllogism in order to share it with someone who might be struggling, but he at least should acknowledge that it is a possible explanation.

76. The "I" strictly refers to the grace given to the elect alone, grace that enables them to repent and believe and thereby receive God's pardon and eternal life. It is called "irresistible" in the sense that—unlike an Arminian position—when it is given to the elect, it is effectual; those who are elect will believe. It is not given to the "reprobate."

Molinism and prayer.

Not only does Molinism explain how both the Bible and God are trustworthy, it also explains how prayer works. Some have explained the mystery of prayer this way: "Sometimes God says 'No.' Other times 'Yes.' And yet at other times 'Wait.'" The author himself has made similar statements. But what are the implications of such a response? To be honest with no desire to be irreverent, does this not let God "off the hook"? He wins every time! And what does thinking this way do with a person's motivation to pray? Does it not subtly undermine serious, expectant praying? Does the person praying ever know if his prayer makes a difference?

To illustrate another approach to praying, a respected teacher asked people at a conference the question: *"Does God answer prayer"*? Of course, they all said "Yes." But had they been perfectly honest, might they not have said, "Well . . . sometimes"? The teacher then asked a second question: *"Do you think your prayers change God's plan"*? There was a silence of puzzlement among the crowd, because people were not certain how to respond. Then the teacher answered the question himself: *"No! Nothing changes God's plan"*! What did he mean by that? He was probably referring to what many Christians believe: that from all eternity past God knows what will occur in our world. Nothing takes him by surprise. Therefore, in the words of a noted evangelical scholar: "If you were to pray individually or if you and I were to join forces in prayer or if all the Christians of the world were to pray collectively, it would not change what God, in His hidden counsel, has determined to do."[77]

Many Christians may not think about the implications of such a position, but with reflection they might ask: "If God has a sovereign plan for the ages—that is, a plan that was determined *before the foundation of the world* and which will be fulfilled to the very detail up to the time when the *Kingdom of this world will become the kingdom of the Lord and his Christ*—what difference will or does prayer make"? Doesn't it lead to what perhaps a growing number of Christians believe: "Why pray? God will do what he wishes anyway." Most, of course, would not say that, but may well think it, and thinking it, have profound doubts about the merit of praying at all.

The believer may wish to hold on to both (1) the instruction to pray (because Scripture does say it makes a difference) and (2) belief in the fixed plan of God, but at the same time find his/her praying timid, lacking in confidence (faith), or worse, doing no praying at all. Such personal doubts and questions, then, have some urgency and must be addressed among believers and in our churches. They are real issues. It seems to this writer that a consistent Calvinist[78] position—that prayer does not

---

77. Sproul, "Does Prayer Change God's Mind"?

78. Calvin addresses prayer in two basic places in his writings: in the *Institutes* (Calvin, 3.20; [708–65]) and in his Commentary on Matt 6:8 (Calvin, *Harmony*, 223). His most extensive treatment in the *Institutes* has been described by Beeke as focusing "more on the practice of prayer than on its doctrine, which shows how practical his theology is," (Beeke, *Taking Hold of God*, 27) a conclusion which he shares with Niesel, *The Theology of Calvin*, 156. Calvin is not as explicit as Sproul

change the plan of God, a plan established from all eternity—leads inevitably and rationally to a pessimism about praying, that is, prayer which expects anything asked for to be done. To express such a position another way, prayer at any time after the creation of the world—since such praying is chronologically after the plan of God was established—cannot retroactively change anything except perhaps the person who is doing the praying.

In contrast, what Luis de Molina proposed provides some unique, motivating insights into the mystery of God's thinking and actions in response to his people's praying. Indeed, his teaching gives a rational foundation for specific praying in a world in which God is sovereignly working out his plan. To the surprise of some, Molina would agree that God's eternal plan will be fulfilled in precise detail.

What makes his position different than that of Calvinists is his insistence on God's thinking in the development of that plan. In God's middle knowledge, he knew

---

quoted above is, but he does address the question whether—given God's "providence" and his eternal plan—prayer makes a difference:

> It is very absurd, therefore, to dissuade men from prayer, by pretending that divine Providence, which is always watching over the government of the universes is in vain importuned by our supplications, when, on the contrary, the Lord himself declares, that he is "nigh unto all that call upon him, to all that call upon him in truth" (Psa 145:18). No better is the frivolous allegation of others, that it is superfluous to pray for things which the Lord is ready of his own accord to bestow; since it is his pleasure that those very things which flow from his spontaneous liberality should be acknowledged as conceded to our prayers (Calvin, *Institutes*, 3.20.3; [714]).

This does not really address the "how" of the common objection. It merely affirms that God's plan and a person's prayers are somehow associated. Calvin is far more direct and spells out more specifically his thinking in his commentary on Matt 6:8:

> But if God *knows what things we have need of, before we ask him,* where lies the advantage of prayer? If he is ready, of his own free will, to assist us, what purpose does it serve to employ our prayers, which interrupt the spontaneous course of his providence? The very design of prayer furnishes an easy answer. Believers do not pray, with the view of informing God about things unknown to him, or of exciting him to do his duty, or of urging him as though he were reluctant. On the contrary, *they pray, in order that they may arouse themselves to seek him, that they may exercise their faith in meditating on his promises, that they may relieve themselves from their anxieties by pouring them into his bosom; in a word, that they may declare that from Him alone they hope and expect, both for themselves and for others, all good things.* God himself, on the other hand, has purposed freely, and without being asked, to bestow blessings upon us; but he promises that he will grant them to our prayers. *We must, therefore, maintain both of these truths, that He freely anticipates our wishes, and yet that we obtain by prayer what we ask.* As to the reason why he sometimes delays long to answer us, and sometimes even does not grant our wishes, an opportunity of considering it will afterwards occur (Calvin, *Harmony*, 223, author's *emphasis*).

It is clear, then, that Calvin ties praying to God's plan, but he does not explain how that can be the case. His purpose appears not to address the apologetic issue, but to urge people to pray. Indeed, people are to pray because prayer is a way of expressing their need for God especially in our times of "anxiety." What he does not explain is how God "freely anticipates our wishes." It is this that Molina addresses and explains by appealing to God's middle knowledge.

about all possible worlds and knew how every person *would* freely think and act and what would happen in every circumstance that would occur. "*Would*" is an important word in Molinism. Molina—as he looked at the complementary teaching of Scripture of human freedom—proposed that God's middle knowledge encompasses the fact (1) that his plan was formulated with his commitment to give man freedom of thinking, choices, and decisions; (2) that his plan was made in the context of giving all persons his grace; and (3) that his plan was motivated by his love and his longing for people to experience his and their best. This does not mean that a person merits a certain destiny—he or she does not—but it does mean that God in formulating the world he *would* create, sovereignly determined the best of all possibilities (either a tied-for-the-best possible world or a best of all feasible worlds according to God's economy) so that those who experience his judgment do so because they have chosen that for themselves, while on the other hand, those whose lot becomes eternity with God enter that destiny solely on the grace of God.

How, then, does this relate to prayer? As God "weighed" all the possible worlds and what each person (whom he would create to inhabit the best of all possible worlds) would freely think, decide, do, he included in that process the prayers (throughout all of human history) of his future children. In other words, he factored in what "his people" would ask in their prayers—when his plan was formulated. Of course, not every prayer was "answered" in the affirmative and thus not included in his plan, because some would be foolish, be harmful, not be possible (if the world created would be the "best" of all possible worlds), or would not be feasible (for example, if it took away human freedom and choice).[79] But some, perhaps many, were consistent with what God in his wisdom desired and thus would be "answered." "Because God middle-knew how each possible individual would freely pray in any set of circumstances, God uses this information providentially to order the world in such a way that at least some of our prayers make a profound difference in the history of the world. As part of the cornucopia of free decisions God makes in his decree to create this world, God decides to respond to some of our prayers in such a way that prayers change the course of the future."[80]

This may be confusing at first, but it resolves the problem of praying. While people do not know God's plan for their world now or the events of the immediate

79. MacGregor (*Luis de Molina*, 127–30) said it this way: "Molina called attention to Jesus's assertion [in Matt 7:7–11] that the Father will give good gifts to those who ask him, [noting that] Jesus did not say that the Father will give his children gifts that are logically impossible, logically infeasible, bad for his children, or beneficial for his children at other people's expense. In all of these cases, the gifts are not objectively good ... Flint captures the gist of Molina's reasoning when he states, 'Perhaps God does always give us the good things we request. Perhaps the prayers he doesn't answer are cases where what we have prayed for wouldn't have been good, for ourselves or for others.'" So Christians can always be confident that God will employ his middle knowledge to answer all and only their prayers that will accomplish objective good. When they pray Christians need never fear, "Be careful what you wish for, because you just might get it," or worry that they brought about some tragedy through some emotionally charged prayer.

80. MacGregor, *Luis de Molina*, 123.

future or after their death, the Scriptures, nevertheless, invite and urge them to pray. God has sovereignly chosen to use the prayers of his people to carry out his plan in the world. Therefore, believers are urged to pray specifically and expectantly. It impacts what will happen. Prayer makes a difference.

This is fascinating to think about! While prayers today shape what happens in the present world, they were known by God from all eternity past and were incorporated into his plan made before the world began. Thus, while prayers *do not* change God's plan—established from all eternity—God knew his people's prayers, and they influenced what has become his plan. That is to say, God created a world in which he knew how each person would freely pray, and factored each specific prayer according to his plan. If one wonders if God chose to create a world in which he or she freely chooses to pray, then one is free to choose to pray (or not) and find out.

Jesus *told them a parable to the effect that they ought always to pray and not lose heart.*

CONCLUSION.

As noted above, there are numerous examples of how Molinism strengthens the faith of Christians while simultaneously challenging the faith of atheists. Therefore, with the apologetic significance of Molinism in mind, it should be clear to see that spending vast amounts of time explaining and defending Molinism is not a "colossal waste of time." In fact, Molinism and divine middle knowledge seem to be keys unlocking many theological mysteries. It explains so much of the data, answers so many of the big questions, and defangs so many objections raised against Christian theism. In the words of the Apostle Paul (2 Cor 10:5) it is fruitful in *destroying arguments and every lofty opinion raised against the knowledge of God.* It has been the attempt not only in this chapter—but especially in chapters 2, 12–15—to show that Molinism has the support of Scripture and even—sometimes unknowingly—by notable theologians throughout the centuries.

Yes, William Lane Craig is right: "Once one grasps the concept of [Molinism and] middle knowledge, one will find it astonishing in its subtlety and power. Indeed, I would venture to say that [Molinism and] middle knowledge is the single most fruitful theological concept I have ever encountered."[81]

This author agrees. Since a plethora of apologetics-based arguments are either compatible with Molinism or supported by Molinism, it only makes sense for Christian apologists to argue for the truth of Molinism. After all, since Molinism is supported by Scripture and it makes sense of and is supported by numerous apologetics-based arguments, it seems that Molinism is *probably* true.

This is all to say: the inference to the best explanation of all the data is Molinism.

---

81. Craig, "The Middle Knowledge View," 125.

Bibliography

Abbott, T. K. *Epistles to the Ephesians and Colossians*. ICC. New York: Charles Scribner's Sons, 1903.

Adams, Robert M. "Middle Knowledge and the Problem of Evil." *American Philosophical Quarterly* 14.2 (1977) 109–17.

Aloisi, John A. "Jacob Arminius and the Doctrine of Original Sin." *Detroit Baptist Seminary Journal* 21 (2016) 183–205.

———. "Understanding Arminius and His Theological Heirs." http://www.dbts.edu/macp-resources-2015/.

Amos, Mark. "How Useful Is Philosophy for Theology"? https://thinktheology.co.uk/blog/article/how_useful_is_philosophy_for_theology.

Anselm. *Proslogion: Discourse on the Existence of God*. Translated by Sidney Norton Deane. http://www.uta.edu/philosophy/faculty/burgess-jackson/Anselm,%20Proslogion.pdf.

Aquinas, Thomas. *On Evil*. Edited by Brian Davies and translated by Richard Regan. New York: Oxford University Press, 2003. https://epdf.pub/queue/on-evil.html.

———. *Questiones Disputatae de Veritate*. Translated by James V. McGlynn. Chicago: Henry Regnery, 1953. http://www.clerus.org/bibliaclerusonline/en/g14.htm.

———. *Summa Contra Gentiles*. Translated by the English Dominican Fathers. London: Burns, Oates, & Washbovrne, 1924.

———. *Summa Theologiae*. Translated by Alfred J. Freddoso. https://www3.nd.edu/~afreddos/summa-translation/TOC.htm

———. *Summa Theologica*. Translated by Fathers of the English Dominican Province. New York: Benziger Bros, 1947.

Aristotle. *De Anima*. Translated by R. D. Hicks. Cambridge: Cambridge University Press, 1907.

———. *Metaphysics*. Translated by William. D. Ross. Oxford: Oxford University Press, 1924. http://classics.mit.edu/Aristotle/metaphysics.html.

Arminius, Jacobus. *The Works of James Arminius*. Translated by William R Bagnall. 3 vols. Buffalo, NY: Derby, Orton, and Mulligan, 1853. CCEL.

The Articles of the Synod of Dort. Translated and edited by Thomas Scott. Philadelphia: Presbyterian Board of Publications, 1841. https://archive.org/details/articlesofsynod01841syno.

Augustine, Aurelius. "Against Two Letters of the Pelagians." Translated by Peter Holmes and Robert Ernest Wallis, and revised by Benjamin B. Warfield. In *NPNF¹* 5:1043–210.

http://www.ccel.org/ccel/schaff/npnf105.html. Revised and edited for New Advent by Kevin Knight. http://www.newadvent.org/fathers/1509.htm.

—————. *The City of God*. Vol. 1. Edited and translated by Marcus Dods. In *The Works Aurelius Augustine*. Vol 1: *The City of God*. Edited by Marcus Dods. Edinburgh: T & T Clark, 1913. In *NPNF¹* 5:5–1151.

—————. *The City of God*. Vol. 2. Edited and translated by John Healey. Edinburgh: John Grant, 1909.

—————. *Confessions*. Edited and translated by Albert C. Outler. Westminster: John Knox, 2006. https://www.ccel.org/ccel/augustine/confessions.html.

—————. "Letter 214 to Valentinus." Translated by J. G. Cunningham. In *NPNF¹* 5:1214–17. Revised and edited for New Advent by Kevin Knight. http://www.newadvent.org/fathers/1102214.htm.

—————. *On the Free Choice of the Will, On Grace and Free Choice, and Other Writings*. Edited and translated by Peter King. Cambridge: Cambridge University Press, 2010. https://philonew.files.wordpress.com/2016/08/augustine-augustine-on-the-free-choice-of-the-will-on-grace-and-free-choice-and-other-writings-2010.pdf.

—————. "On Grace and Free Choice." Translated by Peter Holmes and Robert Ernest Wallis, and revised by Benjamin B. Warfield. In *NPNF¹* 5:141–84.

—————. "On Nature and Grace." (See below, "A Treatise on Nature.")

—————. "On Predestination and Perseverance." Translated by Peter Holmes and Robert Ernest Wallis and revised by Benjamin B. Warfield. In *NPNF¹* 5:1348–491. Revised and edited for New Advent by Kevin Knight. http://www.newadvent.org/fathers/15122.htm.

—————. "On the Spirit and the Letter." Translated by Peter Holmes and Robert Ernest Wallis and revised by Benjamin B. Warfield. In *NPNF¹* 5:301–95. Revised and edited for New Advent by Kevin Knight. http://www.newadvent.org/fathers/1502.htm.

—————. *Retractationes*. In *The Retractationes of Saint Augustine*. Edited and translated by Meredith Freeman Eller. PhD diss., Boston University, 1946. https://open.bu.edu/handle/2144/20452.

—————. "A Treatise on Nature and Grace, Against Pelagius." Translated by Peter Holmes and Robert Ernest Wallis and revised by Benjamin B. Warfield. In *NPNF¹* 5:396–490.

Bangs, Carl. "Arminius and the Reformation." *Church History* 30.2 (June 1961) 155–70.

—————. *Arminius and Reformed Theology*. PhD diss., University of Chicago, 1958.

Banks, J. S. "Hardening." *DB* 2:302–3.

Barnes, Tom. *Divine Sovereignty and Human Choice: Seven Theological Truths That Favor Calvinism over Molinism*. Minden, NE: Independently published, 2018.

Barron, Robert, and Roger Olson. "Grace ~~First~~ or Grace <u>Alone</u>?" *Christianity Today* (April 2017) 43–46.

Barrow, John D., and Frank J. Tipler. *The Anthropic Cosmological Principle*. London: Oxford University Press, 1996.

Bauckham, Richard. "Universalism: A Historical Survey." *Themelios* 4:2 (1979) 47–54.

Bavinck, Herman. *Reformed Dogmatics*. Vol. 2. Grand Rapids: Baker, 2004.

Beebe, James R. "Logical Problem of Evil." *IEP*. https://www.iep.utm.edu/evil-log/.

Beecher, Henry Ward. *Heaven and Hell*. Reprint, Whitefish, MT: Kessinger, 2010.

Beeke, Joel R. "John Calvin on Prayer as Communion with God." In *Taking Hold of God*, edited by Joel R. Beeke and Brian G. Najapfour, 27–42. Grand Rapids: Reformation Heritage, 2016.

Beilby, James K., and Paul R. Eddy, eds. *Divine Foreknowledge: Four Views*. Downers Grove: InterVarsity, 2011.

Bell, Rob. *Love Wins*. New York: HarperOne, 2011.

Bernard, J. H. *The Pastoral Epistles*. CGT. Cambridge: Cambridge University Press, 1906.

Bigg, Charles. *Critical and Exegetical Commentary on the Epistles of St. Peter and Jude*. ICC. New York: Scribner's Sons,1903.

Bignon, Guillaume. *Excusing Sinners and Blaming God*. Eugene, OR: Wipf & Stock, 2018.

———. "A Response to Kevin Timpe's Objections." http://www.associationaxiome.com/wp-content/uploads/2019/03/Response-to-Kevin-Timpe.pdf.

Blomberg, Craig L. *Can We Still Believe the Bible?* Grand Rapids: Brazos, 2014.

Boettner, Loraine. "Predestination." In *Dictionary of Theology*, edited by Everett F. Harrison, 415–17. Grand Rapids: Baker, 1969.

Boice, James Montgomery, and Philip Graham Ryken. *The Doctrines of Grace: Rediscovering the Evangelical Gospel*. Wheaton: Crossway, 2002.

Boyd, Gregory A. *God of the Possible: A Biblical Introduction to the Open View of God*. Grand Rapids: Baker, 2000.

Brandt, Caspar. *The Life James Arminius*. Translated by John Guthrie. Nashville: E. Stevenson & F. A. Owen, 1857.

Bridges, Charles. *Exposition of the Book of Proverbs*. New York: Robert Carter, 1850.

Broadus, John A. *Commentary on St. Matthew*. Philadelphia: American Baptist Publication Society, 1886.

Brock, Stephen L. *The Philosophy of St. Thomas Aquinas*. Eugene, OR: Cascade, 2015.

Broome, John. "Rationality." In *Companion to the Philosophy of Action*, edited by Timothy O'Connor and Constantine Sandis, 285–92. Oxford: Wiley-Blackwell, 2010.

Brown, Christopher M. "Thomas Aquinas (1224/6 to 1274)." *IEP*. https://www.iep.utm.edu/aquinas/.

Brown, Montague. "Augustine on Freedom and God." *The Saint Anselm Journal* 2.2 (2005) 50–65.

Bruce, F. F. *The Book of Acts*. Rev. ed. NICNT. Grand Rapids: Eerdmans, 1988.

———. *The New Testament Documents: Are They Reliable?* 5th ed. Grand Rapids: Eerdmans, 2003.

Brümmer, Vincent. "Calvin, Bernard and the Freedom of the Will." *Religious Studies* 30.4 (1994) 437–55. https://www.jstor.org/stable/20000112?seq=1#page_scan_tab_contents.

Burton, Ernest de Witt. *A Critical and Exegetical Commentary on the Epistle to the Galatians*. ICC. Edinburgh: T. & T. Clark, 1921.

Burton, Kelly Fitzsimmons. *Reason and Proper Function: A Response to Alvin Plantinga*. Phoenix, AZ: Public Philosophy Press, 2019.

Calvin, John. *The Bondage and Liberation of the Will*. Edited by A. N. S. Lane and translated by G. I. Davies. Grand Rapids: Baker, 1996.

———. *Commentary on Acts*. Vol. I. Translated by Christopher Fetherstone and edited by Henry Beveridge. Grand Rapids, MI: CCEL. https://www.ccel.org/ccel/calvin/calcom36.

———. *Commentary on the Catholic Epistles*. Translated and edited by John Owen. Grand Rapids, MI: CCEL. http://www.ccel.org/ccel/calvin/calcom45.

———. *Commentary on a Harmony of the Evangelists: Matthew, Mark, Luke*. Vol. 1. Translated by William Pringle. Grand Rapids, MI: CCEL. https://www.ccel.org/ccel/calvin/calcom31.

———. *Commentary on Isaiah*. Vol. III. Translated by William Pringle. Grand Rapids, MI: CCEL. https://www.ccel.org/ccel/calvin/calcom13.html.

———. *Commentary on John*. Vol. 1. Translated by William Pringle. Grand Rapids, MI: CCEL.

———. *Institutes of the Christian Religion*. Translated by Henry Beveridge. Grand Rapids, MI: 1845. CCEL. http://www.ccel.org/ccel/calvin/institutes/.

Canons of Dort. https://www.crcna.org/welcome/beliefs/confessions/canons-dort.

Carnes, Patrick J. *The Betrayal Bond*. Deerfield Beach, FL: Health Communications, 1997.

Carson, D. A. *Divine Sovereignty and Human Responsibility*. Eugene, OR: Wipf & Stock, 1994.

Charles, R. H. *The Book of Daniel*. New York: H. Frowde, 1875. https://archive.org/details/bookofdanielintroochar.

Clark, Gordon H. *Religion, Reason and Revelation*. Jefferson, MD: Trinity Foundation, 1961.

Clarke, Randolph. *Libertarian Accounts of Free Will*. New York: Oxford University Press, 2003.

Combs, William W. "Does the Bible Teach Prevenient Grace"? *Detroit Baptist Seminary Journal* 10.1 (2005) 3–11.

Cottret, Bernard. *Calvin: A Biography*. Translated by M. Wallace McDonald. Grand Rapids: Eerdmans, 2000.

Craig, William Lane. "Arguing Successfully about God: A Review Essay of Graham Oppy's Arguing about Gods." https://www.reasonablefaith.org/writings/scholarly-writings/the-existence-of-god/arguing-successfully-about-god-a-review-essay-of-graham-oppys-arguing-about/.

———. "The Difference between Possible and Feasible Worlds." http://www.reasonablefaith.org/the-difference-between-possible-and-feasible-worlds.

———. "The Fine Tuning Argument." http://www.finetuneduniverse.com/finetuned.html.

———. "Free Will." http://www.reasonablefaith.org/free-will.

———. "God and Abstract Objects." https://www.reasonablefaith.org/writings/scholarly-writings/divine-aseity/god-and-abstract-objects/.

———. "God Directs All Things." In *Divine Foreknowledge: Four Views*, edited by James K. Beilby and Paul R. Eddy, 79–100. Downers Grove: InterVarsity, 2011.

———. "Is Molinism Biblical? (14 October 2017)." https://www.reasonablefaith.org/media/reasonable-faith-podcast/is-molinism-biblical/.

———. "Men Moved by the Holy Spirit Spoke from God (2 Peter 1.21): A Middle Knowledge Perspective on Biblical Inspiration." *Philosophia Christi* NS 1 (1999) 45–82. http://www.leaderu.com/offices/billcraig/docs/menmoved.html.

———. "Middle Knowledge, Truth-Makers, and the 'Grounding Objection.'" https://www.reasonablefaith.org/writings/scholarly-writings/divine-omniscience/middle-knowledge-truth-makers-and-the-grounding-objection/.

———. "The Middle Knowledge View." In *Divine Foreknowledge: Four Views*, edited by James K. Beilby and Paul R. Eddy, 119–47. Downers Grove: InterVarsity, 2011.

———. "Molinism vs. Calvinism: Troubled by Calvinists." https://www.reasonablefaith.org/writings/question-answer/molinism-vs.-calvinism.

———. "New Questions from Facebook, Part 1 (20 September 2015)." https://www.reasonablefaith.org/media/reasonable-faith-podcast/new-questions-from-facebook-part-1/.

———. *On Guard: Defending Your Faith with Reason and Precision*. Colorado Springs: Cook, 2010.

———. *The Only Wise God*. Reprint, Eugene, OR: Wipf & Stock, 1999.

———. "Questions and Answers with William Lane Craig: #177: Perfect Being Theology." http://www.reasonablefaith.org/perfect-being-theology.

———. "Response to Paul Kjoss Helseth." In *Divine Foreknowledge: Four Views*, edited by James K. Beilby and Paul R. Eddy, 53–62. Downers Grove: InterVarsity, 2011.

———. *Time and Eternity View*. Wheaton: Crossway, 2001.

———. "William Lane Craig vs. Christopher Hitchens, '*Does God Exist*'?" (Biola University, 2009). https://youtu.be/PoXRQd9YOUM.

Crisp, Oliver. *Deviant Calvinism*. Minneapolis: Fortress, 2014.

Crockett, William, ed. *Four Views on Hell*. Grand Rapids: Zondervan, 1996.

Crozat, Elliott R. "Does the Purpose Theory of the Meaning of Life Entail an Irrational God"? *Philosophia Christi* 20.2 (2018) 401–13.

———. "Practical Rationality and Middle Knowledge." https://freethinkingministries.com/practical-rationality-middle-knowledge/#_ftn1.

Davies, Brian. "A Modern Defense of Divine Simplicity." In *Philosophy of Religion: A Guide and Anthology*, edited by Brian Davies, 549–64. Oxford: Oxford University Press, 2000.

———. *The Thought of Thomas Aquinas*. New York: Oxford University Press, 1992.

Deferrari, Roy J. *The Sources of Catholic Dogma*. Fitzwilliam, NH: Loreto Publications, 2002. https://archive.org/details/DenzingerSourcesOfCatholicDogma.

De Greef, Wulfert. "Calvin's Writings." In *The Cambridge Companion to John Calvin*, edited by Donald K. McKim, 41–57. Cambridge: Cambridge University Press, 2004.

De Jonge, Henk Jan. "*Novum Testamentum a Nobis Versum*: The Essence of Erasmus's Edition of the New Testament." *Journal of Theological Studies* NS 35.2 (1984) 397–413.

Dekker, Eef. "Was Arminius a Molinist"? *Sixteenth Century Journal* 27.2 (1996) 337–52.

Den Boer, William. "'Cum delectu': Jacob Arminius's (1559—1609) Praise for and Critique of Calvin and His Theology." *Church History and Religious Culture* 91.1.2 (2011) 73–86.

Denney, James. *The Second Epistle to the Corinthians*. New York: Armstrong, 1894.

Do, Toan. "A Plea for the Novum Instrumentum: Erasmus and His Struggle for a New Translation." *Philosophy and Theology* 28 (2016) 137–59.

Dogmatic Canons and Decrees. New York: The Devin-Adair Company, 1912.

Dolezal, James E. *God without Parts: Divine Simplicity and the Metaphysics of God's Absoluteness*. Eugene, OR: Pickwick, 2011.

Dragseth, Jennifer Hockenbery. "Martin Luther's Views on the Body, Desire, and Sexuality." https://oxfordre.com/religion/view/10.1093/acrefore/9780199340378.001.0001/acrefore-9780199340378-e-354.

Draper, Paul. "The Skeptical Theist." In *The Evidential Argument from Evil*, edited by Daniel Howard-Snyder, 175–92. Bloomington, IN: Indiana University Press, 1996.

Duby, Steven J. *Divine Simplicity: A Dogmatic Account*. New York: Bloomsbury T & T Clark, 2015.

Earle, Ralph. *1,2 Timothy*. EBC. Vol. 11: *Ephesians through Philemon*, 339–90. Grand Rapids: Zondervan, 1978.

"Edwards Center." http://edwards.yale.edu/research/browse.

Edwards, Jonathan. *A Divine and Supernatural Light*. http://edwards.yale.edu/rchive?path=aHRocDovL2Vkd2FyZHMueWFsZS5lZHUvY2dpLWJpbi9uZXdwaGlsbsy9nZXRvYmplY3QucGw/Yy44xNjoyMC53amVv.

———. *Freedom of the Will*. https://www.ccel.org/ccel/edwards/will.html.

————. "Personal Narrative." http://creativescholars.org/wp-content/uploads/2015/09/Jonathan-Edwards-Personal-Narrative-text.pdf.

Ellicott, Charles J. *St. Paul's Epistle to the Ephesians*. 4th ed. London: Longmans, Green, Reader, and Dyer, 1868.

Emerton, Ephraim. "Erasmus." *NSHE* 4:163–6.

Erasmus, Desiderius. *Manual of the Christian Knight*. Reprint, Indianapolis, IN: Liberty Fund, 2006. http://oll-resources.s3.amazonaws.com/titles/191/0048_Bk.pdf.

Erasmus, Desiderius, and Martin Luther. *Discourse on the Freedom of the Will*. Translated and edited by Ernst F. Winter. New York: Bloomsbury Academic, 2013.

Erasmus, Jacobus. *The Kalam Cosmological Argument: A Reassessment*. Cham, Switzerland: Springer International Publishing AG, 2018.

Erickson, Millard. *Christian Theology*. Grand Rapids: Baker, 1998.

Fales, Evan. "Divine Freedom and the Choice of a World." *International Journal for Philosophy of Religion* 35.2 (1994) 83. https://philpapers.org/rec/FALDFA.

Feinberg, John. *No One Like Him: The Doctrine of God*. Wheaton: Crossway, 2006.

Fendt, Gene. "Between a Pelagian Rock and a Hard Predestinarianism: The Currents of Controversy in 'City of God.'" *The Journal of Religion* 81.2 (2001) 211–27.

Fitzgerald, Martin. "Luther and the Divorce between Faith and Reason." https://www.mercatornet.com/above/view/how-martin-luther-helped-the-west-to-lose-its-reason/20590.

The Five Articles of the Remonstrants (1610). Edited by Dennis Bratcher. http://www.crivoice.org/creedremonstrants.html.

Flint, Thomas P. *Divine Providence: A Molinist Account*. New York: Cornell University Press, 1998.

————. "Molinism." In the *Oxford Handbooks Online*. http://www.oxfordhandbooks.com/view/10.1093/oxfordhb/9780199935314.001.0001/oxfordhb-9780199935314-e-29.

————. "Whence and Whither: The Molinist Debate." In *Molinism: The Contemporary Debate*, edited by K. Perzyk, 37–9. New York: Oxford University Press, 2011.

Foster, F. H. "Edwards, Jonathan (The Elder)." *NSHE* 4:80–83.

Fox, F. Earle. "Biblical Theology and Pelagianism." *The Journal of Religion* 41.3 (1961) 169–81.

Frame, John M. *The Doctrine of God*. Phillipsburg, NJ: Presbyterian and Reformed, 2002.

————. "Does the Bible Affirm Open Theism"? In "Real Questions, Straight Answers, Stronger Faith." *The Apologetics Study Bible*, 138. Nashville, TN: Holman Bible, 2007.

————. *No Other God*. Phillipsburg, NJ: Presbyterian and Reformed, 2001.

Franks, W. Paul, ed. *Explaining Evil: Four Views*. New York: Bloomsbury Academic, 2019.

Freddoso, Alfred J. "Molina, Luis de." https://www3.nd.edu/~afreddos/papers/molina.htm.

Frede, Michael. *A Free Will*. Los Angeles: University of California Press, 2011.

Garrigou-Lagrange, Reginald. *The One God*. Translated by Bede Rose. Indiana: Ex Fontibus, 2015.

Gibbens, Sarah. "Woman Swallowed Whole by 23-Foot Python." https://news.nationalgeographic.com/2018/06/python-attack-woman-indonesia-animals/.

Gibson, John Monro. *The Gospel according to Matthew*. New York: Armstrong, 1898.

Gloag, Paton J. *The Book of Acts*. ICC. Vol. 1. Edinburgh: T. & T. Clark, 1852.

————. *The Book of Acts*. ICC. Vol. 2. Edinburgh: T. & T. Clark, 1852.

Godet, F. *The Gospel of John*. Vol. 2. Translated by M. D. Cusin and S. Taylor. Edinburgh: T. & T. Clark, 1885.

Gore, Charles. "The Argument of Romans ix-xi." In vol. 3 *Studia Biblica: Essays in Biblical and Patristic Criticism,* edited by S. R. Driver et al., 37–46. London: Clarendon, 1891.

Grudem, Wayne. *Systematic Theology.* Grand Rapids: Zondervan, 1994.

———. "What's Systematic Theology and Why Bother"? https://www.thegospelcoalition.org/article/whats-systematic-theology-and-why-bother.

Guthrie, Donald. *The Pastoral Epistles.* TNTC. Rev. ed. Grand Rapids: InterVarsity, 1999.

Hagopian, David G., ed. *The Genesis Debate: Three Views on the Days of Creation.* Mission Viejo, CA: Crux, 2000.

Hammond, Joseph. *1 Kings.* PC. Vol. 11. New York: Funk & Wagnalls, 1974.

Hampden, Renn Dickson. *The Life of Thomas Aquinas.* Glasglow: John J. Griffin, 1848. https://ia802605.us.archive.org/2/items/lifethomasaquinoounkngoog/lifethomasaquinoounkngoog.pdf.

Hanson, Anthony T. *The Pastoral Epistles.* NCBC. Grand Rapids: Eerdmans, 1982.

Harris, Sam. *Free Will.* New York: Free Press, 2012.

Hart, Matthew J. "Calvinism and the Problem of Hell." In *Calvinism and the Problem of Evil,* edited by David E. Alexander and Daniel M. Johnson, 248–72. OR: Wipf & Stock, 2016.

Hartung, Christopher. *Thomas Aquinas on Free Will.* BA Diss., University of Delaware, 2013. http://udspace.udel.edu/handle/19716/12979.

Hasker, William. "Explanatory Priority: Transitive and Unequivocal: A Reply to William Lane Craig." *Philosophy and Phenomenological Research* 57.2 (1997) 389–93.

———. *God, Time, and Knowledge.* New York: Cornell University Press, 1989.

———. "Middle Knowledge: A Refutation Revisited." *Faith and Philosophy* 12.2 (1995) 223–36.

———. "The (Non-) Existence of Molinist Counterfactuals." In *Molinism: The Contemporary Debate,* edited by K. Perzyk, 25–36. New York: Oxford University Press, 2011.

Hawking, Stephen, and Leonard Mlodinow. *The Grand Design.* New York: Bantam Books, 2010.

Hay, Charles E. *Luther, the Reformer.* Philadelphia: Lutheran Publication Society, 1898.

Helseth, Paul Kjoss. "God Causes All Things." In *Four Views on Divine Providence,* edited by Dennis W. Jowers and Stanley N. Gundry, 25–52. Grand Rapids: Zondervan, 2011.

Hendriksen, William. *Exposition of the Pastoral Epistles.* Grand Rapids: Baker, 1970.

Hendryx, John W. "Eleven (11) Reasons to Reject Libertarian Free Will: A Critique of *Why I Am Not a Calvinist,*" by Jerry Walls and Joseph Dongell. Downers Grove: InterVarsity, 2004. https://www.monergism.com/thethreshold/articles/onsite/libertarian.html.

Hengstenberg, E. W. *The Revelation of St. John.* Vol. 2. Translated by Patrick Fairbairn. New York: Robert Carter, 1853.

Hicks, John Mark. "The Righteous of Saving Faith: Arminian Versus Remonstrant Grace." *Evangelical Journal* 9 (Spring, 1991) 27–39.

Highfield, Ron. "God Controls by Liberating." In *Four Views on Divine Providence,* edited by Dennis W. Jowers and Stanley N. Gundry, 141–64. Grand Rapids: Zondervan, 2011.

Hill, Amelia. "Star Wars Glossary: The Force." https://www.liveabout.com/star-wars-glossary-the-force-2958017.

Hodge, Charles. *A Commentary on the Epistle to the Ephesians.* New York: Robert Carter and Brothers, 1860.

———. *Systematic Theology.* Vol. 2. New York: Charles Scribner, 1883.

Hoefer, Carl. "Causal Determinism." *SEP* https://plato.stanford.edu/archives/spr2016/entries/determinism-causal.

Howe, Thomas A. "How to Interpret Your Bible Correctly (Part 1)." https://www.equip.org/article/how-to-interpret-your-bible-correctly-part-1/.

———. "How to Interpret Your Bible Correctly (Part 2)." https://www.equip.org/article/how-to-interpret-your-bible-correctly-part-2/.

Hume, David. *Dialogues Concerning Natural Religion*. Reprint, New York: Penguin Putnam, 1990. file:///C:/Users/david/Desktop/FTM/Hume,%20Dialogues%20Concerning%20Natural%20Religion.pdf

Humphreys, A. E. *The Epistles of Timothy and Titus. CBSC*. Cambridge: Cambridge University Press, 1895.

Hunt, David. "Simple-Foreknowledge View." In *Divine Foreknowledge: Four Views*, edited by James K. Beilby and Paul R. Eddy, 55–103. Downers Grove: InterVarsity, 2011.

Hunter, Braxton. "Debating Determinism with Dillahunty." https://freethinkingministries.com/debating-determinism-with-dillahunty/.

———. "Matt Dillahunty vs. Braxton Hunter (Does the Christian God Exist?)." https://www.youtube.com/watch?v=Y9Uktg9nLx8.

Irenaeus, "Against Heresies." Translated and edited by Alexander Roberts and James Donaldson. In *ANF* 1:841–1391.

Irons, Lee, and Meredith G. Kline. "The Framework View." In *The Genesis Debate: Three Views on the Days of Creation,* edited by David G. Hagopian, 217–56. Mission Viejo, CA: Crux, 2000.

Jackson, Samuel M., ed. "Calvin." *NSHE* 2:836–47.

Jensen, Jennifer L. *The Grounding Objection to Molinism*. Notre Dame: University of Notre Dame Press, 2008.

Johnson, Thomas. 2003. "A Wideness in God's Mercy: Universalism in the Bible." In *Universal Salvation? The Current Debate*, edited by Robin A. Parry and Christopher H. Partridge, 77–104. Grand Rapids: Eerdmans, 2003.

Jowers, Dennis W., and Paul R. Eddy, eds. *Four Views on Divine Providence*. Grand Rapids: Zondervan, 2011.

Kaiser, Walter C., Jr., and Moisés Silva. *Introduction to Biblical Hermeneutics*. Rev. and exp. ed. Grand Rapids: Zondervan, 2007.

Kane, Robert. *A Contemporary Introduction to Free Will*. New York: Oxford University Press, 2005.

———. "Introduction: The Contours of Contemporary Free Will Debates." In *The Oxford Handbook of Free Will*, edited by Robert Kane, 3–43. New York: Oxford University Press, 2002.

Kautzsch, E. "Theophany." *NSHE* 11:403–4.

Keathley, Kenneth. *Salvation and Sovereignty: A Molinist Approach*. Nashville: B & H, 2010.

Kelly, J. N. D. *A Commentary on the Pastoral Epistles*. Grand Rapids: Baker, 1981.

———. *Early Christian Doctrines*. 4th ed. London: Adam and Black, 1968.

Kempf, Constantin. "Theodicy." *CE* 14:543. https://www.ecatholic2000.com/cathopedia/vol14/volfourteen543.shtml.

Kennedy, Daniel. "St. Thomas Aquinas." *CE* 14:663–76. https://www.ecatholic2000.com/cathopedia/vol14/volfourteen601.shtml.

Kent, Homer A. *The Pastoral Epistles*. Chicago: Moody, 1986.

Kittelson, James. *Luther: The Reformer*. Minneapolis: Augsburg Fortress, 1986.

Knight, George T. "Universalists." *NSHE* 12 (1950) 95–7.

Knight, George W., III. *Commentary on the Pastoral Epistles.* NIGTC. Grand Rapids: Eerdmans, 1992.

Koons, Robert C., and Timothy Pickavance. *The Atlas of Reality.* 1ˢᵗ ed. Malden, MA: Wiley and Sons, 2017.

Köstlin, Julius. "Luther, Martin." *NSHE* 7 (1953) 69–78.

Koukl, Greg. "Did Calvin Believe in Freewill"? *Vox Evangelica* 12 (1981) 72–90. https://biblicalstudies.org.uk/pdf/vox/vol12/calvin_lane.pdf.

———. "Do Humans Really Have Free Will"? https://www.str.org/videos/do-humans-really-have-free-will#.XKcyUXdFy1e.

———. *Tactics: A Game Plan for Discussing Your Christian Convictions.* Grand Rapids: Zondervan, 2009.

Laing, John D. *Middle Knowledge: Human Freedom in Divine Sovereignty.* Grand Rapids: Kregel Academic, 2018.

Lane, Anthony N. S. 1998. "Bondage and Liberation in Calvin's Treatise against Pighius." Paper presented at the Ninth Colloquium on Calvin Studies, Davidson College and the Davidson College Presbyterian Church. Davidson, NC, January 30–31. http://foundationrt.org/resource/anthony-lane-bondage-and-liberation-in-calvins-treatise-against-pighius-pp-16-45.

Leafe, Scott K. "Prevenient Grace in the Rise of Arminianism." http://www.scriptel.org/wp-content/uploads/2017/06/Prevenient-Grace-in-the-Rise-of-Arminianism.pdf

Leibniz, Gottfried Wilhelm. The *Monadology.* Translated by Robert Latta. https://www.plato-philosophy.org/wp-content/uploads/2016/07/The-Monadology-1714-by-Gottfried-Wilhelm-LEIBNIZ-1646-1716.pdf.

Leibniz, Gottfried Wilhelm. *Theodicy: Essays on the Goodness of God, the Freedom of Man and the Origin of Evil.* Translated by E.M. Huggard. London: Routledge & Kegan Paul Limited, 1951. http://www.gutenberg.org/files/17147/17147-h/17147-h.htm.

Lennox, John C. *Determined to Believe? The Sovereignty of God, Freedom, Faith, and Human Responsibility.* Grand Rapids: Zondervan, 2017.

Lévy, Carlos. "Philo of Alexandria." *SEP.* https://plato.stanford.edu/entries/philo/#page topright.

Lewis, C. S. *Mere Christianity.* Rev. and amp. ed. New York: Harper One, 2015.

Licona, Michael R. "Are We Reading an Adapted Form of Jesus's Teachings in John's Gospel"? https://www.risenjesus.com/reading-adapted-form-jesus-teachings-johns-gospel.

———. "The Basis of Our Biblical Text Manuscripts." https://www.youtube.com/watch?v=F-m8esAfnv8&feature=youtu.be.

———. *Why Are There Differences in the Gospels?* New York: Oxford University Press, 2017.

Liebeschuetz, W. "Did the Pelagian Movement Have Social Aims"? *Historia: Zeitschrift für Alte Geschichte* 12.2 (1963) 227–41.

Lightfoot, J. B. *St. Paul's Epistle to the Philippians.* 3ʳᵈ ed. London: Macmillan, 1873.

Lindsay, Thomas M. "Thomas Aquinas." In vol. 4 *Encyclopaedia Britannica Dictionary,* 250–52. 11ᵗʰ ed. New York: Encyclopaedia Britannica, 1910. https://ia800208.us.archive.org/31/items/EncyclopaediaBritannicaDict.a.s.l.g.i.11thed.chisholm.1910-1911-1922.33vols/02.EncycBrit.11th.1910.v.2.AND-AUS.pdf.

Lockie, Robert. *Free Will and Epistemology,* New York: Bloomsbury Academic, 2018.

Logan, Ian. *Reading Anselm's Proslogion: The History of Anselm's Argument and its Significance Today.* London: Routledge, 2016.

Lonergan, Bernard. *Grace and Freedom: Operative Grace in the Thought of St. Thomas Aquinas.* In vol. 1 *Collected Works of Bernard Lonergan,* edited by Frederick E. Crowe and Robert M. Doran. Toronto: University of Toronto Press, 2000.

Ludlow, Morwenna. "Universalism in the History of Christianity." In *Universal Salvation? The Current Debate,* edited by Robin A. Parry and Christopher H. Partridge, 191–218. Grand Rapids: Eerdmans, 2003.

Luther, Martin. "Lectures on Genesis: Chapters 45–50." In vol. 5 *Luther's Works,* edited and translated by Jaroslav Jan Pelikan, Hilton C. Oswald, and Helmut T. Lehmann. St. Louis: Concordia, 1999.

———. *On the Bondage of the Will.* Translated by J. I. Packer and O. R. Johnston. Grand Rapids: Revell, 1957.

MacCulloch, Diarmaid. "Arminius and the Arminians." *History Today* (October 1989) 28–34.

MacDonald, Gregory. *The Evangelical Universalist.* Eugene, OR: Cascade, 2006.

MacDonald, Scott. "Aquinas's Libertarian Account of Free Choice." *Revue Internationale de Philosophie* 52.204.2 (1998) 309–24.

———. "Review of *On Divine Foreknowledge (Part IV of the Concordia).* Review of Metaphysics* 43.1 (1989) 177–79.

MacGregor, Kirk R. *Luis de Molina.* Grand Rapids: Zondervan, 2015.

———. *A Molinist-Anabaptist Systematic Theology.* Lanham, MD: University Press of America, 2007.

———. "Monergistic Molinism." *Perichoresis* 16.2 (2018) 77–92.

Mackie, J. L. "Evil and Omnipotence." *Mind* 64 (1955) 200–222.

Mann, William. "Divine Simplicity." *Religious Studies* 18 (1982) 451–71.

Mantzavinos, C. "Hermeneutics." *SEP.* https://plato.stanford.edu/entries/hermeneutics/.

Markoupolo, Foitini. "Closer to the Truth Asks Fotini Markopoulou: Why Is the Universe So Breathtaking"? https://www.closertotruth.com/series/why-the-universe-so-breathtaking#video-2655.

———. "Creating Spacetime." https://www.bing.com/videos/search?q=foitini+markoupolo%2c+closer+to+the+truth&view=detail&mid=1B4721E2AA30AC86C09F1B4721E2AA30AC86C09F&FORM=VIRE.

Markovits, Julia. "Ethics." https://ocw.mit.edu/courses/linguistics-and-philosophy/24-231-ethics-fall-2009/lecture-notes/MIT24_231F09_lec25.pdf.

Marsden, George M. *Jonathan Edwards: A Life.* New Haven, CT: Yale University Press, 2003.

Marshall, I. Howard. "The New Testament Does Not Teach Universal Salvation." In *Universal Salvation? The Current Debate,* edited by Robin A Parry and Christopher H. Partridge, 55–76. Grand Rapids: Eerdmans, 2003.

———. *The Pastoral Epistles.* Edinburgh: T & T Clark, 1999.

Martyr, Justin. "The First Apology." Translated and edited by Alexander Roberts and James Donaldson. In *ANF* 1:423–501.

"The Masoretic Text and the Dead Sea Scrolls." https://www.biblicalarchaeology.org/daily/biblical-artifacts/dead-sea-scrolls/the-masoretic-text-and-the-dead-sea-scrolls/.

McInerny, D. Q. *Philosophical Psychology.* Elmhurst Township, PA: The Priestly Fraternity of Saint Peter, 2006.

Melanchthon, Philip. *The Apology of the Augsburg Confession.* Translated by F. Bente and W. H. T. Dau. Paris: Editions de Cerf, 1989. https://www.ccel.org/ccel/melanchthon/apology.

———. *Loci communes theologici.* Quoted in Oswald Bayer. "The Anthropological Concepts in Luther and Melanchthon Compared." *The Harvard Theological Review* 91.4 (1998) 373–87.

McKenna, Michael, and D. Justin Coates. "Compatibilism." *SEP.* https://plato.stanford.edu/entries/compatibilism/.

Menuge, Angus. "Neuroscience, Rationality, and Free Will: A Critique of John Searle's Libertarian Naturalism." *Philosophia Christi* 15:1 (2003) 81–96.

Metz, Thaddeus. "Could God's Purpose Be the Source of Meaning"? In *Exploring the Meaning of Life: An Anthology and Guide,* edited by Joshua Seachris, 200–218. Oxford: John Wiley, 2013.

———. *Meaning in Life.* Oxford: Oxford University Press, 2013.

Meyer, Heinrich A. W. *Critical and Exegetical Handbook to the Epistle to the Ephesians.* 4ᵗʰ ed. Translated by Maurice J. Evans. New York: Funk and Wagnalls, 1884.

Miller, Samuel. "Introductory Essay." In *The Articles of the Synod of Dort,* translated and edited by Thomas Scott. Philadelphia: Presbyterian Board of Publications, 1854. https://archive.org/details/articlesofsynod01841syno.

Molina, Luis de. *On Divine Foreknowledge: Part IV of the Concordia.* Translated and edited by Alfred J. Freddoso. London: Cornell University Press, 1988.

Moreland, J. P. *The Recalcitrant Imago Dei: Human Persons and the Failure of Naturalism.* London: SCM, 2009.

———. *The Soul: How We Know It's Real and Why It Matters.* Chicago: Moody, 2014.

Moreland, J. P., and William Lane Craig. *Philosophical Foundations for a Christian Worldview.* Downers Grove: InterVarsity Academic, 2003.

———. *Philosophical Foundations for a Christian Worldview.* 2ⁿᵈ ed. Downers Grove: InterVarsity Academic, 2017.

Mounce, William D. *Pastoral Epistles.* Nashville: Thomas Nelson, 2000.

Muller, Richard A. "Arminius and the Reformed Tradition." *Westminster Theological Journal* 70.1 (2008) 18–47. http://www.theepiscocrat.com/2014/08/arminius-and-reformed-tradition.html.

———. *Divine Will and Human Choice.* Grand Rapids: Baker Academic, 2017.

———. "Grace, Election, and Contingent Choice: Arminius's Gambit and the Reformed Response." In vol 2 *Historical and Theological Perspectives on Calvinism,* edited by Thomas A Schreiner and Bruce A. Ware. Grand Rapids: Baker, 1995.

Murray, John. *Redemption Accomplished and Applied.* Grand Rapids: Eerdmans, 1955.

Myres, J. N. L. "Pelagius and the End of Roman Rule in Britain." *The Journal of Roman Studies* 50.1–2 (1960) 21–36.

Nagasawa, Mako A. "Human Free Will and God's Grace in the Early Church Fathers." https://blogs.ancientfaith.com/orthodoxbridge/wp-content/uploads/sites/27/2013/11/Mako-Nagasawa-free-will-in-patristics.pdf.

Newman, Alfred Henry. "Calvin, John." *NSHE* 2:836–47.

Niesel, Wilhelm. *The Theology of Calvin.* Philadelphia: Westminster, 1956.

Noebel, David A. *Understanding the Times: The Collision of Today's Competing Worldviews.* Manitou Springs, CO: Summit, 2006.

Olson, Roger E. *Against Calvinism.* Grand Rapids: Zondervan, 2011.

———. *Arminian Theology.* Downers Grove: InterVarsity Academic, 2009.

———. *The Story of Christian Theology.* Downers Grove: InterVarsity, 1999.

Bibliography

Olson, Scott. "Ep. 26: The Problem of Evil (Part 2)." https://freethinkingministries.com/ep-26-the-problem-of-evil-part-2/.

Oppy, Graham. *Arguing about Gods*. Cambridge: Cambridge University Press, 2006.

Osborne, Grant R. *The Hermeneutical Spiral*. Downers Grove: InterVarsity, 1991.

Palmer, Edwin. *The Five Points of Calvinism*. 3rd ed. Grand Rapids: Baker, 2010.

Parry, Robin A., and Christopher H. Partridge, eds. *Universal Salvation? The Current Debate*. Grand Rapids: Eerdmans, 2003.

Pedlar, James. "Why Arminian Theology Is Neither Pelagian Nor Semi-Pelagian." https://jamespedlar.wordpress.com/2012/05/10/why-arminian-theology-is-neither-pelagian-nor-semi-pelagian/.

Pelagius. "Letter to Demetrias." https://epistolae.ctl.columbia.edu/letter/1296.html.

Pelagius. *Pelagius's Commentary on St. Paul's Epistle to the Romans*. Reprint, New York: Oxford University Press, 2002.

Penner, Sydney. "Francisco Suarez (1548 to 1616)." *IEP*. https://www.iep.utm.edu/suarez.

Perzyk, K., ed. *Molinism: The Contemporary Debate*. New York: Oxford University Press, 2011.

Peterson, Michael. L. "The Problem of Evil." In *The Oxford Handbook of Atheism*, edited by Stephen Bullivant and Michael Ruse, 71–88. New York: Oxford University Press, 2013.

Philpott, Daniel. "Sovereignty." *SEP*. https://plato.stanford.edu/cgi-bin/encyclopedia/archinfo.cgi?entry=sovereignty.

Pigliucci, Massimo. "Stoicism." *IEP*. https://www.iep.utm.edu/stoicism/.

Pink, Arthur W. *The Sovereignty of God*. Gearheart, OR: Watchmaker, 2011.

Pinnock, Clark H. *Most Moved Mover: A Theology of God's Openness*. Grand Rapids: Baker, 2001.

Pinnock, Clark H., Richard Rice, John Sanders, William Hasker, and David Basinger. *The Openness of God*. Downers Grove: InterVarsity, 1994.

Pinson, J. Matthew. "The Nature of the Atonement in the Theology of Jacobus Arminius." *Journal of the Evangelical Theological Society* 53/4 (December 2010) 773–85. https://www.etsjets.org/files/JETS-PDFs/53/53-4/JETS_53_4_773–785_Pinson.pdf.

Piper, John. "Are There Two Wills in God"? http://www.desiringgod.org/articles/are-there-two-wills-in-god.

———. "Does God Get More Glory If People Have Free Will"? http://www.desiringgod.org/interviews/does-god-get-more-glory-if-people-have-free-will.

———. "Is God Sovereign over My Free Will"? http://www.desiringgod.org/interviews/is-god-sovereign-over-my-free-will.

———. *The Justification of God*. 2nd ed. Grand Rapids: Baker Academic, 1993.

Piper, John, et al., eds. *Beyond the Bounds: Open Theism and the Undermining of Biblical Christianity*. Wheaton, IL: Crossway, 2003.

Plantinga, Alvin. *Does God Have a Nature?* Milwaukee, WI: Marquette University Press, 1980.

———. *God, Freedom and Evil*. Grand Rapids: Eerdmans, 1989.

———. *The Nature of Necessity*. New York: Oxford University Press, 1974.

———. *Warrant: The Current Debate*. New York: Oxford University Press, 1993.

———. *Warrant and Proper Function*. New York: Oxford University Press. 1993.

———. *Warranted Christian Belief*. New York: Oxford University Press, 2000.

———. *Where the Conflict Really Lies*. New York: Oxford University Press, 2011.

Plummer, Alfred. *A Critical and Exegetical Commentary on the Gospel according to Luke.* 10th ed. ICC. New York: Charles Scribner and Sons, 1914.

———. *The Gospel according to S. Matthew.* London: Elliot Stock, 1909.

———. *The Pastoral Epistles.* New York: Armstrong and Son, 1889.

Plumptre, E. H. *Ezekiel.* Vol. 1. Rep., New York: Funk & Wagnalls, 1974.

———. *The General Epistles of St. Peter and Jude.* CBSC. Cambridge: Cambridge University Press, 1890.

Pohle, Joseph. "Luis de Molina." *CE* 10:349. https://www.ecatholic2000.com/cathopedia/vol10/volten349.shtml.

———. "Pelagius and Pelagianism." *CE* 11:624. https://www.ecatholic2000.com/cathopedia/vol11/voleleven624.shtml.

Polkinghorne, John. *Quantum Physics and Theology: An Unexpected Kinship.* London: SPCK, 2007.

———. *Science and Theology.* Minneapolis: Fortress, 1998.

Qu'ran. Translated by Abdullah Yusuf Ali. http://streathammosque.org/uploads/quran/english-quran-yusuf-ali.pdf.

Rasmussen, Joshua. *How Reason Can Lead to God: A Philosopher's Bridge to Faith.* Downers Grove: InterVarsity Academic, 2019.

Rees, B. R. *Pelagius: A Reluctant Heretic.* Wolfeboro, NH: Boydell and Brewer, 1991.

Reeves, Michael. *The Unquenchable Flame.* Nottingham: InterVarsity, 2009.

Richards, Jay W. *The Untamed God.* Downers Grove: InterVarsity Academic, 2003.

Robertson, Archibald, and Alfred Plummer. *A Critical and Exegetical Commentary on the First Epistle of St Paul to the Corinthians.* 2nd ed. ICC. Edinburgh: T. & T. Clark, 1914.

Rogge, Hendrik C. "Dort, Synod of." In *NSHE* 2:494–95. Grand Rapids: Baker, 1952. http://www.ccel.org/ccel/schaff/encyc03.i.html.

Rosemblum, Bruce, and Fred Kuttner. *Quantum Enigma: Physics Encounters Consciousness.* 2nd ed. New York: Oxford University Press, 2011.

Rosenberg, Alex. *The Atheist's Guide to Reality: Enjoying Life without Illusions.* New York: W. W. Norton, 2012.

Rovelli, Carlo. "Free Will, Determinism, Quantum Theory and Statistical Fluctuations: A Physicist's Take." https://www.edge.org/conversation/carlo_rovelli-free-will-determinism-quantum-theory-and-statistical-fluctuations-a.

Rowe, William. "Divine Freedom." *SEP.* https://plato.stanford.edu/archives/fall2008/entries/divine-freedom.

Rupp, E. Gordon, and Philip S. Watson, trans. and eds. *Luther and Erasmus: Free Will and Salvation.* Westminster: Knox, 1969.

Sanday, William, and A. C. Headlam. *The Epistle to the Romans.* ICC. New York: Charles Scribner, 1902.

Sanders, John. "A Freewill Theist's Response to Talbott's Universalism." In *Universal Salvation? The Current Debate,* edited by Robin A. Parry and Christopher H. Partridge, 169–90. Grand Rapids: Eerdmans, 2003.

———. *The God Who Risks.* Downers Grove: InterVarsity, 2007.

———. "An Introduction to Open Theism." *Reformed Review* 60.2 (Spring 2007) 34–50. http://drjohnsanders.com/summary-of-open-theism/.

Schafer, Thomas A. "Jonathan Edwards." (2020). https://www.britannica.com/biography/Jonathan-Edwards.

Schaff, Philip, ed. *Creeds of Christendom.* Vol. 3. New York: Harper, 1877.

—————. *History of the Christian Church.* Vol. 5: *The Middle Ages. A.D. 1049–1294.* New York: Charles Scribner, 1907. http://www.ccel.org/ccel/schaff/hcc5.

—————. *History of the Christian Church.* Vol. 7: *Modern Christianity: The German Reformation.* 2nd ed. rev. New York: Charles Scribner, 1910. http://www.ccel.org/ccel/schaff/hcc7.

—————. *History of the Christian Church.* Vol. 8: *Modern Christianity: The Swiss Reformation.* 3rd ed. rev. New York: Charles Scribner, 1910. http://www.ccel.org/s/schaff/hcc8/cache/hcc8.pdf.

Schreiner, Thomas A. "Grace, Election, and Contingent Choice: Arminius's Gambit and the Reformed Response." In vol. 2 *Grace of God, Bondage of the Will,* edited by Thomas A. Schreiner and Bruce A. Ware. Grand Rapids: Baker, 1994.

Schultz, Walter J. "'No Risk' Libertarian Freedom: A Refutation of the Free-Will Defence." *Philosophica Christi* 10.1 (2008) 165–81. http://www.academia.edu/7400594/_No-Risk_Libertarian_Freedom_A_Refutation_of_the_Free-Will_Defense.

The Articles of the Synod of Dort. Translated and edited by Thomas Scott. Philadelphia: Presbyterian Board of Publications, 1854. https://archive.org/details/articlesofsynod01841syno.

Searle, John R. *Rationality in Action.* Cambridge, MA: Bradford, 2001.

Siddiqi, Muzammil H. "Salvation in Islamic Perspective." *Islamic Studies* 32.1 (Spring 1993) 41–48. Islamabad: Islamic Research Institute, International Islamic University. https://www.jstor.orgistable/20840106.

Skinner, Otis Ainsworth. *A Series of Sermons in Defense of the Doctrine of Universal Salvation.* Boston: Abel Tomkins, 1842. https://ia800205.us.archive.org/18/items/aseriessermonsi02skingoog/aseriessermonsi02skingoog.pdf.

Smith, R. Payne. *2 Samuel.* New York: Funk & Wagnalls, 1974.

Sprinkle, Preston, et al., ed. *Four Views on Hell.* 2nd ed. Grand Rapids: Zondervan, 2016.

Sproul, R. C. *Can I Know God's Will?* The Crucial Questions Series 4. Lake Mary, FL: Reformation Trust, 2009.

—————. "Does Prayer Change God's Mind"? https://www.ligonier.org/blog/does-prayer-change-gods-mind.

—————. "If God Is Sovereign, Why Pray"? https://www.ligonier.org/blog/if-god-sovereign-why-pray.

Stanglin, Keith, and Thomas H. McCall. *Jacob Arminius, Theologian of Grace.* Oxford: Oxford University Press, 2012.

Starr, William. "Counterfactuals." *SEP.* https://plato.stanford.edu/cgi-bin/encyclopedia/archinfo.cgi?entry=counterfactuals.

Stepp, Edwin. "Martin Luther: The Fearful Philosopher." *Religion and Spirituality* (Fall 2000). https://www.vision.org/fr/node/394.

Steup, Matthias. "Epistemology." *SEP.* https://plato.stanford.edu/entries/epistemology/.

Strange, Daniel. "A Calvinist Response to Talbott's Univeralism." In *Universal Salvation? The Current Debate,* edited by Robin A. Parry and Christopher H. Partridge, 145–68. Grand Rapids: Eerdmans, 2003.

Stratton, Tim. "A Choice apart from Time." https://freethinkingministries.com/a-choice-apart-from-time.

—————. "The Freethinking Argument against Naturalism: An Argument for the Existence of the Soul." MA diss., Biola University, 2014.

—————. "Molinism Is Biblical: Rejoining the Reformed Rejoinder." https://freethinkingministries.com/molinism-is-biblical-rejoining-the-reformed-rejoinder/.

————. "True Love, Free Will, and the Logic of Hell." http://freethinkingministries.com/true-love-free-will-the-logic-of-hell.

Stratton, Tim, and Jacobus Erasmus. "Divine Determinism and the Problem of Hell." *Perichoresis* 16.2 (2018) 3–15.

————. "Mere Molinism: A Defense of Two Essential Pillars." *Perichoresis* 16.2 (2018) 17–29.

Strong, Augustus H. *Systematic Theology*. New York: Revell, 1907.

Studebaker, Richard F. "The Theology of James Aminius." https://www.bethelcollege.edu/assets/content/mcarchives/pdfs/v4n2p4–17.pdf.

Stump, Eleonore. "Aquinas's Account of Freedom: Intellect and Will." *The Monist* 80.4 (1997) 576–97.

Stump, Eleonore, and Norman Kretzmann. "Absolute Simplicity." *Faith and Philosophy* 2.4 (1985) 353–82.

Talbott, Thomas. *The Inescapable Love of God*. Boca Raton, FL: Universal Publishers, 1999.

————. "Universal Salvation." In *Universal Salvation? The Current Debate*, edited by Robin A Parry and Christopher H. Partridge, 3–54. Grand Rapids: Eerdmans, 2003.

Taylor, Justin. "A Bibliography on Open Theism." In *Beyond the Bounds: Open Theism and the Undermining of Biblical Christianity*, edited by Piper, et al., 386–400. Wheaton, IL: Crossway, 2003.

Timpe, Kevin. *Free Will: Sourcehood and Its Alternatives*. N.p.: Continuum International, 2008.

Tomberlin, James E., and Peter Van Inwagen, eds. *Profiles: Alvin Plantinga*. Dordrecht: D. Reidel, 1985.

Tooley, Michael. "The Problem of Evil." *SEP*. https://plato.stanford.edu/archives/spr2019/entries/evil/.

Torrell, Jean-Pierre. *Aquinas's* Summa: *Background, Structure, and Reception*. Translated by Benedict M. Guevin. Washington, DC: The Catholic University of America Press, 2005.

Tozer, A. W. *The Knowledge of the Holy*. http://www.ntcg-aylesbury.org.uk/books/knowledge_of_the_holy.pdf.

Turretin, Francis. *Institutes of Elenctic Theology*. Vol. 1. Edited by James T. Dennison Jr. and translated by George Musgrave Giger. Reprint, Phillipsburg, NJ: Presbyterian and Reformed, 1992.

Tyson, Neil deGrasse. "Does Neil deGrasse Tyson Believe in God? Interview by Chelsea on Netflix." https://youtu.be/jXAokvnv7Mc.

Van Inwagen, Peter. *An Essay on Free Will*. Oxford: Oxford University Press, 1986.

————. "The Problem of Evil, the Problem of Air, and the Problem of Silence." In vol. 5 *Philosophical Perspectives* 5 (1991) 135–65.

————. "The Vision of the Hazelnut." In *Knowing Creation: Perspectives from Theology, Philosophy, and Science*. Vol. 1. Edited by Andrew Torrance and Tom McCall, 181–94. Grand Rapids: Zondervan, 2018.

Wallace, R. Jay. "Practical Reason." *SEP*. https://plato.stanford.edu/entries/practical-reason/#InsStrRat.

Walls, Jerry L. "A Philosophical Critique of Talbott's Universalism." In *Universal Salvation? The Current Debate*, edited by Robin A. Parry and Christopher H. Partridge, 105–24. Grand Rapids: Eerdmans, 2003.

————. *Purgatory: The Logic of Total Transformation*. New York: Oxford University Press, 2012.

————. "What's Wrong with Calvinism? (Part 1)." https://www.youtube.com/watch?v=Dao mzm3nyIg&feature=youtu.be.

Walls, Jerry L., and Joseph R. Dongell. *Why I Am Not a Calvinist*. Downers Grove: InterVarsity, 2004.

Ware, Bruce. *God's Lesser Glory: The Diminished God of Open Theism*. Wheaton, IL: Crossway, 2000.

Webster, Noah. "Deliberate." http://webstersdictionary1828.com/.

Weigel, Peter. "Divine Simplicity." *IEP*. https://www.iep.utm.edu/div-simp/#H1.

Westcott, B. F. *The Gospel according to St. John*. SC. London: John Murray, 1882.

————. *The Gospel according to St. John: The Greek Text and Notes*. 2 vols. London: John Murray, 1908.

Wiggers, G. F. *An Historical Presentation of Augustinism and Pelagianism from the Original Sources*. Translated, with notes and additions by Ralph Emerson. New York: Gould, Newman, and Saxton, 1840. https://www.gospeltruth.net/Wiggers/wiggersindex.htm.

Wilkinson, Maurice. *Erasmus of Rotterdam*. New York: P. J. Kennedy, 1921.

Williams, William C. "Theophany." In *Baker's Dictionary of Biblical Theology*, edited by Walter A. Elwell. Grand Rapids: Baker, 1996. https://www.biblestudytools.com/dictionaries/bakers-evangelical-dictionary/theophany.html.

Willis, John T. *Genesis*. Abilene, Texas: ACU, 1978.

Wolfson, Harry A. "Philosophical Implications of the Pelagian Controversy." *Proceeding of the American Philosophical Society* 103.4 (1959) 555–62.

Wright, R. K. McGregor. *No Place for Sovereignty: What's Wrong with Freewill Theism?* Downers Grove: InterVarsity, 1996.

Yuan, Christopher. *Holy Sexuality and the Gospel: Sex, Desire, and Relationships Shaped by God*. New York: Crown, 2018.

Made in the USA
Monee, IL
27 October 2020